The History of the Clubman's TT Races 1947 - 1956

Fred Pidcock

&

Bill Snelling

Amulree Publications of Laxey

This book is dedicated to all the riders who took part in the Clubman's TT, and who, by so doing, played a part in creating this history.

And to Joanie and Pat, without whose enthusiasm and support it wouldn't have been written.

Cover illustrations:
Main picture: Frank Sheene (67, Royal Enfield), Goo Owen (68, Matchless) and Harry Voice (69, BSA) starting the 1952 Junior Clubman's.
Front cover inset: Bob McIntyre (BSA) flat out on Bray Hill, 1952 Junior Clubman's.
Back cover inset: Bernard Codd (BSA) at Cronk ny Mona, 1956 Senior Clubman's.

The History of the Clubman's TT Races 1947 - 1956

Copyright : © Fred Pidcock & Bill Snelling 2007

ISBN: 978-1-901508-10-9

Published by Amulree Publications
Lossan y Twoaie
Glen Road
Laxey
Isle of Man
IM4 7AN

www.amulree.com

CONTENTS

Introduction   5
Acknowledgements   6
Foreword by Bernard Codd, Double Clubman's TT Winner, 1956   7

Chapter 1 How It All Began - And The Concept Of A Manufacturers 'Team Test'   9
"If I Were You" by Graham Walker   20

Chapter 2 - 1947 The First Clubman's TT - And Off To A Good Start   29
1947 Clubman's Recollections, by Dennis Christian   38
.... as he left a black footrest rubber mark on a wall in Ballaugh village!
My 1947 Clubman's Ride, by Bob Pratt   39
Not going quick enough, mate - off the leader board!

Chapter 3 - 1948 A Full House - And Vincents Rule The Senior   45
My 1948 Junior Clubman's Ride, by Ronnie Hazlehurst   57
This put me in a good position to be on the leader board.

Chapter 4 - 1949 Accomodating A Record Entry, And Two New Stars Emerge   63
My 1949 Lightweight Clubman's Ride, by Cyril Taft   78
Domestic weather situation somewhat "unsettled", decided to come down to a 250cc for 1949

Chapter 5 - 1950 A More Settled Format - TT Wednesday Was 'Clubman's Day'   87
The 1950 Clubman's 1000, by Louis Carr   104
... to help pass the time before moving Sulby Bridge into Ramsey
My Junior Clubman's Ride, by Michael McGeagh   106
I never did find that gear lever.
A. D. (Doug) Brown's Clubman's Stories, by Grace Brown   108
... so they clubbed together to buy the bike.
My 1000cc Clubman's Rides, by Alex Phillip   110
...I got a signal to 'slow down' but I was enjoying the race so much...

Chapter 6 - 1951 Four, Take Away Two, And So Near For Triumph   123

Chapter 7 - 1952 A Win For Triumph At Last, And An Island Debut For 'Bob Mac'   143
My 1952 Senior Clubman's Ride, by Frank Fox   157
...with instructions not to go over 70 mph whilst running it in on the way home!

Chapter 8 - 1953 Coronation Year - And A BSA On The Senior Leaderboard   165
My 1953 Senior Clubman's Ride, by Alf Hagon   178
.... was being passed by more experienced competitors in mist so thick you could hardly see the kerb ....
The Isle of Man And The Clubman's TT, by Ewen Haldane   179
My less than happy state was made even more so as it was raining.

My Clubman's TT Memories, by Derek Powell   182
"There are no gold medals for practice" - sound advice I think
My 1953 Clubman's 1,000cc Ride, by Richard Madsen-Mygdal   184
.... closing fast on a 350, he ignored racing's golden rule - stick to your line!

Chapter 9 - 1954 Changing Times - And What's In A Name?   191
My 1954 Senior Clubman's Ride, by Howard German   202
... the engine coughed and slowed to a seemingly walking pace.
My 1953 and 1954 Senior Clubman's Rides, by Sandy Bowie   204
We drove the bikes from home to the ferry at Liverpool
My 1954 Senior Clubman's Ride, by Percy Tait   205
Being employed as a tester at Triumph, I was barred by the Regulations from riding that company's products

Chapter 10 - 1955 The Clypse Year   209
My 1955 Senior Clubman's Ride, by Jimmy Drysdale   218
The only disappointment was the chequered flag. But that's the way it should be.
My Clubman's Rides, by Jimmy Buchan   219
The next week flew by as we tried to learn the Mountain Course
My Clubman's Rides, by David Hagen   221
"and here comes the American and he is still on the wrong line!"

Chapter 11 - 1956 Back On The Mountain   227
Why the Clubman's?, by John Hurlstone   237
It was the only affordable entry to racing in the Isle of Man
My Clubman's Rides, by Alan Brodrick   239
..... I hit the wall at a corner called 'Morney 3', wrecked the BSA and dislocated my left shoulder

Chapter 12 - The Problems Increase - How And Why It All Ended   245
Riders details   256

INTRODUCTION

Everyone with an interest in motorcycle racing, or in motorcycles of the 'Classic' era, has heard of the Clubman's TT. If asked, no doubt many could add some recollections from magazine articles describing these races held in the Isle of Man in the years following the Second World War. But question further, and it is likely that apart from remembering that the races were dominated by the BSA Gold Star, and maybe that Geoff Duke and Bob McIntyre took part in the early races, little else would be known. In carrying out some private research, the absence of almost any published reference work, or indeed any factual information on the Clubman's TT series was puzzling, particularly as there were so many books written on just about every conceivable aspect of the TT races. In consequence, a number of 'wanted' advertisements were placed, and over a period of time a fairly comprehensive set of original or photocopied race reports and statistics was gathered. It was in the reading of these reports that the realisation began to dawn that there was just so much history there, so many remarkable stories and characters, and high drama, plus some great racing. That was probably the point at which the idea of the book first arose. The aim was to compile as complete a story as possible, a comprehensive record and database of the ten years of the Clubman's TT, such that the men (and it was only men in those days who were allowed to take part), their machines and their exploits would not be lost to motorcycling history.

From the outset, it was decided to intersperse the year-by-year accounts of the races, with a good selection of rider's own recollections of the events, and as soon as the first contacts were made in that regard, the tremendous enthusiasm for the races, both at the time and still to this day, became apparent. Friendships formed then have stood the test of time, and many of the riders have remained in contact with their fellow competitors and rivals, and it was a privilege to hear their stories. An unexpected comment made by many contributors in their replies was along the lines of 'thank you for re-awakening memories of great times'. That simple sentiment was sufficient reward for the effort in producing this book, many times over. An easy decision was that riders' contributions would be included in full and without change to the wording, so as to retain the style of the original writer, and thus preserve their appeal. The only exception to this occurred when an anecdote was removed which would otherwise have appeared more than once.

It would be unfair to single out any individual contribution, certainly in terms of merit or content, but it is appropriate to mention Jimmy Buchan, who was one of the first whose contact details could be obtained, and who was therefore one of the first to contribute. He didn't know it, but the timing of his response and his gentle, genuine enthusiasm for the races and for the book gave impetus to the project just when it was needed. Had his response been negative or 'lukewarm', the book may well have foundered there and then. Thank you, Jimmy.

One other principle adopted from the start of writing was that wherever possible, contemporary written word would be used either as direct quotation (in which case the source was credited) or to compile the text. In so doing, it was hoped that opinions and prejudices inherent in any writing, would be minimised. At least that way such prejudices as did get through would have been those present at the time, and therefore would somehow be more acceptable!

A third objective was to try to ensure that every rider of every year got at least a couple of mentions, and every one of his race laps credited with a time. All riders entered are thus identified, along with machine and the club they represented. (An occasional exception occurs in the case of riders who enter, but for some reason fail to appear, and where as a consequence their places are taken by reserves). If a rider 'finished the course', then his position and every lap time is given. If he were unfortunate enough to retire, then his completed lap times are given and, wherever known, the reason for retirement described. Within the race details, each riders fastest lap is in bold text.

The aim of the authors in creating this book was to produce as complete a record as practical of the 10 years of Clubman's TT racing, 1947 – 1956, and something which might 'fill the gap' between those venerated works, BP's 'History of the TT Races' written by such men as L.R. Higgins, Cyril Quantrill, Peter Arnold and Peter Kneale, and the 'Story of the TT' and 'Story of the Manx Grand Prix' written by the incomparable Geoff Davison. It is our genuine hope that this book can help preserve the memory of the Clubman's TT races, and the efforts and exploits of the many hundreds of clubmen who helped make this history.

Considering the earlier observation that there was no existing reference work on the Clubman's TT, it is hoped that this book might therefore rank high amongst its competitors. 'Number One in a Field of One' was the sub-title of a weird, humorous magazine from our teenage years in the late 1950's. It's a safe bet that both the authors would settle for that high accolade for their endeavours!

Fred Pidcock
Bill Snelling

Acknowledgments

Special thanks for their contributions to:
- Sandy Bowie
- Alan Brodrick
- Jimmy Buchan
- Dennis Christian
- Eddie Crooks
- Jimmy Drysdale
- Frank Fox
- Howard German
- David Hagen
- Alf Hagon
- Ewen Haldane
- Ronnie Hazlehurst
- John Hurlstone
- Richard Madsen-Mygdal
- Goo Owen
- Alex Phillip
- Derek Powell
- Percy Tait
- Jack Wood

Thanks to Alan and Mike Kelly (Mannin Collections) who were always ready to fill in gaps in our reference material, particularly entry lists and official results, and to Eddie Nelson at the ACU for permission to reproduce those results sheets. Also Gary Thompson at the ACU, for arranging access to their archives.

Thanks to Keith Trubshaw and Jim Hunter of the Manx Grand Prix Riders Association for arranging contact with Grace Brown, and to Grace herself for her assistance in compiling her late husband Doug's story.

To Sue and Dick Kingston of the Gold Star Owners Club for their encouragement throughout, and help with finding riders contact details.

To Jane Skayman and Mortons Motorcycle Media, for permission to quote extensively from 'Motor Cycling' and 'The Motor Cycle' and similarly to the Hanks family for permission to quote from the 'TT Special'.

To Annice Collett at the VMCC Library, and the staff of the British Newspaper Library in Colindale, North London.

To Ruth Sutherland for her inspirational cover design.

Thanks also to David Wright for his encouragement for the project.

Foreword

by Bernard Codd, Double Clubman's TT Winner, 1956

There were only two ways to approach the Clubman's TT, either to treat it as an ambition achieved, or as a step towards riding in the International TT. For many riders, it was their one, possibly only, opportunity to follow in the footsteps of their heroes, to have a ride in the TT, to 'be a TT racer'. There is absolutely nothing wrong with that, but for others like myself, it was a vital step in what was hoped would be a successful career in the most prestigious motorcycle races in the world. The progression was straightforward, the Clubman's TT followed by the Manx Grand Prix followed by the TT.

When I started racing in 1955, I was fortunate to have had backing and guidance from four-times Manx Grand Prix winner Austin Munks, and through Austin, advice from Geoff Duke. Although I started on a 350 Gold Star racer, the plan was to ride Manx Nortons in the 1956 Manx Grand Prix, and to prepare by competing in the Clubman's TT, for which Austin ordered a pair of Gold Stars. Weeks before the start of official practice, I went over to the Island and did what seemed to me (and may well have been) hundreds of laps on my Matchless G9 road bike, or in a car with Austin or Geoff. The bikes were standard, mechanic Sam Coupland did all the machine preparation, and a good job he made of it too, as both ran faultlessly throughout practice and the races, and we came home with the 'Double'. In the Junior MGP I finished 4th, and in the following years Golden Jubilee TT 11th, but then I was hit by another rider at a Crystal Palace race meeting, and suffered serious right leg injuries which put a stop to racing.

After the 1956 Clubman's, no-one really knew why the races were stopped, and it is good to see some light being shed on what went on behind the scenes. As a competitor, the tendency is to put the politics to one side and just carry on.

The Clubman's TT was the beginning of many famous rider's Isle of Man careers, but the story of that decade of races following the war has never been fully told. It gives me great pleasure to write the Foreword for this book, reading it has brought back many happy memories, of events and of fellow riders from that era. It does not bear thinking about that even the most recent events described in the book were over half a century ago, I won't dwell on that aspect!

Enjoy the book, and its re-creation of an almost forgotten part of TT and motorcycling history.

Bernard Codd
Wrangle,
Near Boston, Lincs

Goo Owen takes a rodeo ride down Bray Hill on his scrambles G3L Matchless in the 1952 Junior Clubman's. The bike still retained its 21" front wheel fitted with a ribbed tyre. Goo rode the same bike in 1952 and '53, he recalls the engine 'letting go' at precisely this point in '53, "there wasn't much left of it when I stopped at Quarter Bridge". The Owen family have serviced the refuelling depots at the TT since he stopped racing in 1954.

CHAPTER 1

HOW IT ALL BEGAN - AND THE
CONCEPT OF A MANUFACTURERS
'TEAM TEST'

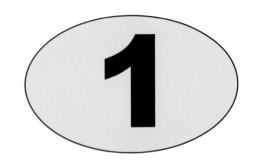

As Europe readjusted to peace in the months after the end of the Second World War, and slowly some semblance of normality began to return to everyday life, British motorcycle enthusiasts began looking forward to the resurrection of their sport, top of the list being the TT and Manx Grand Prix. The first post-war Manx Grand Prix races were held in the September of 1946, with the TT having to wait till the following June. There was much speculation in the motorcycle press over the format of the post-war TT races, as the pre-war 'no restrictions other than engine capacity' would not (or more accurately, could not) be supported by British manufacturers struggling to emerge from six dark years of war effort. Continental manufacturers were in similar if not worse situations. And anyway, it was argued, the immense research and development costs associated with such racing specials would not necessarily benefit the touring motorcycle. Better then, continued the argument, to restrict the technical specification of the machines, thereby encouraging more manufacturers to take part. The competition thus created would benefit those manufacturer's machines, in turn benefiting their customers, and ultimately improving motorcycles in general. Supercharging was banned, exhaust restrictions introduced, and everyone compelled to use the awful 70-75 octane 'Pool' petrol.

From the ACU (Auto-Cycle Union, the governing body of British motorcycle sport) there appeared to be a shift in thinking on the concept of the races, back toward the origins of the TT itself, and the description 'Tourist Trophy', firstly by applying these restrictions on the mechanical development of the highly specialised 'International' racers, and secondly by introducing the concept of additional events for catalogued sports and touring roadster machines. There was nothing new about races based on machines which were basically production sports models. Brooklands had hosted many such events pre-war, and in 1933 had, in association with *'The Motor Cycle'* magazine, initiated a Clubman's Day, in which two or three races and timed runs were added to the usual programme, and open to anyone who would cough up the required five shillings (or half that if the coupon from the magazine could be produced), and who was a member of a recognised club. *'Motor Cycling's'* 'Donington Day' in 1939 staged races for ordinary clubmen on their privately-owned machines, and the possibility of a TT race for 'standard-machines' had also been discussed pre-war. Following a meeting in 1939 between the 'British Cycle and Motorcycle Manufacturer's and Trader's Union' and the ACU, a communiqué had been issued which read *"Representatives of the Manufacturer's Union and the ACU met in Coventry on July 21st and reviewed the proposals for a 'Standard Stock' event in the 1940 TT races. After consideration of the question it was finally agreed not to proceed with the organisation of such an event next year"*.

The Editorial Opinion from *'The Motor Cycle'* of the following Thursday attempted to put some flesh on the bones of the joint announcement. *"While the decision is only in respect of 1940, it can be assumed that the proposal is 'killed'. One reason is the difficulty of ensuring that such a race shall be fair to all. The ideal, of course, is a race for machines exactly as sold to the public - for motorcycles taken straight from dealer's stocks and which, therefore, in the normal course of events would have been bought by the public.*

In these days when prospective purchasers of various popular models have to wait weeks for delivery it is obviously impractical to select the machines in this way. Moreover there are certain makes with a very small output and few agents. The difficulties in this direction are immense - probably insuperable.

Another objection raised is that a true stock-machine race held at the same time as the TT might, to use the words of one manufacturer, appear rather 'silly'. This, however, is not a point that carries much weight with us. We believe that the vast majority of motorcyclists would be extremely interested in learning how the various makes and models compare in high-speed reliability. Whether the speeds were low in comparison with the TT itself would matter little, except that if they were it would reveal how specialised TT racing machines are!

When the ACU again discarded the principle of a standard-machine event (it is no new idea) on account of the difficulties involved, they approached the manufacturers with the proposal of a 'Roadster Race', open to machines on standard lines - machines which might only be altered from the regular specification in certain respects. A race of this type is, in our opinion, practicable, given suitable, clear-cut regulations. How much or how little the ACU's suggested rules permitted deviations from standard is not public knowledge. It is, however, a fact that a big point made against the proposed race was that the event would be neither a real TT nor a Stock-Machine TT. It was felt that the public would not accept the machines as being 'stock' and, therefore, the event would be of little value.

There is much in this, but surely the answer is that the draft rules were permitting too many alterations? No, our view is that the race has been rejected because few manufacturers really wanted it".

Perhaps the most surprising aspect of the meeting was not the inability to agree the basis for the production-based races, but that the meeting took place at all, barely a month before the outbreak of the Second World War.

Although the format for the first post-war Senior, Junior and Lightweight International races was fairly quickly established, that for the new events for roadsters most definitely was not. As late as July 1946, the ACU were presenting proposals for *'a novel high-speed team trial for fully-equipped solo machines, whether singles, twins or fours, atmospheric or forced induction, and of any cc.'* Named at the time as the 'Tourist Trophy Team Test',

it would have had as awards, a Special Tourist Trophy and Certificates of Performance for every manufacturer whose team of three achieved a specified speed for that particular class. There would be no 1st, 2nd, 3rd or any placings. The idea was that the event would not be a race, but a high-speed time trial in which reliability, and not ultra-high speed, was the governing factor. Furthermore, the event was to be promoted as one *'to enable all manufacturers to demonstrate their machines and have the benefit of TT development of their products'.* Scheduled for the Wednesday of race-week, it would cover four laps, and speeds would be set by the ACU.

Industry support for the Mountain Course-based 'Team Test' seemed generally good, and *'The Motor Cycle'* issues of 11th and 18th of July 1946 carried features quoting the manufacturer's reactions to the proposals for the International TT, and to the Team Test concept. The responses dealing with the Team Test are summarised or reproduced below.

Mr. Eric Walker, Managing Director of Excelsior

"Dealing with the proposed programme for Wednesday, here we have, as you remark, 'something for everyone' - a really good idea covering all classes. My thoughts go back to the many times proposed Stock or Standard Motor Cycle Trials. No doubt a good deal can be learnt from this event, always provided the ACU put the speeds to be maintained high enough really to tax the capabilities of the motorcycles on trial.

With 'my tongue in my cheek', I ask, 'What would the 100cc class autocycle speeds be likely to be set at?' for after all, the Wednesday show is to cover all classes and all capacities; why not show the world what the 'little uns' really are capable of standing over 150 miles of the famous course?"

Mr. Peter Goodman, Managing Director of Veloce

"With regard to the racing of tourist types of machines, personally I would rather such events were not run, for touring machines are not intended for racing and, therefore, there may be a crop of unfortunate accidents. I do not wish this last sentence to imply that touring machines are unsafe, but it is quite a different thing to drive a touring motorcycle or a motor car at racing speeds, for which it was not designed, and drive a proper racing machine which has been properly designed for the

work which it has to do."

Mr. George Brough, creator of the Brough Superior.

"How the faster speed of the 'big un' is going to justify itself on the Island course I do not know, but then, that is how we were talking when the TT course was being lapped at 70. One thing I do feel certain about is that the lad on a properly designed 'Thousand' should have the most comfortable ride. Here's good luck to them anyway, and full support."

Mr. F.A. Kimberley, Managing Director of James.

"With regard to us as manufacturers of lightweights, it would appear that the team test is the only event which would probably be of interest to us. I consider that it would be invidious to expect lightweights of 125cc to compete with the larger machines. It follows, therefore, that if such small capacity machines are expected to compete, modifications to the length of course and other essential conditions must be introduced."

Mr. Marians, Director of Phelon and Moore (Panther)

(Note that he made it clear that the expressed opinion was a personal one, not necessarily that of his company).

"With regard to the proposal for a high-speed reliability trial to be introduced during the week, I think the suggestion is a very sound one as an effort to obtain entries from the maximum number of manufacturers, but I am not too sure that the public would want to watch it or that the manufacturers would gain any advantage by entering for it."

Mr. S.F. Digby, General Sales Manager of BSA and Sunbeam (by telegram)

"Have read with great interest suggestions for modifying TT Regulations to encourage development of type of motorcycles suitable for everyday use. Believe that British motorcycle industry would reap maximum benefit from such activity and trust proposals will be fully investigated."

Mr. Tom Davis, Ariel

"We feel that, while this is a step in the right direction, we could not give the suggestions our support owing to the extreme difficulties under which we are working and which, I am afraid, will persist for some considerable time. To maintain our output of standard machines is one long struggle, and to

attempt to prepare special machines for the TT would, I am sure, be the last straw."

Mr. G.F. Halliday, Chief Engineer at Douglas

"In many quarters it is felt that industrial difficulties might exist for a considerable time in directions other than building up commercial stability. Many firms whose interest might be the development and manufacture of motorcycles had their whole attention directed to war production, and it would take at least two years before they could direct their attentions to prepare seriously for, and to take part in, such events as the TT races as they existed pre-war.

The proposal to include a team race somewhat alters this picture, assuming that machines would substantially be to a specification immediately allied to that of machines of immediate production. I think a great mistake would be made if there was any departure from this proviso, and also it is contended that only one team should be allowed to be entered from each firm, the three machines entered being all of the same model. This might be extended so that a firm could put forward two entries, namely, a team of 500cc machines, each of the same type, and a team of 350cc machines each of the same type. This would enable competitive technical progress to be made whereas, if the number of entries is unlimited we should get into the same position as has been the case in the TT events previously, wherein once a certain make of machine is on the up-grade, year after year, the interest of other manufacturers is jeopardized and they eventually lose real competitive interest".

Major F.W. Smith, Royal Enfield

"The Tourist Trophy Team Test is an excellent idea, and one in which we should, no doubt, participate. The only points at issue are the number of laps and the lap speed for each class.

I am very glad to note that there is no attempt to make this into a stock machine test, though I do feel that some effort might be made to ensure that models securing Tourist Trophy Team Awards should be marketed during the following year in substantially the same form as that in which they were demonstrated."

Mr. Eric A. Barnett, Francis-Barnett

"Although my company is continuing to

concentrate upon the manufacture of small-capacity lightweight utility machines and would not, at present, be interested in competing in any TT race or Team Test, I am of the opinion that the suggestions which have been put forward are very sound. In particular, I think there is a great deal to be said for the proposal to run what amounts to a high-speed team trial for fully equipped solo machines. Such an event should provide useful data for those manufacturers who entered teams, as well as being a valuable demonstration to the public of standard machines' staying power."

Mr. Douglas Mayo, Coventry Eagle

"The suggestions for next years TT races interested me greatly, particularly as the opportunity will arise for an entirely new event on Wednesday. May I suggest that this day be reserved for two-strokes only? The race could be in three classes, not exceeding 100cc, 175cc and 250cc, with the proviso that all machines be basically as manufactured, ie. no special injectors and superchargers barred; also normal fuels should be used.

The public are interested in two-strokes. They seldom if ever aspire to freak machines, but a test under IoM conditions of two-stroke lightweights would not only improve the design of the majority of them, but also bring a domestic touch to an otherwise very specialized event.

If Britain wants to lead the world in two-strokes, they must be proved in the acknowledged hard school - the IoM races".

Mr. Gilbert Smith, Managing Director, Norton

His stated view was that the four-lap Tourist Trophy Team Test was, in effect, a Stock TT, and he could not think that the industry wanted such an event when it was not prepared to support a Stock Trial. Questions he raised were: "Will there be any limit on the price of machines that may take part?", "Will any catalogued model be allowed?", "Will any conversion be considered necessary from the safety angle?" He went on to say that he felt that "An event of this character would detract from the value of the substantive TT, and afterwards motorcyclists, seeing the advertisements, might well enquire, 'who then did win the TT?"

Mr. Philip Vincent, Vincent - HRD

"I think that the new TT Team Test is an excellent idea and am naturally very pleased to note that it will be open to machines of any capacity. The proposed regulations seem very fair and should encourage many readers to compete who have hitherto ignored the races for out-and-out racing machines".

Mr. Edward Turner, Managing Director, Triumph

"I regard the ACU proposals for future TT contests as being sensible, rational and helpful, and the proposed Wednesday event should do much to facilitate the so-called non-racing firms demonstrating their products to the sporting public.

It must have been apparent to a great many people interested in the welfare of motorcycling that the TT as it stood before the war was not doing much to develop the ordinary machine which is the market we aim at, because speeds already achieved are almost in excess of those which can be used by the average man. What is now wanted is reliability at those speeds, not only in any particular component but in the machine as a whole, including the electrical equipment. Therefore, more power to their elbow and I hope the trade will fully co-operate and remove the heartburn which is felt by enthusiasts who, though they admire their machine, are disappointed because it does not appear in the Island under contest conditions".

Mr. R.A. Vinter, Managing Director, Scott

"The re-introduction of the Tourist Trophy as a team test on standard machines is very interesting, but the inclusion of all classes in the one event may prove rather a handful; much depends, of course, on the set minimum speed".

Mr. W.S. Banner, General Manager, Levis

"While we are not likely to be interested from the point of view of supporting entrants, my own personal opinion is that the suggestions are excellent indeed and, in fact, the only hope I can see of saving the TT from lapsing into oblivion which everyone even remotely connected with the industry would view with extreme regret.

You emphasise in your leading article the most important point of all and that is the need for speed in going ahead if the event is to be held in 1947".

There was also a response from Mr. D.S. Heather, Joint Managing Director of AMC, but he confined himself to comments on the International TT.

So, with what could be described as a broadly

<u>A.C.U. TO STAGE—</u>

The Clubman's T.T.

Four-lap Tourist Trophy for which Every Affiliated Club Can Enter : Junior and Lightweight Races on the Monday, and the Senior, as Usual, on the Friday

SO the Wednesday of T.T. week will not see the high-speed demonstration of manufacturers' latest productions, the proposed Tourist Trophy Team Test, nor the world's greatest race over rough-stuff, which was another suggestion, but the first Clubman's T.T. The 1947 Tourist Trophy Races' programme, the Auto Cycle Union announces, will be as follows: Monday, June 9th, Junior (350 c.c.) and Lightweight (250 c.c.) T.T. Races held concurrently; Wednesday, June 11th, the Clubman's T.T.; Friday, June 13th, the Senior (500 c.c.) T.T.

The Lightweight, Junior and Senior races will be held over seven laps of the 37¾-mile Isle of Man "Mountain" course and will be under the same general regulations as pre-war except that, following the international decisions, superchargers will be barred and the fuel employed will be straight petrol of 70-75 octane value supplied by the organizers. It is not new, of course, for 250 c.c. machines to race concurrently with three-fifties. In 1920 and 1921 there was a special 250 c.c class of the Junior T.T., with *The Motor Cycle* Trophy for the winner; in 1922 there was the first Lightweight T.T., held concurrently with the Junior; not until 1923 was there an entirely separate race.

Up to 1,000 c.c.

Some of the details of the Clubman's T.T. have still to be decided, but sufficient are announced for clubs and clubmen to start making their plans. The race will be over four laps of the course and open to nominated clubmen riding solo motor cycles of 251 to 1,000 c.c. which are manufacturers' catalogued models, fully equipped. What the last two words will cover has not yet been settled, nor whether a racing machine such as a Manx Norton is eligible; presumably it will be, but what equipment will be demanded?

Those eligible to take part are individual riders or teams of three nominated and entered by clubs affiliated to the A.C.U. Such riders must have been members of the club concerned from February 28th of this year, and must not have been entered for any of the other 1947 T.T. Races.

Practising will be carried out at different times from that for the Junior, Senior and Lightweight. An interesting point is that there will be compulsory refuelling during the race.

A club entering a rider will be called upon to declare that the motor cycle

concerned is according to the manufacturer's catalogue, which must have been printed and published previous to the date on which entries close. Some modifications will then be allowed, as, for instance, changes of plugs and tyres. The entry fee will be £2 2s, and the club entering the winning rider will receive the Clubman's Tourist Trophy, and the rider a replica of the Trophy. Further, every club whose rider finishes within a specified time limit will be awarded a free entry in the 1947 Manx Grand

Prix; it can use this free entry either for the rider who was successful in the Clubman's T.T. or for some other member. The question of whether a trophy should be awarded in each of the three classes, 350, 500 and 1,000 c.c., other than the class which produces the outright winner, is under consideration by the T.T. Sub-committee, who hope in the near future to issue full information in the form of regulations. Editorial comment on the decisions appears on page 39.

*   *   *

It will be noticed that the dates, June 9th, 11th and 13th, are those originally fixed—that they have not been changed following the International Conference in Paris at which Switzerland stated that it required June 1st or 8th for the Grand Prix of Europe. The A.C.U. has discussed the matter with the Manx legislature, which has decided that the dates chosen for the T.T. must stand. Switzerland, too, has been unable to change, so there will be an unfortunate clash which, presumably, will mean that the Grand Prix of Europe is but the G.P. of Europe in name. While over in the Isle of Man, the A.C.U. T.T. Sub-committee, in the form of Mr. Ball and Mr. Huggett, also met representatives of the Manx Grand Prix — the chairman, Mr. Robert Cowell; the secretary, Mr. Ducker; and the chief marshal, Mr. Hanson—who, it is understood, were in full accord with the proposals.

supportive response from the manufacturers, and a need acknowledged by all for a speedy decision in order that the 1947 TT could be staged at all, one might have expected the event to have gone ahead. History shows of course that it didn't, at least not in the 'Team Test' format. Behind the public statements of general enthusiasm lay fundamental difficulties between manufacturer and fellow manufacturer, and between manufacturers and the ACU. *'Motor Cycling'* Editor Bob Holliday, writing in the 23rd January 1947 issue, put the cause down to *"the disappointingly lukewarm response the manufacturers gave to the quite sensible suggestion of a high-speed demonstration"*, and a Mr. Good of Sevenoaks, Kent, in a letter to the same magazine that month probably got as near to the truth as anyone ever will when he said *"It would appear that the ACU was unable to enlist sufficient support for the Manufacturer's Team Trial; presumably the obvious point that the event would be a bad advertisement for all but the best performers, was insurmountable. This seems a great pity, as it would have been a unique spectacle"*. It isn't hard to imagine the difficulties in getting manufacturer's to agree on a set target speed for any given class, each not wanting to show their own models in an unflattering light.

The first meeting between the Competition Committee of the Manufacturer's Union and the ACU to discuss the 'Team Test' had taken place during Manx Grand Prix week, on the 22nd August 1946. What was said and by who was kept within the individual members of the ACU and the manufacturers' representatives at the time, and now, after the passage of almost sixty years, it is difficult to trace how this concept mutated into the Clubman's TT races, but what is clear is who championed it at that time. From reports of the ACU General Council Meeting held on 14th February 1947, a certain Mr. M.D. Ball, who spoke on behalf of the ACU Competitions Committee, was quite obviously one of those enthused by the idea, even saying in answer to a question from one of the Centre delegates, that he could foresee that the Clubman's TT would become the TT of the future [An obituary in the 1955 'Motor Cycling Yearbook' for M.D. (John) Ball described him as "the man who originated the Clubman's TT events"].

Perhaps the change was quite logical. That a 'Wednesday' event would take place was more or less certain, and if the manufacturers could not agree on a set speed for the classes, what better way than let the machines and riders set their own, to go as fast as they could at the same time as the opposition; in other words, make a race of it.

It was to be January 1947 before the public (and therefore prospective entrants) were given first details. From *'Motor Cycling'* of 16th January 1947, *"Congratulations to the ACU on its introduction of a Clubman's TT Race. Here at last is the logical full-scale development of that experiment made in 1939, during 'Motor Cycling's' Donington Day, when the ordinary private owner on his ordinary everyday machine was first given the opportunity to pit his skill against his peers on a recognised road-racing circuit."*

The following commentary on the proposals comes from the same week's *'The Motor Cycle'*. *"Both the date and the programme of TT week in the Isle of Man are now definite. There will be three days racing as usual. On the Monday (June 9th) the Lightweight and Junior Tourist Trophy Races will be held concurrently; the Friday, June 13th, is reserved for the great event of the week, the Senior Tourist Trophy for solo motorcycles not exceeding 500cc. The problem of what to stage on the Wednesday has been solved by the institution of an event fresh in TT annals, the Clubman's TT, which will be open to members of ACU-affiliated clubs nominated by those clubs and riding solo motorcycles of 251 to 1000cc. This race will be over four laps and the intention is that machines shall be fully equipped, though precisely what is meant by the term awaits clarification.*

There is no gainsaying the interest such an event must create among sporting clubmen and, since the machines are to be catalogued models, the race may well have a special significance to motor cyclists in general. On the face of things, the event seems to promise to be almost as informative as the high-speed demonstration, open to manufacturers, which the Auto Cycle Union originally postulated and which the industry decided was undesirable. An objection to the Clubman's TT ruling is that home-

built machines, it seems, will automatically be excluded.

Among the awards are free entries in the September Manx Grand Prix. Using the Clubman's TT as a means of graduating to the Manx Grand Prix is a clever move, but some will wonder whether in this latter there has not already been an event which could without any great stretch of imagination be termed a Clubman's TT.

To judge from experience over the Amateur Road Races, the forerunners of the Manx Grand Prix, the ACU may encounter some little difficulty in its decision that the clubmen's machines must be 'manufacturers catalogued models, fully equipped'. In 1923, the year of the first Amateur Road Race, there were many wrangles, but in that case of course, the ACU was not the organising body and there was division of authority, if not of interests. With strict knowledgeable scrutineering it should be possible to overcome most of the difficulties."

Two weeks later, 'Motor Cycling' carried a selection of views on the announcement of the Clubman's TT from various club, trade and sport individuals, who were all pretty much enthusiastically in support of the event, although one or two had a caution over machine regulations and the general safety aspects of inexperienced riders on such an unforgiving circuit. Some also expressed the very understandable view that the event *"had been wished upon them rather too swiftly"*, and that the various Centre Competitions Committees should have been consulted before any announcement had been made. Not as many manufacturers cared to make public comment on the new proposals as did on the previous 'Team Test' idea, but reaction was forthcoming from four.

Mr. Philip Vincent, of Vincent-HRD, said that he was naturally rather pleased that the 'big uns' were going to be given a chance to gallop round the Island. *"But,"* he added, *"I hope they select the riders carefully. Otherwise it is going to be like the first half-hour after the roads are opened each June - only more prolonged!"* He foresaw difficulties arising over the defining of standard machines, but was sure that could be overcome. And a race for over-the-counter models he said (quoting the Le Mans 24-hour car race), could be the finest proving ground,

and the finest advertisement for the successful, that any manufacturer could desire.

A statement from the Triumph factory considered that a Clubman's TT run on the right lines was an excellent idea. It continued *"The practical difficulties which must be successfully catered for are, however, considerable, and final judgement of the ACU's decision to hold such an event in June must be reserved until fully detailed rules and regulations are available. We consider that, provided the event is such that the clubman can compete on a reasonably standard sports machine and have a real chance of winning, great interest will be created by an event which will give opportunities of a type which have not in the past been available."*

Jock West, Sales Manager for AMC, and himself a top-line TT rider, gave the following (and somewhat surprising) statement. *"I have discussed the proposal of a Clubman's TT with a number of knowledgeable racing folk, and we are all agreed that it is a most ill-advised thing, liable to have most unfortunate repercussions. In my view, the requirements of the clubmen are fully catered for by the Manx Grand Prix, and the June event provides sufficient interest and entertainment without this added complication. Looked at from the safety angle only, the results of the Clubman's TT might be catastrophic and, far from putting racing in a favourable light to the public, might easily have the very opposite effect."*

George Savage, Sales Manager for BSA, issued on their behalf a statement which was described by 'Motor Cycling's' correspondent as being *"as diplomatic as a Government pronouncement"*. *"We are always keenly interested in motorcycle sport, and believe that the Clubman's TT motorcycle race will create considerable interest, particularly to riders of machines not manufactured for road racing."*

The changes that were made to the Team Test concept were simple and effective. The size of the likely entry was increased by inviting individuals and teams to be fielded by clubs, irrespective of machine selection (but still only catalogued same-as-you-could-buy machines would be eligible), rather than requiring two or three teams from each manufacturer. Crucially though, they would be 'proper' races over the same circuit as the International TT. The organiser's intention was to thus improve the breed of road-going sports motorcycles by pitting them against each other in direct competition, to be held in the full view of the world, in the spotlight of TT fortnight, over the most demanding race circuit in the world. Above all, for the riders, it represented a realistic way of achieving what was otherwise an almost impossible dream, that of competing in the TT or Manx Grand Prix (not many in those early post-war days of shortages and restrictions could afford to buy, transport and run a dedicated racing motorcycle). Nonetheless, ordering and obtaining new machines were two very different things in those post-war years, and, in the 'export everything' years that followed, demand outstripped supply (for some models anyway) for most if not all the ten years of the Clubman's.

As highlighted by the comments above, the wisdom of letting dozens of inexperienced clubmen loose on the TT Mountain circuit in their own race was, to some, questionable. These misgivings were increased when the meagre allocation of dedicated practice periods was made known, especially bearing in mind that the majority of riders would be newcomers (already for safety reasons the decision had been made to keep the Clubman's practice separate from the International sessions). Therefore, in order to provide some degree of qualification and selection, riders were to be nominated and entered by a club affiliated to the ACU, either as individuals or teams of three, with the riders having been members of that club at least from the end of February of the same year. The clear intention was that the clubs themselves would perform this screening process by nominating known riders who could claim some experience and who had demonstrated their racing capabilities on the mainland short circuits. On the other hand, for the first year of the Clubman's at least, there was no 'upper' limit on qualification, the only stipulation being that the rider had not entered the International TT of the same year. This meant that overseas riders, pre-war TT riders and Manx Grand Prix riders of any year were all eligible, as were past winners of either the June or September races. The eligibility requirements changed for 1948, when riders who had gained a replica in any TT, or finished in the first three of a post-war Manx Grand Prix, were barred. Later, for 1950, this was tightened

further so as to bar riders who had:

a) started in an International TT or International road race, or

b) won a replica in any Manx Grand Prix or finished in any three Manx Grands Prix, or

c) finished in 1st, 2nd or 3rd place in any Junior, Senior or 1000cc Clubman's TT, or

d) finished in any three previous Clubman's TT races.

Also in subsequent years, the Lightweight class was treated a little differently, barring only past winners from competing again in that class (but presumably they would have been allowed to enter a bigger class). Entry fee in 1947 was two guineas (£2.20). The initial proposals included for machines of 251 cc and over, and caused much criticism and debate, but were probably realistic. All the clamour for a Lightweight category to be included was eventually successful, but in the end only eight entries were actually received.

On machine eligibility there was some initial confusion, as the ACU requirements for *"manufacturer's catalogued models, fully equipped"*, left room for interpretation. Even *'The Motor Cycle'* in mid-January 1947, took this to include such production racing machines as the Manx Norton, but wondered what 'equipment' would be required. Later that month, the matter seemed to be settled by detailed proposals from the ACU, which stated *"Every motorcycle entered for these Races shall be a two-wheeled vehicle propelled by an engine and shall be a fully equipped model according to the manufacturer's catalogue which shall have been published before 28th February 1947, such catalogue to be submitted to the Union by the entrant not later than 3rd May 1947. At least 25 of each model entered shall have been produced by the makers and such motorcycles shall include in their equipment, kick-starters and full lighting equipment".* Although lights and kickstarters had been identified as being part of the required equipment, still some misinterpretations persisted. *'Motor Cycling'* of 13th March 1947 contained the following; *"As for the Clubman's TT, the country is just seething with rumour and, if all the prospective riders do eventually send in their entries, the ACU will have little difficulty in fielding its anticipated 80 starters. Unfortunately, so many would-be competitors are banking on new-machine deliveries which are now problematical. Incidentally the 'Manx' Nortons are now catalogued with lights, silencers etc. which would seem to make them eligible for the event. Velocette have, according to the rules proposed at the recent ACU Council meeting, got until April 30 to amend their catalogue similarly in respect of the KTT".*

The kickstarter requirement would have needed the Manx and KTT to be specially equipped with roadster gearboxes or with modifications to the race box, neither of which were impossible, but in the end neither manufacturer produced the required 25, and therefore the models were simply ineligible. Whether any were made, or attempted to be made, is an interesting question.

Number plates, stands, horns, head and tail lamps had to be removed, but the removal of luggage carriers, speedometers, electrical equipment and dynamos was optional. Riders were allowed to alter the position of footrests and the brake operating mechanism, but changes to original equipment were limited to 'consumables' such as plugs, tyres and chains. No change from standard ignitions, carburettors and gearboxes was allowed, although gear ratios could be altered. Exhaust pipes had to be *"approximately the same diameter throughout"*, thus barring megaphones. Many riders used plain pipe extensions in place of the silencer(s), but actual removal of the silencer was optional, not compulsory. Any attempt at lightening by metal removal (eg. drilling) or the substitution of lighter metal, was prohibited. 'Pool' petrol was mandatory, as was the use of the kick-start for the start of the race and following the (compulsory at the end of the 2nd lap) fuel stop. The method of re-starting from any other stop, whether scheduled or not, could be run-and-bump if the rider so wished. A 15-minute warm-up period was permitted prior to the off, riders using the Glencrutchery Road back down toward Governors Bridge. Nowhere in the Rules and Eligibility Regulations was there any stated intention to prevent the use of a 'tuned' engine, provided that whatever work had been done did not infringe the 'equipment' regulations.

The Clubman's TT was not, nor was it the intention that it ever should be, an 'amateur' status event. In addition to the Tourist Trophy itself for the race-winner, cash prizes were awarded to the winners and place-men.

On the question of rider eligibility, particularly the ineligibility of Motor Cycle Union of Ireland (MCUI) members when foreign nationals were allowed to start, the ACU made it clear that they had graded the event as 'National' status, and as a result MCUI members would not be eligible unless that organisation was to surrender its independence and become affiliated to the ACU. That was not very likely to happen, nor was it likely that the ACU would make direct approaches to selected MCUI-affiliated riders. At first this appears to be another example of ACU pomposity, but the then ACU Secretary, Mr. Sam Huggett, put the situation into common-sense language, saying that as the event was run as a National, clubs outside the ACU's jurisdiction could not enter riders. However, it would not *"matter a toot what a man's nationality was"* if he were selected, and entered by, an ACU club, and was a member of that club before 28th February 1947.

Graham Walker's Editorial in the 27th March 1947 issue of *'Motor Cycling'* was enthusiastic in support of the races, but was critical of some aspects of the Reulations *"... the regulations for the new Clubman's TT will evoke criticism in varying degrees. Again we feel sympathy with the ACU in tackling a formidable task, but that does not prevent us expressing the view that a brilliant conception has been marred by weak planning. The basic idea of a full-scale road race for the ordinary clubman is excellent. Why, then, largely defeat that object by making the rules so elastic that a club may apparently nominate a team of ex-TT winners? Surely, as the avowed purpose of the event is to provide potential entrants for the Manx Grands Prix, it would have been fairer to restrict entries to riders who have never competed in a race listed on the International Calendar. As it is, there would appear to be nothing to prevent competitors in past Manx Grands Prix putting in practice for next September's events.*

The more we study the regulations, the more convinced do we become that the Clubman's TT has fallen between two stools. At the one extreme the event might have been a virtually unrestricted 'free-for-all' race; at the other, an opportunity for the industry to learn much about its standard products. It is neither the one nor the other. For example, to permit the fitting of racing footrests and brake pedals, yet to insist on the use of kick-starters, may result in riders fitting folding rests, which are by no means safe. The permission apparently granted to fit close gear ratios will necessitate in some instances the making of special parts not normally available to the public. What is there to prevent such parts being made of non-standard materials, and what is to prevent replacement of standard valves, brake linings, chains and other vital equipment with equipment of special quality? The wholesale removal of accessories, presumably in the interest of safety, will destroy an invaluable opportunity for research into components which would benefit from a high-speed test of this nature. On balance, the machines on the grid will approximate in their equipment, or lack of it, very closely to the genuine racers, thus such regulations as the kick-starting rule and the insistence upon the retention of speedometer gearing savour somewhat of straining at a gnat and swallowing a camel. The fact is that the 'fully-equipped' rule, designed to exclude machines incorporating racing components, has been so emasculated as to be scarcely worthwhile.

The most serious criticism, however, concerns the meagre practising period allocated to this new event. We say without hesitation that four periods, representing under the most favourable conditions a total of 12 laps, are insufficient. We are aware that there is nothing to prevent riders covering an unlimited number of laps during unofficial hours, but this a practice to be discouraged for obvious reasons and is also one which is useless in gaining the knowledge of the circuit which is essential to safe navigation at maximum speeds. We appeal to the ACU to endeavour by some means to increase the number of periods to six for the Clubman's event.

Despite our criticisms, we believe this new race

has very great possibilities when experience has dictated where regulations should be strengthened or modified. But the first event can so easily be a tragedy instead of a triumph - and inadequate practising is the one risk which competitors must not be called upon to face".

One aspect of the introduction of the Clubman's event to the International TT race-week of 1947 may come as something of a surprise to us now, especially so because in later years the Clubman's itself became so one-make dominated. However, at the time of their introduction, the new races brought with them the priceless attribute of machine variety. The great days of Italian, German and British factory teams, head-to-head in the early and mid-50's International TT's were then still to arrive, and the 1947 Junior and Senior races were stocked by virtually two makes, Norton and Velocette. There was serious concern that the lack of different makes contesting the International TT could reduce the stature of the races, whereas the entries for that first Clubman's TT represented no fewer than twelve British manufacturers. How enthusiastic the race-goers would be to the new races would become apparent during June, but support from manufacturers, dealers and accessories suppliers was by and large very strong indeed. The sales possibilities created by a 'Clubman's Day' in the middle of TT race-week, show-casing the latest sports models in front of an enthusiastic, knowledgeable, and above all numerous, audience, were not lost on the trade. Some even expressed a hope that the 1948 TT would be 100% 'Clubmanised', which is interpreted as meaning that all the TT races should be contested using production sports machines. Thankfully that never happened, and the 'Golden Age' of International TT racing was soon to begin. There is some irony in that now, sixty years on, the TT races are 100% 'Clubmanised' in terms of machinery, the last TT races held for purpose-designed and built racing motorcycles were the 2004 Lightweight and Ultra-Lightweight events.

IF I WERE YOU . . .

In 1946 Graham Walker. then Editor of *'Motor Cycling'* produced a series of articles about preparing for the forthcoming Clubman's TT races.

Graham drew on his many years of experience through the 1920s and 1930s, he raced solo and sidecar on the Island, winning the 1931 Lightweight and finishing in the top six on twelve occasions. He ran the Sunbeam solo and sidecar race team in the 1920s and was a member of the Rudge team comprising Ernie Nott, Tyrell Smith and himself which swept all before them in the late 1920s and early 1930s with wins in Lightweight, Junior and Senior classes.

The following nine pages were scanned from bound volumes, which explains the dark line on the inside edge of the pages.

We are indebted to Mortons Motorcycle Media for allowing us to reproduce the following article.

Preparing for the Clubman's T.T.

DOTTED about all over the British Isles are some 80 or more lucky people. They are the chaps who will be nominated by various A.-C.U. clubs to ride in the first Clubman's T.T. on Wednesday, June 11. Several will have already raced over the extraordinarily difficult Manx circuit, but for the majority, I imagine, that experience will be a new one. It is for the latter that I am writing this short series of articles, in the hope that the advice I offer will help them to avoid the twin pitfalls of over-confidence and undue awe of the occasion.

Sitting in my study on this Sunday night I have recalled my impressions of the T.T. course as I saw it first in 1920. Those impressions are still very vivid. I had crossed to the Island full of a confidence based on a considerable experience of short hill-climbs, speed trials and sand races, but when I got there I was petrified with fear. The task of mastering the difficulties of the 37¾ miles circuit seemed altogether too big to be tackled in the brief space of 12 practising periods. I secretly wanted to pack my bags and beat it back to Birmingham but, thank goodness, I was too much of a coward to be a coward in public and stayed to learn many lessons the hard way. As you, the newcomer to the Island, will probably feel much the same and will apparently have only four official practising periods, I have tried to-night to picture what I should do were I in your shoes.

I should, for a start, try to see the problem in the right perspective. With the obvious exception of the original 1907 event, no rider has succeeded in winning a T.T. on his first visit to the Island. And that applies, too, to the Manx Grand Prix save only in the case of Tim Hunt, who, I think, was a newcomer when he won the 1927 "Amateur," as it was then called. You may be a second Tim, but that's unlikely. Thus, common sense suggests that the winner of the first Clubman's T.T. will almost certainly be someone who knows the Mountain course intimately, because that knowledge is worth several m.p.h. in average speed, all other things being equal.

Worries Vanish!

Once that viewpoint is accepted, half your anxieties will disappear. Regard yourself in your first year as serving an apprenticeship to the world's toughest circuit and you will cease to worry because your lap times may not be so hot compared with others put up on models just like your own. I know it is difficult, but what you want to do is to ignore everyone else. All you should be interested in is finding your right line on the corners, your safe maximum speeds on those corners, your latest possible braking points and, of course, the individual idiosyncrasies of your mount.

And that is plenty on which to concentrate in 12 laps! They are essentially personal problems and your limits will differ, however slightly, from those of other riders. So don't be drawn into friendly time-and-attention-wasting scraps—unless, perhaps, the other chap is known to be a better rider, in which case you may learn something if you remember not to be led into corners at a speed "too fast for owner!"

Now, about this line business. Divorced from the glamour associated with their famous names, the corners on the T.T. circuit are precisely the same as the corners of similar radii, camber and surface on any other road. There is no magic which will enable you to take them faster merely because they are in the Isle of Man. So if someone tells you that Harold Daniell takes a certain bend flat out in top and you feel happier in third with a bit of throttle in hand, don't get rattled. You are not interested in Harold Daniell, only in yourself. Maybe Harold took that particular bend in third when he first came to the Island, anyway. It was because he had the sense to "learn how" safely that he eventually worked up to that "flat out in top" routine.

It is better to enter a corner slow and leave it fast than vice versa. If you will always remember that advice, 'you, too, may learn to be a Harold Daniell." In other words, if you can take a certain corner at 50 m.p.h. maximum enter it at 49 and leave it at 51. The secret in maintaining a high average is to do all your braking on the straight and to

A4

Some Advice on Road-racing Technique
Offered to Competitors in the
Forthcoming I.o.M. Innovation

enter the bends at speeds which permit you to accelerate all the way round them, so that you emerge on the next straight with the motor mounting towards peak revs.

A vital factor in this procedure is the "straight line" technique with which the shortest possible route is taken through the curves. There are umpteen corners and bends on the course which can be cut in this manner, some flat out in top and others with the use of brakes and gears, but the right-handed right-angle at Craig-ny-Baa will serve for a classic example.

Hurtling down the steep drop from Kate's Cottage, the plot is to change down through the gears and brake in a straight line, whilst working towards the left gutter on the approach, to a point where you can "see through" the

Follow in the wheel tracks of the experts and you won't go wrong. Our arrow indicates where Bob Foster (A.J.S. 4) banked hard over to take the straight-line route through Craig-ny-Baa corner.

bend—well beyond where one would normally turn right if faithfully following the curve of the road. The model is then banked hard over and aimed at the right-hand gutter on the apex of the curve, the natural camber here enabling full acceleration to be used safely.

Maybe that reads rather like "Teachings For Tiny Tots," but it is surprising how many people manage to wallop the protective haybags at "the Craig" because of their failure to remember that elementary lesson! Maybe you've done some grass tracking, or perhaps you've raced at Donington or Cadwell. Well, that experience will help a lot but, believe me, there's a world of difference between rushing round a short circuit for 10 minutes and the Isle of Man course for two hours or more. That is why I stress something that may seem obvious but which can cease to be so if you allow your concentration to wander momentarily.

But it is not the famous corners which present the biggest

Instruction by numbers!
Three Manx Grand Prix
riders demonstrate the
three stages in the straight
line technique as applied to
Quarter Bridge.

remember. It blows a bit at times up on the Mountain. Beware of the sudden calm when you enter the lee of the Bungalow. You may have been subconsciously leaning into the wind and the resultant swerve when the building shelters you from the draught can be very frightening if it catches you unawares. And Windy Corner is so named because of a similar fright-making effect.

That, in turn, reminds me of another very important precaution. When riding in perfect visibility, you are normally looking many yards ahead of your actual position. Without realizing it, you are cutting lots of minor curves, making a straight line through gentle right- or left-hand bends. But when you find yourself in a swirling mass of Mountain mist you instinctively look to one side, following closely the curvature of the road. At least one famous rider has crashed because he thought he knew the course better than he did in such conditions

He knew that after three right-hand bends on the Mountain there was a longish straight. What he didn't realize was that there is an initial slight right-hand sweep before entering those curves—he had always regarded it as straight because in clear weather he went through it on a bee-line—and following its actual curvature in the fog he counted it as No. 1 of the big bends only to open flat out on the last and worst of them.

Take my tip, don't trust your memory in the mist and don't try to pass someone until you can see sufficiently far ahead; better to remember that in your first year the big idea is to finish the race and good luck to those who can go faster

dangers for the newcomer. Rather is it the host of unnamed bends which look faster than they really are—the left curve approaching the Bungalow is the perfect example of what I have in mind—and that's why it will pay you to make haste slowly during your initial lappery.

Which reminds me of a useful tip. If you find yourself wafting round a long bend a bit too briskly and easing the throttle doesn't produce the desired deceleration, turn your "inside" knee out as far as you can; your leg acts as a sail and wind pressure will help to pull you round on to your line. And that's no fairy story. The effect may be largely psychological, but it certainly works.

Using the Wind

In that connection much the same thing applies to braking. Make full use of the wind resistance to save wear and tear on the linings. If you flatten yourself, at great personal discomfort, to reduce wind resistance in your endeavours to go faster, it is logical enough deliberately to increase that resistance when you want to slow up. And not only will you have better control of the model if you sit squarely in the saddle on the slowish corners; you will also give cramped muscles and restricted circulation a sporting chance. Never mind about those pictures of famous riders rushing round Governor's Bridge on the rear pad. Stanley Woods has won twice as many T.T.s as anyone else and *he* always sits in the saddle on the slower curvery.

And talking of wind pressure, there is another thing to

Fine Weather Tips

Conversely, fine weather has its especial danger, particularly during the second lap period in morning practising. From Kirkmichael to Ramsey there are many points at which the low-set rising sun can blind you very completely, so take particular heed of the starter's warning on such a day. In this connection, the long Sulby Straight can be particularly dangerous as it is possible to miss one or other of the big warning signs for the bridge bend and to overshoot your braking point on the approach.

Other notorious spots are Bishopscourt, Ballaugh Bridge, the Quarry bends before Sulby, and several unnamed stretches between the Ginger Hall Hotel and Milntown, whilst a most disconcerting "fluttering" effect is produced on the eyes by sunlight shining through the trees along the approach to Ramsey. And, of course, this danger applies to other points during evening practice when the sun is setting.

Despite the all-too-short practising period you've been allotted there is much you can do to improve your knowledge of the course outside official practising hours. Merely to go lapping round and round on a hack model during the daytime is largely a waste of effort; besides, on roads open to traffic it can be highly dangerous—there is always some fool prepared to rush round too fast, and not always the right way of the circuit at that.

No, the thing to do is to divide the course up into, say, five sections. I would suggest (1) The Grandstand to Ballacraine, (2) Ballacraine to Kirkmichael, (3) Kirkmichael to Ramsey, (4) Ramsey to the Bungalow, and (5) The Bungalow to the Grandstand. Then got out on a spare

With their braking done on the short downhill approach these two riders have a clear view round Signpost Corner as they accelerate.

A5

Beware of wet tar on a sunny day! Not everyone is blessed with the ability shown here by Tim Hunt, who extricated himself from this embarrassing situation in the 1932 Senior T.T.

model and concentrate on one or other of these sections in turn, getting off frequently to view the main corners at their points of entry and exit. Then later compare notes with a friend and see how many corners, bends and so forth on each section you can jot down on a piece of paper. You'll find the special milestones a very useful guide in mentally sub-dividing each section.

And don't forget the wonderful opportunity presented by the separate practising times allotted to the competitors in the actual T.T. races. Whatever you do, don't let the claims of sleep or the delights of Douglas deprive you of the chance to watch the stars on such bends as Windy Corner, Kate's Cottage and its approach, Craig-ny-Baa, Hillberry, Signpost (watch that one; it's downhill after an upgrade and apt to catch people on their braking), Quarter Bridge, Braddan Bridge and Union Mills—all points within easy reach of your digs. And it wouldn't be a bad idea to stop once or twice towards the end of Clubman's practising to see how your fellow competitors do things!

But if you must stop on the course for any reason, *get your machine off the road immediately.* More than one well-known T.T. rider has been guilty of imperilling himself and others through foolishly parking on the line taken by the fast men. It's not the sort of mistake one makes twice, but even once may be too often.

On race day, by the way, you will probably suffer from nerves on the grid. Rest assured you won't be unique in that respect. Everyone else will be feeling the same, although each will disguise it in a different way. It may comfort you to know that that complaint lasts throughout one's racing career, but the symptoms invariably disappear so soon as the model fires and you are in the saddle.

But there are other things to guard against on race day. The happy-go-lucky atmosphere of the practising period has been exchanged for a more purposeful air. Familiar corners appear different and the reason may puzzle you. It is due to crowds of spectators—and be careful lest they mask some of your braking landmarks. But don't get flustered. Seldom has a T.T. been won in the first lap and it's certain your race won't be. Ignore the crowds. Don't be distracted by fluttering programmes and waving hands. Try to kid yourself you are still practising and, above all, give your model a chance to settle down. If I were you, I'd go really carefully to Kirkmichael or at the very least to Ballacraine. Many a chap has crashed at Quarter Bridge through trying to do his stuff in the first mile.

By the way, if it's a fine day there will be a narrow black line approaching the principal corners worn by the tyres of the Junior T.T. chaps. It will be a useful guide, but don't let it distract you from paying attention to your braking points.

And what if it's wet? Well, if you use your common sense you'll be all right. All you need do is brake a shade earlier, take even greater advantage than usual of the favourable cambers and be sure the model is on an even keel when accelerating or decelerating. During practice make a mental note of the few shiny patches where there may be danger in banking over at speed—and have large squares of chamois leather stitched to the back of your gloves with which to give frequent sweeping wipes to your goggles. By the way, *never*, if you can possibly avoid it, lift your goggles in rain. The delicate eye muscles cannot stand the tattoo of the drops at high speed and the lids will slowly close, however much will power you exert.

If you must lift them, they'll be misty inside when you slip them on again. Usually a gloved thumb can be inserted to wipe each eyepiece. Incidentally, a sucked finger quickly applied on a fine day will remove squashed flies before they congeal into case-hardened sugar!

Towards the end of the race the near side of the rear tyre will probably be covered in oil thrown off by the chain. Bear that in mind when taking fast left bends—try to pick a line which keeps the model more vertical than usual. And if you are a late number, don't forget another danger, particularly prevalent when it's wet—thoughtless spectators on the Bungalow-to-Hillberry section walking in the road during the closing stages. They usually appear to be stone deaf as well as daft!

Well, that seems to be that so far as the riding part of things is concerned. I am confident that if you will accept my advice and your model "resists," you will see that finest of all flags, the one with the black and white squares.

In the next instalment I will go into the matter of machine preparation.

Cheerio, chaps; keep well into the left this Easter. There will be a lot of odd people going round the other way on your road, so don't start a premature spot of "straight line" cornering!

(To be continued)

THIS
IS
YOUR
AIM!

Caution is necessary to the very end. More than one competitor has crashed on crossing the finishing line through over enthusiastic braking after an otherwise faultless ride.

Preparing for the Clubman's T.T.—Part II

"IF I WERE YOU . . ."

THE first instalment in this three-part series dealt with riding methods whereby the newcomer to the famous Isle of Man circuit can make the best use of the very limited practising time at his disposal. Obviously, mechanical breakdowns or any vicious qualities in his model which prevent complete concentration on mastery of the difficult course are things to be eliminated beforehand by the rider if the tight time schedule is not to be completely upset.

You may be riding a machine which you know inside and out. On the other hand, you may be astride something pretty potent in June which you have yet to see other than as a catalogue illustration. Again, you may be a star turn on the mechanical side, or a public menace when let loose with a spanner, but for whichever category you qualify, let me please impress upon you that yours is the ultimate responsibility for appearing on the starting grid with a roadworthy machine between your knees. Thus, you should have a complete knowledge of everything that is done to your machine, and if someone else does the work, you should check every little detail before the model is handed in.

You owe that attention not only to yourself, to your club and the other competitors, but also to any mechanic who may have helped you. Rest assured the latter will not be insulted if you cross-examine him. Indeed, if he has any sense, he will be relieved by your acceptance of responsibility for your own performance.

If I were you, I should have attended to all of the following points—and a good many more besides—before the first official practice. They would have been points jotted down on the backs of envelopes or in a pocket book, just as they came into my head at odd moments, later to be transferred to an orderly list, each item being crossed off when completed. Note that the majority deals with navigation or transmission—far too many chaps are apt to concentrate on the power unit to the exclusion of other details of a less spectacular nature, but of equal importance in sustained high-speed motoring.

Continuing the Series of Tips for Intending Competitors in Next June's "Everyman" Race

—— By ——

GRAHAM WALKER

That Taut Feeling

Briefly, your model should have that taut all-in-one-piece feel which is obtained only where wheels are correctly aligned and balanced, bicycle bearings are free without side play, and every control works without conscious effort. There is no magic in achieving this desirable state of affairs, all that is required being patience, common sense with tools, and, above all, the determination not to be satisfied until each item is as perfect as you can make it.

First, then, I should check wheel bearing adjustment and the tyres for truth on the rims—and I assume you will have fitted a ribbed front cover. Next, with brake plates and shoes removed, each wheel would be balanced *in situ* by means of lead wire wound round appropriate spokes, taped in position and shellacked. At high speeds the tyre tread "lifts," so protruding mudguard bolts would be cut short or reversed. When reassembling, check that tightening the spindle nuts does not also tighten the wheel bearings.

Don't adjust the brakes too closely if light-alloy shoes are fitted in a steel drum—they are apt to expand more than the drum when used for long periods, thereby bringing the friction material into constant rubbing contact. If you see blisters around the drum paint, you will know the answer! Incidentally, make sure that brake adjustment nuts are really free all the way up their threads—you may need the adjustment in a hurry during the race! Finally, check the tyre pressures and make a point of using the same gauge at all times—they have been known to vary.

Next, I should strip and examine the steering head bearings; if the machine is new, it is possible the races are not bedding down squarely, due to a spot of enamel on their seatings. On a well-used model the ball tracks may be pitted slightly, in which case the remedy is obvious. Smooth rotation from lock to lock with absence of up and down play in the bearings is *absolutely essential* to good navigation. Next, check the steering damper; very few in my experience are so perfectly set that the friction pressure is constant from lock to lock. The trouble usually lies in a cockeyed torque arm. A large spanner, used as a twister, and possibly a file will work wonders. By the way, where girder forks are used it is best to remove the shackle bolts and to examine them for high spots. As with the steering head, perfect freedom of movement without side play is essential if steering is not to be impaired.

Then the chains should be checked for tension. It is better for them to be very slightly on the easy side than too tight, and remember that, with spring frames of the plunger type, the rear chain is at its tightest at top or bottom of plunger movement, whilst with the swinging-arm pattern the tightest point is reached when the chainstays are horizontal and the wheel spindle in line with pivot point and gearbox mainshaft.

Whatever you do, ensure that the gearbox fixing bolts and adjuster are *really* tight, otherwise on your first practice run the box will probably be pulled back, thereby over-tightening the front chain. As for wheel alignment, a long wooden straight-edge is a pleasant possession, but equally good results can be obtained with a piece of string plus the aid of an intelligent helper. Held taut as high as the crankcase and other obstructions will permit, the string should touch each tyre at two points; this test should, of course, be carried out on both sides of the machine. If the front tyre is of smaller cross-section than the rear, the clearance between string and front cover should, of course, be equal on each side.

The next operation would be to remove all cable clips, most of which are merely ornamental anyway, but where some form of restriction is necessary (such as the possibility of cables fouling fork shackles) make it a slack-fitting narrow strap or a loose loop of insulating tape. When this has been done, check adjustment of clutch, air, ignition and throttle cables, as they will almost certainly want resetting with the clips out of the way. If you are really painstaking, you will make a point, at this stage of the proceedings, of lubricating each cable.

Two Vital Controls

Next, I should concentrate on the twistgrip with throttle cable removed; it should turn smoothly and evenly throughout its range. If it doesn't—and it probably won't—look for high spots on the handlebar and check the operation of the cable drum inside the large split clamp member. Provided the rotating sleeve is free on the bar, careful adjustment of the two locking pins in the clamp will usually solve most problems. Finally, tighten the central nuts or screws on ignition and air levers and increase the friction load on the twistgrip by means of its adjuster until it is on the tight side—controls which vibrate shut unless held in position provide a nerve-racking handicap. Don't forget to make sure—by turning the bars on both locks—that the throttle slide really shuts when the twistgrip is closed.

Oh, yes, that reminds me! If your model is fitted with one of those piffling little half-pint size, one-finger-operated exhaust lifter levers, scrap it and fit a man-sized device. The exhaust lifter is a grand standby in emergencies. I once

A sound knowledge of the circuit is useless without complete reliability in the machine. The scene depicted is typical of any "Works" camp during T.T. week. Those in search of Clubman's T.T. replicas, please note!

covered six and a half laps in a Senior T.T. using the litter as a substitute for a clutch, the operating mechanism of which had ceased to function at Sulby Bridge on the first tour; without that aid, Ramsey Hairpin, Governor's Bridge and one or two other spots would have provided a pretty problem.

And besides, think of that kickstart you have to make both on the grid and after refuelling—and probably with close-ratio gears! On single-cylinder models, at any rate, a hefty exhaust lifter will be more than a trifle useful. Whilst on the subject of control levers, square or hexagon headed setpins are much better than the usual cheese-head affairs, which are apt to work loose in the clips. If in doubt as to their security, don't be afraid of insulating tape —the Clubman's T.T. is a race, not a Concours d'Elegance.

Fuel and Oil Pipes

The next item on the agenda would concern the free and uninterrupted flow of fuel and oil. If I found that a kindly manufacturer had installed flexible pipelines, that would be just dandy, but if they turned out to be rigid things of chromium-plated copper I should want to anneal them and check the re-sweating of nipples before I should feel really happy. At the very least, each pipe would be sawn in half and sheathed with a length of rubber-canvas tubing wired or hose-clipped into position.

And I should certainly enlarge the air vent in the petrol filler cap or its attachment neck. Of course, a central separate racing type vent, complete with long rubber tube to carry away fumes and fuel spray, would be the ideal thing, but would be a trifle tricky to fit to the modern welded tank. A good makeshift, however, can be fashioned by soldering a short curved length of copper pipe into a suitable hole drilled in the filler cap, the inset end of the pipe being swaged over for additional security.

To this, of course, you can attach a length of rubber-canvas pipe, preferably leading backwards to a point below the saddle. If you do this, however, make sure that the cap can be opened and closed really quickly and that it seats securely when slammed shut. And don't forget that petrol taps of the "turn down for on" type should be fairly tight in operation, otherwise they may vibrate shut; a light tap with a spanner on the "handle" end of the taper spigot does the trick.

It would be a good idea, too, to check the tightness of the float chamber cap locking pin and the knurled ring which retains the cable stop-block in the top of the spraying chamber, as both these fitments have been known to work loose, a remark which also applies to the air inlet funnel.

Nothing is more infuriating than a flapping exhaust pipe; besides it is dangerous and may lead to the black flag, which at the least means a stop for inspection by the marshals and at the worst enforced retirement. Therefore, gaze with some suspicion on any but really sturdy clips and ensure that there is one at the bottom of the bend forward of the crankcase in addition to the chainstay support.

Some standard pipes are prone to rub on the road when the model is heeled over smartly—and odd things happen in the Island with cambers, which are apt to reduce pipe clearance with remarkable rapidity! If, therefore, you find scratch marks under your pipe, you may be able to get a little extra clearance by crafty manipulation of the support clips whereby the pipe is pulled in closer to the crankcase. If not, I suggest a little professional aid, as "snake charming" is very definitely an art and something not to be tackled lightly by the inexperienced.

And now for what I consider to be the most important of all the pre-practice tasks—adjustment of riding position. I know that I created a lot of amusement amongst my fellow competitors in the old days because I spent many hours alternately sitting in the saddle or on the mudguard pad and then tweaking a footrest here or a brake pedal there, shifting the kneegrips a shade or bending a control lever a few degrees north or south. But in the long run—and the T.T. is a very long run—I had the last laugh, because that apparently excessive faddiness enabled me to last the distance without getting unduly tired despite several pretty serious physical handicaps.

Probably you don't suffer from similar disabilities, but that's no reason why you should put up with energy-wasting discomfort. Your aim in preparing your machine is to make it so much a part of yourself that you are scarcely conscious of the thousands of movements you must make with your hands and feet during the race. Believe it or not, so little as a quarter of an inch error in the ideal position for your footrests, or a few degrees out in the correct inclination of the saddle, can make the difference between a comfortable ride and one which can become sheer purgatory

A5

with braking and gearchanging finally becoming physical agony.

So don't worry if your pals chip you, but just carry on bending things until you are satisfied. And, by the way, the position which seems ideal when you are wearing flannel bags and a sports coat will be too cramped when you've got full riding kit on; so fine is the margin between perfection and imperfection that thicker boot soles and clothing must be allowed for.

Most footrests and pedals can be bent cold with the aid of a long, stout tube applied intelligently—and that last word means that the part to be operated on should sometimes be detached and held in a vice lest the wrong bit be bent by your efforts! Watch small points, too, in the search for comfort and control. Footrest rubbers, for example, which are a slack fit on their spindles are a curse; a wrapping of insulation tape around the spindles will fix the pads firmly in position.

You will probably come up against one difficulty which I have never had to tackle, namely, the provision of the perfect position for your feet whilst allowing for the use of a kickstarter. Frankly, I don't know how you are going to solve this particular problem because I have a shrewd suspicion that folding or sliding rests will be frowned upon, but I can assure you that none of the time spent in getting rests, brake and gear pedals just the way you want them for perfect control will be wasted. And more particularly will you reap the benefit of patience if the race turns out to be wet. In this connection make sure that the saddle nose pivot pin has no side float; this can be a most disconcerting fault and especially so when roads are slimy.

With regard to security of the machine as a whole, don't be afraid to use spring washers; it is amazing just how many bits can come loose on the Island circuit. Some machines employ tank fixing bolts which must not be fully tightened; in such cases the bolt heads should be drilled and wired in pairs—and that may be a sound precaution to take also with the oil tank bolts.

Well, if you have attended to all the points I have men-

tioned not much remains to be done, other than topping up, before turning out for the first practice morning. When filling the petrol tank, do so with an accurate measure and note exactly how much it will hold. And don't overfill the oil tank; if you do, it will simply "boil over" through the filler cap or air vent and probably smother the rear tyre. Which, in turn, reminds me that when topping up the gearbox it is possible with some designs to get an airlock and, therefore, a false level reading. The secret of security lies in tilting the machine "away" from the filler orifice two or three times whilst pouring in the lubricant, so that the air bubbles may escape. But whatever you do, don't overfill the box or you will certainly plaster the back tyre with the finest skid producer known to science.

Be careful, too, with the oil level in the primary chaincase if one is fitted. Don't overdo things or you may drown the clutch—just enough oil to reach the lowest point of the chain is all that is necessary. Incidentally, should you have a mysterious form of "clutch slip" when accelerating, but no obvious signs of trouble in the clutch itself when examined, have a look at the engine shaft cushdrive member. The spring-loaded face cam may be riding right over the fixed cam with which it mates, in which case the tips of the cams will show signs of distress. This cannot happen if the shock absorber spring is sufficiently strong, or if it goes solid with the cams in reasonably deep engagement. The cure, therefore, is to fit a stouter spring if available, or a thick washer between the spring and its abutment.

In the next and final instalment I intend to outline what I should do, if I were you, about the daily routine check which should be given to the model; what I should endeavour to find out during the practising; what should be done in the way of final adjustments and replacements before handing in the machine, combined with a few observations on clothing, food and so forth. Meanwhile, if you think I can be of any help in tackling some problem which I have so far not mentioned in this series, don't hesitate to write to me.

(To be concluded.)

Preparing for the Clubman's T.T.—(Part III)

IF time-saving be the essence of the contract in a race, it is certainly the quintessence of the problem to be solved during the practising period by the rider who is making the Clubman's T.T. his first long-distance affair. The previous instalments in this series outlined (I) a method of learning the difficult Snaefell circuit in the shortest possible time, (II) the adjustments which should be made on any machine, new or old, so that no time will be wasted through mechanical faults during the all-too-brief practising period. And now—if I am not to offend those readers who suggest that " Motor Cycling " devotes too much space to sport!—I have got to crowd into three pages a host of additional time-saving points which you, the competitor, should have dealt with before you hopefully kickstart on the morning of Wednesday June 11

The first thing to remember is that you will be in the Island on a serious bit of business—to do the best you can for your club. Obvious? Agreed; but it is so *very* easy to relax in the Island and there just isn't time to do so. The first thing, then, is to lay down a routine with the determination to stick to it. If I were you, the following would be my daily practising schedule:—

the glamour inseparable from its long T.T. history, the Island seems to endow competitors with a remarkable ability to do without sleep. But that is not a good thing, because Nature takes a serious view of it in the long run. So don't be tempted—either nip back into bed before breakfast, or make a vow, short of serious trouble with the model, to be asleep by 11 p.m. each night. In this connection, if you drink, beer or stout in moderation during the practising period will do you more good than harm; but, if I were you, I should lay off spirits.

"IF I WERE YOU

Whatever your decision about this sleep business, however, make the following routine check a " must "—and do it immediately you return to the garage, as it will give your mechanic (or yourself) a chance to get on with essential jobs immediately after breakfast.

First, check oil and fuel consumptions by the simple process of refilling with carefully measured quantities. Next, check both chains for tension and the possibility of missing rollers. Then, test tyre pressures and examine the treads for

Awards can be won or lost at the Pits. The first-year competitor and his attendant should practise pit drill to ensure that no vital seconds are wasted on race day.

cuts, nails or embedded flints. Feel the wheel and steering head bearings and check brake adjustments. Next, test the compression and valve clearances, whilst noting any obvious oil leaks and, finally, give a quick glance round for loose nuts or suspicious cracks on enamelled surfaces. You will enjoy your breakfast all the more if all is well.

I have said nothing so far in this series about engine examination, but, if I were you, after the first full morning's practice, I should remove the cylinder head and barrel and have a general gaze round. Whilst on this subject, if you decide to fit any new part, be it a piston ring, a tyre, a chain or what-you-will, *don't* do so immediately before handing-in the model. The part should be given a chance to settle down and for any nuts and so forth to be checked for tightness after running. If time is short, a tour over the Mountain to Ramsey and back is almost as good as a practice lap for this purpose.

The Daily Routine

During the actual lappery I should, of course, concentrate on weighing up the bends, braking points and so forth; but on the straights I would memorize defects in carburation, the riding position or action of controls, steering faults and other features demanding immediate attention in the garage.

On completing the first morning's practice, however, and before toying with thoughts of a " cocoa with Cadbury " or a " coffee with Dunlop " in those very hospitable Paddock tents, I should remove the sparking plug and gaze at its business end, preferably with one of the resident plug or carburetter wizards in attendance. Don't forget that, if they are to pass their expert opinion, it is essential you should have come absolutely flat out down the Glencrutchery Road, and that the throttle was snapped shut as you whipped out the clutch. Don't attempt to trickle into the Paddock on the pilot jet, or all the invaluable evidence will have been destroyed.

Duly depressed or elated by your lap times—and, if I were you, I certainly wouldn't worry too much about these—you will eventually return to your digs. What to do then? Some chaps will go for a swim in Noble's baths, some will go back to bed; others will prefer a hot bath and leisurely shave, wondering meanwhile how soon it will be possible to scrounge breakfast. I leave the decision to you, but with this caution: Due to its wonderful atmosphere, and possibly

On the second morning of practising, make an endeavour to get the pit situation weighed up. Many a valuable second has been lost in races through lack of this knowledge, and, besides, you'll feel such a fool if you overshoot and have to wheel the model backwards! For practising purposes, select any pit and arrange with your attendant to be in it at the conclusion of your final lap. Memorize the position, and as you come down the road, weighing up the braking distance, flick open your fuel and oil caps, just as you would in the race, and try to pull up right opposite your man. Don't worry if spectators grin should you and your assistant go through the motions of operating an imaginary filler and oil gun—you will have the last laugh if this bit of practice saves seconds in the race. And don't forget, if it's a dry morning, you will have to allow a bit more distance on race day if the latter turns out to be wet.

You might try the same experiment in the third practice period, but on the last day concentrate on memorizing the circuit and bedding down any new bits which may have been fitted.

Practising over, you must set about the final preparation of the model prior to handing-in. If I were you I should insist upon my primary and magneto chains being riveted up, thus dispensing with spring links. The chain experts, who will be in the Island, are the people best equipped to

A4

The Concluding Instalment in a Series of Hints and Tips for Newcomers to the Difficult Isle of Man Circuit

"
. . **"**

—— By ——
GRAHAM WALKER

The last chance to satisfy yourself that all is well will come with the warming-up parade prior to the start. Don't forget afterwards to fit that "hard" race plug before wheeling the model down to the starting grid.

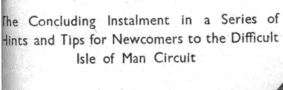

do the job, but if you tackle it yourself remember that you will need the proper soft-nosed riveting links and that the ignition timing should be checked carefully before you remove the magneto chain. Unless you are highly skilled, *don't* attempt in situ riveting; that is just asking for trouble. The rear chain can either be riveted or the spring member of the detachable link made secure with a thin strip of tin.

A Clutch Point

When reassembling the primary drive, note particularly if the clutch-retaining nut has a locking washer. Several designs employ a tab washer; if so, this should be replaced by a new one if the "ears" show signs of cracking across the bend. The constant reversal of load on the gearbox shaft caused by acceleration and braking can loosen that particular nut very quickly.

I should also fit a hexagon locking plate on the blind cap nut below the carburetter jet. If the "gasworks" experts have none in stock, it is a simple matter to make one up and to tape its shank to the neck connecting the float and spraying chambers. And check once again that the locking

ring retaining the air and throttle cable block is also tight.

Fuel and oil filters should be examined, cleaned and replaced after the tanks have been flushed out. All pipes should be blown through, and don't forget, when reassembling the oil pipes, to allow lubricant to flow r ght through the main feed from tank to pump before attaching the bottom union, otherwise you may get an air lock in the system.

Make a real workmanlike job of attaching your three race number plates. Proper bolted clips are the thing, but if you use copper wire don't be stingy with it, and wrap insulating tape round the stays to give it something to bite into.

Next, check the condition of all cables (and particularly their nipples), and ensure that no control lever is likely to work back under vibration. Tape the high-tension cable so that it doesn't drop down when you remove the plug terminal. Check that your spare plugs really spark and have the right gap, also that their washers are firmly in position and that they screw easily into the cylinder head. Finally, test every visible nut and screw *yourself*, and slip on to some part of the machinery half-a-dozen rubber bands—you may find them handy!

Roadside Repairs !

What about tools? You're not Freddie Frith or Harold Daniell, charged with winning a T.T., and therefore concerned with every ounce of superfluous weight. Right? Then a few tools seem to me to be indicated! They may make the difference between an award and a retirement, and, at the least, may save a long wait or a longer walk. I always carried—either in a tank-top toolbox-cum-tummy pad, or in two cycle-type toolbags on a waistbelt—a medium adjustable, a small pair of pliers, two tappet spanners and a short, stout screwdriver, plus some copper wire, a tiny roll of insulating tape and two short lengths of rubber-canvas piping.

In my waistcoat pockets—and I knew *which* pockets—I also carried dismantled chain links (saves time if they are in separate pieces) two spare plugs, with their business ends sealed by dirt-excluding caps; several spring plug terminals, spring clips for throttle needle and float needle, and also a magneto spanner.

Tucked down my right boot, secured by an easy-fitting rubber band, was a plug spanner with the outer edges of the hexagon ground "round" so that it didn't bind against the cylinder fins. Down my left boot was tucked a pipe. If you smoke, take some tobacco or cigarettes; even at current prices they will prove a grand solace if you are unlucky but still conscious! By the same token, carry a pound note; it takes up little room and free beers don't last for ever, even for the most favoured competitor—besides, the Isle of Man

Thousands of spectators will line the approaches to the principal corners on race day, but on each only one man should catch the competitor's eye—the man in white, the official flagman—in this instance standing in front of the hotel at Craig-ny-Baa.

The end of a perfect day. If you follow the advice given in this series you may be that chap behind the Villa Marina microphone on Wednesday, June 11.

pressures, but be careful to use your own gauge if you alter them at all.

If the day be wet, you might consider smearing a little Plasticene round the contact breaker cover and the high-tension lead socket. And as you may be in rather a nervous flap after the official warming-up period, don't forget to fit your new " hard " race plug before wheeling the model down to the grid.

Anything else? Yes; but all small details. First, among the local curiosities in the Isle of Man are vast numbers of " HALT " signs. They appear in the most unexpected places. So do the local police. Both mean what they say, so even if no one is looking *always* obey the signs and thus save possible practising period prosecutions.

By the way, in the first instalment I mentioned the danger of becoming blinded by the sun during early-morning practising. Please add to the list of places quoted Laurel Bank and the long, steep, right-hand sweep just after Ramsey Hairpin. These two points really mark the beginning and end of the stretch—roughly 14 miles—over which this particular hazard is encountered.

On race morning don't forget to mark carefully your pit position and to check over with your attendant on agreed signals. Don't forget to give the petrol cocks a gentle " one for luck " tap with a spanner to ensure they stay open. Don't forget that the race is not won in the first mile, and that a cool, calculated kickstart will be much better than a frenzied dig followed by a disconcerting backfire. If I were you, I should practise kickstarting quite a lot. With " close " gears it is not going to be easy unless pilot setting and throttle opening are dead right.

Railway has to pay its way and you may have to use its services!

On the subject of tools once more, should one take a tyre pump? True, it is awkward to house and a possible danger if it comes loose. I feel, nevertheless, that with a couple of rubber bands to increase its security it *might* get you home if you get a slow puncture. And one of your waistcoat pockets should contain spare Schrader 'caps and' valve " insides " just in case. . . .

And now back again to clothing. The muscles on the underside of the upper arms are apt to " flap " if not supported, and the agony can become intense. For that reason I always saw to it that the sleeves of my waistcoat were made a reasonably tight fit by means of a sleeved sweater. Conversely, don't lace your boots too tight or you will suffer the tortures of the damned. Woven elastic wrist cuffs can be a great help and I found that adhesive plaster wound round the bottom thumb joints eased the strain created by constant braking, whilst a strip of the same material across the bridge of the nose prevents soreness created when goggles are rubbed frequently in a wet race. If you wear a scarf, make sure its ends are pinned to your shirt, whilst spare gloves and goggles (with elastic correctly adjusted) should, of course, be placed in your pit.

On race day, keep pit signals to a minimum and of the maximum simplicity. Before you start, find out which way the tap turns on the quick-filler (your job), and make sure you know how to stand so that your assistant can do his job of replenishing the oil tank—and impress upon him not to leave the cork in the spout of the gun! You should also know instantly the meanings of the various official coloured signal flags—in addition to the black and white chequered one! Likewise, intelligent deductions made from strange movements on the part of the white-coated Dunlop flagmen on the main corners can often save the rider from an unfortunate happening.

Have you given any thought to race-day breakfast? Probably not, because it seems a long way off. The fact remains that some chaps can race on a real I.O.M. meal— and that is quite something!—whereas others literally cannot stomach it. The trouble is that, as a " first year " man, you may not know the answer in your case until it is too late. I made the painful discovery in 1920, after which my race-day diet always consisted of two eggs beaten up in a pint of milk and laced with a double brandy, the delightful concoction being taken precisely two hours before starting time. Expensive maybe—and possibly hard to obtain nowadays—but none the less very sustaining.

When handing-in your machine, make sure that it is tied securely to its numbered post in the tent, that both valves are closed, and all taps turned off. When drawing it on race morning check immediately fuel and oil levels. If the latter has dropped appreciably, the lubricant has probably drained into the crankcase, so remove the drain plug— *not forgetting to replace it afterwards!* Check the tyre

Watch the Weather !

Maybe, when your turn comes to leave the grid the weather at the Grandstand will be dry but doubtful. If I were you, I should try to listen to the reports of conditions around the circuit broadcast over the public address system prior to 11 a.m. If you can't spare the time to do so, at least your pit attendant can. In any case, you should keep a wary eye open throughout the race because frequently it can be perfectly dry on one side of the Island and wet on the other. More than one famous competitor has discovered this phenomenon on rounding a perfectly dry bend only to skid on a patch suddenly made slippery by a local shower.

There is another important point to remember after your compulsory refuelling stop at the end of the second lap; be careful to keep your face turned away from the vicinity of the filler-cap for a few miles, and more particularly when braking hard. The sudden forward surge of fuel in a full tank is apt to force spray out of the cap and all over your goggles, whilst the fumes can make you feel very sick. I know of at least two instances where riders have crashed through failure to take this precaution. The danger, of course, should not be great in your case, because there will be no need completely to fill the tank for the remaining one or at the most, two laps.

And don't forget that it's your job to finish. Cut out the fireworks and concentrate on learning all you can this year with a view to bigger and better things next year. If all " first year men " will do just that, there should be no accidents, the event should be a huge success, and everyone will be happy. Remember, the secret of success is to go steady *for the first 15 miles*, thus giving your machine and yourself a reasonable chance to get in the groove. Those few seconds' sacrifice in the early stages will save minutes in the later stages. You are the master of your own destiny, but if you will accept these hints in the spirit in which they are given, I am sure you will make the grade.

Good luck to you!

" If I were you . . ." I only wish I were!

1947

THE FIRST CLUBMAN'S TT -
AND OFF TO A GOOD START

Three classes were announced for the inaugural Clubman's TT. The Lightweight and Junior classes followed the capacity limits of the International events (250cc and 350cc respectively), but the Senior allowed machines up to 1000cc to compete. The awards, which actually were to be made to the entrant (the club nominating the rider, not to the rider himself), were the Clubman's Tourist Trophy for each class, with cash awards of £50.00 for 1st place down to £20.00 for 4th. In addition, finishers within sixth-fifths (i.e. the winners time plus 20%) would win for their club a free entry in that year's Manx Grand Prix. There were no replicas to be won nor were there any Club Team or Centre Team awards.

Race-day was set for the Wednesday of the International race-week, with total entries restricted to a maximum of 80, although in the event the number received reached 64, 4 of which were never taken up. When the entry lists were published, it was apparent that one of the primary aims of the ACU in staging the event, the hoped-for variety in machinery, had indeed been achieved. Entries for the Senior represented ten different makes of machine,

with twelve Nortons, six Triumphs, three Ariels, three BSA's, two AJS's, two Vincent-HRD's, two Rudges, and one each of Excelsior, Scott and Sunbeam. Four of these makes (Triumph, Scott, Vincent-HRD and BSA) included twin-cylinder machines. The Junior entry provided eight different makes, nine Nortons, four BSAs, two Ariels, two Triumphs, two Excelsiors, one AJS, one Matchless and one Velocette. The Lightweight produced four, with three Excelsiors, three Velocettes, one AJS and one Triumph.

Among the rider entry of eight for the Lightweight were Arthur Wheeler, Bill McVeigh, Don Crossley, Les Archer and Basil Keys, with John Simister, Eric Cheney, Willy Wilshere, Ted Pink, Fron Purslow and Denis Parkinson contesting the twenty-two strong Junior race. Amongst the thirty entries in the Senior were Allan Jefferies, Phil Heath, Eric Briggs, Syd Lawton, George Leigh and Jack Cannell, totalling sixty for the whole event.

Reflecting the likely speed differentials between some clubmen and the International TT competitors, four separate practice sessions were held, and on the evening of Monday 2nd June, the clubmen were let loose on the Mountain circuit for the very first time in practice for their own event. In near perfect weather conditions, a packed grandstand welcomed the 49 riders who presented themselves at the start-line on the Glencrutchery Road, and from the comments by *TT Special* reporters stationed around the course, spectators were out in good numbers all the way around too. The honour of being the fastest man in that first practice went to Manxman Jack Cannell on his Senior Triumph, using his course knowledge to good effect in registering 29m 40s (76.32 mph). Slower by some 52 seconds was Allan Jefferies also on a Tiger 100, with third fastest being the Norton of Eric Briggs. Course familiarity also

First Clubman rider to set wheel on the course, Jack Cannell (Senior Triumph). Jack was a riding extra in the 1933 George Formby TT film 'No Limit'. No. 2 is Lightweight winner Bill McVeigh (Triumph)

helped the fastest man in the Junior class, Denis Parkinson on his Norton, three times a winner in the Manx Grand Prix, to lap at 31m 40s (71.5 mph). Les Archer Junior turned in the fastest lap by a Lightweight on his Velocette, at 36m 23s (62.2 mph). Only one spill was reported, that of H. Cooper who came off his Vincent-HRD at Braddan, resulting in a trip to hospital with concussion and bruises.

The 'TT Special's' reporting of speeds along a one mile stretch of the Sulby straight made for some interesting reading (and no doubt provided ammunition for some learned debate in the pubs and hotel bars), with Eric Briggs' Norton fastest at 98.2 mph, followed by Jack Cannell's Triumph at 94.74 mph. Denis Parkinson's Norton set fastest Junior speed at 93.28 mph, with Bill Jenness fastest Lightweight on his Excelsior at 74.09 mph. J. Howard Marshall's brand new Scott Flying Squirrel was not particularly fast at 78.26, but made up for that for many spectators with a sound that had not been heard on the Island for a good many years. Compare these speeds with those recorded in the previous years Manx Grand Prix, where Ken Bills recorded 104.7 mph on his Senior Norton, Freddie Hawken 97.3 mph on his Junior Norton, and Don Crossley 85.7 mph on his Lightweight Excelsior.

The second practice, again in perfect weather conditions early on the following morning, tempted out a total of 31 riders. No incidents of any kind were reported during the session, in which fastest laps in their respective classes were set by Allan Jefferies (30m 22s, 74.55 mph), Ted Pink (33m 55s, 66.76 mph), and Les Archer (36m 10s, 62.60 mph). A smooth-running incident-free session, with riding standards praised by all, just what was needed to ease the nerves of organisers, race officials, and in fact everyone involved.

Thursday morning's third practice was greeted by rain and mist, with visibility down to 50 yards in places. From the 48 riders who braved the conditions, the fastest lap was recorded by Allan Jefferies, with 34m 4s (64.47 mph), from Len Uttley's Norton and Manxman George Parsons riding an Ariel Red Hunter. Jack Cannell stopped on the Mountain with gearbox problems, a seized gearbox some reports said. Denis Parkinson headed the Junior class, and Bill McVeigh the Lightweight,

everyone's speed down because of the conditions. A casualty during the session was F. R. Price who dropped his 'daily-transport' Tiger 100 at Glentramman, suffering back injuries. By the end of the session fourteen riders still had to qualify, although three were club 'entries' without nominated riders, and in the end were not taken up.

The fourth and final practice took place in fine, if cold, and mainly clear conditions, and attracted 47 riders. Speeds recorded were generally a little lower than earlier in the week, Allan Jefferies again fastest with 30m 22s (74.5 mph). Jack Cannell put in two steady laps on the repaired Triumph, and his Monday time of 29m 40s remained the class fastest. Joe Moore was fastest Junior of the morning on his BSA, with 34m 0s (66.6mph), but Denis Parkinson still led the class overall. Les Archer improved on his best lap time by 13 seconds, clocking 30m 10s (75.1 mph), fastest lap of the week in the Lightweight class.

Of those still to qualify, seven had, for whatever reason, failed to put in an appearance at all during practice. Included in the unfortunate five who had practiced but had failed to qualify were the first session faller H. Cooper, as was the only other 1000cc machine entered, that of G. Whittaker. Thursday's faller F. R. Price was the third Senior non-qualifier, and in the Junior W. H. Singleton failed to qualify his Norton, and similarly R. J. Edwards his Lightweight Excelsior. Geoff Davison, writing in the 11th June issue of the 'TT Special' expressed great sympathy with these latter two, Singleton and Edwards, since both were well known Manx Grand Prix competitors, and had finished in the previous September's races. They could therefore claim considerably more experience and knowledge of the course than many who were being allowed to start, but the Rules required each rider to have completed at least three practice laps, and the way they were worded left no room for interpretation. In his editorial role, Geoff Davison put forward the hope that the Rules be altered for the following year, or simply phrased so as to allow for the possibility of some discretion being applied by the Race Stewards.

For most people following the races, and certainly the organisers, there was a feeling of relief that the first major hurdle had been overcome, that at least practice had ended satisfactorily in terms of rider safety. All reports told a similar story of a generally high standard of riding by the clubmen, the majority of whom were new to the course. There had been spills, but no serious injuries had occurred by the close of practice, certainly none of the carnage and mayhem predicted by some!

The Lightweight Race (Wednesday, 11th June)

Starters

	Rider	Club	Machine
1	A F Wheeler	Leatherhead & DMC	Excelsior
2	W McVeigh	Pathfinders MCC Ltd	Triumph
3	D G Crossley	Peveril (IoM) MC & CC	Velocette
4	W J Jenness	Ashford Kent MC	Excelsior
5	R W Fish	Ringwood MC & LCC	Velocette
6	L R Archer	BMCRC	Velocette
8	B E Keys	Worthing Eagle MC	A.J.S.

Race-day weather was near perfect, with sunshine, blue skies and only an occasional gentle breeze. The three classes were to run concurrently, the first time in TT history that more than two races had been run together. The decision to send the Lightweights off first for their three laps, followed by the Juniors, then the Seniors for their four laps, caused minimal comment at the time, but looks very strange and suspect now. The interval between classes was insufficient for it to be likened to a handicap type race, in which riders were intended to close up toward the end of the race, because it was certain that the faster machines would catch and have to pass the slower long before the end, and the possibility existed that some Seniors would be catching the Juniors at the same time as they in turn were catching the Lightweights. Thankfully, it is good to record that no serious incidents occurred, but a few awkward moments around the course can be imagined.

The riders were flagged away singly, at 15 second intervals, and the distinction of being the first man away in the very first Clubman's TT fell to Arthur Wheeler, who kick-started his Excelsior into life

Leatherhead MCC's Arthur Wheeler (Excelsior) leads the field away in 1947. Unsuccessful in this event, Arthur's MGP and TT career spanned an amazing 52 years. On the second row are No. 2 Bill McVeigh, the helmet and goggles of Don Crossley, and No. 4 Bill Jenness. No. 15 is the Junior entry of John Simister

without difficulty. Second away was a Triumph with Bill McVeigh on board, followed by the remaining five, none of whom had any starting difficulties. McVeigh was the first to reach Ramsey, and had further extended his lead by Creg-ny-Baa, and by the end of the lap he had pulled out a 47 second lead over 2nd place-man Basil Keys on the AJS.

First Lap Leaderboard

1 W. McVeigh (Triumph)   34m 31s   (65.61 mph)
2 B. E. Keys (AJS)   35m 18s   (64.15 mph)
3 L. R. Archer (Velocette) 35m 27s   (63.88 mph)
4 A. F. Wheeler (Excelsior) 35m 45s   (63.34 mph)
5 D. G. Crossley (Velocette) 35m 51s   (63.16 mph)
6 W. J. Jenness (Excelsior) 38m 44s   (58.46 mph)

McVeigh had increased his lead almost to two minutes as he pulled in to refuel at the end of the second lap, but the following group of four were within seconds of each other. Four reduced to three when Wheeler retired his Excelsior at the pits after stopping at the Gooseneck, an unfortunate result after his efforts to completely rebuild a worn out 1935 model especially for the event.

Second Lap Leaderboard

1 W. McVeigh (Triumph)   1h 8m 51s   (65.78 mph)
2 B. E. Keys (AJS)   1h 10m 14s   (64.48 mph)
3 L. R. Archer (Velocette) 1h 10m 50s   (63.94 mph)
4 D. G. Crossley (Velocette) 1h 11m 19s (63.50 mph)
5 W. J. Jenness (Excelsior) 1h 20m 33s   (56.23 mph)
6 R. W. Fish (Velocette)   1h 23m 43s   (54.10 mph)

Leaderboard places remained almost the same during the third and last lap, the only change being that Fish overtook Jenness on corrected time by the finish, to take 5th. McVeigh was flagged in as the winner, covering the last lap in 35m 11s, a speed of 64.4 mph.

Finishing Order

1 W. McVeigh (Triumph)   1h 44m 2s   (65.30 mph)
2 B. E. Keys (AJS)   1h 45m 42s   (64.27 mph)
3 L. R. Archer (Velocette) 1h 46m 36s   (63.73 mph)
4 D. G. Crossley (Velocette) 1h 47m 58s (62.91 mph)
5 R. W. Fish (Velocette)   2h 5m 8s   (54.34 mph)
6 W. J. Jenness (Excelsior) 2h 5m 8s   (54.29 mph)

Fastest Lap: W. McVeigh (2nd lap) 34m 20s (66.0 mph)

After the finish came the real drama, when the winning engines were stripped and measured. McVeigh's Triumph was a 1939 Model 70 with a good number of miles under its belt, and sometime in its life had received a well-earned re-bore, with a fractionally oversize piston that took the measured capacity past the limit. The race officials discussed, voted and argued for hours, until 4.45 pm in fact, when the official announcement came that the calculated capacity of 251.86cc disqualified machine and rider. Basil Keys was declared the race winner, and everyone else moved up a place.

The Junior Race (Wednesday, 11th June)

Starters

	Rider	Club	Machine
10	W Sleightholme	West Wilts MC	A.J.S.
11	A Symonds	Wickham MC	Excelsior
12	A Johnstone	South Liverpool MC	Excelsior
14	R Pratt	B.M.C.R.C.	Norton
15	J Simister	Manchester '17' MCC	Norton
16	J K Beckton	Middlesborough & DMC	Triumph
17	H R Holding	Wirral '100' MC	B.S.A.
18	W Evans	Antelope MCC	Matchless
19	W E Quine	Dewsbury & DMC & LCC	Triumph
20	E R Cheney	X.H.G. Tiger MC	Triumph
22	H Pilling	Bury & DMC	Norton
23	W Wilshere	Watford & DMC & LCC	Ariel
24	W T Pink	West Middlesex Amateur MCC	Norton
25	F Purslow	Salop MC	B.S.A.
26	D Parkinson	Wakefield & DMSC	Norton
27	J W Moore	Peveril (IoM) MC & LCC	B.S.A.
28	R W Spavin	Scunthorpe MCC	Velocette
29	R Pennycook	South Liverpool MC	Norton
30	J Terry	Kings Norton MCC	Ariel
31	P Moss	Salop MC	B.S.A.
32	M Sunderland	Rochdale & DMC	Norton

First man to show in the 350cc Junior was Wilf Sleightholme on his AJS, Andrew Johnstone's Excelsior and Harvey Pilling's Norton both being reluctant to start. All did get away eventually, and by Kirkmichael Denis Parkinson (Norton) had passed half a dozen or so riders and was obviously going well. Sleightholme still led on the road at Ramsey, and was still there at the end of the lap, followed by Bob Pratt (Norton) and Denis Parkinson. Ted Pink was the first retirement, his Norton stopped at Cregny-Baa with a split tank. J. K. Beckton gave a 'thumbs down' to his pit as he passed indicating trouble with his Triumph 3T twin, and J. Terry (Ariel) took a fall at Governor's Bridge. He remounted, but retired at the pits with a buckled front wheel.

First Lap Leaderboard

1 D. Parkinson (Norton)	31m 3s	(72.92 mph)
2 J. W. Moore (BSA)	32m 5s	(70.57 mph)
3 W. Sleightholme (AJS)	32m 27s	(67.70 mph)
4 W. Evans (Matchless)	33m 49s	(66.96 mph)
4 P. Moss (BSA)	33m 49s	(66.96 mph)
5 J. Simister (Norton)	33m 55s	(66.76 mph)

By Ramsey on the second lap, Sleightholme and Parkinson were almost together on the road, and by the end of the lap the Matchless of Evans had also drawn ahead of the AJS, relegating Sleightholme to 4th place, but both riders were over two minutes behind Moore on the BSA. R. W. Spavin became the second retirement after he came off his borrowed Velocette at Braddan, suffering minor injuries. The engine on Manxman Edgar Quine's 1938 Triumph Tiger 80 seized temporarily at Union Mills, again at Glen Helen and then terminally on the Mountain, putting him out of the race. He had been persuaded by Triumph to fit a high-compression piston after practice, not a good idea as a 10 to 1 compression ratio and Pool petrol were not good bed-fellows! H.R. Holding dropped his BSA at Cruickshanks, without injury, and he returned to Ramsey to spectate for the remainder of the race. With a second lap slightly slower than his first, the compulsory fuel stop at the end of the lap saw Parkinson with a reduced lead of some 34 seconds over Moore.

Second Lap Leaderboard

1 D. Parkinson (Norton)	1h 3m 35s	(71.22 mph)
2 J. W. Moore (BSA)	1h 4m 9s	(70.59 mph)
3 W. Evans (Matchless)	1h 6m 20s	(68.27 mph)
4 W. Sleightholme (AJS)	1h 6m 21s	(68.26 mph)
5 J. Simister (Norton)	1h 6m 46s	(67.83 mph)
6 R. Pratt (Norton)	1h 6m 55s	(67.68 mph)

Two well-earned leaderboard placings disappeared during the third lap, with the engine of Evans' Matchless expiring at Ballacraine, and Moore's gearbox forcing his retirement of the BSA at Union Mills. Sleightholme inherited 2nd place temporarily, but by the end of the lap it was Pratt's Norton holding the place, closing a little on Parkinson, but four minutes down on corrected time. A further retirement was that of Pilling's Norton, which came to a halt in Ramsey.

Third Lap Leaderboard

1 D. Parkinson (Norton)	1h 35m 37s	(71.08 mph)
2 R. Pratt (Norton)	1h 39m 50s	(68.04 mph)
3 W. Sleightholme (AJS)	1h 40m 2s	(67.91 mph)
4 J. Simister (Norton)	1h 41m 14s	(67.08 mph)
5 F. Purslow (BSA)	1h 41m 51s	(66.62 mph)
6 P. Moss (BSA)	1h 43m 34s	(66.30 mph)

The lead held by Parkinson as he began the last lap was sufficient for him to ease back on a machine that was beginning to sound a little rough, and despite Pratt going faster again on the lap, the winning advantage was three and a half minutes. Other leaderboard places remained more or less the same, but the runner-up slot was in doubt right to the end, staying eventually with Pratt, who put in his fastest

Denis Parkinson waits to start his winning ride. He had already won three Lightweight Manx Grand Prix by this time, and was to add a Junior and Senior Manx victories after this, his only TT ride.

lap of the race at 31m 41s (71.46 mph). Bob Pennycook (Norton) overhauled Moss's BSA to claim 6th place, and, riding in his first ever road race, Fron Purslow took a fine 5th place on a BSA. No further retirements were reported on the last lap, and 13 riders were classified as finishers.

Finishing Order

1 D. Parkinson (Norton)	2h 8m 1s	(70.74 mph)
2 R. Pratt (Norton)	2h 11m 31s	(68.87 mph)
3 W. Sleightholme (AJS)	2h 12m 39s	(68.28 mph)
4 J. Simister (Norton)	2h 14m 34s	(67.30 mph)
5 F. Purslow (BSA)	2h 15m 40s	(66.75 mph)
6 R. Pennycook (Norton)	2h 18m 6s	(65.59 mph)

Fastest Lap: D. Parkinson (1st lap) 31m 3s (72.92 mph).

The Senior Race (Wednesday, 11th June)

Starters

	Rider	Club	Machine
34	W Reeve	Wakefield & DMCC	Excelsior
35	J W White	Gainsborough & DMC	Triumph
36	A A Jefferies	Bradford & DMC	Triumph
39	F P Heath	Leicester Query MC	Norton
40	J E Stevens	Oswestry & DMC	B.S.A.
43	P H Waterman	Bristol MCC	A.J.S.
44	R Tolley	Kings Norton MCC	Ariel
45	H B Iremonger-Watts		
		X.H.G. Tiger MC	Triumph
47	P Lingard	Southport MC	Norton
48	E E Briggs	Bradford & DMC	Norton
50	S Lawton	Southampton & DMCC	Rudge
51	F Fairbairn	Scarborough & DMC	Norton
52	J T Wenman	North Berks MC	Sunbeam
53	G E Leigh	Southport MC	Norton
54	J H Marshall	Sunbeam MCC	Scott
55	A R Bateman	Wolverhampton MC & CC	Ariel
56	A Crocker	Southern Amateur MC	Triumph
58	H J Bacon	B.M.C.R.C.	Norton
60	J Cannell	Chester MC	Triumph
61	W Myers	Louth & DMC	Rudge
62	G F Parsons	Peveril MC & CC	Ariel
64	N Kirby	Accrington & DMCC	B.S.A.
65	H F Hunter	Gosport & DMC	A.J.S.

Having elected to ride his AJS in the Junior, the eventual 3rd placeman in that class Wilf Sleightholme, was quite obviously a non-starter for the Senior, others were Phil Carter, Len Uttley and Wilf Dobson (all Nortons). A little before 11.10am, the first of the Senior riders got away, or at least attempted to. Bill Reeve suffered that most frustrating of all retirements, still at the pits, with his Excelsior refusing all efforts to fire up. Philip Lingard's 1934 Norton showed some reluctance to start, but eventually got away just in front of Syd Lawton's Rudge. The remainder of the field made good starts, and Allan Jefferies was reported as first to reach Ballacraine, with Phil Heath and Eric Briggs fast and obviously in the running. Out of the running though, even before Ballacraine, was one of the pre-race favourites Jack Cannell, with a broken fuel pipe. Unofficial timekeepers at Ramsey put Briggs already an amazing one minute and forty seconds ahead of 2nd placed Heath, closely followed by Jefferies, with James Stevens 4th on a BSA A7 twin. First lap retirements were John Wenman (1935 '95' Sunbeam) at Hillberry, and A. R. Bateman who came off his Ariel on the Mountain, suffering 'a bad case of gravel rash' and other minor injuries. As it passed the pits, the Scott of J. Howard Marshall also appeared to be showing evidence of having 'been down the road', but continued for a while before eventually retiring.

First Lap Leaderboard

1 E. E. Briggs (Norton)	28m 38s	(79.09 mph)
2 F. P. Heath (Norton)	30m 22s	(74.57 mph)
3 A. Jefferies (Triumph)	30m 31s	(74.17 mph)
4 J. E. Stevens (BSA)	31m 01s	(72.99 mph)
5 R. Tolley (Ariel)	31m 05s	(72.84 mph)
6 S. Lawton (Rudge)	31m 40s	(71.51 mph)

Last-starter H. F. Hunter was reported as having had a close call at Quarter Bridge, running so wide as to clout a sandbag with his AJS, but was able to continue. Jefferies still led on the roads at Kirkmichael on the second lap, but was closely followed by Heath and Briggs, and by the time they reached the Mountain, Briggs led Jefferies, with Heath dropping back a little. 5th placeman Dick Tolley was forced to retire his spring-framed Ariel Red Hunter at Ballacraine, when the rear mudguard and stay assembly collapsed onto the tyre. First into the refuelling stop was Briggs, leading by well over three minutes, and in fact headed on the roads only by one of the earlier-starting Juniors, Sleightholme's AJS. Jefferies pitted very soon after, and as a result of a quicker stop actually left the pits just ahead of Briggs. Heath was slower in the stop, but was still comfortably ahead of Lawton. J. W. White came off his Tiger 100 at Governor's Bridge, but was able to rejoin the race. With Tolley out, and Stevens stopped near Glen Helen, George Parsons and P. H. Waterman found themselves on the leaderboard in 5th and 6th places respectively, making for five different makes in the first six places. Further down the field, Norman Kirby retired his BSA A7 with a broken fuel union, while Jack Cannell who had managed to repair his similar problem (with his bootlaces!) on the Triumph, was circulating quickly.

Second Lap Leaderboard

1 E. E. Briggs (Norton)	56m 56s	(79.56 mph)
2 A. Jefferies (Triumph)	1h 0m 11s	(75.24 mph)
3 F. P. Heath (Norton)	1h 0m 19s	(75.08 mph)
4 S. Lawton (Rudge)	1h 2m 23s	(72.60 mph)
5 G. F. Parsons (Ariel)	1h 2m 55s	(71.99 mph)
6 P. H. Waterman (AJS)	1h 4m 43s	(69.68 mph)

About halfway into the race, a sudden thick sea mist threatened to envelope part of the Mountain section, but then just as suddenly retreated and evaporated, to the relief of all. Leading positions remained unchanged through the lap, but with

It's self-service for Hilary Iremonger-Watts (Triumph) as he refuels at the end of his second lap.

Lawton closing considerably on Heath.

Third Lap Leaderboard

1 E. E. Briggs (Norton)	1h 26m 24s	(78.63 mph)
2 A. Jefferies (Triumph)	1h 30m 25s	(75.13 mph)
3 F.P. Heath (Norton)	1h 32m 10s	(73.71 mph)
4 S. Lawton (Rudge)	1h 32m 21s	(71.21 mph)
5 G.F. Parsons (Ariel)	1h 36m 30s	(70.39 mph)
6 P.H. Waterman (AJS)	1h 37m 4s	(69.99 mph)

The fourth and final lap saw Briggs and Jefferies maintain their positions and they duly came home in relatively safe 1st and 2nd places, but behind them all kind of difficulties arose. Heath's Norton ran out of fuel at the Bungalow, and he pushed and coasted to an eventual 15th (and last) place. Lawton also hit problems, pushing him down to 8th by the finish. Their misfortune brought the Nortons of George Leigh and Freddie Fairbairn onto the leaderboard. On the last lap, Alan Crocker came off his Triumph Speed Twin at Ballaugh, injuring three spectators in the process, thankfully none seriously.

Finishing Order

1 E. E. Briggs (Norton)	1h 53m 8s	(78.67 mph)
2 A. Jefferies (Triumph)	2h 0m 23s	(75.23 mph)
3 G. F. Parsons (Ariel)	2h 7m 6s	(71.26 mph)
4 P. H. Waterman (AJS)	2h 8m 8s	(70.68 mph)
5 G. E. Leigh (Norton)	2h 8m 25s	(70.53 mph)
6 F. Fairbairn (Norton)	2h 9m 47s	(69.80 mph)

Fastest Lap: E. E. Briggs (2nd lap) 28m 18s (80.02 mph)

Reflections

In his ride in the Senior, taking out one and a half minutes on each of the first two laps from strong opposition, Eric Briggs was almost in a class of his own that day. Even so, it has to be concluded that his machine, an 'International' Norton, was more than equal to the task. It no doubt benefitted from the attention it received prior to the races from Steve Lancefield, although it actually belonged to a customer of his. It was a 1939 model, the view taken at the time that the slight advantage of the telescopic forks on the 1946 model being more than compensated by the light alloy head and barrel catalogued on the pre-war model. Photographs of Denis Parkinson's Junior winning Norton indicate similar thinking. Steve Lancefield described the Senior-winning Norton as *"a 1939 Norton Model 30 with a compression ratio of 7.4:1, standard cams and standard everything else. All I did was just to make sure that everything was right"*. He then went on to say that it had been run very carefully for several hundred miles, then stripped, inspected, rebuilt, tested, stripped and so on until he was satisfied. Briggs reported no problems during his winning ride, other than having a chicken cross his path (feathers found on the speedo drive evidenced the closeness of the encounter).

Denis Parkinson had a similarly good run, free from mechanical problems, saying only that he had experienced some difficulty with the riding position, the footrest position being incorrect but the kick-start position precluded any useful change. The machine variety provided by the entry carried through reasonably well into the results, and despite both the larger classes being won by Norton, no one make of bike dominated the results, with four makes in the first six in the Senior, three in the Junior, and four in the Lightweight.

The motorcycling press were unanimous in congratulating the clubmen over the way they had conducted themselves, describing their riding as restrained, skilful, and safe. They had acquitted themselves very well indeed in what was for many,

their first taste of riding the TT circuit, in a number of cases also, their first road race. A few spills had occurred, but no serious injuries had resulted. Although the number of non-starters and non-appearances were slight disappointments, the proportion of starters who actually finished the races was encouraging, particularly as the bikes' reaction to sustained high speed on 'Pool' petrol had not been previously tested. Compression ratios had certainly been dropped from pre-war levels, but how far it was necessary to go was not known. Brake performance (or eventual lack of it), had also been a concern before the races, particularly for the heavier and faster machines, but in the end was not a general problem. For the record, six of the seven Lightweight starters finished, thirteen of twenty-one Juniors, and fifteen of twenty-three Seniors, a total of thirty-four from fifty-one.

Geoff Davison's editorial in the 13th June issue of the *'TT Special'* was encouraging and supportive, saying, *"The ACU is to be congratulated on the extremely successful result of a bold experiment"* and *"On the whole a host of difficulties that looked almost insuperable was overcome - by tact and compromise. Apart from clear-cut cases of non-compliance with the Rules, there were no exclusions"*. Again from the same editorial *"The Clubman's TT may well be the training ground for the September races, just as they in turn are the training ground for the TT proper. Good luck to the Clubman's! May it prosper and become recognised as the junior house in our great TT school"*.

Problem areas? Entry numbers would need to increase to make the event a viable proposition, but there was nothing to suggest that this wouldn't happen in subsequent years, once the races had established themselves. The difficulties caused by shortages of just about everything in those early post-war years must not be overlooked, not the least of which was a general shortage of money. Transport to and from the Isle of Man, plus accommodation and normal racing expenditure meant that a racing holiday in the Island was not, is not, and

The victors: left to right. Bill McVeigh (Lightweight), Denis Parkinson (Junior) and Eric Briggs (Senior)

probably never will be, a cheap option! Two specific aspects of the races though, did need to be addressed. The first was the 'letter-of-the-law' exclusion mentioned earlier of two experienced Mountain Circuit competitors who hadn't completed the number of practice laps required by the Regulations. The second was the disqualification of McVeigh's 'over-size' Triumph from victory in the Lightweight. At the Wednesday evening prize distribution (as it was then described) there was a great round of applause when McVeigh's name was mentioned, even though he didn't appear on the platform. Included amongst those who did go onto the platform, and who voiced support were Major Watling on behalf of the ACU and the race stewards, and Allan Jefferies who was particularly vociferous in favour of the reinstatement of McVeigh's win. But 'rules are rules', and it seemed that nothing could be done. Thankfully, McVeigh appealed against the ruling, and although it took some two months to sort out, he was finally declared as the Lightweight winner. However fair and correct the final decision, and most folk did agree with it, the uncertainty over the result did no-one any favours, and one can only then sympathise with Basil Keys, who, so long after the prize presentation, had to accept that he was not in fact, the winner.

The future of the 'Lightweight' category was causing concern however, the 3rd July issue of 'Motor Cycling' pointed out that neither McVeigh nor Keys rode models then in production, and only three ohv and one side-valve models were currently in manufacture, none of which had any 'racing background'. The industry was apparently ignoring the class, whereas in the mid-1930s virtually all British manufacturers catalogued 250's, many of which were 'adequate sports machines'. *"Neglect of the class now means that there is much experimental work in store for any manufacturer seeking to revive his 250 field. The TT of 1947 proved that in this sphere the Continentals have learned a great deal that we have forgotten. To catch up with their lead and to pass it will require extensive research and testing. They have never hesitated to use racing for this purpose. Nor must we"*.

Looking back, a seemingly insignificant change of machine for the Junior race might be seen as having a far-reaching effect on the Clubman's TT. A motorcycle spares shop owner from Shrewsbury, and riding in his first road race, Fron Purslow was down to ride an AJS in the Junior. The *'TT Special'* records that he completed eight practice laps riding an AJS, but in the list of starters and in the 'Who's Who' feature he is indicated to be on a BSA B32. There is inconsistency in race reports of the time, some reports and even results still have him on the Ajay, some on the BSA, but there is no doubt that he rode a BSA in the actual race. Writing an engine analysis of the Gold Star in the December 1996 issue of *'The Classic Motorcycle'*, Brian Woolley had the following to say. *"Everyone will recall the Gold Star's remarkable record in the Isle of Man - in particular the Junior Clubman's TT. The BSAs entered for the inaugural 1947 race were not Gold Stars at all but B31's fitted with lightweight aluminium alloy cylinders and heads. They were tuned by Jack Amott and Cyril Halliburn. Two machines were entered, but at the last minute another was offered to AJS entrant Fron Purslow (for many years a flyer of the BSA flag) who finished in fifth place."* Jack Amott and Cyril Halliburn were two of the best development engineers in the motorcycle industry of the time, both of whom were to be central players in the later Gold Star story. Two other BSA 'names' attending the races (who were photographed in the *'TT Special'* alongside James Stevens on his A7 Senior entry), were Bill Nicholson and Bert Perrigo. The results of the Junior race (Purslow 5th, Moss 7th, and Moore 2nd until retirement) were sufficient to convince the BSA Board to back the development of the Gold Star, concentrating initially on the 350 model.

Nothing directly to do with the Clubman's TT or the International TT, but an insight into those days of post-war austerity, shortages and subsequent rationing, also comes from the pages of the *'TT Special'*. An editorial from 9th June 1947 explained that paper shortages had restricted the number of issues to three. There were none available during practice, and to enable the three that were produced during race-week to be comprehensive 24-page issues it meant that their allocation of paper would be used up for that year. There could therefore be no issues at all during September's Manx Grand Prix.

Quoting from the same editorial, *"Supplies [of the 11th and 13th June issues] will be limited, so readers are asked to share their copies with their friends. Next year we hope to produce some practice issues,* *but that is in the hands of Paper Control!"* (The upper case used in Paper Control, and the exclamation mark following, are in the original editorial).

1947 Clubman's recollections
by Dennis Christian

In 1947 I was in the second year of my apprenticeship with the Salisbury Garage in Fort Street, Douglas. After the excitement of the previous MGP in 1946 I was looking forward to the TT and the Clubman's races. An extra interest to me was the participation of several local riders; being a member of the Peveril Club we were fielding a team in this new event.

The Salisbury Garage had several agencies including Velocette and Ariel and two of our machines were supplied to team members. An MOV Velocette to Don Crossley and a 500 Ariel Red Hunter to Jack Harrison who was sponsoring George Parsons.

I was given the job of helping to prepare these bikes. Although the regulations were very strict, a lot of the jobs were making the bikes fit the riders such as footrests, brake and gear levers. One job on the Ariel I remember was pegging the taper footrests on the Ariel to stop them dropping down on a jump.

We took the bikes to the Mountain Mile and they set off together. The Ariel led but Don was tucked in behind and we were suprised that there was hardly any difference in the speed at the top of the mountain. Both riders were quite pleased and there were no serious problems.

I was put in charge of cleaning and polishing the Velo and Don made me his 'gofor' and pit attendant. One job that was most important was the draining of the sump before starting it if left overnight otherwise the engine flooded with oil and oiled up the plug.

The machines were left overnight in a tent behind the Start the day before the race after going through scrutineering.

Riders only were permitted to remove their machines from the tent fifteen minutes before the start of the race at which time I could help to make adjustments if required. I was waiting with a spanner and draining tin waiting for Don to turn up.

Don arrived a little worse for wear, after the time period allowed to make adjustments had expired; he had expected me to collect the bike, by then it was too late for me to drain the engine as the time had elapsed.

When the starter dropped the flag the rider was required to kick start his bike from cold and dash off down Bray Hill.

Don kicked and kicked and by some miracle it burst into life blotting out the start with smoke, he set off to start his first lap. I was dissapointed with his lap times and it was only on the last lap he started to fly. He eventually finished fourth but we celebrated just the same.

George Parsons finished a superb third behind two of the superstars of their day, Allan Jefferies and Eric Briggs. George must have had an exciting moment during the race at Ballaugh as he left a black footrest rubber mark on a wall in Ballaugh village!

Recently at a grass meeting I heard the name Tolley mentioned. This reminded me when Dick Tolley arrived at the Salisbury Garage with a problem. The scrutineers had rejected his Ariel because he had a plunger rear suspension and tele forks. The Ariel sales catalogue did not list this machine with this specification. So Dick elected for a spring frame and girder forks, which then had to be fitted very quickly.

Dick at that time was a famous speedway and grass track rider from the Midlands and was quite mad on the road.

Unfortunately his race ended at Ballaugh Bridge, he did some low flying on the bridge and ended up completely collapsing the frame and wheels!

My 1947 Clubman's Ride
by Bob Pratt

My experiences in the Junior Clubman's TT last year may interest those competing this June. A little over a year ago I had just started my demob. leave, and was hoping to watch the TT. Weeks later, when the Clubman's regulations had been published, a crowd of Worcester Auto Club lads were discussing them and egging each other on to have a go. They finally directed all their sarcasm at me, as I was always bragging about road-burning and high averages. I promised to compete, and in that rash statement my future was sealed!

Within a week my entry (by B.M.C.R.C.) was in, and boat, hotel and everything booked up. Ten days before, I had been hoping to watch! My 348 c.c. International Norton, on order for many moons, came through one week before 'on the boat' and I had to put 400 miles on the clock by the time we pushed on board. I relate the events leading up to my arrival in the Island to emphasize the fact that I entered only at the last minute, with no previous idea of being 'out for blood.'

We docked at Douglas on the Saturday morning, and as practice (for us) started the following Monday evening, I lost no time in having a look round the course—the course! I had never been on it before and didn't even recognise half the famous places at first; those I did seemed very different from the photographs. It was a great thrill to ride round, following the arrows and warning boards, and to realize that I was actually on the TT circuit of world renown. The glamour soon passed, and I began visualizing the course as an adversary to be learned and conquered.

My first impression was of the great length of a lap—$37\frac{3}{4}$ miles of 'country' going with only two towns is a long way. I toured along slowly, having a good look-see; it took me nearly two hours and I felt quite tired. Four laps—whew! But I was genuinely relieved to find that the course wasn't quite such a horrible, tortuous monster as I had imagined. Not a 'race-track' by any means, but just the sort of local road stuff I had been used to at home.

I did six touring laps by Monday evening, and was beginning to get an idea of 'where it was going round the next corner,' but couldn't fit all the bits together yet. I think this was more sensible than the practice of some lads, who spent all Sunday morning practising Governor's Bridge hairpin! On the great evening when I first donned leathers and crash hat to gallop over the Mountain I intended to take things steadily and feel my way. The one part of the course which did scare me was from the Grandstand to Quarter Bridge—via Bray Hill! The Inter. was capable of a genuine 95 m.p.h. on the flat, due to much 'breathing upon it' beforehand.

On the first 'do' at Bray I had the steering damper gripping, and went down at about 85; it felt safe, and I cheered up a bit. At the end of the lap I descended at a shade over 90 and was really enjoying myself. Then, all the way round the Island I was promising myself I would have a real go next time. I came through with everything full on in third, changed into top by the Grandstand, and hung on tight with the grip against the stop. I just touched 100 m.p.h. on the speedometer at the bottom, and felt that I had made real progress—I could go down Bray flat out any time from then on.

My serious approach to learning the circuit paid unexpected dividends—I was the third fastest 350cc of the evening. Next morning I moved up to second fastest, and was one of only two Juniors to have put in six official laps to date. I suddenly thought that 'fame was within my grasp,' which was a bad thing, as I started worrying about all the little things that could go wrong, and could hardly sleep at night! My mechanic, George Wakefield, advised me to lie low and take it easy, as it would be silly to damage either the machine (his main concern) or myself, now that we had got so far.

Funnily enough, I did as I was told, but managed to fall off twice during the second half of the practising. The first occasion was due to short-comings in machine preparation rather than riding. The front brake cable was not taped up very securely, and we can only surmise that it was nipped against the steering lock at Signpost Corner. I approached the Nook at over 70 m.p.h., and when the front anchor was called upon to do its stuff the lever just snapped against the grip—nothing there! I thought—'Here it is!' Having lost as much speed as possible, a lot of rear rubber, and no doubt a few teeth out of the cogbox, I sailed up the grass bank and reclined in the hedge.

Aside from a few aches and pains, which departed before the next practice, I was none the worse for the experience, but firmly resolved to proceed with all due caution during the race. I had changed my mind again: 'Finish at all costs' was the motto after all. Strangely enough, my head had changed in another sense. Afer the acrobatics my crash-hat wouldn't fit any more; one of us had altered shape. Since it was the easier thing to do, we warmed the helmet and bent it to fit again, but I'm not sure which of us it was that suffered in the first place!

The second incident occurred on the last practice morning, when we did a dress-rehearsal pit stop. I had been pushing myself along fairly hard—in case it rained on race day—and at the end of Lap 1 George waved to let me see the pit he had chosen for the practice stop on the next lap. Round again we went. Up the Glencrutchery Road from Governor's I was promising myself that this was going to be some pit stop. It was! I was in neutral with the engine stopped, opening the filler cap and coasting in about 50 m.p.h. I started to brake, and George was waving everything in the pit like mad.

I thought, "All right, fool, I can see you, can't I?" About ten yards further on I found out what he meant, arriving on my back, head first, with a 348cc Norton in my lap! We all laughed at this one, but as George said, "We've learned something mate!" In his opinion we should have seen several others make the same mistake had it been a wet Clubman's race.

The story of the race itself has been told before, but I can add a few personal incidents. Clubman's Day was ideal for racing; warm and dry, with a light breeze, but with a few misty patches on the west side, between Ballacraine and Kirkmichael. Somehow the motor didn't like the damp air (we had set up for warm

Bob Pratt receives the congratulations of mechanic and fellow rider George Wakefield in the winners enclosure.

and dry, as forecast), and on the first lap I could get only 80-82 mph on the level. I was going all out everywhere, and suffered a big disappointment when Denis Parkinson overtook me along the Glencrutchery Road at the end of the first lap—number 26 and I was 14! On the second lap the bike was doing just over 85, and I was expecting a horde of three-fifties in Denis's wake to come howling by. But I didn't see any, although I had a look behind pretty often; and a really quick pit stop at the end of the lap helped to hold my position, whatever it was.

The stop itself still stands out clearly in my mind as the most vivid memory of the whole race, perhaps because of the jolt George gave me. I had stopped with the cap open and everything set for a quick kickstart and was just reaching for a clean pair of goggles and a drink when George shouted "Not going quick enough, mate—off the Leader Board!" I felt almost ready to weep, after my practice times, but G. had never said "Faster" before; he always advised me to go steadily and finish. I expect he was a bit het-up too!

I was off like a shot with the fly-spattered goggles still on and with no drink. Then flat out down Bray Hill . . . and I had forgotten the steering damper slackened right off for the stop. Though I willed it with all my might, I could not get my hand off the bar to turn it. That was the beginning of two rather hectic laps—I had changed my mind again! "What's the use of finishing, anyway, if you finish last?" I asked myself. "No blessed use at all" I said, "Get your blinkin' 'ead down!" On that lap I took Ballaugh Bridge a lot faster than ever before (or since) and the mighty wallop when we finally got back to the ground snapped off my welded-up folding footrest. Luckily, I had to swerve to the right anyway, but didn't have much say in the matter at the time.

That left me with a lap-and-a-half to go, with one leg waving in the breeze. I was scared to rest my foot on the gear lever, as that would be the next thing to go, and the kick-starter boss was by now a bit oily and my toe kept slipping off that at awkward moments. So I let it wave.

At the end of Lap 3 George held out a board marked 5, —4 which I took to mean fifth, four seconds behind the fourth man. After the race I saw the board and it was clearly a figure 3—third—and the 4 was intended to mean four minutes behind the leader. Perhaps they thought I might catch that up! Thinking I was 4s behind number 4, I really hammered the bike, and myself, on the last lap. I don't know which was the hottest part of the machine—the engine or the brakes. It felt like the saddle. My right leg was playing up, but the idea of stopping at the roadside and saying "Enough!" seemed too fantastic to think about.

After all, every place I passed through was for the last time, and riding the bike was the quickest way of getting back to the Cadbury Tent—and peace at last! A great thrill was on that last lap was passing Wilf Sleightholme (push-rod AJS), who finished third. He had started in front of me, and I had wondered where he was; I didn't know he was still in front! (I had passed the other Juniors and had been passed only by Parkinson). I followed Wilf for miles on the Mountain, closing the gap surely but very slowly; he was going great guns. I finally got past him above Keppel Gate, and once in front seemed to gain ground more quickly. The Norton was clocking 102 mph on the speedometer down to the Craig!

The chequered flag in my first race over the IoM course was the biggest relief of a lifetime. Although feeling pretty tired, I went though the start hard down to it, still hoping to clip that second off to get fourth place, and so had to turn off at the top of Bray and return by the side streets. Some boys even tried to stop me on the corner; they thought I felt like signing autographs! When, after a few seconds wait, I found that I could not be beaten for second place I could scarcely believe it, and stood there like an idiot watching my number and times going up on the Board.

And so ends a personal story of a first visit to the Isle of Man I hope it won't be my last—for very many years. Even if I never again have the luck, the machine, and all the little things that others contribute to make success possible, I shall still be happy as long as I can don leathers with the rest of the lads and do battle over that wonderful Mountain course.

After that—I may even go to watch!

(First published 'The Motor Cycle', June 3rd, 1948)

1947 Clubman's Lightweight

	Rider					
1	W. McVeigh, Triumph	34.31	**34.20**	35.11	1 44 02	65.30
2	B. Keys, AJS	35.18	**34.56**	35.28	1 45 42	64.27
3	L. R. Archer, Velocette	35.27	**35.23**	35.46	1 46 36	63.73
4	D. Crossley, Velocette	35.51	**35.28**	36.39	1 47 58	62.91
5	R. W. Fish, Velocette	42.10	41.33	**41.17**	2 05 00	54.34
6	W. J. Jenness, Excelsior	**38.44**	41.49	44.35	2 05 08	54.29
	A. F. Wheeler, Excelsior	**35.45**	90.39	R		

LAP POSITIONS

1947 CLUBMAN'S LIGHTWEIGHT

RIDER AND MACHINE	FIRST LAP POSITION		FINAL POSITION	RIDER AND MACHINE
W MCVEIGH TRIUMPH	1		1	W MCVEIGH TRIUMPH
B KEYS A.J.S.	2		2	B KEYS A.J.S.
L R ARCHER VELOCETTE	3		3	L R ARCHER VELOCETTE
A F WHEELER EXCELSIOR	4		4	D CROSSLEY VELOCETTE
D CROSSLEY VELOCETTE	5		5	R W FISH VELOCETTE
W J JENNESS EXCELSIOR	6		6	W J JENNESS EXCELSIOR

Destined to be denied a Clubman's win in controversial circumstances, Basil Keys waits in a crowded paddock.

1947 Clubman's Junior

1	D. Parkinson, Norton	**31.03**	31.32	33.02	32.24	2 08.01	70.74
2	R. Pratt, Norton	34.04	32.51	32.55	**31.41**	2 11 31	68.87
3	W. Sleightholme, AJS	33.27	32.54	33.41	**32.37**	2 12 39	68.28
4	J. Simister, Norton	33.55	**32.51**	34.28	33.20	2 14 34	67.30
5	F. Purslow, BSA	34.07	**33.31**	34.19	33.43	2 15 40	66.76
6	R. Pennycook, Norton	35.16	34.35	34.35	**33.40**	2 18 06	65.59
7	P. Moss, BSA	**33.49**	34.20	35.25	37.51	2 21 25	64.05
8	M. Sunderland, Norton	35.31	**34.25**	36.15	35.28	2 21 39	63.95
9	E. R. Cheney, Triumph	37.14	36.32	36.26	**34.46**	2 24 58	62.48
10	W. H. Wilshere, Ariel	35.10	36.26	42.42	**34.54**	2 29 12	60.71
11	A. Symonds, Excelsior	**38.59**	40.46	40.00	39.06	2 38 51	57.02
12	J. K. Beckton, Triumph	35.30	**34.59**	58.35	38.40	2 47 44	54.00
13	A. Johnstone, Excelsior	35.10	**34.54**	40.01	85.52	3 15 57	46.22
	J. W. Moore, BSA	32.05	**32.04**	R			
	W. Evans, Matchless	33.49	**32.31**	R			
	H. Pilling, Norton	34.41	**34.36**	R			
	H. R. Holding, BSA	34.56	R				
	R. W. Spavin, Velocette	35.22	R				
	W. E. Quine, Triumph	42.29	R				
	J. Terry, Ariel	45.40	R				
	E. T. Pink, Norton	R					

LAP POSITIONS

1947 CLUBMAN'S JUNIOR

RIDER AND MACHINE	FIRST LAP POSITION		RIDER AND FINAL POSITION	MACHINE
D PARKINSON NORTON	1		1	D PARKINSON NORTON
J W MOORE BSA	2		2	R PRATT NORTON
W SLEIGHTHOLME AJS	3		3	W SLEIGHTHOLME A.J.S.
W EVANS MATCHLESS	4		4	J SIMISTER NORTON
P MOSS BSA	5		5	F PURSLOW B.S.A.
J SIMISTER NORTON	6		6	R PENNYCOOK NORTON

1947 Clubman's Senior

1	E. E. Briggs, Norton	28.38	**28.18**	29.28	28.44	1 55 08	78.67
2	A. Jefferies, Triumph	30.32	**29.39**	30.14	29.58	2 00 23	75.23
3	G. F. Parsons, Ariel	31.50	31.05	33.35	**30.36**	2 07 06	71.26
4	P. H. Waterman, AJS	32.59	31.44	32.21	**31.04**	2 08 08	70.68
5	G. E. Leigh, Norton	32.43	32.01	32.41	**31.00**	2 08 25	70.53
6	F. Fairbairn, Norton	33.12	32.14	33.08	**31.13**	2 09 47	69.80
7	H. B. Iremonger-Watts, Triumph	33.36	32.25	33.05	**31.48**	2 10 54	69.23
8	S. Lawton, Rudge	31.40	**30.43**	33.01	38.56	2 14 20	67.43
9	H. J. Bacon, Norton	34.20	33.14	34.46	**32.52**	2 15 12	66.99
10	W. Myers Rudge	**33.19**	33.36	37.03	35.41	2 19 39	64.85
11	J. Cannell, Triumph	43.06	34.43	31.40	**31.38**	2 21 07	64.19
12	H. F. Hunter, AJS	**34.26**	36.07	38.06	35.55	2 24 34	62.64
13	J. W. White, Triumph	34.01	**33.12**	34.56	42.40	2 24 49	62.54
14	P. Lingard, Norton	37.34	38.14	39.04	**36.50**	2 31 42	59.70
15	F. P. Heath, Norton	30.22	**29.57**	31.51	69.05	2 41 15	56.17
	A. Crocker, Triumph	36.08	**35.48**	36.14	R		
	J. E. Stevens, BSA	31.01	R				
	R. Tolley, Ariel	31.05	R				
	N. Kirby, BSA	49.20	R				
	J. H. Marshall, Scott	55.32	R				
	W. Reeve, Excelsior	R					
	J. T. Wenman, Sunbeam	R					
	A. R. Bateman, Ariel	R					

LAP POSITIONS

1947 CLUBMAN'S SENIOR

RIDER AND MACHINE	FIRST LAP POSITION		RIDER AND FINAL POSITION	MACHINE
E E BRIGGS NORTON	1		1	E E BRIGGS NORTON
F P HEATH NORTON	2		2	A A JEFFERIES TRIUMPH
A A JEFFERIES TRIUMPH	3		3	G F PARSONS ARIEL
J E STEVENS BSA	4	R	4	P H WATERMAN A.J.S.
R TOLLEY ARIEL	5	R	5	G E LEIGH NORTON
S LAWTON RUDGE	6		6	F FAIRBAIRN NORTON

1948

A FULL HOUSE - AND VINCENTS RULE THE SENIOR

The format for the second Clubman's TT followed the same basic pattern as 1947, with three classes, Lightweight (240 - 250cc), Junior (251 - 350cc) and Senior (351 - 1000cc), and the Wednesday of International TT race-week was retained as the Clubman's 'slot'. A change to the running order on race-day meant that the Seniors led the way, followed by the Juniors then the Lightweights, which seemed an eminently more sensible arrangement.

The Manx Highways Board had been at work since the previous year, and improvements to the course included the removal of some adverse cambers in the Ramsey area, and relaying part of the Glencrutchery Road in front of the Grandstand. The

Felix Green (Scott) gets picked up and dusted down after a Governors Bridge spill in practice. This machine is still in existence and still bears the bent footrest, evidence of its all-to brief TT history.

most significant change as far as the riders were concerned was to Hillberry, where the road had been widened and the right-hand bank cut back, easing the corner and making it considerably faster as a result. The widening had also been carried through into the Cronk-ny-Mona section immediately following Hillberry. A notable and much-needed addition to the course rather than a modification for the benefit of the riders was nearing completion, a footbridge at St. Ninian's crossroads just before Bray Hill, thus allowing access to and from the inside of the course when the roads were closed.

'Pool' petrol was still the mandatory fuel, with an octane rating of about 69-70.

Machines entered were required to have been standard models catalogued before 1st January 1948, and of which at least 75 (three times the previous qualification number) had been produced and delivered to the general public by the closing date for entries. All machines had originally to be equipped with full lighting sets, although most such equipment either had to be removed for the race (lamps, horns), or was permitted to be removed (batteries and dynamos, plus luggage carriers, speedometer and drive, air cleaners) at the rider's discretion.

'Machine Regulations', and the interpretation thereof, was a topic of much discussion in the lead up to and during practice. Bert Perrigo had obtained ACU agreement that the gear-change pedal could be reversed, which made possible the use of the rear-mounted footrests and thus considerably improved the riding position on the BSAs, but the internal mechanism could not be modified to restore the gear-change direction (apparently not a problem for the scrutineers in 1948, this issue was to return in 1949). Another, far more contentious issue, was that any machine was permitted to fit after-market rear springing, and that meant that pre-war girder-fork

Nortons, for example, could have such rear suspension, but not telescopic forks, even though the current models had them as standard. The almost-universal wire gauze fly-screen was also a forbidden luxury for the clubmen.

It was in the interpretation of the Regulations requiring the primary drive to be fully enclosed that a ridiculous and (for two competitors) very unfortunate 'rules are rules' situation developed. Simple enough, one might have thought, but at the time J. Beagley's 1933 Norton was manufactured, 'fully-enclosed' simply meant a pressed-steel case covering the chain, and that was how the machine left the factory. Scrutineer Vic Anstice, however, maintained that the meaning of 'fully-enclosed' was to require an oil-tight oil-bath chain-case. Furthermore, fitting a back-plate to the chain-case in an attempt to comply with the Regulations would break the 'according to the manufacturer's catalogue' rule. Deadlock, and it stayed that way. The Norton was not allowed to start. Fortunately the rider was offered, and took, a reserve place offered in the International Junior. Felix Green's Scott Flying Squirrel entered in the Senior, although of 1937 vintage, was in 1948 still a current model and, in common with all Scott's did not have a primary chain-case, the chain running between the two crankshafts. Again, modifications to enclose the offending chain were not allowed, and letters flew between the Scott works in Shipley, Yorkshire, the rider and the ACU, all to no avail. The situation was not resolved, and Felix was denied his TT ride. He was allowed to practice, during which he managed to drop the machine in the dip at Governors Bridge. The total stupidity of the ruling was apparent when a journalist from the weekly press raised the question *"didn't the removal of the dynamo from an AJS, Matchless or EMC create a similar situation, by making the chain-case no longer oil-tight?"* The answer given was that although it was conceded that the effect was the same, dynamo removal came into the category of *'permitted removals'*, and was therefore was acceptable. How that went down with Mr. Green and with the good folk of Shipley is, perhaps fortunately, not recorded.

Entries and Practice

In the Supplementary Regulations, the ACU reserved the right to reduce, if necessary, the total number participating in the races to a maximum of 80. The great popularity of the event can be gauged by the fact that no fewer than 135 clubs applied to enter 205 riders. The ACU allowed the total to rise to 100, making an initial selection on the basis of one-club-one-rider, with priority given to clubs who had supported the 1947 event, thereafter entries were accepted in order of receipt, 5 reserves being accepted on top of the 100.

The breakdown of entries by class showed 16 Lightweights, 40 Juniors and 44 Seniors, of which 12 were 1000's (not quite all were Vincents, as Charles Howkins had entered an Ariel Square Four). Three makes contested the Lightweight, Velocette the most popular with 8, Triumph and Excelsior with 4 each. The Junior entry comprised a very healthy eight makes with AJS supplying the majority (13), Velocette (7), Norton and BSA (6 each), Matchless (3), Ariel and Triumph (2 each), and a lone EMC. Eight makes also contested the Senior, this time the clear favourite was Norton with 16, followed by Vincent HRD with 11, Triumph with 9, Ariel with 3, BSA with 2, and single representatives from Matchless, Scott and Rudge.

For 1948, riders who had gained a replica in any International TT, or finished in the first three in a post-war Manx Grand Prix, were no longer eligible, although Clubman's winners from 1947 were. In order to qualify, riders had to complete at least three practice laps, unless they had competed in the previous year's Clubman's when two were required. Either way, one of the laps had to be completed within the qualifying time of 45 minutes for Junior and Senior, 50 minutes for the Lightweight class.

Names to note from the entry list were Jack McVeigh (brother of 1947 Lightweight winner Bill), Ian Telfer and Frank Cope in the Lightweight, Wilf Sleightholme and Bob Pratt, (who finished 3rd and 2nd respectively in 1947), Cecil Sandford, Ron Hazlehurst, Arthur Wheeler and Jack Difazio in the Junior, and Phil Carter, Jack Daniels, Phil Heath, Allan Jefferies, Bill McVeigh, Ivor Arber, George Brown, Don Crossley and Harold Clark in the Senior.

After a pleasant, sunny afternoon, torrential rain sweeping in over Douglas Bay on a stormy easterly wind, arrived at the Glencrutchery Road at more or less the same time as the 79 who turned out for the first practice, on the evening of Monday 31st May. By the time the riders were starting their first lap, parts of the road at Ballig and Laurel Bank were already partially flooded, and warning flags were displayed to riders on the approaches. Further round the course conditions weren't so bad, and by contrast Ramsey was at first quite dry, and the wind prevented any chance of mist forming higher up the Mountain. 'The Motor Cycle' commented on the turnout for the first practice *"It was an unusual and welcome spectacle to see so many makes of machine represented. A very high percentage were current models in showroom condition, and 'Feridax-McCandless' rear suspension conversions were popular"*. Allan Jefferies' second lap was fastest of the session on his Triumph, with Phil Heath and Harold Clark some 10 seconds slower. L. Peverett was fastest Junior on his AJS, although *'The Motor Cycle'* credited the place to Tom Westfield (Triumph), and Tom Bryant fastest Lightweight on his Velocette. Most riders seemed to settle for just one lap then pulled in for a hot drink, but Jack Daniels (father of 1969 Senior Manx Grand Prix winner Gordon) on his Vincent-HRD completed three laps in the dreadful conditions, all in respectable times. N. H. Garden crashed his Junior Norton at Laurel Bank, and was taken to hospital with jaw injuries, and there were other spills notably at Governors Bridge, which claimed B. J. Simpson (Junior Matchless), D. Brereton (Lightweight Velocette) and Bill Dehany (Lightweight Excelsior), all without injury, although the forks on Dehany's machine were somewhat bent. There were apparently a few more spills which went unreported, and 'The Motor Cycle' estimated that *"nearly a dozen machines were seen carrying grass and earth which suggested encounters with the bank, and one or two riders came in with torn leathers"*. The *'TT Special'* again published speeds taken over the Sulby mile, and while conditions were very different, the fastest speed (Heath's 1000 Vincent HRD at 104.7 mph) was considerably faster than Eric Briggs' 1947 speed, set on his 500 Norton at 98.92 mph.

Leathers would not have dried very much before they were dragged out again for the following morning's early practice, delayed slightly until 5.15 am because of poor visibility on the Mountain. The rain continued, and speeds were if anything, slower than the opening session, this time Heath clocked fastest Senior lap, Wilmot Evans (Matchless) fastest Junior, and Monty Lockwood (Excelsior) fastest Lightweight. For nearly all riders, caution was the order of the day, and happily no spills were recorded, although Ronnie Hazlehurst (Junior Velocette) needed the slip road at Ballacraine after a far-too-fast approach.

Thursday morning provided the clubmen their first opportunity to practice on reasonably dry roads, although conditions were still far from ideal, with an occasional drizzle and cold, blustery winds. In total 103 riders were out on the course (including reserves) after a short delay caused by difficulties with a telephone link to one of the control points around the course. Heath again posted fastest Senior lap, with Bob Pennycook (Norton) and Frank Fletcher (Excelsior) heading up the Junior and Lightweight respectively. The difference in lap times between the fastest 1000's and 500's was negligible, 8 seconds covering the first three, with Allan Jefferies's Triumph splitting the Vincent-HRD's, Daniels being 3rd fastest. However, all were slowed by the weather, and times were still almost two minutes off Eric Briggs' 1947 lap in 28m 18s. The session though was marred by two serious accidents, one of which unfortunately proved fatal. Riding a Lightweight Velocette, 23-year-old Tom Bryant from Bournemouth, entered by the Ringwood Club, ran wide on the exit from Brandish, touched the bank, and was thrown down the road. A group of riders following closely behind narrowly avoided him, but he suffered severe head injuries and died in Nobles Hospital shortly after arrival. Tom Bryant was the younger son of Tom Bryant Snr., an ex-rider and then partner in a Bournemouth motorcycle business with Joe Huxham. C. Robinson (Senior Norton) broke his thigh and received facial cuts in the other incident, at Ballaugh.

The storm which had badly affected Thursday evening's International TT practice had passed by the morning when the clubmen emerged for their final session. Except for a few damp patches the roads were dry, but it was still quite cold for the 80 riders, some of whom still needed a couple of laps to qualify (and whose cause would not have been helped by a short delay while Travelling Marshall Harold Rowell cleared some stray sheep from the Mountain road). During this fourth and final session, the 1000's began to show their pace and impose themselves on the practice leaderboard, with the first five places occupied by the Stevenage-built twins. Phil Heath still led, and fifth-fastest was Reserve 'J', Chris Horn. The new surface on the Glencrutchery Road had looked treacherous throughout practice, but had not caused any incidents until the Friday morning, when a few of the faster men had slides, including Allan Jefferies, who 'spun' his Triumph under power whilst accelerating up the hill, escaping with cuts and bruises. Always the joker, Allan no doubt appreciated the humour occasioned by the location of these bruises, to a part of his anatomy which would have made sitting down a little uncomfortable! Pennycook was again fastest Junior, and Fletcher fastest Lightweight.

Allan Jefferies and Tiger 100, Governors Bridge.
This photograph from the Jefferies family album bears the caption: "Pa Jefferies in a somnambulant position"

By the end of practice, only two riders had failed to qualify, both in the Junior, B. Ternouth (Norton) and B. J. Simpson (Matchless). As a consequence mainly of the bad weather, many of those who did qualify had only managed the minimum number of laps or just over, and therefore faced the prospect of starting their race with only three or four closed-roads laps experience.

As if to reward the competitors for enduring a miserable week of weather during practice, race-day dawned with clear skies, brilliant sunshine and only a slight breeze. *'The Motor Cycle'*, reporting the races in its 17th June, was in romantic mood, and described the scene thus.

"Motorcyclists are distinguished from all other sportsmen by a merry and passionate enthusiasm, displayed both individually and corporately. Never and nowhere is this unique emotion more conspicuous than in TT week at Douglas. On the Monday and Friday it focussed in the form of hero-worship around the persons of the famous professional stars. On Clubman's Day it is evinced in a more domestic and affectionate version as dad and mum, sis and assorted brothers, girl friends and club-mates, with fans from the home towns, fore-gather to hail (they hope) the triumph of 'our' Tom, Dick and Harry.

These lads are dreamers all. They are risking their beloved and cherished personal property in the perils of the race, hoping at the least to earn some small credit, at the best to magnetize some Big Shot by their skill and aplomb, and so find a golden key into the magic circle of the world-famous aces. All roads up the hills are crammed with eager pals and relations, their faces beaming, their tongues discussing the prospects of their family champion. Add sun and sport to such an emotional foundation, and result is a happy day, which warms every heart, even if about a third of the would-be stars fail to last the appointed laps. These will grin, blush, and have another shot in 1949."

The three classes were run concurrently, with two minutes between classes, riders setting off in pairs at 20-second intervals. Of the 100 entries plus reserves, 91 made the start line. As in 1947, starting the race by means of the kick-start was mandatory, as was the re-start following the compulsory stop at the end of the second lap.

The Lightweight Race (Wednesday, 9th June)

Starters

	Rider	Club	Machine
1	F Fletcher	West Leeds MC	Excelsior
2	W J Jenness	Ashford, Kent MC	Triumph
3	H Warburton	Blackpool MC & LCC	Excelsior
4	J J McVeigh	Grimsby MC	Triumph
5	I F Telfer	West Middlesex Amateur MCC	Velocette
6	W G Dehany	Wirral '100' M.C.C.	Excelsior
7	A Henthorn	C.S.M.A. Ltd.	Velocette
8	A G Crighton	Aberdeen & D.M.C.	Velocette
9	G S Wakefield	Cambridge Centaur MCC	Triumph
11	D Brereton	Southport MC & LCC	Velocette
12	E F Cope	Birmingham M.C.C.	Velocette
14	M V Lockwood	Ipswich Triangle M.C.C.	Excelsior
15	J Smith	Chester M.C.	Velocette
16	R Carvill	Coventry & Warwickshire M C.C.	Triumph
17	H J Downing	Manchester Ace M.C.	Velocette

Of the entries, only the unfortunate Tom Bryant was a non-starter. For the eventual winner, the race had the added incentive of the 'Wal Handley' Trophy, awarded and to be presented by Wal's mother in memory of the great pre-war ace who had lost his life in a flying accident during the war, while serving with the Air Transport Auxiliary.

A Henthorn and A G Crichton kick their MOV Velocette's into life. The Dowty front forks gave a softer ride than the girders, but were undamped and prone to lose air and gently deflate!

At 10.30 am, machines were allowed out of the assembly area onto the Glencrutchery Road, for a 15-minute 'round the barrels' warm up, prior to the off at 11.00 am.

Starting at Number 1, Frank Fletcher got away smartly on his Excelsior Manxman, as did most of the field, except for Frank Cope and J. Smith (both on Velocettes), and H. Warburton (Excelsior) who lost time before setting off. By Ballacraine, Jack McVeigh had closed up on Fletcher, whose machine appeared not to be running quite as it ought. McVeigh was much closer by Hillberry, and he crossed the start/finish a few yards ahead, some 20 seconds up on corrected time, but both their times were beaten by Monty Lockwood (Excelsior) who led the race by 17 seconds. Fletcher's starting partner Bill Jenness was in trouble on his Triumph, and McVeigh's starting partner H. Warburton's troubled race continued when he lost a minute and a half in the pits at the end of the lap, wiping oil off the back end of the Excelsior.

First Lap Leaderboard

1	M. Lockwood (Excelsior)	34m 45s	(65.16 mph)
2	J.J. McVeigh (Triumph)	35m 02s	(64.63 mph)
3	F. Fletcher (Excelsior)	35m 23s	(64.00 mph)
4	R. Carville (Triumph)	35m 40s	(63.49 mph)
5	G.S. Wakefield (Triumph)	35m 59s	(62.92 mph)
6	W.G. Dehany (Excelsior)	36m 03s	(62.80 mph).

The first retirement reported was that of 5th place-man George Wakefield, with engine trouble at Marown Bridge on his Triumph. Lockwood extended his lead throughout the lap over McVeigh, who took a tumble right at the end of the lap at Governor's Bridge, and retired. One of the pre-race favourites, Frank Fletcher's race also ended when the engine in his Excelsior expired at the Gooseneck, and the net result was to increase Lockwood's lead to over two minutes, elevate Bill Dehany into 2nd place, and move everyone else up a place, except for Ian Telfer, whose Velocette stopped at the Sulby crossroads with engine trouble. Jenness's first lap machine problems also proved to be terminal, and he eventually retired at Sulby with the magneto sprocket adrift on his Triumph, and Warburton retired his Excelsior at Ramsey Hairpin.

Second Lap Leaderboard

1 M. Lockwood (Excelsior)   1h 8m 51s   (65.78 mph)
2 W.G. Dehany (Excelsior)   1h 11m 06s   (63.70 mph)
3 R. Carville (Triumph)   1h 12m 24s   (62.55 mph)
4 A.G. Crichton (Velocette)   1h 14m 47s   (60.55 mph)
5 J. Smith (Velocette)   1h 16m 28s   (59.22 mph)
6 E.F. Cope (Velocette)   1h 17m 07s   (58.73 mph)

Lockwood had the race in his pocket barring accident or mechanical difficulties, and he held the lead through the last lap, slightly increasing the margin over Dehany, and finishing a little over two and a half minutes ahead. Carville's last lap almost cost him his 3rd place when he came off at the Waterworks, but he was able to re-mount very quickly and rejoin the race, still with 3 minutes in hand over Crichton. D. Brereton was a last lap retirement with his Velocette, and 6th place went to Frank Cope, making his TT debut when already in his 50's, who continued racing well into his 70's. In fact when he turned out for the first practice session, it had been the first time he had sat astride a motorcycle since before the war!

Finishing Order

1 M. Lockwood (Excelsior)   1h 44m 37.6s (64.93 mph)
2 W.G. Dehany (Excelsior)   1h 47m 13.8s (63.35 mph)
3 R. Carville (Triumph)   1h 48m 38s   (62.53 mph)
4 A.G. Crichton (Velocette)   1h 52m 24s   (60.44 mph)
5 J. Smith (Velocette)   1h 55m 33.4s (58.79 mph)
6 E.F. Cope (Velocette)   1h 57m 28.2s (57.82 mph)

Fastest Lap: M. Lockwood (2nd lap) 34m 06s (66.40 mph). (Record)

The Junior Race (Wednesday, 9th June)

Starters

	Rider	Club	Machine
18	D E R Morgan	North East London MCC	A.J.S.
19	A Broadey	Stockton & DMCC	Norton
20	M Sunderland	Bury & DMC	Norton
21	A Klinge	Salop MC	B.S.A.
22	W Sleightholme		
		West Wilts MC	A.J.S.
23	R Pratt	Worcester AC	Norton
24	A D Bassett	Newbury MC	B.S.A.

25	J Terry	Kings Norton MCC	Ariel
26	D Moncreiff	Lanarkshire MC & CC	B.S.A.
27	H Roberts	Manchester '17' MCC	A.J.S.
28	E J Bowman	Barham & DMC & LCC	A.J.S.
29	T A Westfield	North Lincs MC	Triumph
30	C C Sandford	Broadway MCC	Velocette
31	R H King	Bedford Eagles MCC	B.S.A.
33	R V Slinn	South Birmingham MC	B.S.A.
34	J K Beckton	Middlesborough & DMC	Triumph
35	C Julian	Ilkeston DM.C & LCC	Velocette
37	S A Milne	Sunbeam MCC	E.M.C.
38	I D Drysdale	Edinburgh St. George MC	A.J.S.
39	L Peverett	Harringay & DMC	A.J.S.
41	J F Jackson	Bradford Vagabonds MCC	Velocette
44	R J Hazlehurst	Solihull MCC	Velocette
45	A F Wheeler	Leatherhead & DMC	Velocette
46	W Evans	Antelope (Coventry) MCC	Matchless
47	R A Rowbottom		
		Scunthorpe MCC	A.J.S.
48	J Difazio	Frome & DMC & LCC	B.S.A.
49	W J Mundy	Sheffield & Hallamshire MC	A.J.S.
50	E N Peterkin	Sidcup & DMCC	A.J.S.
51	R Pennycook	South Liverpool MC	Norton
52	J Fisher	Portsmouth MCRC	Ariel
53	W M McLeod	Edinburgh Southern MC	A.J.S.
54	O P Hartree	Ely & DMCC	Velocette
55	A Peatman	Kircaldy & DMC	A.J.S.
56	A S Herbert	O.W.L.S. MC	Matchless
57	G W Robinson	Newcastle & DMC	A.J.S.

In addition to the two riders who had failed to qualify, G. W. Harrison (Norton), N. H. Garden (Norton) and K. Rickard (Velocette) non-started, leaving 35 to face the starter. Dennis Morgan's AJS was fast away, as was the Norton of the 1947 runner-up Bob Pratt, getting away in the third pairing, alongside Wilf Sleightholme's AJS. Delayed starts were experienced by A. D. Bassett (BSA), E. N. Peterkin (AJS), O. P. Hartree (Velocette), Ron Hazlehurst (Velocette) and Cecil Sandford (Velocette). D. Moncrieff (BSA) fell foul of the 'tank-full-of-petrol-rider-full-of-adrenalin' combination, and crashed at the first corner, Quarter Bridge. No serious damage seemed to have been done, and he re-mounted and continued, but only got as far as Kirkmichael before retiring with clutch trouble. Milton Sunderland (Norton) had made up the starting interval on Morgan by Kirkmichael, and led on the roads, but Pratt was not very far behind. Sunderland led at Ramsey on corrected time, and also led on the roads as they completed the first lap, but Pratt had picked up time over the Mountain, and led by 2 seconds from Sleightholme, and 12 seconds from Sunderland when the lap times were announced. 4th, 5th and 6th places were separated by just 2 seconds, Jack Difazio leading the trio. O. P. Hartree came off his Velocette at Ramsey Hairpin, but re-mounted, eventually to finish just one place off the leaderboard, in 7th place. There were problems elsewhere round the course for A. D. Bassett, who retired after coming off in the dip at Governors Bridge, without serious injury, R. H. King (BSA) who retired at the East Mountain Gate with engine trouble, and reportedly stopped also were Cecil Sandford and Wilmot Evans (Matchless).

First Lap Leaderboard

1 R. Pratt (Norton)	31m 43s	(71.40 mph)
2 W. Sleightholme (AJS)	31m 45s	(71.32 mph)
3 M. Sunderland (Norton)	31m 55s	(70.94 mph)
4 J. Difazio (BSA)	32m 20s	(70.04 mph)
5 G.W. Robinson (AJS)	32m 21s	(70.00 mph)
6 R. Pennycook (Norton)	32m 22s	(69.96 mph)

Pratt turned on the style on the second lap with a new record of 30m 42s (73.76 mph) and drew out a 21-second lead over Sunderland, while Sleightholme's lap, almost a minute slower, dropped him to 3rd. It would appear though, that he had hit some kind of trouble, because when he arrived at his pit at the end of the lap for his mandatory stop and fill-up, he retired. Later, it was reported that the Ajay had lost compression. 4th place-man Difazio and Bob Rowbottom (AJS) both retired at Hillberry, and prompted some amusement to the spectators by catching a Douglas-bound bus, still clad of course in full racing leathers! Reg Slinn (BSA) was another retirement, stopped near the 12th Milestone with engine trouble. With Difazio's departure, and E. J. Bowman's AJS suffering a broken oil pipe, forcing his retirement at Ramsey, a new name appeared on the leaderboard, that of Ron Hazlehurst (Velocette).

Second Lap Leaderboard

1 R. Pratt (Norton)	1h 2m 25s	(72.56 mph)
2 M. Sunderland (Norton)	1h 2m 46s	(72.16 mph)
3 W. Sleightholme (AJS)	1h 3m 24s	(71.43 mph)
4 R. Pennycook (Norton)	1h 4m 25s	(70.30 mph)
5 G.W. Robinson (AJS)	1h 4m 27s	(70.27 mph)
6 R.J. Hazlehurst (Velocette)	1h 4n 28s	(70.25 mph)

Still the minor leaderboard places were very close at the start of the third lap, with 3 seconds covering the 4th, 5th and 6th places, and with Sleightholme stuck in the pits, they all moved up a place, the vacant 6th being taken up by L. Peverett riding an AJS. A loudspeaker announcement that Hazlehurst had retired at the Guthrie Memorial turned out to be a case of mistaken identity, the unfortunate rider quickly identified as being Wilmot Evans, who had hit problems on the first lap. Sandford's troubles continued, and he toured in to retire at the pits at the end of his second lap. Pratt had a comfortable minute and a half lead as he completed the lap, but spectators in the grandstand saw him give a 'thumbs-down' signal to his pit as he raced through. Hazlehurst moved up to 3rd, but 6th place-man Peverett came off at Creg-ny-Baa on his third lap. He was able to re-mount and limp the few miles back to his pit to straighten out a bent mudguard and gear lever, and complete the race in 10th place. Another of the AJS's went out, that of W. J. Mundy, who stopped at his pit and retired, apparently with engine trouble.

Third Lap Leaderboard

1 R. Pratt (Norton)	1h 33m 36s	(72.58 mph)
2 M. Sunderland (Norton)	1h 35m 10s	(71.39 mph)
3 R.J. Hazlehurst (Velocette)	1h 36n 55s	(70.10 mph)
4 G.W. Robinson (AJS)	1h 37m 25s	(69.74 mph)
5 R. Pennycook (Norton)	1h 37m 40s	(69.56 mph)
6 J.F. Jackson (Velocette)	1h 38m 56s	(68.65 mph)

The 'thumbs-down' from Pratt turned out to be well founded, and what looked like a certain victory for the Norton rider ended in retirement at Union Mills, and bitter disappointment. Initially reported as a 'split tank', it later transpired that the petrol tap had pulled out of the tank bottom. His rivals were all behind him on the roads at the time of his stoppage, and may well have seen his machine by the side of the road, as a free-for-all ensued. Sunderland began the last lap over a minute and a half ahead of Hazlehurst, and so he looked certain to inherit the win, but his last lap time of 35m 3s was by far his slowest of the race, indicating that possibly he had struck trouble which was not apparent to onlookers or to reporters by the trackside. Slow enough that he was passed on corrected time not only by Hazlehurst but by the AJS of Robinson, eventually taking 3rd place. (Post-race machine examination showed the cause of his slow final lap, with several scores in the barrel indicating a partial seizure.) In contrast to Sunderland's time, Hazlehurst's last lap was 31m 52s, Robinson 4 seconds slower. Pennycook was another Norton rider to hit last lap difficulty, in his case terminal engine trouble, and his likely 4th place ride ended at The Highlander. Angus Herbert's Matchless split its tank and ran out of petrol, but he had reached Cronk-ny-Mona by the time it happened, and he was able to coast and push to the finish, and 14th place.

Finishing Order

1 R.J. Hazlehurst (Velocette) 2h 8m 47.2s (70.33 mph)
2 G.W. Robinson (AJS) 2h 9m 21.6s (70.02 mph)
3 M. Sunderland (Norton) 2h 10m 13.4 (69.58 mph)
4 J.F. Jackson (Velocette) 2h 12m 13s (68.56 mph)
5 I.D. Drysdale (AJS) 2h 14m 0s (67.60 mph)
6 T.A. Westfield (Triumph) 2h 14m 3s (67.57 mph)
  [O.P. Hartree (Velocette) 2h 15m 26s (66.88 mph)
was elevated to 6th place after Westfield's exclusion]

Fastest Lap: R. Pratt (2nd lap) 30m 42s (73.76 mph) (Record)

The Senior Race (Wednesday, 9th June)

Starters

Rider	Club	Machine
58 C A Stevens	Streatham & DMC	Norton
59 A Crocker	Southern Amateur MCC	Vincent H.R.D.
60 S Parsons	Wisbech MC	Triumph
61 G E Leigh	Southport MC	Norton
62 J D Daniels	Swansea MC	Vincent H.R.D.
63 W J Netherwood	Huddersfield MC	Norton
64 A R King	Tollerton MCTC	Triumph
65 P H Carter	Winsford & DMC	Norton
66 C Howkins	Sphinx MC	Ariel
67 N Osborne	Blackmore Vale MCC	Triumph
68 F P Heath	Leicester Query MC	Vincent H.R.D.
69 H F Hunter	Gosport & DMCC	Triumph
70 L Uttley	Rochdale & DMC	Norton
71 A Jefferies	Bradford & DMC	Triumph
72 P Cousins	North Lancs MC	Vincent H.R.D.
73 T G Wycherley	Oswestry & DMC	Ariel
74 A A Sanders	Midland MCSC	Triumph
75 A A F Burton	West of England MC	B.S.A.
76 W McVeigh	Pathfinders MCC Ltd	Triumph
77 H J D Boynton	Redditch MC & CC	B.S.A.
78 J E Carr	Gravesend Eagles MCC	Vincent H.R.D.
79 J T Wenman	North Berks MCC	Norton
82 C Horn	South Shields & DMC	Vincent H.R.D.
83 L J B R French	Norwood MC	Norton
84 J H Colver	Bexleyheath & DMCC	Matchless
85 A M S Smith	Vintage MCC	Norton
86 J Harrison	Cumberland County MCC	Ariel
87 T H Hodgson	Whitehaven MCC	Triumph
88 W C Reed	Stockport MCRC	Norton
90 R J Vernon	Bolton MCC	Vincent H.R.D.
91 R P Sifleet	X.H.G. Tigers MCC	Triumph
92 W F Beckett	Bermondsey MCC	Vincent H.R.D.
93 G Brown	Louth & DMC	Vincent H.R.D.
94 D G Crossley	Peveril (IoM) MC & LCC	Triumph
95 F Fairbairn	Scarborough & DMC Ltd	Vincent H.R.D.
96 E Andrew	Mansfield & DMCC	Norton
97 W M Lamb	Wakefield & DMSC	Norton
98 D Whelan	Burton M.C. & LCC	Rudge
99 H Clark	Manchester Eagle MC	Norton
100 R F Walker	Rotherham & DMC	Norton
101 E J Davis	Six Hills MC	Vincent HRD

Senior non-starters were E. J. Beagley (Norton), C. Robinson (Norton), I. K. Arber (Norton) and F. I. Green (Scott). The first pair away at 11.13 am were Cyril Stevens (Norton) and Alan Crocker (Vincent HRD), and both made good starts. Phil Heath, one of the favourites for the race win, made a similarly good start in the sixth pair on his Vincent HRD, followed

George Brown (Vincent-HRD) in action at Quarter Bridge, inset: just about on the point of collapse after pushing in.

20 seconds later by another possible winner Allan Jefferies (Triumph). Jack Daniels got his Vincent HRD away without delay, not so P. Cousins and Chris Horn who both lost considerable time starting their similar machines. Stevens was the first to reach Ballacraine, and the first into Kirkmichael, by which point Jefferies had closed to within a second or so of Heath. Unfortunately, Jefferies was forced to retire a little way up the road at Ballaugh, with a split petrol tank. By Creg-ny-Baa it was Daniels who led on the road from Stevens and George Leigh, as they all began to catch some of the Junior entry. R. P. Sifleet, another who had been expected to do well, got no further than Greeba before being sidelined by a flat rear tyre on his Triumph. Daniels' standing-start first lap was announced as being within one second of Briggs' 1947 record. With his late starting number (93), George Brown's rapid progress though the field was maybe not quite so obvious, but when the first lap times were posted he was 8 seconds inside the record, and 9 seconds ahead of Daniels, who in turn led Heath by 16 seconds. This was George Brown's first visit to the Island, and he had cheerfully

admitted that after practice he thought he had learned all the course *"with the exception of the bit between Braddan and Ramsey"!*. The big Stevenage twins held the first three places, with the previous year's Lightweight winner Bill McVeigh in fourth place riding a Triumph. H. J. D. Boynton was reported to be pushing in his BSA from Governors Bridge, and Charles Howkins retired after coming off the Square-Four at Keppel Gate as a result of, in his own words *"a combination of lack of experience and over-exuberance"*. Another faller was Jack Colver, who came off his Matchless at the Waterworks, but was able to re-mount and continue.

First Lap Leaderboard

1 G. Brown (Vincent HRD)	28m 10s	(80.39 mph)
2 J. D. Daniels (Vincent HRD)	28m 19s	(79.97 mph)
3 F. P. Heath (Vincent HRD)	28m 35s	(79.23 mph)
4 W. McVeigh (Triumph)	29m 27s	(76.90 mph)
5 C. A. Stevens (Norton)	29m 41s	(76.29 mph)
6 H. Clark (Norton)	30m 05s	(75.26 mph)

The order remained the same during the second

lap as the riders approached the compulsory fuel stop, but Brown posted a new lap record of 27m 24s (82.65 mph) as he extended his lead to 44 seconds over Daniels, who held a similar advantage over Heath. R. J. Vernon was reported as having dropped his Vincent HRD at Sulby, but still he managed to get onto the Leaderboard in 6th place. L. Uttley stopped near the Mountain Box to attempt repairs to his Norton, but eventually had to retire, as did W. C. Reed whose Norton ran out of fuel at the Gooseneck, and A. Burton, who retired at the pits with clutch trouble on his BSA. Another retirement was that of P. Cousins, after a fall from his Vincent HRD at Hillberry which caused considerable damage to the machine and the countryside. He was able to walk away from the wreckage.

Daniels retained his lead on the road throughout the third lap, and as the leaders crossed the line to start their last lap, the '*TT Special*' clocked Heath 2m 9s after Daniels, which on corrected time maintained the placings, Brown a minute and a half ahead. Well behind the leaders on time, but going great guns was R. J. Vernon, who was up to 4th place at the end of the lap. Don Crossley came off his Triumph at the Hairpin, but was able to restart and continue, while W.M. Lamb was not so lucky in a fall on his second lap a few hundred yards before the Hairpin, at Cruickshank's. He was taken to the Cottage Hospital with head injuries which thankfully turned out to be none-too-serious. Just off the leaderboard in 7th place was Harold Clark, riding the Norton on which Eric Briggs had won in 1947.

Second Lap Leaderboard

1 G. Brown (Vincent HRD)   55m 34s   (81.48 mph)
2 J.D. Daniels (Vincent HRD) 56m 18s   (80.44 mph)
3 F.P. Heath (Vincent HRD)   56m 59s   (79.48 mph)
4 W. McVeigh (Triumph)   58m 14s   (77.77 mph)
5 C.A. Stevens (Norton)   59m 10s   (76.55 mph)
6 R.J. Vernon (Vincent HRD) 59m 41s   (76.03 mph)

Third Lap Leaderboard

1 G. Brown (Vincent HRD)   1h 23m 20s (81.49 mph)
2 J. D. Daniels (Vincent HRD) 1h 24m 54s (80.02 mph)
3 F. P. Heath (Vincent HRD)   1h 26m 05s (78.92 mph)
4 R.J. Vernon (Vincent HRD)   1h 28m 47s (76.52 mph)
5 C. A. Stevens (Norton)   1h 29m 45s (75.77 mph)
6 W. McVeigh (Triumph)   1h 30m 05s (75.40 mph)

Charles Howkins may have attributed his spill at Keppel Gate to 'a lack of experience' but he was certainly no spring-chicken in this, the first of his three Clubman rides. Note the 'racing' rear tyre!

As the scoreboard clock reached 1.00 pm, riders' progress 'clocks' had Daniels on the Mountain section of the course, with Heath and Brown in Ramsey, Brown only a few seconds behind as they began the climb. As Daniels crossed the finish line, Heath and then quickly after, Brown, were indicated at Creg-ny-Baa, and the finishing order seemed set to be maintained as it had been from the start. What the indicators couldn't say, but what spectators on the course near Keppel Gate had picked up on, was that Brown was in trouble. His Vincent HRD had used the last of its fuel in the area of the 33rd, and he was coasting. Momentum and the gradient carried him past Hillberry, but then on the climb up Cronk-ny-Mona toward Signpost he was having to push. He was not the first to have to push in to finish a race, and he wasn't the last, but few have had to push so heavy a machine. The crowd along the course gave him the only support they could, with cheers, and he stopped a couple of times out of sheer exhaustion, but make it home he did, his last lap taking just short of 40 minutes, twelve and a half minutes slower than his fastest. The Grandstand crowd gave him a standing ovation, but that and the record lap would have been little consolation for a 6th place instead of a deserved win. The reason for lack of fuel would seem to have been simple misreading of the tank level in the hustle of the pit-stop, and his consequent departure with something less than a tankful. Brown's misfortune lifted the other leaderboard men a place, which brought Ted Davis into 5th, as on the last lap Vernon also hit trouble, eventually finishing 13th, and Chris Horn finishing 8th, never able to make up time lost at the start. A last lap retirement for unspecified reasons was George Leigh's Norton.

Finishing Order

1 J.D. Daniels (Vincent HRD) 1h 52m 29.6s (80.51 mph)
2 F.P. Heath (Vincent HRD)   1h 53m 49s (79.58 mph)
3 C.A. Stevens (Norton)   1h 59m 03.4s (76.07 mph)
4 W. McVeigh (Triumph)   1h 59m 47s (75.61 mph)
5 E.J. Davis (Vincent HRD)   2h 01m 4.4s (74.81 mph)
6 G. Brown (Vincent HRD)   2h 03m 18.6s (73.48 mph)

Fastest Lap G. Brown (2nd lap) 27m 24s (82.65 mph)
(Record)

Reflections

There was particular interest in the Senior class to see how the 998 Vincent HRD's would compare over four laps of the Mountain Circuit, under the exact same race conditions, as the 500 Triumphs and Nortons, whether the weight of the vee-twins was more of a handicap than their extra capacity was an asset. Practice times had indicated that the Vincents were quicker, but not completely dominant. The race positions were a better indicator of relative performances, and were, despite the variable introduced by the differing abilities of the riders, quite convincingly in favour of the 1000's. Ten Vincents started, nine finished, with six in the first ten places, an impressive demonstratiion of high-speed reliability (and in 11th place was a Vincent Comet). George Brown's second lap set a record for the class, and in fact was 4 seconds faster than Freddie Frith's fastest lap in the Monday's International Junior. Predictably, the wisdom in pitching the 1000's and the 500's together was questioned by some. 'The Motor Cycle' said "Since the results of the Senior Clubman's TT have shown the tremendous advantage the 1000cc machines have over the smaller machines, many clubmen wonder if there will be a separate 1000cc class next year". Also their handling and cornering drew favourable comment, 'The Motor Cycle' again, "Contrary to uninformed speculation the big fellows were obviously easy to handle, both at maximum speed and on the bends. Heath, Brown and Davis, in particular, ran down Bray Hill as if on rails, so safe and so smooth as to camouflage their real speed, while at Highlander Inn their cornering was of the highest class. Properly balanced weight is no great hindrance."

The winner of the Senior, Jack Daniels, was riding in his very first road race, although he had raced on the sand in his native Wales, and was an experienced trials and scrambles competitor. A prominent member of the Swansea Club, he sadly was to lose his life in a road accident in October of the same year. His son Gordon, was the winner of the 1969 Senior Manx Grand Prix. A website featuring historic racing in Wales describes Daniels during the race as the *"determined private entrant, out-riding the* works teams (including the Vincent HRD works team)". It then gets a bit carried away with enthusiasm for its subject and claims that Daniels was ahead of Brown and pulling away from him toward the end of the race. From the published race reports and times in the 'TT Special', 'The Motor Cycle', 'Motor Cycling' and the times included in the ACU Report of the Stewards of the Meeting, this is clearly incorrect. That Daniels did take a fine win, and in so doing beat Phil Heath and Ted Davis on similar models, is fact, and should be remembered as such. As should George Brown's misfortune.

The Model 16 AJS which finished 2nd and 5th in the Junior race were specially prepared for the event by the AMC Competition Shop, under the supervision of Wally Wyatt, and any machine which received special attention from this man was going to be near the front in whatever branch of the sport it was intended for. At that time, the same basic engine powered the works trials bikes to great success with riders of the calibre of Hugh Viney and Artie Ratcliffe on board, later by the three Gordons (Jackson, Blakeway and McLoughlin) and then Mick Andrews. In 500 form, generally 'badged' as a Matchless, the scrambler version won countless events ridden by the likes of Basil Hall, Geoff Ward and Dave Curtis, then Chris Horsfield and Vic Eastwood. For such a bike to finish 2nd in a race on the TT Course to an overhead-camshaft Velocette was a fine achievement. The factory also experimented with open-class road racing and hill climb variants of the basic engine design, Les Graham's 'Cadwell Ajay' of 1948 and 'Shelsley Matchless' both being highly successful 'one-offs', built by the Competition Shop using a mix-and-match of AMC road and competition parts, and whose exploits are now the stuff of legend.

After the races were over, there were unfortunate shades of Bill McVeigh's 1947 're-bore' controversy, when the 6th place machine in the Junior, the Triumph of Tom Westfield, was found to be 'oversize'. Francis Beart issued a public statement following the rider's exclusion, admitting that the error (a re-bore at 0.020" instead of a bore clean-up) had been his, and was the result of an *"unfortunate mistake at his works, in the rush of preparing many racing engines"*. He went on to make it clear that the situation was unknown to Westfield, who was completely blameless, and he apologised both to the rider and to the entrant club, the North Lincs. Despite Westfield being innocent of any attempt to gain unfair advantage, the exclusion of the desperately unlucky rider, unlike that of McVeigh the previous year, was upheld.

Overall enthusiasm for the races ran high, and Major H. R. Watling, Director of the Manufacturer's Union summed up the feeling of many when addressing those present at the prize distribution for the Clubman's TT. He said that motorcycling history had been made that day, that it had proved that the big machines were fast and reliable, and the results *"would send our exports flying far above what they were. What finer advertisement was there for British machines than the results of the Clubman's TT"*. This was further supported by the conditions of the machines at the finish. 'The Motor Cycle' again: *"One of the most interesting aspects of this years TT was the magnificent condition of the engines at the conclusion of the Clubman's races. Ordinary sports and semi-sports engines covered their three or four laps at speed - remarkably high speed in many cases - yet showed no sign of any ordeal. It was telling testimony to the design and inbuilt excellence of Britain's same-as-you-can-buy motorcycles"*.

Jack McVeigh's bid for Clubman glory ended in a heap at Governors Bridge at the end of the second lap: marshals pick up his stricken Triumph

My 1948 Junior Clubman's Ride
by Ronnie Hazlehurst

The records show that I won the 1948 Clubman's TT, but it should be said that it was not a sure thing and my win was as a result of bad luck for some of the others. Bob Pratt was leading for the first and second laps with Wilf Sleightholme (Norton) close behind. I started my first lap a little slower than these two, I am told, but that was my plan. I was determined to finish and rode with care, although my lap times started to improve and I steadily gained on the leaders.

This put me in a good position to be on the leader board so that when Bob Pratt went out with a broken petrol tap (and out of petrol), I was in a position to take the lead and win. I did not know this as I crossed the finish line. However I had been trying hard and as I started to brake to turn into the pits the brakes had faded, I guess due to heat, and I went boring on to the top of Bray Hill. All this time I am still happy because I had finished. I turned left at the cross roads and then left again into the park and arrived back at the grandstand to be met by my mechanic Stan Felton who said "WHERE THE HELL HAVE YOU BEEN. We have to take the bike down to be measured. YOU WON THE RACE".

It was a great race and we took home a great trophy plus fifty pounds prize money. However I shall always be disappointed that no replica was awarded. Now we have nothing to show for the 1948 Clubman's TT and I do think the ACU should have considered this award most important for beginners, which most of us were at that time.

Ronnie Hazlehurst at Quarter Bridge and (inset) with mechanic Stan Felton. His KSS has been 'looked at' by Bill Stuart from the Norton works, who had cleaned up the inlet tract, removing the lower portion of the guide which protuded into the inlet tract, "it will shorten the life, but will last the race" was his comments. A founder member of the Solihull MCC, Ronnie still returns to the TT most years from his Los Angeles home.

1948 Clubman's Lightweight

	Rider					
1	M. V. Lockwood, Excelsior	34.45	**34.06**	35.46.6	1 44 37.6	64.93
2	W. G. Dehany, Excelsior	36.03	**35.03**	36.07.8	1 47 13.8	63.35
3	R. Carvill, Triumph	**35.40**	36.44	36.14	1 48 38.0	62.53
4	A. G. Crighton, Velocette	38.03	**36.44**	37.37	1 52 24.0	60.44
5	J. Smith, Velocette	**38.00**	38.28	39.05.4	1 55 33.4	58.79
6	E. F. Cope, Velocette	38.35	**38.32**	40.21.2	1 57 28.2	57.82
7	H. P. Downing, Velocette	39.34	**38.17**	40.17.4	1 58 08.4	57.50
8	A. Henthorn, Velocette	42.11	40.09	**39.57.2**	2 02 17.2	55.55
	D. Brereton, Velocette	40.35	**39.22**	R		
	J. J. McVeigh, Triumph	35.02	R			
	F. Fletcher, Excelsior	35.23	R			
	G. S. Wakefield, Triumph	35.59	R			
	I. F. Telfer, Velocette	42.14	R			
	H. Warburton, Excelsior	43.00	R			
	W. J. Jenness, Triumph	R				

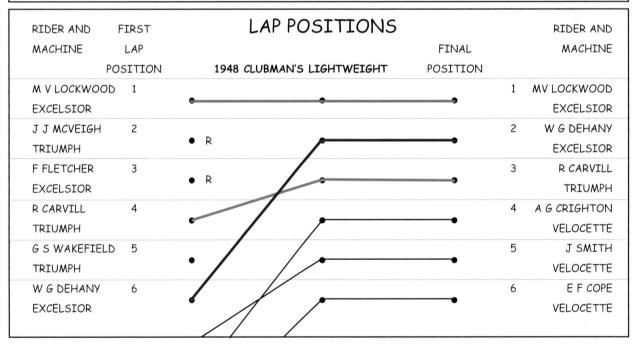

LAP POSITIONS

58

1948 Clubman's Junior

1	R. W. Hazlehurst, Velocette	32.38	**31.50**	32.27	31.52.2	2 08.47.2	70.33
2	G. W. Robinson, AJS	32.21	32.06	32.58	**31.56.6**	2 09 21.6	70.02
3	M. Sunderland, Norton	31.55	**30.51**	32.24	35.03.4	2 10 13.4	69.57
4	J. F. Jackson, Velocette	32.44	**32.20**	33.52	33.09	2 12 05.0	68.56
5	I. D. Drysdale, AJS	33.28	**33.08**	33.59	33.25.8	2 14 00.8	67.60
6	O. P. Hartree, Velocette	33.41	34.00	34.50	**32.55.8**	2 15 26.8	66.88
7	A. F. Wheeler, Velocette	36.29	**32.36**	33.43	32.43	2 15 31.0	66.85
8	C. Julian, Velocette	34.32	34.42	35.19	**34.31.2**	2 19 04.2	65.13
9	D. E. R. Morgan, AJS	35.16	34.28	36.02	**34.15.2**	2 20 01.2	64.68
10	L. Peverett, AJS	32.52	**32.08**	35.35	39.43.8	2 20 18.8	64.55
11	E. N. Peterkin, AJS	36.08	**34.52**	35.56	34.56	2 21 52.0	63.85
12	J. K. Beckton, Triumph	33.12	**32.27**	34.05	42.51	2 22.35.0	63.68
13	A. S. Herbert, Matchless	40.19	**33.56**	35.01	35.22.2	2 24 38.2	62.62
14	W. M. McLeod, AJS	37.08	36.43	37.19	**35.29.6**	2 26 39.6	61.76
15	J. Fisher, Ariel	35.06	**34.53**	35.20	42.24	2 27 43.0	61.31
16	H. Roberts, AJS	**34.15**	40.52	39.01	36.23.8	2 30 31.8	60.17
17	S. A. Milne, EMC	38.19	37.24	38.41	**36.19**	2 30 43.0	60.10
18	A. Peatman, AJS	37.29	38.58	39.18	**37.14**	2 32 59.0	59.21
19	J. Terry, Ariel	38.49	39.02	38.44	**37.25.6**	2 34 00.6	58.82
20	A. Broadey, Norton	39.26	38.28	40.00	**37.16.8**	2 35 10.8	58.37
21	A. Klinge, BSA	37.37	**34.14**	34.52	51.37	2 38 20.0	57.20
	R. Pratt, Norton	31.43	**30.42**	31.11	R		
	R. Pennycook, Norton	32.22	**32.03**	33.15	R		
	W. S. Sleightholme, AJS	31.45	**31.39**	R			
	E. J. Bowman, AJS	34.57	**34.21**	R			
	W. J. Mundy, AJS	**34.38**	37.17	R			
	J. Difazio, BSA	32.20	R				
	R. A. Rowbottom, AJS	33.59	R				
	R. V. Slinn, BSA	36.18	R				
	C. C. Sandford, Velocette	85.32	R				
	A. D. Bassett, BSA	R					
	D. Moncrieff, BSA	R					
	R. H. King, BSA	R					
	W. Evans, Matchless	R					

LAP POSITIONS

1948 CLUBMAN'S JUNIOR

RIDER AND MACHINE	FIRST LAP POSITION		FINAL POSITION	RIDER AND MACHINE
R PRATT NORTON	1		1	R J HAZLEHURST VELOCETTE
W S SLEIGHTHOLME A.J.S.	2		2	G W ROBINSON A.J.S.
M SUNDERLAND NORTON	3		3	M SUNDERLAND NORTON
J DIFAZIO B.S.A.	4		4	J F JACKSON VELOCETTE
G W ROBINSON A.J.S.	5		5	I D DRYSDALE A.J.S.
R PENNYCOOK NORTON	6		6	O P HARTREE VELOCETTE

Junior class riders Bill Mundy (AJS) and Jack Difazio (BSA) round Quarter Bridge on the first lap. Neither were destined to finish.

1948 Clubman's Senior

1	J. D. Daniels, Vincent HRD	28.19	27.59	28.36	**27.35.6**	1 52 29.6	80.51
2	F. P. Heath, Vincent HRD	28.35	28.14	29.06	**27.44**	1 53 49.0	79.58
3	C. A. Stevens, Norton	29.41	29.29	30.35	**29.18.4**	1 59 03.4	76.07
4	W. McVeigh, Triumph	29.27	**28.47**	31.51	29.42	1 59 47.0	75.61
5	E. J. Davis, Vincent HRD	30.17	**29.15**	31.02	30.30.6	2 01 04.6	74.81
6	G. Brown, Vincent HRD	28.10	**27.24**	27.46	39.58.6	2 03 18.6	73.48
7	H. Clark, Norton	30.05	30.08	33.45	**29.52.2**	2 03 50.2	73.13
8	C. Horn, Vincent HRD	31.08	30.46	32.09	**30.21.8**	2 04 24.8	72.79
9	F. Fairbairn, Vincent HRD	31.31	31.20	31.33	**30.58**	2 05 22.0	72.25
10	E. Andrew, Norton	31.18	31.23	33.08	**30.32.2**	2 06 21.2	71.69
11	J. E. Carr, Vincent HRD	31.50	**31.20**	32.22	31.20.4	2 06 52.4	71.40
12	A. A. Sanders, Triumph	**31.17**	31.18	33.11	31.48.6	2 07 34.4	70.99
13	R. J. Vernon, Vincent HRD	30.46	**28.55**	29.06	39.31.6	2 08 18.6	70.59
14	R. F. Walker, Norton	32.15	31.51	33.27	**31.34.4**	2 09 07.4	70.15
15	A. M. S. Smith, Norton	32.23	32.03	33.17	**31.28.4**	2 09 11.4	70.11
16	D. G. Crossley, Triumph	**31.07**	31.29	33.14	33.33.4	2 09 23.4	70.00
17	W. J. Netherwood, Norton	33.16	32.09	32.46	**31.13.6**	2 09 24.6	69.99
18	J. Harrison, Ariel	33.11	31.48	32.55	**31.36**	2 09 30.0	69.95
19	W. F. Beckett, Vincent HRD	32.10	35.43	33.03	**30.00**	2 10 56.0	69.18
20	J. H. Colver, Matchless	32.33	32.55	34.37	**32.22**	2 12 27.0	68.39
21	T. G. Wycherley, Ariel	33.23	**33.10**	33.43	33.36	2 13 52.0	67.66
22	T. H. Hodgson, Triumph	33.48	33.10	34.12	**32.58.4**	2 14 08.4	67.53
23	N. Osborne, Triumph	34.18	**33.14**	34.08	33.53.6	2 15 33.6	67.16
24	J. T. Wenman, Norton	33.49	36.16	35.50	**32.58.2**	2 18 53.2	65.21
25	H. F. Hunter, Triumph	34.53	35.01	35.32	**34.42.4**	2 20 08.4	64.63
26	A. Crocker, Vincent HRD	**35.53**	36.57	36.29	36.02.4	2 25 11.4	62.38
27	P. H. Carter, Norton	37.03	36.16	38.11	**35.22.2**	2 26 52.2	61.67
28	A. R. King, Triumph	**35.53**	36.28	38.05	36.47.2	2 27 13.2	61.52
29	D. Whelan, Rudge	50.07	32.06	34.35	**31.47.4**	2 28 35.4	60.95
30	L. J. B. R. French, Norton	39.03	**38.01**	**38.01**	42.24.2	2 37 29.2	57.52
31	S. Parsons, Triumph	49.30	47.34	**40.46**	42.07	2 59 57.0	50.33
	G. E. Leigh, Norton	**31.01**	31.37	71.24	R		
	A. A. F. Burton, BSA	**30.59**	32.09	R			
	P. Cousins, Vincent HRD	31.20	R				
	W. C. Reed, Norton	31.35	R				
	L. Uttley, Norton	32.33	R				
	W. M. Lamb, Norton	35.17	R				
	C. Howkins, Ariel	R					
	A. Jefferies, Triumph	R					
	H. J. D Boynton, BSA	R					
	R. P. Sifleet, Triumph	R					

LAP POSITIONS

1948 CLUBMAN'S SENIOR

RIDER AND MACHINE	FIRST LAP POSITION		FINAL POSITION	RIDER AND MACHINE
G BROWN VINCENT HRD	1		1	J D DANIELS VINCENT HRD
J D DANIELS VINCENT HRD	2		2	F P HEATH VINCENT HRD
F P HEATH VINCENT HRD	3		3	C A STEVENS NORTON
W MCVEIGH TRIUMPH	4		4	W MCVEIGH TRIUMPH
C A STEVENS NORTON	5		5	E J DAVIS VINCENT HRD
H CLARK NORTON	6		6	G BROWN VINCENT HRD

Governors Bridge seems to have caught out many Clubman riders. Dennis Morgan (AJS) runs wide as George Brown (Vincent-HRD) sweeps past.

Dennis rode the Manx for many years as well as doing a stint as travelling marshall.

George Brown was one of the world's foremost sprinters in the 1960 and 1970s, setting many world records with his Vincent powered 'Nero' and 'Super Nero'. His last road race was the 1953 Senior TT, when he was brought down by the wreckage of Les Graham's fatal Bray Hill crash.

1949

ACCOMMODATING A RECORD
ENTRY, AND TWO NEW STARS
EMERGE

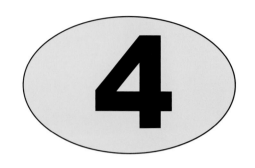

The mutterings over the inclusion of the 1000's with the 500's continued after the 1948 event. Much was said and written on the affair, and at a winter meeting in Birmingham the whole issue was thrashed out between ACU officials, Isle of Man representatives and riders, although as it turned out, the number of riders who actually attended was very few. As Geoff Davison commented, *"The absence of many of those who had said and written so much was regrettable, but the meeting bore fruit in that for 1949 it was decided that four Clubman's races should be held, two in the morning and two in the afternoon, with a maximum of a hundred competitors in each period"* This was twice the number of competitors in 1948, and the additional race, of course, was for machines between 500cc and 1000cc.

Junior and Senior races in 1948 had covered four laps, but it was felt that with the new format there would be insufficient time to maintain that race distance in the bigger classes, and consequently they were all set to cover three laps, and the Lightweight two. Awards in each class were as for 1948, with £50.00 for the winning entrant club, down to £10.00 for 6th place, plus thirty free entries for the Manx Grand Prix divided up between the classes in proportion to the number of starters in that class. The Dunlop Trophy was awarded to the rider (not the club) whose fastest lap improved on the existing class record by the greatest amount. Riders were promised fuel of a marginally better quality than previous, but still nominally at 72.5 octane.

Entries and Practice

Entries were high, not quite as high as had maybe been expected, but this meant that no problems of selection arose, and all the 174 who met the entry qualifications were able to be accepted. Eligibility requirements and restrictions were more or less the same as before, the only real difference being that the bar on riders who had finished in the first three in a previous Manx Grand Prix, was extended to the first five. Twelve entered the 1000cc class and eighty-five the Junior, to be held concurrently in the morning, with fifty-five Senior and twenty-two Lightweights following in the afternoon.

Machine eligibility and equipment regulations remained pretty much as 1948, with fully equipped models according to the manufacturer's catalogue or published specification, of which 50 (reduced from 75 in 1948) had been sold to the public before the closing date for entries. The previous year's primary drive cover fiasco had resulted in a change of wording to the effect that what was required was *"fully enclosed primary drive except in the cases of motorcycles having external flywheel(s) or where the primary drive is taken from between the crankcases"*. It would be good to have been able to record here, given that his machine would have been eligible, the entry of Mr. Felix Green and his Scott, but he never rode in the Isle of Man again.

Permitted additions to equipment included flyscreens, rev-counters, steering dampers, tyre security bolts, rear-springing, air vents and water excluders to brakes, and mudguard pads. Within the seventeen 'optional modifications to equipment', which generally allowed for preferences in spark plugs, brake and clutch linings, cables and the like, were introduced flexible oil and petrol pipes, presumably in response to the number of problems with, or caused by, the standard rigid pipes (and the safety hazard caused by leaked fluids to the rider and other competitors). The effect of vibration on fuel and oil tanks and lines was a major headache in those days, but such failures under race conditions resulted

The Race Transporter of the 1940s! Cyril Hopwood brings his Bullet ashore; the sidecar is probably full of leathers, helmets, tools . wife etc., so the only luggage space was on the bow of the sidecar.

in improved materials and design. Racing was improving the breed.

Machine variety was again most evident in the Junior, with eight different manufacturer's represented, including four entries on Douglas's, the first time for many a year that the Bristol-made flat twin had appeared in the Island. Most popular was BSA with over 20, then Norton, AJS and Velocette, 5 Royal Enfields and Matchless, and 2 Triumphs. The Senior had six manufacturer's, predominantly Norton and Triumph, then BSA, but after the practice period had taken its toll, three manufacturer's (Ariel, AJS and Vincent HRD) were down to being represented by just a single machine. In the Lightweight class, a solitary BSA was to start against a fairly even spread of Velocette, Triumph and Excelsior machinery. Nor was the 1000cc class entirely made up of Vincent HRDs, as Charles Howkins had again entered on his Ariel Square Four.

Names from the entry list included George Brown, Dennis Lashmar and Chris Horn on 'thousands', Phil Carter, Robin Sherry, Reg Dearden, Allan Jefferies,

Ivor Arber, Ken James, Jack Bottomley and a certain G. E. Duke on 500's in the 'Senior'. The line up for the Junior included Willy Wilshere, Milton Sunderland, Arthur Lavington, Brian Jackson, Harold Clark, Sam Seston, Cecil Sandford, Bill Lomas, Jack Difazio, and Ted Pink. The Lightweight's included Bernard Hargreaves, Frank Cope, Cyril Taft, Jack McVeigh and Fron Purslow. The Junior and Senior entry therefore contained no less than three future World Champions 'before they were famous'!

Riders were to start their races as in 1948, in pairs at 20-second intervals, and by the customary kick-start. However, changes to the Regulations reflecting the reduction in race distances, meant that not only was the compulsory pit and re-fueling stop after two laps removed, but that re-fuelling at any stage of the race was barred. Regulation 22 read *"Fuel sufficient for one tank full will be supplied by the ACU for each competing motorcycle, free of charge. No replenishment, other than topping-up immediately prior to the Race, is permitted"*. Not surprisingly, this was to have a profound effect on race strategies, particularly in the 1000 cc class.

80 clubmen turned out early on the morning of Saturday 4th June, for the first of their allotted five practice sessions. Conditions were by no means perfect with a strong head-wind as they crossed the Mountain, but unlike the previous year, at least the roads were dry and visibility was good. Lap times and speeds were not spectacular, but the names of George Brown, who put in the fastest time of the session with 28m 44s (78.80 mph), and Geoff Duke headed the bigger classes, while John Simister and Cyril Taft led the smaller. Two fallers were reported, Horace Barnes on his Junior BSA went into the hedge at the fast Handley's Corner and was taken to hospital, while Frederick Burns, also on a Junior BSA, came off at Glen Helen, but was able to re-mount and complete the lap, to then take himself off to hospital to have his injuries dressed.

With the arrival of more riders on the weekend boats, there was a much larger turn-out of 148 for the second session, held on Monday evening. Speeds were a little down on the previous session, as the riders found low cloud and reduced visibility in the south and east of the course, but bright sunshine elsewhere. George Brown and J.A. Edwards (1947 Rapide) shared fastest lap of the evening in the 1000cc class with 30m 7s (75.18 mph), while Allan Jefferies was fastest overall with 29m 41s (76.32 mph). A dozen or so minor spills were reported, the only one of which requiring first aid being that of the same Mr. Edwards on a later lap.

Always of interest to riders and race-goers alike, the results of the 'TT Special' Sulby Mile timings showed good speeds, and for this year there was a strong following wind to help those whose confidence allowed them to keep the throttle wound on for the full distance. George Brown clocked fastest at 120.0 mph, with five more Vincent HRD's before the fastest Senior, Allan Jefferies' Triumph with 104.7 mph. Only two Nortons managed to get into the top ten in the Senior, those of Duke and Arber, the rest a solid block of Triumphs. No less than five riders tied for fastest Junior at 96.3 mph (Eric Harvey, Frank Weller, Tommy Cookson, Cyril Julian and John Wenman), the machinery split being three Nortons and two BSA's, and two tied for fastest Lightweight at 81.8 mph, Dennis Ritchie (Velocette) and Fron Purslow (BSA). The Square Four of Charles Howkins recorded a creditable 93.7 mph.

By the third session on Tuesday evening, weather

Bill Lomas was working at Royal Enfield at the time and was using a fairly standard 350cc Bullet in his TT debut. His career encompassed works rides (both racing and trials) with James, Royal Enfield, Vincent, Velocette, AJS, Benelli, MV, NSU, Moto Guzzi. His TT career spanned seven years, and he holds a unique double of winning two TT's in the same year, on separate courses, the 1955 Junior on a Moto Guzzi, and the Lightweight, MV-mounted on the Clypse Course.

Willy Wilshere awaits another practice lap on his 3T Triumph. He was probably wearing the brown leathers that made him recognisable in Vintage racing and hill-climbing right through to the 1970s.

conditions had deteriorated to the 'Clubman's Practice Standard', with mist, heavy rain, and visibility down to 25 yards in places, even less on the Mountain. Speeds were naturally low for all the 109 riders who ventured out, and it was the Vincent HRD of Chris Horn that was quickest of the period with 32m 11s (70.36 mph). Peter Carr crashed his Senior Triumph into the hotel wall at Creg-ny-Baa, and although he escaped with shock and minor injuries, he later

A practice-session sensation who came good in the race, Alan Taylor (Junior Norton) rounds Governors Bridge.

complained of head pains, and was taken to Nobles hospital for observation. T. W. Brown came off his Senior AJS at the Nook, but was uninjured. Mechanical casualties included Cyril Taft, whose Excelsior dropped a valve, Hilary Iremonger-Watts hit magneto trouble with his Lightweight Triumph, and James McMeeken's Junior AJS suffered a split tank.

The weather for the fourth session on Thursday morning was ideal, with clear blue skies, dry roads and no visibility problems whatever, the first time that riders had been able to see properly the stretch of the Mountain between Guthrie's and Keppel Gate. A total of 133 riders turned out, and this despite the fact that about 20 BSA's were not allowed out. This dramatic action apparently followed a warning on the Monday after the preliminary examinations that many machines did not comply with the maker's specification in respect of the gearchange. The cause of the problem was simply that when using the rear footrest position provided on the Gold Star, the gear lever was repositioned on the splines 180 degrees round. To re-instate the 'down-for-up, up-for-down' which was the specified arrangement, a modified (reverse) cam-plate was used, and it was this modification which had upset the Scrutineers. Some of the riders had been able to make the necessary alteration using BSA parts obtained either before they came over or from parts obtained locally in the

Island, but the unfortunate 20 had not been able to do either. Once again, 'rules are rules', and they were barred. From those who were out, speeds were high, George Brown quickest overall with 27m 46s (81.55 mph), Geoff Duke fastest Senior with 29m 4s (77.90 mph), Alan Taylor fastest Junior with 30m 42s (73.76 mph), and Bernard Hargreaves heading the Lightweights with 36m 9s (62.65 mph). George Wakefield's Lightweight Triumph was another to have a valve drop in, after it over-revved on the downhill run to Creg-ny-Baa, and Allan Jefferies stopped at Kirk Michael with carburettor problems. Raymond Allen stopped with a seized engine on his AJS, the resulting damage forcing him to non-start. W. Lishman (Junior Royal Enfield) was apparently temporarily blinded by the sun toward the end of Sulby Straight, and hit the bridge. After receiving some attention at the Cottage Hospital he was able to spectate in Parliament Square. Ivor Arber dropped his Senior Norton near the Mountain Box, suffering cuts and minor injuries. J .J. Pache had a narrow escape when he found after finishing his session that he'd lost one rear wheel spindle nut, and the other had only a couple of threads still engaged, on his Speed Twin Triumph.

Friday morning's final practice was held in perfect conditions. The 'problem BSAs' were allowed out for this one, and a total of 123 riders were out on the course, the session yielding the fastest lap in each class thus far in practice. George Brown again topped the 1000's with 27m 13s (83.19 mph), Allan Jefferies the Senior with 28m 27s (79.59 mph), Alan Taylor the Junior with 30m 42s (73.76 mph) and Dennis Ritchie the Lightweight with 33m 46s (67.02 mph). The name of Alan Taylor was not then known on the Island or even on the mainland, for the simple reason that the Clubman's was the first ever road race, or two-wheeled competition of any sort, for the

19-year-old. A casualty of the last practice was K. H. King, who had set third fastest time in his class, but crashed his 250 Triumph at Brandish, and who was taken to hospital with knee and other injuries.

Early laps in the practice period had served to confirm the fear that the no-refuelling rule would seriously affect the 1000's. The combination of tank size and fuel consumption meant that the big vee-twins simply could not go the three laps ridden at race pace. It was true that some riders had actually managed three laps on a tank-full, but only as a result of running carburettor settings which were weak, and the machines were over-heating as a consequence. The race itself would demand an awkward combination of lean-as-you-dare jetting and judicious use of the throttle, more like a 'fuel economy run' than a TT race! Similarly affected, although to a lesser extent, were riders of competition-model AJS's and Matchless's, with their small capacity fuel tanks.

The Lightweight Race (Wednesday, 15th June)

Starters

	Rider	Club	Machine
57	B J Hargreaves	Ribble Valley MC	Velocette
59	A B Barton	Liverpool Imperial MC	Triumph
60	A Henthorn	C.S.M.A. Ltd.	Velocette
61	J R Dulson	South Liverpool MC	Velocette
63	E F Cope	Birmingham MCC	Excelsior
64	C V Taft	Alcester & DMCC	Excelsior
65	J Smith	Wrexham MC	Excelsior
66	G A Northwood		
		Wolverhampton MC & LCC	Velocette
68	G S Wakefield	Cambridge Centaur MC	Triumph
69	H B Iremonger-Watts		
		X.H.G. Tigers MCC	Triumph
71	W J Jenness	Tenterden & DMC & LCC	Triumph
72	T W Swarbrick	Preston & D.M.C.	Excelsior
73	L C Bolshaw	Nantwich & DMC	Triumph
74	D A Ritchie	Aberdeen & DMCC	Velocette
75	V J Holcroft	Leamington Victory MC & LCC	
			Velocette
76	J J McVeigh	Grimsby M.C.	Triumph
77	F Purslow	Salop MC	B.S.A.

Race-day began dull and cloudy, but from 10.00 am the sun began to break through, and a very fine day was in prospect for the four events. Five of the twenty-two entrants were non-starters, Frank Price (Excelsior), Arthur Hutchinson (Rudge), P. Moss (BSA), J. Makaula-White (Rudge) and K. H. King (Triumph). The Lightweights were despatched two minutes after the last of the Seniors for their two-lap 'sprint', the first man away being Bernard Hargreaves on a Velocette. Two machines reluctant to fire up were the Triumph of Hilary Iremonger-Watts, and the Excelsior of T. W. Swarbrick, and two machines to give trouble almost from the off were the Triumphs of Bill Jenness and Jack McVeigh, the latter riding his brother's 1947 Lightweight winning machine, in fact a 1939 model. Both stopped before Ballacraine, McVeigh re-starting eventually to finish in 8th place, but Jenness retired. Bill Jenness was one of two over-50 riders in the race, the other being Frank Cope. After changing plugs a couple of times, including one scrounged from a spectator, he accepted the inevitable, and settled down to watch the race at the Highlander, with a pint of Guinness! First into Ramsey was Hargreaves, followed by Taft, who was closer than his starting time difference, and Dennis Ritchie (Velocette) and Fron Purslow (BSA) had also gained ground on earlier starters. Eventual 4th place-man Wakefield stopped briefly in Ramsey to look at something on his Triumph before

Leading from flag fall to finish, Cyril Taft takes his pre-war Excelsior Manxman down Bray Hill.

continuing. By the end of the lap, Hargreaves still led Taft on the road, but by a diminishing margin. A. B. Barton was credited with 5th place at the end of lap one, but he had to make a stop at his pit with what was reported as a leaking oil gauge, which he was able to repair and continue. Not so fortunate was Purslow, who, after a strong showing as far as Ramsey had been forced to stop, eventually making it as far as his pit, where he retired. Other first lap retirements were Iremonger-Watts whose Triumph had not been right from the start, with engine trouble at Kirkmichael, and V. J. Holcroft (Velocette) with a seized engine at the Mountain Box.

First Lap Leaderboard

1 C. V. Taft (Excelsior)	33m 33s	(67.50 mph)
2 B.J. Hargreaves (Velocette)	33m 57s	(66.69 mph)
3 D.A. Ritchie (Velocette)	34m 05s	(66.43 mph)
4 G.S. Wakefield (Triumph)	35m 41s	(63.46 mph)
5 A.B. Barton (Triumph)	35m 53s	(62.89 mph)
6 L.C. Bolshaw (Triumph)	36m 00s	(62.89 mph)

As the leaders approached Ramsey on their second lap, Taft was close enough to occasionally catch a glimpse of Hargreaves ahead of him, and by the time they reached Creg-ny-Baa they were together, with Ritchie also closing on Hargreaves. Taft's second lap set a new class record of 32m 57s (68.70 mph). and with his second lap only 8 seconds slower, Ritchie, who was riding a tele-forked post-war MOV Velocette in contrast to the mainly girder-forked field, took 2nd place by a comfortable 35 seconds. Bolshaw's last lap effort lifted him above Barton into 5th place, less than 2 seconds behind 4th placed Wakefield.

Finishing Order

1 C.V. Taft (Excelsior)	1h 6m 30.2s	(68.10 mph)
2 D.A. Ritchie (Velocette)	1h 7m 10.2s	(67.43 mph)
3 B.J. Hargreaves (Velocette)	1h 7m 45.2s	(66.84 mph)
4 G.S. Wakefield (Triumph)	1h 10m 30.8s	(64.23 mph)
5 L.C. Bolshaw (Triumph)	1h 10m 32.6s	(64.21 mph)
6 A.B. Barton (Triumph)	1h 11m 29.6s	(63.34 mph)

Fastest Lap: C.V. Taft (2nd lap) 32m.57s (68.70 mph) (Record)

Handley Trophy: C.V. Taft

Dunlop Trophy: C.V. Taft

The Junior Race (Wednesday, 15th June)

Starters

Rider	Club	Machine
14 G Milner	Hull MC Ltd.	B.S.A.
15 W J Mundy	Sheffield & Hallamshire MCC	A.J.S.
16 A C Taylor	Oldham Ace MC	Norton
17 L D Boult	Antelope MCC	B.S.A.
18 J McMeeken	Galloway MC & LCC	A.J.S.
19 J Green	Berwick & DMC	Triumph
20 W H Wilshere	Watford & DMC & LCC	Triumph
21 L Bertorelli	Wansbeck MC	Royal Enfield
22 J F Cook	Eltham & DMC	Matchless
23 J Fisher	Portsmouth MC	B.S.A.
24 C M Hopwood	Oldham Ace MCC	Royal Enfield
25 W C Reed	Stockport MCRC	Norton
26 E Harvey	Taunton MC	B.S.A.
28 E J Bowman	Barham & DMC & LCC	A.J.S.
29 F B Burns	Streatham & DMCC	B.S.A.
31 W Camier	Ashford, Kent MC	Norton
32 W Reeve	Wakefield & DMSC	B.S.A.
34 C W Davis	Sidcup & DMCC	B.S.A.
35 E H C Baker	Wellingborough MC	B.S.A.
36 J D Warren	Leicester Query MC	B.S.A.
37 T R Cookson	Blackpool M.C. & C.C.	Norton
38 F G Edgar	Edinburgh Southern MC	A.J.S.
39 L Price	Crewe & Southern Cheshire MCC	B.S.A.
40 F W Haines	Swansea MC	Norton
41 J D Haines	South Birmingham MC	B.S.A.
42 R Hallett	Sittingbourne & DMC	B.S.A.
43 M Sunderland	Rochdale & DMC	Norton
44 B A Jackson	Oswestry & DMC	A.J.S.
46 E A Lavington	Wimbledon & DMC	Velocette
47 A Raynor	Stocksbridge & DMC	Norton
48 H Walmsley	East Lancs MC & LCC	Velocette
49 A S Herbert	O.W.L.S. MC	Matchless
50 E Proctor	Kettering & DMCC	Matchless
51 K Talbot	Scunthorpe MCC	Velocette
52 E F Collings	Surrey Hills MC	Velocette
53 A A F Burton	West of England MC	B.S.A.
54 J Simister	Manchester '17' MC	Norton
56 H Clark	Manchester Eagle MC	B.S.A.
57 F H Weller	Goring & DMC & MCC	Norton
58 S Seston	Bourneville MC	Royal Enfield

61	D E R Morgan	North East London MCC	A.J.S.
62	D Moncrieff	Lanarkshire MC & CC	B.S.A.
63	C C Sandford	Broadway MCC	Velocette
64	'S Franklen'	Grasshopper (Romford) MCC	A.J.S.
65	A R Brassington	Potteries Clarion MCC	Norton
66	B Morris	Southampton Vikings MC & LCC	B.S.A.
67	H Grant	Falkirk & DMC	A.J.S.
68	C. Bruce	Glasgow Lion MCC	A.J.S.
69	J Warr	Leicester Query MC	Velocette
70	C Julian	Ilkeston & DMC & LCC	B.S.A.
73	A Klinge	C.S.M.A. Ltd. (Shropshire)	B.S.A.
74	W F Wood	Hartlepool & DMC	Douglas
75	W A Lomas	Redditch MC & CC	Royal Enfield
76	D A Wilcocks	St Albans & DAC	Velocette
77	F O Coleman	Wolverhampton & DMC & CC	Velocette
78	D H R Gray	Rochester & Chatham DMC	A.J.S.
79	R Porter	Peterborough MCC	B.S.A.
80	F Pados	Ashford, Kent MC	Douglas
81	W S Corley	Mont' Christie MCC	A.J.S.
83	J Difazio	Frome & DMC & LCC	B.S.A.
84	R H King	Bedford Eagles MCC	Matchless
85	G N Camfield	London Douglas MCC	Douglas
86	R W Mouat	Edinburgh & DMC Ltd.	A.J.S.
87	G W Robinson	Tynemouth & DMC	Norton
88	J S Basinger	Harringay & DMCC	Velocette
89	J A Thomson	Croydon MC	A.J.S.
90	E T Pink	Sunbeam MCC	Norton
92	W A G Auld	Waterloo & DMMC	Matchless
93	A D Brown	Stewarts & Lloyds (Corby) MCC	Norton
94	K G Adcock	Leicester Query MC	Royal Enfield
95	W F Barker	Rushden & D. Query MC	B.S.A.
96	W J Hill	Newbury & DMC	Douglas
97	J T Wenman	North Berks LC & MCC	Norton
98	R D Briscoe	Leatherhead & DMC	Norton

This was the largest entry of any Clubman's race in the series thus far, with 74 making it through to the start from an entry of 85, made up of 21 BSA's, 15 Nortons, 13 AJS's and single figure numbers of Douglas, Enfield, Matchless, Triumph and Velocette. Non-starters were D.C. Birrell (BSA), H. Barnes (BSA), D. T. Pugh (Norton), R. A. Smith (BSA), W. Lishman (Royal Enfield), J. McDermott (Velocette),

R. Allen (AJS), A. Williams (BSA), C. S. Mason (Velocette), T. A.Westfield (Triumph) and P. H. Waterman (AJS).

First away at 10.34 am should have been Number 14 G. Milner, the other of the starting 'pair' being the unused number 13, but his BSA refused to play, and although he eventually did get away, it was alongside riders with starting numbers in the 30's, a penalty of some 3 minutes. Other problem starters were L. Price (BSA), A. Raynor (Norton), and H. Walmsley (Velocette) who all lost up to half a minute, and F. H. Weller (Norton), J. Warr (Velocette) and A. Klinge (BSA) who lost a little less time. Alan Taylor and his Norton led on the roads at Ballacraine, continuing to display the fine form he had shown during practice, pulling away a little more by Ramsey and over the Mountain. At the end of the lap he had a good lead on the road, although when the corrected times were posted his lead was some 8 seconds over the BSA's of Ray Hallett and Harold Clark who were tying for 2nd place, and the first six were separated only by 19 seconds. In fact, not much more than a minute separated the first dozen riders, mounted on four different makes, at the end of that lap. Two early

Arthur Lavington takes Ballaugh Bridge on his Velocette KSS. His spectacular fall at Hillberry was caused by a broken front fork spring. At this time, Arthur was working as foreman at L. Stevens of Shepherds Bush, but later opened his Velo workshop in Tooting, London. He was fatally injured in a practice crash for the 1966 Junor TT.

spills were reported, Cyril Julian coming off his BSA at Quarter Bridge, and John Warren getting only a little further before dropping his BSA on the first left-hander into the Braddan Bridge 'S'-bend. Julian was able to restart after straightening his gear lever, and make it to the finish, Warren retired. Engine trouble accounted for Adrian Burton retiring his BSA at Ballacraine, and Harry Grant retired his AJS at the Stonebreakers Hut also with engine problems. Other first lap retirements were Jack Warr's Velocette, after a fall at Keppel Gate, Bill Camier's Norton, no reason specified, and John Cook's Matchless, after a crash at the Nook. Cook was taken to Nobles Hospital with head injuries, but they were stated as being none-too-serious.

First Lap Leaderboard

1 A.C. Taylor (Norton)	30m 26s	(74.41 mph)
2 R.Hallett (BSA)	30m 34s	(74.09 mph)
2 H. Clark (BSA)	30m 34s	(74.09 mph)

Geoff Duke in the winners enclosure. His mechanic was Doctor Stephen Darbishire, a pre-war Manx GP star

4 G.W. Robinson (Norton)	30m 38s	(73.92 mph)
5 J. Simister (Norton)	30m 41s	(73.80 mph)
6 E. Harvey (BSA)	30m 45s	(73.64 mph)

Reports from the Mountain on the second lap indicated that Hallett had lost some time to Taylor, but the main leaderboard mover during the lap appeared to be Eric Harvey on the BSA, with a new lap record of 30m 5s to lead Taylor by just 1 second. However, it was a short-lived record, as Clark, starting well behind Harvey, went even faster, and in doing so registered the first ever sub 30 minute lap by a 350, with 29m 52s (75.81 mph). Bill Lomas and Arthur Lavington were second lap retirements, Lomas with engine trouble on his Royal Enfield, Lavington in spectacular fashion with a fall at the very fast Hillberry, when he ran wide on the exit and hit the left-hand bank, rolling over in the road so many times that the '*TT Special*' reporter there was fearful for Lavington's very life! As it turned out, he was able to walk away from the accident, bruised and battered, but with nothing broken, much to the correspondent's relief. David Moncrieff's BSA cut out as he passed the pits, and it was reported that he had retired a short while after.

Second Lap Leaderboard

1 H. Clark (BSA)	1h 0m 26s	(74.94 mph)
2 E. Harvey (BSA)	1h 0m 50s	(74.45 mph)
3 A.C. Taylor (Norton)	1h 0m 51s	(74.43 mph)
4 J. Simister (Norton)	1h 0m 56s	(74.33 mph)
5 R. Hallett (BSA)	1h 1m 15s	(73.95 mph)
6 C.C. Sandford (Velocette)	1h 1m 39s	(73.46 mph)

Harvey's race came to an end on the third and last lap with a broken chain at Handley's Corner, as Taylor continued to lead on the road all the way to the finish, where he had to wait and see what the interval was between himself and Clark. For whatever reason, his last lap was his slowest of the race, some 38 seconds slower than Clark who duly took the win, and in fact also allowed Simister to catch and pass to snatch runner-up spot. Last lap disappointments in the form of retirements came for W. A. G. Auld (Matchless), Bill Mundy (AJS), Charles Bruce (AJS), Douglas Wilcocks (Velocette), Angus Herbert (Matchless), J. D. Haines (BSA) and

G. N. Camfield (Douglas). The reason given for the stoppages of both Mundy and Herbert was that of dry tanks, the latter after a determined effort to get to the point on the Mountain where he could coast home, pushing some distance before calling it a day at the Bungalow. Once Milner did get away from his disastrous start, he put in three good laps to finish a creditable 13th. Had he not lost those precious minutes, a leaderboard place may well have been his.

Finishing Order

1 H. Clark (BSA)	1h 30m 21.4s	(75.18 mph)
2 J. Simister (Norton)	1h 31m 11s	(74.51 mph)
3 A.C. Taylor (Norton)	1h 31m 24.6s	(74.32 mph)
4 R. Hallett (BSA)	1h 31m 51.6s	(73.97 mph)
5 C.C. Sandford (Velocette)	1h 32m 23.4s	(73.52 mph)
6 E.T. Pink (Norton)	1h 32m 32.8s	(73.42 mph)

Fastest Lap: H. Clark (2nd lap) 29m.52s (75.81 mph) (Record)

The Senior Race (Wednesday, 15th June)

Starters

	Rider	Club	Machine
1	J Smith	Aberdeen & DMC	Norton
2	D A Wayne	Southall & DMC	Norton
3	L Starr	Bar None MCC	Triumph
4	A A Sanders	Coventry & Warks MC	Triumph
6	J Wright	Wirral '100' MC	B.S.A.
7	G F Slater	Southern Amateur MCC	Triumph
8	J E Brookes	Northwich MC	B.S.A.
9	H F Hunter	Gosport & DMCC	B.S.A.
10	R McDonald	Tenterden & DMC & LCC	Norton
11	T P Crebbin	Peveril (IoM) MC & LCC	Triumph
12	J K Beckton	Middlesborough & DMC	Ariel
15	D W N Brereton	Southport MC & LCC	Triumph
16	R Kenworthy	Royton A.T.C. MCC	Triumph
18	L J B R French	Norwood MC	Triumph
19	D Marshall	Scarborough & DMC	Triumph
21	P H Carter	Winsford & DMC	Norton
22	M S Featherstone	Grantham Pegasus MCC	Triumph
23	G E Duke	B.M.C.R.C.	Norton
25	R H Sherry	Ilford MC & LCC	Triumph
26	E Andrew	Mansfield & DMCC	Norton
27	L Uttley	Todmorden & DM & MCC	Norton
29	D J P Wilkins	Mendip Vale MC & LCC	Triumph
30	T Hodgson	Whitehaven MC	Triumph
31	K S Watling	Garforth & DMCC	Norton
32	W H Hartley	Bolton MCC	Triumph
33	A Johnstone	South Liverpool MC	Triumph
34	J Fisher	Furness & DMCC	Triumph
37	J R Burrows	Bradford & DMC	Triumph
38	S Woods	Warrington & DMC	Triumph
39	R F Austin	West Middlesex Amateur MCC	Triumph
40	A Jefferies	Bradford & DMC	Triumph
41	L Newcombe	West Ealing MCC	Triumph
42	I K Arber	Irthlingborough Bats MCC	Norton
43	K R James	Ringwood MC & LCC	A.J.S.
45	R E Paxton	Cheltenham H.G. MC. & LCC	Triumph
46	R W Holywell	Alnwick & DMCC	Triumph
47	J J Pache	Southall & DMC	Triumph
48	F Passmore	Hayes & DMCC	Norton
49	M J Chefneux	Manchester 48th MC	Triumph
50	J Bottomley	Moccasin (Manchester) MC& LCC	B.S.A.
51	E Kirby	Bolton MCC	Triumph
52	R W C Kerr	Ayr MCC	Norton
54	J E Carr	Gravesend Eagles MCC	Vincent H.R.D.

As the start time of 2.00 pm approached, prospects looked good for a record-breaking Senior, with the existing lap record of 27m 24s (82.65 mph) held by George Brown on his 1000cc Vincent HRD likely to be threatened by Duke and Jefferies. A Triumph was the choice of the majority of starters with 25, Norton mustered 11, BSA 4 and AJS, Ariel and Vincent-HRD 1 each. Twelve non-starters were posted, A.J. Braithwaite (Norton), T. W. Brown (AJS), T. Moore (Norton), G .L. D. Newman (Triumph), R.H. Burns (Triumph), W. Middleton (Triumph), T. C. Squance (Ariel), R. Dearden (Norton), A. Johnson (Norton), G. A. Naylor (Norton), J. Harrison (Triumph) and P. Carr (Triumph).

Most of the Seniors got away easily, and the '*TT Special*' report of the race drew a direct comparison between that and the starting difficulties which had affected so many in the morning's Junior. The Triumph of J. R. Burrows was perhaps worst affected, losing the rider about 30 seconds, and the similar machines of D. W. N. Brereton and R. Kenworthy proving to be just a little reluctant to go. First to reach Ramsey on the opening lap was Leo Starr (Triumph), but 5th man through was the rider who had started number 23, Geoff Duke. Allan Jefferies had overhauled a dozen or more riders by the time he reached Ramsey, so was obviously going well also. By the Bungalow, Duke was 3rd on the roads, and was closer to the two in front as the lap was completed, Starr still in front, followed by Manxman Peter Crebbin (Triumph). T. J. K. Beckton's Ariel developed gearbox problems forcing his retirement on the Sulby Straight, and D. A. Wayne retired after he took a fall from his Norton at Braddan Bridge. H. F. Hunter's BSA hit engine trouble even before he reached Braddan, and he was joined on the retirement sheet by Roland Austin (Triumph). Duke's standing-start lap time was 27m 32s (82.25 mph), only 8 seconds outside the record, and in consequence he held a lead of almost half-a-

Jack Harding at Governors Bridge. When the Vincent engine was prepared for competition work, it was common practice to remove a roller from the crowded-roller big end to increase oil flow; they forgot to omit the roller on Jack's bike and the big end locked up!
Jack later became one of the long-standing travelling marshals for the races.

minute over Jefferies. Nortons held 1st and 6th, with four Triumphs sandwiched between.

First Lap Leaderboard

1. G.E. Duke (Norton)	27m 32s	(82.25 mph)
2. A. Jefferies (Triumph)	28m 01s	(80.81 mph)
3. T.P. Crebbin (Triumph)	28m 46s	(78.72 mph)
4. M. Featherstone (Triumph)	29m 16s	(77.37 mph)
5. L. Starr (Triumph)	29m 33s	(76.64 mph)
6. P.H. Carter (Norton)	29m 52s	(75.81 mph)

Duke stepped up the pace on the second lap, and by Ramsey held more than a minute advantage over Jefferies, Crebbin still fairly comfortable in 3rd place. In fact, 'stepped up the pace' is an understatement. This was one of the great TT laps, one of those moments in sport that spectators recall for years after, recounting their "I was privileged to be there" stories with great satisfaction. Completed in 27m 3s, an average speed of 83.70 mph, it was 21 seconds faster than Brown's record set on a machine of twice the capacity, and, to put it into true perspective, was only 71 seconds slower than the best International TT practice time that year, set by Artie Bell on the factory Norton. Others down the field were having mixed fortunes, John Burrows had experienced a troubled first lap, and although he made it to his pit, he retired the Triumph there with carburettor trouble. Mick Featherstone lost his 4th place when he came off at Ramsey Hairpin, and retired, while a mile or so back down the course, in Parliament Square, Douglas Marshall retired his Triumph with clutch problems. Jack Bottomley made a spectacular entrance to the Square when oil on the back tyre of his BSA A7 twin brought him down. After checking for damage he was able to get going and rejoin the race, as was L. J. B. R. French who also stopped for a while in the Square. Out on the course, Jacques Pache also stopped on the second lap, and retired his Triumph. Ernest Kirby was another faller who was able to rejoin the race, after parting company from his Triumph at the Gooseneck, and Stanley Woods (of Warrington, not his namesake the TT winning Irishman) was forced to retire his Triumph in the pits after completing the second lap.

Second Lap Leaderboard

1. G.E. Duke (Norton)	54m 35s	(82.98 mph)
2. A. Jefferies (Triumph)	56m 02s	(80.81 mph)
3. T.P. Crebbin (Triumph)	58m 04s	(77.98 mph)
4. L. Starr (Triumph)	59m 05s	(76.66 mph)
5. P.H. Carter (Norton)	59m 21s	(76.31 mph)
6. E. Andrew (Norton)	1h 0m 27s	(74.92 mph)

Barring mechanical problems or accidents, the leaderboard places looked fairly secure as the riders began their third and final lap. Just as Cyril Taft was taking the chequered flag to win the Lightweight class, Duke was signalled at Ramsey. By Creg-ny-Baa he was leading on the road, and when he crossed the line a few minutes later he was over 2 minutes ahead of Jefferies. Finishing in 3rd place was the rider whose occupation was described in the '*TT Special*' Who's Who as 'actor, author, playwright and scenic designer', Leo Starr. (The same newspaper feature had Geoff Duke's employment down simply as 'trials rider'). Unfortunately for 3rd placeman Crebbin, the 'mechanical problems' or 'accident' both combined, as front brake trouble caused him to fall at the Guthrie Memorial. He was able to remount, and made it to the finish to a well-deserved 5th place. Not so Jack Bottomley, who similarly fell and restarted, but was forced to retire his BSA shortly after. Frederick Passmore (Norton) and John Brookes were other last lap retirements, Brookes riding his pre-war Gold Star.

Finishing Order

1 G.E. Duke (Norton)	1h 21m 53s	(82.97 mph)
2 A. Jefferies (Triumph)	1h 24m 04s	(80.79 mph)
3 L. Starr (Triumph)	1h 29m 13.2s	(76.15 mph)
4 P.H. Carter (Norton)	1h 29m 43.8s	(75.69 mph)
5 T.P. Crebbin (Triumph)	1h 29m 46.8s	(75.65 mph)
6 E. Andrew (Norton)	1h 30m 35s	(74.99 mph)

Fastest Lap: G.E. Duke (2nd lap) 27m 3s (83.70 mph) (Record)

Robert Kerr (Senior Norton) about to abandon ship on a suspiciously light patch of tarmac at Quarter Bridge. The presence of a marshal with a broom in the background would indicate that someone else had fallen earlier in the race and that cement dust had been applied. He remounted, checked the bike and then proceeded. After two slow laps he got back into the groove, his last lap was the fifth fastest of the race.

The 1000cc Race (Wednesday, 15th June)

Starters

	Rider	Club	Machine
1	J B Netherton	West Ham & DMC	Vincent H.R.D.
2	D G Lashmar	Watford & Bushey MC	Vincent H.R.D.
4	J Wright	Bromley MC	Vincent H.R.D.
5	C Horn	South Shields & DMC	Vincent H.R.D.
7	C Howkins	Sphinx MC	Ariel
8	G Brown	Louth & DMCC	Vincent H.R.D.
9	G Manning	Leicester Query MC	Vincent H.R.D.
10	J Harding	Solihull MCC	Vincent H.R.D.
11	P C Wilson	Southampton & DMCC	Vincent H.R.D.

There was just the one non-starter for the 1000cc race, starting at 10.00 am after the traditional round-the-barrels warming up period on the Glencrutchery Road between the Grandstand and Governors Bridge, and that was the Series 'B' Rapide of J.A. Edwards. James Wright had a few problems getting away on his similar model, and was to pull over at Ballacraine to attend to something, before continuing. Pre-race favourite and 'almost' winner of the previous year's race, George Brown started alongside one of the most unlikely TT leaderboard machines ever, the Ariel Square Four of 48-year-old Charles Howkins. Setting off at number 5, Chris Horn began as he intended to continue, paying no regard whatsoever to fuel consumption, he would go as fast as he could, as far as he could, and would run out of petrol somewhere on the third lap. Perhaps it was his way of making a protest at the 'economy run'. His first lap was completed in 26m 50s (84.39 mph), 13 seconds faster than that posted by Duke in the Senior, and fastest of the week (It was not officially a record, as riders first laps were some 70 yards short of the full lap as a consequence of the start line position. Brown was 22 seconds behind Horn, and 3rd placeman Geoffrey Manning was another minute behind Brown, but in trouble. Instead of going through to start his second lap, he pulled in to his pit, but overshot by 30 yards or more, and had to manoeuvre the big twin back before he could begin to tackle the problem. Whatever was wrong with the Vincent proved terminal, as he later retired

without having left his pit. Jack Netherton stopped at Hillberry apparently to re-attach a plug lead, and completed the lap, only to retire finally at Crosby on his second lap.

First Lap Leaderboard

1 C. Horn (Vincent HRD)	26m 50s	(84.39 mph)
2 G. Brown (Vincent HRD)	27m 12s	(83.25 mph)
3 G. Manning (Vincent HRD)	28m 19s	(79.97 mph)
4 A. Phillip (Vincent HRD)	28m 56s	(78.25 mph)
5 J. Harding (Vincent HRD)	29m 11s	(77.59 mph)
6 D. Lashmar (Vincent HRD)	29m 30s	(76.77 mph)

Brown's record lap in 1948 had been at a speed of 82.65 mph, and his first lap this year had been faster, on what was basically the same machine, so he was obviously 'racing' and not going for economy. Whether he could have challenged Horn for the lead, or whether he would have been able to conserve enough fuel to take advantage of Horn's inevitable retirement, will never be known, as he struck trouble mid way round that second lap, and was only able to limp around to record a lap in 58m 32s, well over twice his first lap time. Horn on the other hand, had no such trouble, and went ever faster, setting a new record lap with a magnificent 26m 28s, a speed of 85.57 mph. Riding his Stan Pike prepared machine, Lashmar's second lap was not particularly quick by comparison, but he was the only other rider to put in consistent laps at good speed, and likely to actually make it to the finish, and by so doing leapt from 6th place at the end of the first lap, to second by the end of the next. Placed 4th and 5th after the first lap, Harding and Phillip also hit trouble, both retiring after marathon second lap times.

Second Lap Leaderboard

1 C. Horn (Vincent HRD)	53m 18s	(84.98 mph)
2 D. Lashmar (Vincent HRD)	59m 18s	(76.38 mph)
3 P. Wilson (Vincent HRD)	1h 0m 32s	(74.82 mph)
4 J. Wright (Vincent HRD)	1h 3m 22s	(71.47 mph)
5 C. Howkins (Ariel)	1h 7m 39s	(66.94 mph)
6 G. Brown (Vincent HRD)	1h 25m 44s	(52.22 mph)

Riders progress round the course at that time was recorded from six points, 'B' represented Ballacraine (7½ miles out), 'K' Kirkmichael (15 miles), 'R'

Ramsey (24 miles), 'M' East Mountain Gate near the end of the 'Mountain Mile' (28½ miles), and 'C' for Creg-ny-Baa (34½ miles). A light above the riders number went on when he reached Governors Bridge. Horn's lead starting the last lap was exactly 6 minutes over Lashmar, and all eyes in the Grandstand watched his progress 'clock', waiting for it to stop, as it had to. It reached 'B' and 'K', but never moved on to 'R'. In fact the fuel had given out as he passed through Glentramman, and he coasted to a halt in Parliament Square, Ramsey. As Lashmar rounded Hillberry for the last time, Brown pulled into his pit temporarily, then set off again almost a lap adrift, with the Vincent only firing on one cylinder, determined to make it to the finish. Challenging hard for the runner-up spot, there was drama for 3rd placeman Pat Wilson, who hurt himself in a fall at Governors Bridge, but managed to pick up and re-start the machine, and ride the last half-mile or so to a deserved 3rd place, still almost 10 minutes ahead of Howkins and the 'Squariel'. Brown made it round the lap and was credited with a finish, 5th and last, having pushed home with an empty tank for the second year running.

Finishing Order

1 D. Lashmar (Vincent HRD)   1h 29m 1.8s (76.30 mph)
2 J. Wright (Vincent HRD)   1h 33m 27.6s (72.68 mph)
3 P.C. Wilson (Vincent HRD) 1h 34m 6.6s (72.19 mph)
4 C. Howkins (Ariel)   1h 43m 33.4s (65.61 mph)
5 G. Brown (Vincent HRD)   2h 16m 45s   (49.67 mph)

Fastest Lap: C. Horn (2nd lap) 26m 28s (85.57 mph) (Record).

Reflections

Taking the 1000cc race first, it is difficult to credit the ACU with anything other than an obstinate stupidity for not allowing refuelling. As 'The Motor Cycle' said in its race report

"....that the machines had to be tuned for petrol economy, ie. a lean mixture, which might induce serious overheating. Even at that they might run dry on the third lap, and obviously were quite unable to demonstrate their real speed. The ACU was obdurate to all protests, and spiteful spectators almost hoped that all the Vincent tanks might empty on lap 3, leaving the solitary 'Squariel' to toddle home alone, exposing the rules to ridicule".

George Brown's remarks at the Prize Distribution

Frank Cope takes the chequered flag on his Lightweight Excelsior. Frank was still racing in his 80s in South Africa

75

My 1949 Lightweight Clubman's Ride
by Cyril Taft

My Last Race

From TT Tales (edited by Geoff Davison)

[Cyril Taft is one of those individuals who takes any happening as the normal state of affairs. The fact of being the father of nine children is to him just normal, though he admits that the job of rearing them borders on the miraculous. He certainly relies on the fact that all things are directed and come out right in the end.

The record he established in 1949—when, aged forty-six and the father of nine, he won a race in the Isle of Man at his first attempt—should stand for all time. His recent reply to a note from me is typical of his outlook on things. He wrote as follows :

"Dear Geoff (Davison), Have been delayed doing the write-up. Tenth child arrived three weeks ago. Followed by 'flu all round. What a panic! Cyril."—Editor.]

Several things which had happened to me in the past contribute to that 'little extra' that allowed me to win the Clubman's Lightweight TT in 1949. After all, a slide is not so fearful a problem after six years professional speedway racing; further, being more interested in tuning than riding on the dirt, I had picked up a few clues that were useful when it came to tuning a 250 Excelsior; also, I had long since got past the nervous tension that is usual in a first TT race; and finally the TT Course had no bad psychological effect on me because a bend is a bend, to me, whether in the Isle of Man or elsewhere. So I must admit that I felt confident when I faced the starter. The last that I expected was a win—that was the shock of all shocks. But read on, because I write as it comes to me.

I had always got a tremendous kick out of watching the TT races during the last twenty-five years, and had thought that perhaps, one day, I might get the chance to ride myself. The Clubman's Series seemed to offer that chance even at this late stage of life—so over to the 1947 'Clubman's' to see how it was done.

Yes, it *could* be done. Must get a try-out this season. My BSA twin was duly fitted with two carbs. (probably the first to be so), and entered for Scarborough. Got badly slated by the domestic department and had to drop it, but a few weeks later entered Dunholme and told no one. The BSA got me a fourth in the three lap race (forty starters) and I was lying about seventh in the 100-mile event when I went out with a leaking petrol tank at the ninetieth mile.

But the try-out has said: "Yes, Have a Go!" Entered a Rapide in good time for the 1948 Clubman's but got slung out with the rest of the unfortunates. Domestic weather somewhat "unsettled", decided to come down to a 250 cc for 1949.

It took some to buy a 1939 Excelsior Manxman that looked good. Reduced it to little bits before Christmas, but landed in hospital on 8th January for a nice quiet stay of three months. Sent off the entry while still laid out; caused a thought, so to speak, but seemed a normal thing to do.

Long and hard work in April and May, tuning, assembling and fitting my own idea of a spring frame. A grim determination to do all the work before getting to the Island so that it could be a holiday, mainly. On arrival, paid Albert Moule and Co. a visit to their workshop where they were busy—working! Roared with laughter at the darned fools, mentioning something about organisation, and told them I had come for a holiday. Albert smiled one of his sweet smiles, and said little.

Went out on my first practice the following morning and did two laps. Finished with no brakes to speak of and discovered several snags in the rear springing device; but made the fastest time in my class.

At breakfast, Albert Moule, with a broad grin, enquired how the holiday was going—he had heard of the vast amount of work I had in hand. I replied: "Later." (And so it was later—the holiday came after I finished the race!) The engine blew up at the thirteenth milestone on the following practice period, causing me to miss the next time out. In all, I did five practice laps, which, added to five touring laps the year before, constituted my total "lappery" of the TT Course. Ninety-nine per cent hard work, half per cent racing, and half per cent holiday—that's just how it was. But I got the model ready in time. It, and I, were on the line on race day.

My knowledge of the Course was first acquired by hours of study of the detailed description of it in 'The Story of the Manx'—this after a few laps touring in 1948. Finding that it was possible to get through certain sections at full bore, such as from Union Mills to Greeba Castle (three miles), Kirk Michael Corner to Ballaugh (three miles) and so on, simplified matters considerably. The major bends I did not bother about, simply shutting off very late, grabbing for everything and just scrambling round. There were two places, however, that frightened me particularly—Bray Hill and Kate's Cottage. One day I took them both absolutely full bore—and that was the end of any worry about them; make your mind up and do it, sort of style.

On the line at the start I felt good, the awful backache (hangover from the hospital do) from which I had been suffering had gone after a few days 'holiday'; I felt fit and ready to enjoy myself. Down went the flag, and I gave a nice swinging kick. Nothing happened; but Frank Cope, my companion on the line, shot off after one kick, leaving me still prodding away. The engine fired at last and I passed Frank before the bottom of Bray, catching four of the five early

starters before Ballacraine, from then onwards I had the road to myself until the second—and last—time round at Ramsey.

I had had a 'comfortable' run up to that point, except for a horrible two-wheel slide at Bedstead on lap one, so at Ramsey I said to myself: "This is precisely where one decides to get home," and managed to remember this until I reached the Gooseneck.

Then I must have forgotten, for the father and mother of the wickedest slide occurred. Women screamed, etc., etc., but my speedway training helped me, and I managed to hold it. Well, oil was the answer to that one; the bike was floating in it. So with a firmer resolution to get home, I eased down on the major corners, but kept flat on the tank on the rest, as indeed I had been all the way.

Watching the revs. go up over 8,000 towards Brandish, I thought: "My word, I'm whizzing along in top," and in a flash realised I was still in third! Dabbed for top—over 7,000 at that—and so on to the finish, with oil on the brain!

I look back with a great thrill on over twenty years of racing and the climax of them, which was my little win in the Clubman's 250, 1949. And so, with a wife, ten children and an age of forty-seven, they must remain. "Those were the Days."

Too bad; but there is always the rising generation...

" . . . the father and mother of the wickedest slide occurred."

1949 Clubman's Lightweight

1	C. V. Taft, Excelsior	33.33	**32.57.2**	1 06 30.2	68.10
2	D. A. Ritchie, Velocette	34.05	**33.05.2**	1 07 10.2	67.43
3	B. J. Hargreaves, Velocette	33.57	**33.48.2**	1 07 45.2	66.48
4	G. S. Wakefield, Triumph	35.41	**34.49.8**	1 10 30.8	64.23
5	L. C. Bolshaw, Triumph	36.00	**34.32.6**	1 10 32.6	64.21
6	A. B. Barton, Triumph	35.53	**35.36.4**	1 11 29.4	63.34
7	E. F. Cope, Excelsior	36.18	**35.53**	1 12 11.0	62.73
8	J. J. McVeigh, Triumph	38.02	**35.03.8**	1 13 05.8	61.95
9	G. A. Northwood, Velocette	37.44	**36.23**	1 14 07.0	61.09
10	J. R. Dulson, Velocette	38.00	**37.42.8**	1 15 42.8	59.82
11	J. Smith, Excelsior	38.00	**37.57.4**	1 15 57.4	59.62
12	T. W. Swarbrick, Excelsior	39.17	**36.54.8**	1 16 11.8	59.43
13	A. Henthorn, Velocette	39.21	**38.35.4**	1 17 56.4	58.10
	F. Purslow, BSA	38.15	R		
	H. B. Iremonger-Watts, Triumph	R			
	W. J. Jenness, Triumph	R			
	V. J. Holcroft, Velocette	R			

LAP POSITIONS

1949 CLUBMAN'S LIGHTWEIGHT

RIDER AND MACHINE	FIRST LAP POSITION		FINAL POSITION	RIDER AND MACHINE
C V TAFT EXCELSIOR	1		1	C V TAFT EXCELSIOR
B J HARGREAVES VELOCETTE	2		2	D A RITCHIE VELOCETTE
D A RITCHIE VELOCETTE	3		3	B J HARGREAVES VELOCETTE
G S WAKEFIELD TRIUMPH	4		4	G S WAKEFIELD TRIUMPH
A B BARTON TRIUMPH	5		5	L C BOLSHAW TRIUMPH
L C BOLSHAW TRIUMPH	6		6	A B BARTON TRIUMPH

1949 Clubman's Junior

1	H. Clarke, BSA	30.34	**29.52**	29.55.4	1 30 21.4	75.18
2	J. Simister, Norton	30.41	**30.15**	**30.15**	1 31 11.0	74.51
3	A. C. Taylor, Norton	30.26	**30.25**	30.33.6	1 31 24.6	74.32
4	R. Hallett, BSA	**30.34**	30.41	30.36.4	1 31 51.4	73.97
5	C. C. Sandford, Velocette	30.50	30.49	**30.44.4**	1 32 23.4	73.52
6	E. T. Pink, Norton	30.46	31.10	**30.36.8**	1 32 32.8	73.41
7	E. F. Collings, Velocette	31.20	**30.44**	30.56.4	1 33 00.4	73.03
8	W. C. Reed, Norton	31.30	30.55	**30.32.4**	1 33 17.4	72.80
9	A. R. Brassington, Norton	32.06	31.18	**31.11.4**	1 34 35.4	71.83
10	R. D. Briscoe, Norton	31.39	**31.30**	31.46.4	1 34 55.4	71.58
11	J. Fisher, BSA	32.23	31.51	**30.57.2**	1 35 11.2	71.37
12	T. R. Cookson, Norton	32.23	**31.18**	31.32.6	1 35 13.6	71.35
13	G. Milner, BSA	34.35	30.40	**30.30.2**	1 35 45.2	70.94
14	M. Sunderland, Norton	32.26	31.48	**31.38.2**	1 35 52.2	70.85
15	W. Reeve, BSA	32.02	32.24	**31.40**	1 36 06.0	70.68
16	F. Pados, Douglas	32.31	32.10	**31.58.6**	1 36 39.6	70.28
17	J. Difazio, BSA	32.27	32.22	**32.04**	1 36 53.0	70.11
18	F. O. Coleman, Velocette	32.50	**32.10**	32.13.4	1 37 13.4	69.89
19	B. Morris, BSA	32.50	**32.00**	32.32.8	1 37 22.8	69.75
20	A. D. Brown, Norton	33.04	32.30	**32.17.8**	1 37 51.8	69.38
21	K. Talbot, Velocette	33.29	32.34	**32.02.8**	1 38 05.8	69.26
22	W. H. Wilshere, Triumph	33.24	32.35	**32.11**	1 38 10.0	69.20
23	D. H. R Gray, AJS	33.15	**32.22**	32.59.4	1 38 36.4	68.87
24	'S. Franklen', AJS	33.12	**32.40**	32.53	1 38 45.0	68.78
25	B. A. Jackson, AJS	32.59	**32.36**	34.06.4	1 39 41.4	68.15
26	F. B. Burns, BSA	**33.15**	33.21	33.15.2	1 39 51.2	68.03
27	J. T. Wenman, Norton	32.02	**31.00**	36.55	1 39 57.0	67.97
28	L. Bertorelli, Royal Enfield	33.31	33.33	**33.28.6**	1 40 32.6	67.56
29	W. F. Barker, BSA	34.17	33.12	**33.07.8**	1 40 36.8	67.53
30	G. W. Robinson, Norton	**30.38**	37.53	32.50.2	1 41 21.2	67.03
31	L. D. Boult, BSA	34.32	33.36	**33.19**	1 41 27.0	66.96
32.	D. E. R. Morgan, AJS	34.02	33.55	**33.45.4**	1 41 42.4	66.78
33	C. Julian, BSA	39.29	**30.57**	31.20	1 41.46.0	66.75
34	A. Rayner, Norton	34.40	33.51	**33.23.4**	1 41 54.4	66.65
35	W. J. Hill, Douglas	35.00	33.57	**33.22**	1 42 19.0	66.39
36	W. S. Corley, AJS	34.29	**33.59**	34.00.2	1 42 28.2	66.29
37	J. F. Basinger, Velocette	34.55	34.55	**33.49.6**	1 43 39.6	65.54
38	H. Walmsley, Velocette	34.54	**34.25**	35.07.2	1 44 26.2	65.04
39	C. W. Davis, BSA	37.31	33.57	**33.34.4**	1 45 02.4	64.67
40	F. H. Weller, Norton	36.47	34.51	**33.43.4**	1 45 21.4	64.47
41	F. G. Edgar, AJS	35.11	**34.54**	35.25	1 45 30.0	64.39
42	K. G. Adcock, Royal Enfield	38.20	34.10	**33.49.4**	1 46 19.4	63.90
43	E. Proctor, Matchless	34.17	**33.15**	39.20.2	1 46 52.2	63.57
44	S. T. Seston, Royal Enfield	35.32	**34.20**	37.10.2	1 47 02.2	63.47
45	J. A. Thomson, AJS	36.18	35.27	**35.18.8**	1 47 03.8	63.44
46	R. W. Mouat, AJS	38.00	**34.28**	34.40	1 47 08.0	63.41

1949 Clubman's Junior (cont.)

47	L. Price, BSA	33.34	**32.06**	41.38	1 47 18.0	63 31
48	E. H. C. Baker, BSA	**35.44**	36.06	36.08.2	1 47 58.2	62.91
49	J. McMeeken, AJS	35.30	**35.04**	39.05.4	1 49 39.4	61.95
50	W. F. Wood, Douglas	38.08	36.18	**35.19.2**	1 49 45.2	61.90
51	R. H. King, Matchless	33.35	**33.21**	48.39.2	1 55.35.2	58.77
52	A. Klinge, BSA	**33.54**	39.46	42.03	1.55 43.0	58.70
53	F. W. Haines, Norton	32.27	**32.08**	52.01.6	1 56 36.6	58.25
54	C. M. Hopwood, Royal Enfield	32.40	**32.37**	52.25.2	1 57 42.2	57.71
55	J. Green, Triumph	39.21	**38.40**	40.21.4	1 58 22.4	57.39
56	R. Porter, BSA	**34.52**	48.25	38.55.6	2 02 12.6	55.59
57	E. J. Bowman, AJS	33.45	**33.15**	55.41	2 02 41.0	55.37
	E. Harvey, BSA	30.45	**30.05**	R		
	G. N. Camfield, Douglas	32.40	**31.48**	R		
	D. Moncrieff, BSA	33.24	**32.54**	R		
	J. D. Haines, BSA	**33.08**	33.44	R		
	A. S. Herbert, Matchless	33.52	**33.19**	R		
	D. A. Wilcocks, Velocette	35.54	**35.07**	R		
	C. Bruce, AJS	**32.13**	39.18	R		
	W. J. Mundy, AJS	**37.51**	38.45	R		
	W. A. G. Auld, Matchless	**38.37**	95.41	R		
	W. A. Lomas, Royal Enfield	31.44	R			
	E. A. Lavington, Velocette	32.50	R			
	J. F. Cook, Matchless	R				
	W. Camier, Norton	R				
	J. D. Warren, BSA	R				
	A. A. F. Burton, BSA	R				
	H. Grant, AJS	R				
	J. Warr, Velocette	R				

LAP POSITIONS

1949 CLUBMAN'S JUNIOR

RIDER AND MACHINE	FIRST LAP POSITION	FINAL POSITION	RIDER AND MACHINE
A C TAYLOR NORTON	1	1	H CLARK B.S.A.
R HALLETT B.S.A.	2=	2	J SIMISTER NORTON
H CLARK B.S.A.	2=	3	A C TAYLOR NORTON
G W ROBINSON NORTON	4	4	R HALLETT B.S.A.
J SIMISTER NORTON	5	5	C C SANDFORD VELOCETTE
E HARVEY B.S.A.	6	6	E T PINK NORTON

82

Sunshine and shadows at Governors Bridge. Cyril Julian (BSA) heads for the Dip.

Harold Clark in the winners enclosure.

1949 Clubman's Senior

1	G. E. Duke, Norton	27.32	**27.03**	27.18	1 21 53.0	82.97
2	A. Jefferies, Triumph	**28.01**	**28.01**	28.02	1 24 04.0	80.79
3	L. Starr, Triumph	29.33	**29.32**	30.08.2	1 29 13.2	76.15
4	P. H. Carter, Norton	29.52	**29.29**	30.22.8	1 29 43.8	75.69
5	T. P. Crebbin, Triumph	**28.46**	29.18	31.42	1 29 46.8	75.65
6	E. Andrew, Norton	30.23	**30.04**	30.08	1 30 35.0	74.99
7	J. E. Carr, Vincent HRD	30.34	**30.11**	30.16.4	1 31 01.4	74.64
8	R. H. Sherry, Triumph	30.52	30.13	**30.00**	1 31 05.0	74.59
9	A. Johnstone, Triumph	30.58	**30.17**	30.17.8	1 31 32.8	74.21
10	D. J. P. Wilkins, Triumph	31.56	31.19	**31.11.4**	1 34 26.4	71.94
11	J. Wright, BSA	**31.33**	31.45	31.36	1 34 54.0	71.59
12	J. Smith, Norton	32.03	**31.26**	31.27	1 34 56.0	71.57
13	T. Hodgson, Triumph	31.57	**31.11**	31.53	1 35 01.0	71.50
14	A. A. Sanders, Triumph	**31.56**	32.24	32.08.8	1 36 28.8	70.40
15	W. H. Hartley, Triumph	32.05	**31.15**	33.10	1 36 30.0	70.39
16	R. E. Paxton, Triumph	**31.58**	32.45	32.38.6	1 37 21.6	69.79
17	J. Fisher, Triumph	31 01	**30.49**	35.51.6	1 37 41.6	69.54
18	D. W. N. Brereton, Triumph	33.36	32.20	**32.17.8**	1 38 13.8	69.15
19	E. Kirby, Triumph	**31.45**	36.34	31.48.8	1 40 07.8	67.84
20	L. Uttley, Norton	32.36	**31.18**	36.46.6	1 40 40.6	67.49
21	R. McDonald, Norton	36.49	32.23	**32.11.8**	1 41 23.8	66.99
22	L. Newcombe, Triumph	35.04	34.17	**34.04.8**	1 43 25.8	65.68
23	M. J. Chefneux, Triumph	35.04	**34.21**	34.30	1 43 55.0	65.37
24	K. S. Watling, Norton	38.05	**34.07**	34.08	1 46 20.0	63.88
25	R. W. Holywell, Triumph	36.12	35.17	**35.14.2**	1 46 43.2	63.66
26	R. Kenworthy, Triumph	36.19	35.30	**35.02.6**	1 46 51.6	63.57
27	I. K. Arber, Norton	31.03	**30.17**	44.34.2	1 46 54.2	63.55
28	R. W. C. Kerr, Norton	41.03	38.36	**29.44.2**	1 49 23.2	62.11
29	L. J. B. R. French, Triumph	37.00	39.24	**36.38.4**	1 53 02.4	60.10
30	G. F. Slater, Triumph	37.58	**37.26**	38.08	1 53 32.0	59.83
31	K. R. James, AJS	32.25	**32.08**	61.48	2 06 21.0	53.76
	J. E. Brookes, BSA	34.32	**32.59**	R		
	S. Woods, Triumph	**31.10**	36.45	R		
	F. Passmore, Norton	37.08	**32.56**	R		
	J. Bottomley, BSA	**30.52**	49.25	R		
	M. S. Featherstone, Triumph	29.16	R			
	D. Marshall, Triumph	30.30	R			
	J. J. Pache, Triumph	43.28	R			
	J. R. Burrows, Triumph	53.58	R			
	D. A. Wayne, Norton	R				
	H. F. Hunter, BSA	R				
	T. J. K. Beckton, Ariel	R				
	R. F. Austin, Triumph	R				

LAP POSITIONS

1949 CLUBMAN'S SENIOR

RIDER AND MACHINE	FIRST LAP POSITION			FINAL POSITION	RIDER AND MACHINE
G E DUKE NORTON	1			1	G W DUKE NORTON
A A JEFFERIES TRIUMPH	2			2	A A JEFFERIES TRIUMPH
T P CREBBIN TRIUMPH	3			3	L STARR TRIUMPH
M S FEATHERSTONE TRIUMPH	4 ● R			4	P H CARTER NORTON
L STARR NORTON	5			5	T P CREBBIN TRIUMPH
P H CARTER NORTON	6			6	E ANDREWS NORTON

Peter Crebbin (Senior Triumph). To his right is Don Crossley, a local baker who won three Manx Grand Prix races. Peter was another Clubman who also acted as a Travelling Marshal.

1949 Clubman's 1000 c.c.

	Rider and Machine					
1.	D. G. Lashmar, Vincent HRD	**29.30**	29.48	29.43.2	1 29 01.2	76.30
2.	J. Wright, Vincent HRD	31.21	32.01	**30.05.4**	1 33 27.4	72.68
3.	P. C. Wilson, Vincent HRD	**29.49**	30.43	33.34.6	1 34 06.6	72.19
4.	C. Howkins, Ariel	**33.02**	34.37	35.54.4	1 43 33.4	65.61
5.	G. Brown, Vincent HRD	**27.12**	58.32	51.01	2 16 45.0	49.67
	C. Horn, Vincent HRD	26.50	**26.28**	R		
	A. Phillip, Vincent HRD	**28.56**	68.32	R		
	J. Harding, Vincent HRD	**29.11**	84.46	R		
	G. Manning, Vincent HRD	28.19	R			
	J. B. Netherton, Vincent HRD	33.28	R			

LAP POSITIONS

1949 CLUBMAN'S 1000 cc

RIDER AND MACHINE	FIRST LAP POSITION		FINAL POSITION	RIDER AND MACHINE
C HORN VINCENT HRD	1	R	1	D G LASHMAR VINCENT HRD
G BROWN VINCENT HRD	2		2	J WRIGHT VINCENT HRD
G MANNING VINCENT HRD	3	R	3	P C WILSON VINCENT HRD
A PHILLIP VINCENT HRD	4		4	C HOWKINS ARIEL
J HARDING VINCENT HRD	5		5	G BROWN VINCENT HRD
D G LASHMAR NVINCENT HRD	6			

A study in race tactics: A measured race saw Dennis Lashmar (left) progress through the field from 6th to win. Throwing conservatism to the winds, Chris Horn (right) raced hard and fast, and ran dry!

1950

A MORE SETTLED FORMAT - TT WEDNESDAY WAS 'CLUBMAN'S DAY'

The fourth running of the Clubman's TT saw the races again held in what many had become to hope would be their permanent 'slot', on Wednesday of the International TT race-week. The initial intention to run two races in the morning and two in the afternoon as in 1949 had to be re-thought when the entries for the Junior class exceeded those of the other three classes put together, and it was decided to run the 1000cc, the Senior and the Lightweight classes in the morning, starting at 10.30am and in that order, leaving the afternoon exclusively for the Juniors, the start to be at 2.00pm. Each race was increased in length by one lap, and this removed the 'economy run' aspect, particularly for the 1000cc race, because refuelling became essential, albeit limited to a maximum of two gallons. Riders were now to be despatched in groups of four at 20-second intervals, again by kickstart only (although there would no longer be a requirement to kick-start after the pit-stop). However, there would no longer be a warm-up period prior to the start of the race, and riders had to kick-start cold engines on the plugs that they were to use for the race. One can only presume that this was an attempt to restrict the 'tune' of the engines, and in so doing reinforce the links with the 'ride-to-work' model. Also, the clubmen were restricted to 'Pool' petrol, while the International races were allowed 80-octane fuel.

More limitations were placed on rider qualifications, barring those who had:
a) started in any International TT;
b) won a replica in a Manx Grand Prix;
c) finished in the first three of any Clubman's TT (excepting the Lightweight);
d) finished in any three previous Clubman's TT races. Lightweight winners were allowed to enter any of the bigger classes.

The intention and reasoning behind these restrictions was understandable, to keep the races a training ground for the 'real thing', to help sift out those with the ability and the resources to enter the Manx Grand Prix and the TT, whilst keeping costs (at least of machinery) down. However, as with any such limitation, there were those for whom it worked against rather than for. One can understand the winner of a race being expected to move onward (and presumably upward), but consider the case of a 2nd or 3rd place-man who would have dearly loved to come back and try for the win he'd always dreamed of. Perhaps a rider had led a race, only to hit mechanical problems and drop back a place or two, he too would be unable to try again. And after three finishes, maybe on uncompetitive machinery to begin with, as he slowly climbed the ladder and was able to buy a faster machine, just when his knowledge of the course was starting to come together, he too would be barred, and have to face the reality of buying a race bike for the Manx Grand Prix, or stop racing in the Island. Further bars to acceptance were based on those riders who could be considered as 'being in the trade'. They were thus ineligible if they, in the 12 months preceding the entry closing date, were
a) a manufacturer;
b) a registered dealer;
c) a sub-dealer for the particular make of motorcycle to be ridden in the race or
d) anyone who was in the employ of any such manufacturer, registered dealer or sub-dealer.

Finally, despite a small but increasing lobby to the contrary, the rider must still to have been *a male person over 18 years of age'*.

In addition to the 196 entries, which were split up as 100 in the Junior, 66 in the Senior, 17 in the Lightweight and 13 in the 1000cc class, there were 6 reserves for the Junior. Machine variety was still good in three classes, the 1000's were all Vincent-HRD's. Five makes contested the Senior, Triumph being the most popular with 32, Nortons with half that number, then 11 BSA's, 4 Vincent-HRD Comets, and 3 AJS's. The 106 Juniors included nine manufacturers, and, no doubt influenced by their 1949 success, BSA's were beginning to dominate numerically, and fielded 48. Perhaps surprisingly now, the next most popular make was Douglas, with 25 examples, well ahead of Norton's ageing 'Inter' with 18, then 6 from AJS, 5 from Velocette, and single entries of EMC, Royal Enfield, Matchless and Triumph. The Lightweight class mustered four makes, comprising 10 from Velocette, 4 from Triumph, 2 Excelsiors and a single Panther.

Awards remained at £50 for the entrant club for each race winner, down to £10 for 6th, and 25 free entries to the Manx Grand Prix for entrant clubs for the fastest finishers in relation to the winners time, divided between the classes in proportion to the number of race starters. The Dunlop Trophy was awarded to the rider, in any race, who improved on the class lap record by the biggest margin.

Entries and Practice

Course improvements from 1949 were minor; the approach to Quarter Bridge had been resurfaced, in the braking area under the trees, as had Ramsey Hairpin and Waterworks corner, and there was a different look about the Start/Finish, with the scoreboard moved back a little, and the old timekeeper's hut apparently cut in two, with one half placed on top of the other making for a two-storey edifice.

Charles Howkins had abandoned his attempts in the 1000cc class with his Square Four Ariel, and joined the rest of the field on a Vincent-HRD, where, among the 12 other entries were Louis Carr, Roy Organ (a popular misconception is that the rider was Rod Organ, a name familiar to many for his superb motorcycle paintings Rod Organ the artist would have been three years of age in 1950, and as he says, *"he would have been a trifle young to be riding a 1000cc Vincent on the Mountain course,"*) Alex Phillip, and a certain 'J. Alexander', which was known to be an assumed name. In the Senior were

Harry Plews, Ivan Wicksteed, Mick Featherstone, Jack Bottomley, Ivor Arber, Phil Carter, Ted Kempson and Arthur Newstead, and in the Junior entry appeared the names of Frank Sheene, K.V.R. (Ken) James, Willy Wilshere, Brian Jackson, Ian McGuffie, Jack Difazio, Eric Houseley, Jimmie Davie and Sam Seston. Frank Fletcher, who had shown well in the 1948 event before retiring contested the Lightweight, along with 1949 Leaderboard men Bernard Hargreaves, Len Bolshaw and George Wakefield, the latter riding the solitary Panther.

Weather conditions which greeted the clubmen were a little better than what had become to be expected, and for the first session on the morning of

Bracebridge Street, Hall Green and Plumstead have produced superb racing machines. Cleckheaton, home of Panther does not immediately spring to mind as the home of sports motorcycles. Nevertheless, George Wakefield chose this 250cc Model 65 (Lightweight could not be a term to describe the model) as his mount for 1950.

A low sun brings long shadows over Charles Robinson at Barregarrow as he practices with the Reserve 'F' plate on his Douglas.
After three Clubman rides Charles returned to ride the Island once more in the 1962 Junior Manx Grand Prix on a Honda.

Saturday 27th May, the roads were dry at the start, but further round the course early starters found that it was raining in Kirkmichael and Ramsey, and that on the Mountain the rain was joined by mist and low cloud, with visibility down to 20 yards at times. Conditions were however, improving, and after delaying the first man away (E. H. C. Baker on a BSA) for a while to allow the situation on the Mountain to ease, eventually 106 riders took to the course, although a number of hopefuls were initially turned away with instructions from the ACU Scrutineer Vic Anstice to remove the tax discs from their machines. Fastest of the session was Allan Jefferies' protégé Mick Featherstone on his Triumph Tiger 100 who clocked 29m 38s (76.39 mph), the only rider to break the half-hour, Allan of course was ineligible to enter as a result of his 2nd place the previous year. Reg Pilling, younger brother of 'International' TT competitor Harvey, escaped injury when he came off at Ramsey Hairpin, but his machine was not so fortunate, catching fire in the incident. One of the 1000's, that of J.B. Netherton, hit the wall of the Villa Stella Maris, the right-hander leaving Ramsey just before the hairpin, but the rider was unhurt. It all seemed to be happening in Ramsey that morning, *'Motor Cycling'* later carried a barely credible story from its reporter in Ramsey where *"there were several spills, and whilst marshals were attending to one mishap, a pair of newcomers,*

engaged in a private dice, and having no-one to direct them, mistook the course at May Hill, swerved left instead of right, and disappeared into the environs of Ramsey, still giving furious battle!" Another faller, but not so lucky in the outcome, was Junior Norton rider J. McLoughlin, who crashed at Ballaugh, breaking his left arm and suffering cuts and shock. Unhappily, the arm injuries were so severe that later in the week it was learned that the fore-arm had had to be amputated.

By Monday evening's second session, the weather was back to its 'traditional' worst, with pouring rain and Mountain mist. Nevertheless, 176 riders ventured out, many so wrapped in waterproofs that *'Motor Cycling'* likened the scene on the Glencrutchery Road to the start of the London-Exeter trial. Because of the conditions, riders were warned at the start to take things easy, and the fastest lap of the evening was just a little over 70 mph, Manx Grand Prix rider John Boynton (Norton) registering 32m 4s, (70.61 mph). There were a couple of none-too-serious spills, Ken Willis (Junior BSA) at Sulby Bridge, and Charles Howkins (who had been fastest 1000 runner in the first practice by quite a margin) at Creg-ny-Baa. John Curphey came off his Triumph Tiger 100 at May Hill, in his home town of Ramsey, but escaped serious injury. Unfortunately, an incident at the fast and unforgiving Handleys Corner proved to be far more serious, and the session was halted for half an hour to allow an ambulance onto the course to reach J. Makaula-White, who had come off his Senior Triumph. He was taken to Nobles Hospital, where he succumbed to his injuries early the following morning. Aged 24, he was a single man, a coal miner from Eythorne, near Dover, entered by the Folkestone Club.

Completely contrasting conditions met riders for Tuesday's evening session, with bright sunshine, blue skies, dry roads and perfect visibility. There was not even anything more than a light breeze either, and 200 riders took full advantage, or at least they tried to. *The Motor Cycle* reported numerous spills and, unusually for the clubmen, a generally poor standard of riding, commenting on *"sheer carelessness and lack of sense of caution by the riders"*. It is perhaps a little unfair, immediately after that quote, to name the reported fallers, but since none of the accidents were serious, and a little bit of 'joie-de-vivre' on a beautiful evening can be

forgiven, they are included where known. Fred Collings (Senior Triumph) completely misjudged the entry into Braddan, and failed to either follow the course or take the Strang road, hit the bridge wall, and suffered bruises and facial cuts; Norman Banks (Junior Douglas) had a miraculous escape, going over the edge at the Verandah, flying 20 yards down the rocky slope, and ending up with a broken arm and bruising; Stanley Hall (Velocette) received similar injuries and slight concussion in a fall at the Gooseneck; J. Smith (Junior BSA) suffered a dislocated shoulder when he overshot Kate's Cottage; J. W. (Chick) Taylor amazingly escaped with bruises and facial cuts after he went straight on at Brandish; A. J. Hart (Junior Velocette) was unhurt when he hit the wall at Sulby Bridge; J. L. Watkin was reported as having broken an ankle when he came off his Vincent-HRD; John Cowling received a severe shaking and cuts when he came off his Junior Douglas at Ballaugh Bridge; and Willy Wilshere slid

John Clark (Douglas) relaxes after a practice lap. Clark rode every year from 1950 to 1957 on machines ranging from Douglas, Norton, works Matchless (on which he suffered the ignomy of falling off at the start of the 1954 Senior) through to works Guzzi rides in the 1957 TT.

off his Junior Triumph at Kirkmichael. Fastest lap of the evening was the 28m 42s (78.88 mph) recorded by Featherstone, and in fact all the Senior leaderboard six were faster than the 1000's, which were led by Alex Phillip with 30m 14s (74.90 mph).

The 1000's may have been slower than the 500's in this session, but it was not for want of trying, and their exploits that evening provided the material for an oft-repeated anecdote concerning three well-known spectators out on the course. As *Motor Cycling* described the scene, *"At the 'Highlander', two of the greatest thrills were provided by Vincent riders. First Charles Howkins went through such a sickeningly frightful repertoire of wobbles that spectators Allan Jefferies, George Rowley and Bert Perrigo had, in their own words, to switch instantly from beer to whisky, whilst A. Phillip almost caused them to give up drinking altogether when he brought the house to its feet with a simply staggering performance. He took the whole section - down the hill, across the bump, and out to the Hall Caine's Castle [Greeba Castle] bends with the throttle hard against the stop. The sight of the 'thousand' twin roaring through the air like some giant flying saucer compelled even the 'Highlander's oldest inhabitant to confess that he'd never known anything like it.*

Nor, it is suspected, had A. Phillip".

The speed at which these antics were taking place can be judged by looking at the 'Sulby Mile' speed check results taken by the *'TT Special'* reporters, as the machines would have been travelling at more or less the same speed in these two places. (In years to follow, when electronic devices were employed to check maximum speeds, the 'Highlander' became synonymous with the TT Speed Trap). Conditions for 1949 and 1950 timed mile speeds were effectively the same, and comparisons clearly indicate the improvements (or not!) in equipment and machine performance. Alex Phillip in 1950 and George Brown in 1949 recorded identical speeds, 120.0 mph, but in the Senior, Allan Jefferies 1949 speed of 104.7 mph was well beaten by Mick Featherstone at 111.14 mph, bigger improvements still were recorded in both Junior and Lightweight classes, John Wenman's Norton and Ken James' BSA set fastest in the former at 103.46 mph, over 7mph faster than E. Harvey's BSA, and Len

Bolshaw's Triumph clocked 89.12, a similar margin faster than Ritchie's Velocette (81.8 mph) a year earlier. In fact, Bolshaw's 1940-model Triumph was the same machine he had ridden the previous year, but fitted with rear springing, telescopic forks, a close-ratio gearbox and a racing carburettor. It would have been useful to compare his speeds taken the year apart, but he doesn't appear in the 1949 listings. It would be safe to assume that he wouldn't have been much faster than Ritchie, if at all. Triumph provided the fastest three Seniors, after which Norton and BSA had a roughly equal share of the placings down to the next Triumph, which was well down the list in 17th place, over 8 mph slower than Featherstone's machine. In the Junior, Norton and BSA were more or less equally spread from 1st to 15th, where a Royal Enfield and an AJS clocked 97.30. The fastest Douglas was 94.74 mph. After Bolshaw in the Lightweight came three Velocettes, then a couple more Triumphs and a Velocette, before Fletcher's Excelsior at 83.72 mph.

The fourth practice on Thursday was another dry, clear and reasonably warm morning session, with the fastest laps thus far being set in all four classes. Leading the way was the Senior Triumph of Ivan Wicksteed, with a lap in 28m 25s (79.63 mph), while the fast-improving Phillip led the 1000's with 28m 48s (78.62 mph). Two BSA's led the Junior, Ken James two seconds faster than Brian Jackson with 30m 49s (73.47 mph), and Dean Boult (Triumph) headed up the Lightweight with 35m 02s (64.63 mph). Improving course knowledge and a more restrained approach by most meant that riding standards improved considerably, but there were still some alarming errors, the *'TT Special'* reporter at Signpost noted that in the first half-hour *"no fewer than seven riders had to take to the slip road, some of them approaching with obviously no idea that the corner existed."* A small number of spills were reported, two of which were at Kate's Cottage. Donald Hutt came off his Douglas, and was taken to Nobles Hospital with head injuries, and F. Price received facial injuries and was briefly knocked unconscious when he crashed his Junior BSA. Ronald Choules (Junior BSA) came off at Creg-ny-Baa and injured his ankle, and Lennox Broughton was reported to have been thrown from his Douglas at Glentramman, both escaping injury. John Bean ran wide at Brandish on his Junior BSA, climbing the bank and brushing the hedge before returning to the tarmac.

One practice session remained, that on the Friday morning. Wicksteed's performance on Thursday had lifted him into the reckoning for a race win, and the final practice cemented that, when he put in the fastest lap of all the clubmen, recording 27m 46s (81.54 mph). Another to draw favourable comment from observers around the course was Lightweight runner Bernard Hargreaves, who impressed particularly with his high cornering speeds. As might be expected in the final session, most of the 150-odd riders took it steady, content to learn the course and make sure their machines were set up correctly for the race, and some to bed in new chains or tyres. Two fallers were reported, both at the Nook, the tight right-hander just before Governors Bridge, but neither J. E. Carr (Senior BSA) or Arthur Newstead (Senior AJS) were injured.

The Lightweight Race (Wednesday, 7th June)

Starters

No. Rider	Club	Machine
101 J R Dulson	South Liverpool MC	Velocette
102 L D Boult	Leicester Query MC	Triumph
103 A J Liddiard	Wolverhampton MC & LCC	Velocette
104 T W Brown	Newcastle & DMC	Excelsior
105 J P Barker	C.S.M.A. Ltd.	Velocette
106 A J Wellsted	Pathfinders & Derby MC Ltd	Triumph
107 F Desborough	Wolverhampton MC & LCC	Velocette
109 A Hutchinson	East Lancs MC & LCC	Velocette
111 R W Porter	Peterborough MCC	Triumph
112 D W Mustard	Aberdeen & DMC	Velocette
113 F Fletcher	West Leeds MC	Excelsior
114 G S Wakefield	Dunstable & DMC	Panther
115 L C Bolshaw	Nantwich & DMC	Triumph
116 B J Hargreaves	Ribble Valley MC	Velocette

Despite a generally good forecast for the day's weather, by 10.00 am there was still a heavy, damp mist which restricted visibility in the Douglas area, not badly, but the Mountain was somewhat more affected. The western and northern sections of the course were better, and conditions over the Island were expected to improve as the day wore on. Three non-started, T. Salthouse, K. Taylor and P. R. W. Mayo, all entered on Velocettes.

With the ban on warming-up, there was a slightly different atmosphere to the build-up to the off, an uneasy 'things not being quite right' feeling. This was dispelled with the departure of the 1000's, then

Looking very à la Stanley Woods, D W Mustard takes Quarter Bridge on the first lap. It was also his last lap, a Parliament Square spill ended his Clubman's career.

the Seniors, until, 11 minutes later, the Lightweights were sent on their way. Most of the 14 facing the flag made good starts, exceptions were Tommy Brown (Excelsior), Frank Desborough and Arthur Hutchinson, both on Velocettes, particularly the last-named, who lost almost 18 minutes. Reports around the course had Arthur Wellsted (Triumph), Donald Mustard (Velocette) and Frank Fletcher (Excelsior) running pretty close in the first three places, but one who had been expected to be challenging hadn't reached Kirkmichael. Bernard Hargreaves had come a cropper at Laurel Bank, and, although it was announced that he had retired there, he did re-start, only to retire later at Governor's Bridge. Anthony Liddiard's Velocette stopped at Brandywell with engine trouble. At the end of the lap, Fletcher led Wellsted by 150 yards on the road, and by a comfortable 45 seconds on corrected time, with 3rd place-man Mustard a further 26 seconds adrift.

First Lap Leaderboard

1 F. Fletcher (Excelsior)	34m 8s	(66.33 mph)
2 A. J. Wellsted (Triumph)	34m 53s	(64.91 mph)
3 D.W. Mustard (Velocette)	35m 19s	(64.12 mph)
4 L.C. Bolshaw (Triumph)	36m 16s	(62.44 mph)
5 J.R. Dulson (Velocette)	37m 12s	(60.87 mph)
6 R.W. Porter (Triumph)	37m 47s	(59.93 mph)

By the time he reached Ramsey for the second time, Fletcher had extended his lead over Wellsted to more than a minute, but drama followed soon after when Mustard crashed in Parliament Square, damaging the gearbox on his Velocette, and forcing his retirement. Some oil deposited in the road during the spill caught out 6th placed Ross Porter before it was able to be cleaned up, and he too came off. After taking time to straighten the mudguard of his Triumph, he was able to restart and rejoin the race. Frank Desborough retired his Velocette at the pits after a troubled first lap, and the sole Panther of George Wakefield also dropped out, the reason not specified.

Second Lap Leaderboard

1 F. Fletcher (Excelsior)	1h 8m 1s	(66.85 mph)
2 A.J. Wellsted (Triumph)	1h 9m 23s	(65.29 mph)
3 L.C. Bolshaw (Triumph)	1h 11m 52s	(63.01 mph)

4 J.R. Dulson (Velocette)	1h 13m 18s	(61.78 mph)
5 L.D. Boult (Triumph)	1h 15m 45s	(59.79 mph)
6 J.P. Barker (Velocette)	1h 17m 26s	(58.48 mph)

Wellsted's cornering and course knowledge was equally as impressive as the leader, and there may well have been less of a time advantage to Fletcher given equal machinery, but the Triumph was simply no match for the Excelsior, and in fact he lost even more time to Fletcher as a result of his fuel stop at the end of the second lap. As they were signalled in Ramsey, Hutchinson passed the Grandstand to start his third and last lap, pressing on well despite the handicap of his awful start. Len Bolshaw, who had been in 3rd place, went into his pit at the end of the second lap, and eventually retired his Triumph there, and Tommy Brown retired at The Highlander, his Excelsior having dropped a valve. The gap between Wellsted and Fletcher increased steadily during the last lap, and as everyone below 2nd place moving up a place with Bolshaw's exit, Hutchinson actually made it onto the leaderboard at the flag, helped a little by more retirements. Out of the race at Ballaugh went Ross Porter, and George Barker retired his Velocette out on the course on his final lap. Only five managed to reach the finish.

Finishing Order

1 F. Fletcher (Excelsior)	1h 41m 34.4s	(66.89 mph)
2 A.J. Wellsted (Triumph)	1h 45m 6.2s	(64.63 mph)
3 J.R. Dulson (Velocette)	1h 50m 5.2s	(61.73 mph)
4 L.D. Boult (Triumph)	1h 52m 0.2s	(60.65 mph)
5 A. Hutchinson (Velocette)	2h 08m 35s	(52.16 mph)

Fastest Lap: F. Fletcher (3rd lap) 33m 33.4s (67.30 mph)

The Junior Race (Wednesday, 7th June)

Starters

No.	Rider	Club	Machine
1	P B Davies	Huddersfield MC	B.S.A.
2	J R Clark	Waterlooville MCC	Douglas
3	W S Corley	Mont' Christie MCC	Norton
5	W V S Leech	Gt. Yarmouth Seagull MCC	B.S.A.
6	G Arnold	Warrington & DMC	Velocette
7	C G Griffiths	Lewes Unity MCC	Douglas
8	J T Wenman	North Berks MC & LCC	Norton

The chaos that the no-warming-up rule caused, especially to the Douglas riders in the Junior race.

Top: Charles Robinson is still trying to prod his Douglas into life whilst No's 85, 86 and 87 await the starters flag, over a minute after he should have been away. Despite the handicap, he pulled through to fifth.

Below left: is that a broken kick start shaft just behind the back wheel of J A Cowling's 90+? J A Hedley's problem was the kick start pedal went awol; did he borrow the part from Cowling to make his start?

Below right: All the way from Ceylon to spend half an hour getting the machine to fire; Collin Silva works on his BSA

9	A C R Collins	Bristol MC & LCC	B.S.A.
10	J A Cowling	Thornton Cleveleys MCC	Douglas
11	P J Price	Ashford Kent MC	B.S.A.
14	A C T Turk	Tenterden MC & CC	A.J.S.
15	W G Hutt	Oxfordshire MRC	Douglas
17	C Bruce	Glasgow Lion MCC	Royal Enfield
16	F Sheene	Douglas MCC (Bristol)	Douglas
19	A A F Burton	West of England MC	Douglas
20	R Jones	Salop MC	B.S.A.
21	M R McGeagh	Sunbeam MCC	B.S.A.
22	J W Moore	Peveril (IoM) MC & LCC	B.S.A.
23	T Williams	Foden's MC	B.S.A.
24	W C Reed	Stockport MCRC	Douglas
25	R J Dear	Whitley MCC	B.S.A.
26	K Willis	Chelmsford & DAC	B.S.A.
27	F Hilditch	Crewe & South Cheshire MC	Douglas
28	R H King	Bedford Eagles MCC	B.S.A.
29	B C Norwood	London Douglas MCC	Douglas
30	J F Basinger	Southampton & DMCC	B.S.A.
31	J H Cooper	Halifax & DMC & LCC	Velocette
32	B A Jackson	Oswestry & DMC	B.S.A.
33	A Rayner	Stockbridge & DMC	Norton
34	R Brassington	Potteries Clarion MC	Norton
35	L H Stevenson	Harworth & DMC	B.S.A.
36	C Macartney	Taunton MC	B.S.A.
37	K R V James	Ringwood MC & LCC	B.S.A.
38	W H Wilshere	Chalfont & Amersham AC	Triumph
39	R Rees	Gloucester & Cotswold MC	A.J.S.
40	S A Milne	Vintage MCC	E.M.C.
41	J Wade	Sheffield & Hallamshire MC	B.S.A.
42	P Beaney	South Harrow & District MCC	Norton
43	A McIvor	Bolton MCC	Norton
44	J Cantrill	Notts & District MCC	B.S.A.
45	A Bates	C.S.M.A. Ltd.	Douglas
46	I McGuffie	Galloway MC & LCC	B.S.A.
47	P Simister	Macclesfield MCC	Norton
48	H L Stephen	Coventry & Warwickshire MC	B.S.A.
49	L Price	Liverpool Imperial MCC	B.S.A.
50	J Hockin	Bermondsey MCC	Douglas
51	C Silva	Ceylon MCC	B.S.A.
52	A E Morrow	Horsham & DMC & LCC	Douglas
53	T Clegg	Bury & DMCC	B.S.A.
54	A E Heath	Pendle Forest MC	Norton
55	E H C Baker	Finedon 'Dolben' M.C.	B.S.A.
56	G Milner	Louth & DMCC	Douglas
57	T H Silk	Warrington & DMC	B.S.A.
58	A D Bassett	Mid Bucks MCC	B.S.A.
59	J Difazio	Frome & DMC & LCC	Norton
60	J Havercroft	Hull MC Ltd.	A.J.S.
62	H Brown	Berwick & DMC	B.S.A.
63	C E Robinson	Louth & DMCC	Douglas
64	P Bagshaw	Manchester '17' MCC	A.J.S.
65	E Houseley	Chesterfield & DMCC	B.S.A.
66	H Vinall	Portsmouth MC & LCC	B.S.A.
67	J W Davie	Kircaldy & DMC	B.S.A.
68	J Hedley	Balmoral MCC	Douglas
69	W Zoellner	Runcorn & DMCC	B.S.A.
70	J A Ure	Glasgow Sporting MCC	B.S.A.
72	A G Mollan	Bradford & DMC	B.S.A.
73	L J B R French	Norwood MC	Douglas
74	C W Davis	Sidcup & DMCC	B.S.A.
75	J A Thomson	Worthing Eagle MC	A.J.S.
76	L Broughton	Wye Valley A.C.	Douglas
77	G R Brown	Boston DMC & LCC	B.S.A.
78	C Ellerby	Scunthorpe MCC	Velocette
79	B J Smith	Streatham & DMC	Norton
80	C L Carter	Bar None MCC	Douglas
81	W F Barker	Rushden & District Query MC	B.S.A.
82	L Dunham	Thorne & DMC	A.J.S.
83	J F Bean	Middlesborough & DMC	B.S.A.
84	R Choules	Ilford Amateur MC	B.S.A.
85	A J Hart	Wigan AC	Velocette
86	G P Ellison	Wallasey MC	Norton
87	A D Brown	Stewarts & Lloyds (Corby) MCC	Norton
89	S Cooper	Banovallum MCC	Douglas
90	H Nowell	Preston & DMCC	Norton
91	R M Thomson	Falkirk & DMC	B.S.A.
92	J Boulter	Staverton RC	Douglas
93	G N Camfield	X.H.G. Tiger MCC	Douglas
94	K S Watling	South Leeds MC	B.S.A.
96	S T Seston	Bourneville Works MC	B.S.A.
97	T R Cookson	Preston & District MCC	Norton
98	J Cox	Manchester Eagle MCC	B.S.A.
99	A Klinge	C.S.M.A. Ltd	Norton
100	J L Kendall	Cricklewood & DMC & LCC	B.S.A.
101	A J Chefneux	Manchester 48th MCC	Douglas

Starting later the same day, at 2.00 pm, the Junior race enjoyed better weather conditions, but still there lingered some slight drifting mist for the largest-ever Clubman's entry to contend with. Of the 100 original entries, non-arrivals and practice problems had reduced the field so that, even though the 6 reserves all rode, 93 riders lined up for the start. Those recorded as non-starters were N. Banks (Douglas), J. Smith (BSA), H. S. Hall (Velocette), F. Price (BSA), D. N. Hutt (Douglas), J. M. McLaughlin (Norton), G. Walls (BSA), T. Hodgson (BSA), A. C. Kirby (Norton), P. R. Sproat (Douglas) and D. Spain (Norton). The six reserves taking rides were G. Arnold (Velocette), Charles Robinson (Douglas), P. J. Price (BSA), H. Nowell (Norton), B. J. Smith (Norton), and A. Klinge (BSA).

John Clark (Douglas) led away from the off, his two starting companions P. B. Davis (BSA) and W. S. Corley (Norton) taking time to coax their cold engines into life (the intended fourth member of the group was the non-starter Norman Banks). This rather set the scene for the rest of the field, as many riders found their machines reluctant to fire up. If a machine wouldn't start on the line, a marshal was obliged to usher the rider to one side to avoid having his presence hinder the following group. In effect, given the starting interval, a rider had a little over 15 seconds to kick-start his machine before he was asked to leave the start line and continue his efforts in the pits. It was not surprising then, that a 'pit-queue' soon formed (at one point, it was noted that an entire starting group of four had to be so removed, none of them having succeeded in starting their machines). From *The Motor Cycle*, "At one time, the left of the road was so packed with sweating, swearing, frantic kickers that the marshals had to shoo them along toward Bray Hill. Several were still leaping and plunging after No. 101 had gone. Never can a yowling exhaust have sounded so sweet in human ears". Gradually the assembly thinned, and most eventually got away, although Collin Silva (BSA), who hailed from Ceylon (as it was then, Sri Lanka now), did not do so until after the leaders had completed their first lap. Two unfortunates who didn't, were G. N. Camfield (Douglas) and J. A. Cowling, who broke his kick-starter in his efforts to start his Douglas. A similar breakage also befell the Douglas of James Hedley, but as reported by *Motor Cycling* "he manages a start somehow"!

On the other hand, the Douglas of Clark was going very well indeed, and was first to reach Ballacraine and Ramsey, followed on the road by William Leech (BSA). As well as Clark was riding, the 'Duggies'

were no match for the BSA's, and at the end of the first lap he was in 5th position, over a minute behind the leader, one of the pre-race favourites Ken James, who in turn held a 34-second advantage over Ian McGuffie, with Brian Jackson 12 seconds further back in 3rd. Other Douglas entries to fall by the wayside were those of Walter Reed, who went out with unspecified mechanical problems at Glen Helen, and L.J.B.R. French who had a seized engine at Sulby. The bridge at Sulby also claimed two fallers, Harry Stephen (BSA) who was forced to retire with hand injuries, and John Bean (BSA) who was able to continue, but was reported to have had another fall later on that eventful lap, at Windy Corner. J. H. (Bert) Cooper retired in the Glen Helen section with 'back wheel trouble' on his Velocette, which turned out to be a broken wheel spindle, and was joined by Trevor Williams who had engine trouble on his BSA (which was Harold Clark's 1949-winning machine). The unhappy Douglas story continued with the retirements of Bernard Norwood, George Milner and J. Hockin.

First Lap Leaderboard

1	K.V.R. James (BSA)	30m 9s	(75.10 mph)
2	I. McGuffie (BSA)	30n 43s	(73.70 mph)
3	B.A. Jackson (BSA)	30m 55s	(73.20 mph)
4	R. Jones (BSA)	31m 19s	(72.30 mph)
5	J. R. Clark (Douglas)	31m 25s	(72.10 mph)
6=	R.H. King (BSA)	31m 53s	(71.0 mph)
6=	W. F. Barber (BSA)	31m 53s	(71.0 mph)

Clark continued to lead on the road all the way round the second lap, with Jones and James getting ever closer, but the sensation of that lap was the speed of Jackson, who took 7 seconds off the lap record with a time of 29m 45s (76.12 mph), and in so doing overhauled McGuffie to move into 2nd place, and close the deficit on James to 16 seconds. As always, fuel stops may have slightly masked leaderboard movements, particularly as a number of the BSA riders elected to top up in the relatively quiet slot at the end of the first lap, rather than risk being hindered in the busy end-of-second-or-third lap periods. However, there was no disputing the fact that Jackson's second lap had been some 30 seconds faster than James. A. J. Hart and Clifford Ellerby retired their Velocettes at the pits, the latter with a seized engine, Arthur Klinge (BSA) stopped at Union Mills with engine trouble, and Charles Bruce retired the solitary Royal Enfield at Lezayre, on the approach to Ramsey. A. J. F. Basinger (BSA) and A. McIvor (Norton) were also reported as having retired, the Norton rider after a fall, without injury, at the Nook.

Second Lap Leaderboard

1 K.V.R. James (BSA)	1h 0m 24s	(74.98 mph)
2 B.A. Jackson (BSA)	1h 0m 40s	(74.66 mph)
3 I. McGuffie (BSA)	1h 1m 27s	(73.68 mph)
4 R. Jones (BSA)	1h 1m 40s	(73.44 mph)
5 J.R. Clark (Douglas)	1h 2m 26s	(72.54 mph)
6 J. Difazio (Norton)	1h 3m 18s	(71.55 mph)

Weather conditions continued to improve, and although the southern part of the course remained obstinately cloudy and dull, visibility on the Mountain improved, and spectators were sunbathing in Ramsey. Jackson continued to close on James all around the third circuit, and unofficial timing on the Mountain had him ahead by about a minute on the road, from which the starting interval of 40 seconds had to be deducted. Ron Jones, who had been in 4th place at the end of the second lap, took a fall at the Gooseneck, and retired later at his pit. Clark's Douglas still led on the road, in 4th place on corrected time, and a couple of Nortons had eased their way into the top six, those of Doug (Buster) Brown and Phil Simister, Phil riding the 'Inter' which had finished 2nd in the 1949 event, ridden by brother John. William Leech, Leslie Stevenson, Tom Clegg and Tom Silk (all on BSA's), were third lap retirements with mechanical bothers.

Third Lap Leaderboard

1 B.A. Jackson (BSA)	1h 31m 35s	(74.16 mph)
2 K.V.R. James (BSA)	1h 31m 48s	(73.98 mph)
3 I. McGuffie (BSA)	1h 32m 59s	(73.10 mph)
4 J.R. Clark (Douglas)	1h 33m 45s	(72.44 mph)
5 A.D. Brown (Norton)	1h 34m 38s	(71.76 mph)
6 P. Simister (Norton)	1h 34m 46s	(71.66 mph)

Entering the final lap, James' indicator moved on to 'B' for Ballacraine, but no further, as he was forced to retire at Glen Helen with engine trouble, leaving Jackson with an almost 2-minute lead over McGuffie, which he duly held to the finish. Clark also seemed to have problems on that lap, putting in a time over a minute slower than his best, and this coincided with Brown putting in his fastest lap of the race. At the finish, and as the corrected times were calculated, the Norton rider had a 40-second advantage over Clark, catching out the PA commentators who had already announced the third place-man as being Clark! The early disappointment of retirements from the Douglas contingent was somewhat compensated by the arrival on the leaderboard of Charles Robinson, who had put in three fast laps after a rather slow opener. There was a lengthy list of last-lap retirements, although in fact some were simply 'red-flagged' as no laps were able to be started after the 4.00 pm cut-off. They were A. C. R. Collins (BSA), Michael McGeagh (BSA), John Moore (BSA), Willy Wilshere (Triumph), John Wade (BSA), Collin Silva (who had been running well on his BSA after that most awful start, his first lap was recorded as just 40 seconds short of the hour), A. E. Morrow (Douglas), A. D. Bassett (BSA), Maurice Chefneux (Douglas), James Hedley (Douglas), Harry Vinall (BSA), and Laurence Dunham (AJS). In fact,

Phil Carter (Norton) takes Bray Hill with the throttle well cracked open.

both Vinall and Dunham had earlier had (separate) falls in the Ramsey area, and managed to re-join after 'straightening things out'. Rowland Dear came off his BSA at the Bungalow, and George Arnold took a fall after the engine of his Velocette seized at Sulby. Both retired without serious injury.

Finishing Order

1 B.A. Jackson (BSA)   2h 1m 58.2s   (74.25 mph)
2 I. McGuffie (BSA)   2h 3m 54.8s   (73.07 mph)
3 A.D. Brown (Norton)   2h 5m 15s   (72.42 mph)
4 J.R. Clark (Douglas)   2h 5m 54s   (71.97 mph)
5 C.E. Robinson (Douglas) 2h 6m 22.4s   (71.70 mph)
6 P. Simister (Norton)   2h 6m 33s   (71.59 mph)

Fastest Lap: B.A. Jackson (2nd lap) 29m 45s (76.12 mph) (Record)

The Senior Race (Wednesday, 7th June)

Starters

No.	Rider	Club	Machine
20	H Plews	Wakefield & DMSC	Norton
21	J E Brookes	Northwich MC	B.S.A.
22	H L Williams	Dursley MC & LCC	Norton
23	W Hillary	Rochdale & DMC	Triumph
24	A J Pollitt	Widnes & DMC	Norton
25	F Passmore	Hayes & DMCC	Norton
26	A S Avis	Border MC	Triumph
27	D A Gadd	Bristol MCC	Vincent H.R.D.
28	"W Workman"	Rochdale & DMC	Triumph
29	V G Hyland	North Hants MC	Norton
30	R W C Kerr	Ayr MCC	Norton
31	E M Kempson	Sidcup & DMCC	Norton
32	D J P Wilkins	Mendip Vale MC & LCC	Triumph
33	R F Austin	West Middlesex Amateur MCC	Triumph
34	J Curphey	Ramsey & DMC & LCC	Triumph
35	L C Newcombe	Wayfarers MCC	Triumph
36	W Kay	Antelope MCC	B.S.A.
37	H E Gilbert	Sanderstead & DM & LCC	Triumph
38	J Fisher	Furness & DMCC	Triumph
39	A Johnstone	South Liverpool MC	Triumph
40	W Dobson	Accrington & DMC & LCC	Norton
41	H Beck	Hull MC Ltd.	Vincent H.R.D.
43	R V Hunt	Ramsey & DMC & LCC	Triumph
44	A Newstead	Newark 'Eagle' MC & LCC	A.J.S.
45	H Wall	North Lancs MC	Triumph
46	D R A James	Malden & DMC	Triumph
47	J Wright	Wirral '100' MC	B.S.A.
48	I B Wicksteed	Royston & DMCC	Triumph

Despite starting the race with two pairs of goggles, Ivan Wicksteed had shed both pairs as he headed down Bray Hill, seconds later he was out with a split tank.

49	H L Mills	Diss & DMC & LCC	Triumph
50	R K Pilling	Bury & DMCC	Triumph
52	J N Buck	Stratford-on-Avon MC & LCC	Norton
53	A Hill	Bradford & DMC	Triumph
54	M S Featherstone		
		Grantham Pegasus MC & LCC	Triumph
55	P J Orton	Hinckley MC & LCC	Vincent H.R.D.
56	F C J Collings	West Bristol MC & CC	Triumph
57	J Bollington	Sheffield Ace MC	Triumph
58	F O Coleman	Birmingham MCC	B.S.A.
59	R E Paxton	Cheltenham Home Guard MCC	
			Triumph
60	'T Southward'	Reading Ace MCC	Triumph
62	M Hird	Worksop & DMCC	Triumph
63	H J Ollerenshaw		
		Hillsborough MCC	Vincent H.R.D.
65	W Howard	Warrington & DMC	B.S.A.
66	J J E Porter	Norwood M.C.	A.J.S.
67	A S Herbert	O.W.L.S. MC	Norton
68	R F Keen	Birmingham Speedway MC & LCC	
			Triumph
69	K Dixon	South Liverpool MC	Norton
72	H J D Boynton	Alcester MCC	Norton
73	F F Parry	B.M.C.R.C.	Triumph
74	P J Fetherston	Builth Wells MC	Triumph
75	J E Carr	Dart M & MC	B.S.A.
76	R Yates	Mansfield & DMC & CC	Norton
77	I K Arber	Wellingborough MCC	Norton
78	D C Millar	Seaton Delaval & DMC	A.J.S.
79	W F de Zylva	Ceylon MCC	Triumph
80	R A Rowbottom		
		North Lincs MC	Triumph
81	P H Carter	Winsford & DMC	Norton
82	J C Duncan	Lincoln & DMC	B.S.A.
83	C Scott	Sheffield N. End MC & LCC	Norton
84	D Bogie	Perth & DMC	B.S.A.

Senior non-starters were P. Carr (Triumph), J. W. Taylor (BSA), R. Kenworthy (Triumph), Jack Bottomley (BSA), J. G. Davis (BSA), A. R. King (Triumph) and the unfortunate J. Makaula-White.

Run in the morning simultaneously with the Lightweight and 1000cc races, and starting 2 minutes after the last '1000' had departed, the Senior riders obviously faced the same damp and misty conditions over the southern end of the course.

From the first group to go, Harry Plews (Norton),

J.E. Brookes (BSA) and W. Hillary (Triumph) got away without difficulty, but H.L. Williams (Norton) had to join the 'pit-queue' of kickers. The first of the Seniors to show on the road was Plews, who was rewarded for his efforts in the *'TT Special'* with a very personal 'tribute' from Geoff Davison, who wrote *"Plews, in spite of his girth - which has increased considerably since he was a driver/mechanic in my Army Unit - is now well ahead on the roads, reaching Ramsey 1m 15s ahead of the next man, Kerr (Norton) who started 40 seconds behind him."* Arthur Pollitt's Norton was one of the more reluctant starters, while Reg Pilling's moment of distraction when faced with a similar situation, led to his exclusion. He stopped some way past his pit, from where his mechanic rushed, armed with replacement plugs and a spanner. He was in full view of all the start-line officials, and, according to the rulebook, the taking-on of replacement parts outside the pit area was cause for exclusion.

Out on the course, the race began to take shape, although some of the faster riders were somewhat hidden in the pack, and when the first lap times were announced it was pre-war Brooklands habitué Ivan Wicksteed who led on his Triumph, followed by the Nortons of John Boynton and veteran Angus Herbert. Wicksteed and H. L. Williams (Norton) stopped to refuel at the end of the first lap, and Wicksteed in fact took time to clean his goggles, suggesting to onlookers that he felt he had time in hand, and was relatively comfortable with the situation. Roger Hunt came off his Triumph at Ballaugh, suffering facial cuts, Wally de Zylva (Triumph), another rider from Ceylon, retired at Creg-ny-Baa with mechanical trouble, and Roland Austin retired his Triumph at the pits with front brake problems. Other retirements with various mechanical 'maladies' were Arthur Pollitt (Norton), John Fisher (Triumph), and Roger Paxton (Triumph), while Albert Gadd retired his Vincent/HRD at Keppel Gate with 'footrest trouble', as *'Motor Cycling'* commented, *'a not uncommon bother on that fast left-hander'.*

First Lap Leaderboard

1 I. B. Wicksteed (Triumph)	28m 55s	(78.30 mph)
2 H. J. Boynton (Norton)	29m 19s	(77.24 mph)
3 A. S. Herbert (Norton)	29m 57s	(75.60 mph)

4 A. Hill (Triumph)	30m 01s	(75.43 mph)	
5 M. Featherstone (Triumph)	30m 02s	(75.39 mph)	
6 J. E. Brookes (BSA)	30m 22s	(74.57 mph)	

If anything, the mist and damp around Douglas worsened after the start of the race, before things finally began to improve later. Despite these conditions, and the fact that it was his first Isle of Man experience, Wicksteed continued to pull away on the second lap, his position strengthened by the retirement of 2nd place-man Boynton at Glentramman, with engine trouble. Brookes' consequent elevation to 5th was short-lived as he retired the BSA at Barregarroo with magneto problems, and then Featherstone was forced out with a split fuel tank. Another retirement with a split tank, this time oil, was the Triumph of 'Wilf Workman', at Sulby, while an improved second lap lifted Allen Hill (Triumph) into 3rd place, only 6 seconds behind Herbert.

Second Lap Leaderboard

1 I. B. Wicksteed (Triumph)	57m 59s	(78.12 mph)	
2 A. S. Herbert (Norton)	59m 26s	(76.20 mph)	
3 A. Hill (Triumph)	59m 32s	(76.07 mph)	
4 H. Plews (Norton)	59m 53s	(75.64 mph)	
5 P. H. Carter (Norton)	1h 0m 16s	(75.14 mph)	
6 R. W. C. Kerr (Norton)	1h 4m 43s	(69.94 mph)	

After a slow first lap, at the end of which he was 11th, and aided by the retirements, Phil Carter's leaderboard appearance meant that it was four Nortons and two Triumphs doing battle at the front. The 2nd, 3rd and 4th place-men were all lapping in similar times, but were being closed down by Carter all the time, while Wicksteed pulled further away with a lap in 28m 29s (79.51 mph). Mechanical problems accounted for the retirements of Stanley Avis (Triumph), Harry Beck (Vincent), Derek James (Triumph), Jack Orton (Vincent), Maurice Herd (Triumph), and Dennis Millar (AJS). John Curphey (Triumph) retired at the pits with clutch trouble, but the most significant retirement was that of 2nd place-man Herbert, who had been baulked by a slower rider approaching Signpost, and had come off. Although uninjured, he was unable to continue.

Third Lap Leaderboard

1 I. B. Wicksteed (Triumph)	1h 26m 28s	(78.53 mph)
2 H. Plews (Norton)	1h 29m 36s	(75.81 mph)
3 A. Hill (Triumph)	1h 30m 6s	(75.39 mph)
4 P.H. Carter (Norton)	1h 30m 25s	(75.14 mph)
5 I. K. Arber (Norton)	1h 32m 2s	(73.84 mph)
6 H.L. Williams (Norton)	1h 32m 6s	(73.76 mph)

As he crossed the line to start the last lap, with only the leader of the '1000's in front on the roads, race-long leader Wicksteed held a 3-minute-plus advantage, but his race was over before he reached Quarter Bridge, forced to retire with a split petrol tank. Suddenly the race was wide open. Plews was leading, but Hill and Carter were close and any one of the three was capable of winning. The Public Address commentator at Cronk-ny-Mona was watching for the first man to appear, and announced that it was Plews as expected, but that his engine was 'spluttering'. So Hill looked favourite until Carter put in a spurt right at the end, to record a lap 45 seconds quicker than Hill, and snatch the win by 26 seconds. 6th place-man Williams also hit mechanical trouble in the closing miles, and finished up in a 'pushing race' with Plews, to finish in 10th place, less than 10 seconds behind Plews. All of which, together with a final lap only 6 seconds slower than Wicksteed's fastest, hoisted Ken Dixon into 3rd place, 14 seconds ahead of Arber. Fred Collings (Triumph) and Cyril Scott (Norton) were last lap retirements.

Finishing Order

1 P. H. Carter (Norton)	1h 59m 50.4s	(75.60 mph)
2 A. Hill (Triumph)	2h 0m 17.0s	(75.30 mph)
3 K. Dixon (Norton)	2h 1m 29.4s	(74.57 mph)
4 I. K. Arber (Norton)	2h 1m 43.8s	(74.41 mph)
5 R.W. C. Kerr (Norton)	2h 3m 10.4s	(73.56 mph)
6 F. Passmore (Norton)	2h 5m 38.4s	(72.08 mph)

Fastest Lap: I.B. Wicksteed (3rd lap) 28m 29s (79.51 mph).

The 1000cc Race (Wednesday, 7th June)

Starters

No. Rider   Club   Machine

1	L Carr	Newcastle & DMCC	Vincent H.R.D.
2	G Lund	Southall & DMC	Vincent H.R.D.
3	F E Taylor	Vincent HRD OC	Vincent H.R.D.
4	J B Netherton	West Ham & DMC	
			Vincent H.R.D.
6	R F Organ	North East London MC	Vincent H.R.D.
7	J D O Davis	Birmingham MCC	Vincent H.R.D.
8	C W G Taylor	Cambridge Centaur MC	Vincent H.R.D.
9	C Howkins	Leamington Victory MCC	
			Vincent H.R.D.
10	A Phillip	Vincent HRD OC	Vincent H.R.D.
11	F J Young	Luton & DMC & CC	Vincent H.R.D.
14	"J Alexander"	Rhyl & DMC	Vincent H.R.D.

J. L. Watkin and W. D. Francis were non-starters, leaving a field of 11 for the 10.30 am start, all on Vincent-HRD's. F. E. Taylor took the lead away from the start, closely followed by Gerald Lund and J. B. Netherton. Louis Carr had problems starting his machine, and was moved toward the pits to continue his efforts. He unfortunately lost his balance with the heavy bike, and it fell on its side, and he was faced with further delays as he struggled to right the massive bike, and then push to his pit to inspect for damage. Netherton was first into Kirkmichael, but by the Mountain climb Alex Phillip led from Lund and 'J. Alexander', but 'Alexander' passed Phillip on the drop toward Douglas, as the mist thickened. Only the

first three covered the first lap in under the half-hour, and three others were in trouble on the opening lap. Roy Organ was reported as having come off at the Bungalow, and the clocks of Netherton and Taylor were stuck at Kirkmichael and the Mountain respectively. In fact Netherton had stopped at Ballaugh with engine trouble, and both Taylor and Organ had crashed at the Bungalow, without injuring themselves seriously. Both men had suffered shoulder injuries, Organ some head wounds too, and as they both required further medical attention they were helped to the Snaefell Electric Railway and thence to Nobles Hospital via Laxey!

First Lap Leaderboard

1	'J. Alexander' (Vincent-HRD)		
		29m 17s	(77.33 mph)
2	A. Phillip (Vincent-HRD)	29m 37s	(76.46 mph)
3	C. Howkins (Vincent-HRD)	29m 57s	(75.60 mph)
4	G. Lund (Vincent-HRD)	31m 28s	(71.97 mph)
5	F. J. Young (Vincent-HRD)	32m 5s	(70.57 mph)
6	L. Carr (Vincent-HRD)	32m 10s	(70.36 mph)

'Alexander' and Phillip remained very close together on the road for the whole of the second lap, both lapping almost a minute faster than their opener, thus the 20 second margin also remained. They pitted almost together, and left still close to each other, to

John Wright (BSA) leaves Governors Bridge. BSA's influence on the development of the Gold Star was beginning to make its mark.

many is that what was actually wrong with the Clubman's series, and what in the end would prove to be the downfall of the races in terms of the lack of spectacle of all-out battles between rival manufacturers, was not the fact of the BSA factory's direct involvement and eventual dominance, but the absence of similar involvement by any of the others.

The 1950 Clubman's l000
by Louis Carr

(From the 'TT Special' 10th June, 1963)

I think my very first race in the Isle of Man was as interesting as any, for everything went wrong — even before I got there. I was, and still am, a member of the Newcastle Motor Club. Well, back in 1949 they decided to enter me in the following year's 1,000 cc Clubman's TT I don't really know why, but I did have a pretty quick Vincent that I had been working on very hard, so that must have been it.

I was very thrilled by all this, but there was one big snag — I had no money, though I did have a lot of good friends. They were all

as hard up as I was, but when you have friends there is always a way out.

Bert Ellis, who, by the way, had been with me on every trip to the Isle of Man, had a 1937 Ariel Hunter with a chassis on it, so that was the transporter sorted out. He couldn't come with me for the start of practice, but would be over a few days later. So far so good.

On the big day I set off from Whitley Bay with what looked like half-a-ton on the poor combination.

All went well till just after Barnard Castle when, on a long downhilll moorland bit of road, a small flock of sheep decided to try the grass on the other side for some reason or other — mad fools. Oh I tried, yes, indeed, but the Ariel had the bit between its teeth

and it just refused to slow down, never mind stop. The outcome was that a dirty big old ram got the lot full in the mush. It had a great big pair of curly horns and its head went between the exhaust pipe and cylinder. The horns were then locked good and firm.

At this stage the Ariel's steering was very poor indeed, so we hit the left-hand bank with a hell of a thud. I decided to go on in front for a spell, landing flat on the grass verge. Even after all that the machine was still on its way, and it ran over me. This was the last straw — I had never before managed to run over myself.

When everything finally came to rest, I was stuck under the sidecar, with no help for miles, it must have taken me some ten minutes to get out, but that was not all, I couldn't get that sheep's horns from behind the exhaust pipe, even though it was very dead. I pulled and I pushed; in the end I had to take the pipe out of the head.

After a bit a few cars did go by, and I couldn't help feeling that at least one of them must belong to the farmer and owner of said sheep. So each time a car came along I tried to look as innocent as possible till it passed, and then started pulling like mad again.

The main reason for all this worry was that I had only my boat fare with about £6 to spare — no digs money, even; the plan was to win the cash to pay the good lady at our digs. So you see, if I'd had to pay some £10 for the sheep that would have been the end — no boat fare!

After dumping the meat in the heather I took stock of the machine. What a mess! The forks were bent, and so was the frame. The wheels were a good six inches out of line, but it would run, so I had to press on. After collecting tools and gear, which were spread all over the road, off we went. It took everything I had to hold the machine straight, and by the time I got to Fleetwood my arms felt like lead; but I made it.

I then set about learning the course. The practice went off all right, though a Vincent is not the best machine to learn on. Came race day and the model wouldn't start. In the end I got off with the 500cc machines, but once under way we were going very well, until on the second lap the zip on my borrowed leathers bust. I covered some two miles, no hands, trying to do it up. In the end I gave up and just pressed on to the pits where Bert laced me up like a football while I filled the tank.

Off we went again in fine style as far as Sulby Straight, down which the Vincent was tramping big licks till the point where I decided some braking was called for. Everything went on with a bang, and then I was struck a sharp blow on the conk. On looking down I was rather annoyed to see the front brake cable standing on end right in front of my face — the nipple had pulled off. As you know, the rear brake on a Vincent is not very powerful by itself, so I started to think all sorts of things, funny stories, etc., to help pass the time before moving Sulby Bridge into Ramsey.

At this point I remember seeing a small hole in the wall leading down to the river. I decided to try for it, still doing a good 60 m.p.h. One snag — a marshal was in the gap; not to worry, he was doing a good 65 m.p.h. So I shot through, but fell off whilst trying to keep out of the river. After some heaving and kicking, however, I managed to restart and finish fifth, so I was able to pay for my digs after all.

By the way, I never told the landlady; she was such a trusting old girl.

Big Louis even dwarfs a Vincent! How he was able to wrap himself round a Junior Clubman Goldie in '52 is a mystery.

My Junior Clubman's Ride
by Michael McGeagh

machines from the tent and set them up in rows upon the grid. Stone cold engines, ice-encrusted plugs, a tank full of treacle, and a kick-start to set the whole high-compression issue in motion. The year of the cold start.... when men aged a month in a minute.... when the air on the Glencrutchery Road turned blue – and not with exhaust fumes either!

The B32 finally burst into song $7\frac{1}{2}$ minutes late. I recall being marshalled to the roadside to join the

(From the 'TT Special', 11th June 1956)

After eight rather hectic rides over the Mountain circuit in the Isle of Man, I find it a little difficult to describe which one ranks highest in the 'tough' category. The '51 Manx was a little hair-raising at times; '52 had its moments, while '54 was a fight all the way towards a tail-end bronze replica.

I think, however, that it must be the 1950 Junior Clubman's TT which takes the honoured place. Not because it was my first race ever, but because it involved more people than just myself in headaches, heartaches and worries.

My machine was a B32 BSA, quite standard, with all the iron fittings and rigid rear end associated with the '49 version of this marque. It blew up shortly before practice started, and was only rebuilt just in time to receive the 'doubtful' approval of Mr. Anstice at the pre-practice weigh-in.

The training period was not unduly memorable – a slight seizure in the Quarry Bends through a retarded ignition lever and a carburettor base nut which went AWOL at the Bungalow one evening – that was about all that happened.

And then to that great day when we wheeled the

throng of other unfortunates, and I remember changing a plug and hurling the offending article at the feet of the unfortunate Rep. who happened to be standing alongside offering advice. Being a wise man, he picked up the plug, slipped it into his pocket, and disappeared into the crowd, muttering his opinions on the whole fiasco. I finally got moving, right at the back of the field and in a very sour mood.

Somewhere between Laurel Bank and Glen Helen the gear lever fell off. I know it was missing because I stopped at the hotel wondering why the cogs wouldn't swap around. A marshal asked me, quite pleasantly, if I had retired? In fact he phoned through to say that I was there and looked like staying. Whatever I looked like (and I could hazard a few guesses), I didn't say, and amidst much clutch slip and footing, the Beeza gained sufficient momentum to stagger over the top of Creg Wyllies' – still in 3rd gear and with little likelihood of getting out of it for the remainder of the race.

On the run into Ballaugh, a cow in a field took a notion and launched itself out into space, landing just ahead of my machine. Luckily it took a second notion and charged the opposite hedge. I informed the marshal that there was an interloper on the course, slipped the clutch and wafted onwards through the village, wondering what else could possibly happen.

Those who have raced in one gear will realise the mental strain involved – not so much on the rider as on the spectators. Accustomed as they were to rapid gear changes, sharp braking, and the howl of potent motors, the approach of Number 21 at a corner began to upset their calculations, and amazed and worried expressions appeared on their faces. At last I started to enjoy myself. Tramping down the Sulby Straight at a steady 78 mph and making no attempt to change gear sent the flagmen into a frenzy. Even the normally imperturbable Ned in Ramsey's Parliament Square became a trifle apprehensive – and so did I when I found the brakes fading!

The crowds at the Creg were full of sympathy the first time I coasted down from Kate's Cottage with the clutch out and the motor ticking over (I still treasure the memory of that stalwart clutch). The second time down they were suspicious, whilst the third lap produced shouts of "Get a move on", to which I duly and rather rudely responded.

I was too late to start a fourth and final lap. There were red flags all over the Glencrutchery Road, so that was that. Perhaps it was a good thing, for the process of circulating all on one's own, in one gear, tends to become monotonous.

I never did find that gear lever. Perhaps it still lies by the roadside, perhaps it doesn't. But wherever it rests, it may be assured that its sudden retirement from the racing scene produced a lot of worried looks in the Island that day.... and they weren't all on my face either!

Michael McGeagh gets the red flag at the end of the third lap

A D (Doug) Brown's Clubman's Stories
by Grace Brown

[Doug (Buster) Brown passed away on 1st August 2005. Later that year, a short letter appeared in the Christmas Newsletter of the Manx Grand Prix Riders Association "Out of the Mist", written by his widow Grace informing the Association of his passing. There was such a mix of emotions in that letter, obvious sadness at the loss, love for the man and pride in his achievements, and also a kind of gratitude to the Isle of Man and the races for giving him so much pleasure over the course of his lifetime. Through Keith Trubshaw and Jim Hunter at the MGPRA contact was made with Grace to ask permission for the letter to be reproduced here. To this she kindly agreed, and also was able to provide some additional recollections.]

"In 1948, Doug bought a second-hand 350 ohc Velocette KN, a 1929 model, and rebuilt it into a racing machine. He rode in his first race with it with little success, but had enjoyed the racing so much he rode in several races before the end of the year. That same year, with a group of like-minded friends he visited the Isle of Man for the first time to watch the racing. He was hooked! He loved the motorcycle racing, and could not wait to return to take part. There were five good and best friends who formed a 'syndicate' that bought a 350 International Norton, Doug Rose, Bill Hodge, Eddie Danks, Stan Tyack and Doug Brown. No-one could afford one on their own and they were all really interested in the Clubman's TT, so they clubbed together to buy the bike. They each contributed £50 as the bike had cost about £250. They all wanted to ride the bike but Doug Rose and Doug Brown had the necessary experience, and it was Doug Brown who won the draw for 'who should ride'. The bike was brought to Doug's home, Rockingham

A paddock shot of Buster Brown, 1950 Clubman

Station, and to the home-made workshop in the backyard. The syndicate came to view the Norton with great admiration and enthusiasm. It was the best motorcycle in the Club. Doug entered it in the 1949 Clubman's TT as had been agreed and planned.

All the syndicate members and their girlfriends, of the Corby Motor Cycle Club, travelled to the Isle of Man for the two Clubman's TT races that Doug and the Norton rode in. They had to go, to make sure Doug did not ill-treat the bike! They had formed themselves into a good humoured and busy team of timekeepers, mechanics, advisors and helpers.

At the finish of the race, number 93 Doug Brown had finished 20th and the Norton was covered in oil at the back end, all the Nortons were the same. There was a problem. The engine was sent to Geoff Monty and Allen Dudley-Ward engine tuners in London. They fixed the oil breather and tuned the engine. The next year it was the cleanest Norton in the race.

The syndicate could not sell the Norton as planned to recover their outlay, and it was stored in Doug's mothers' front room behind the piano, under a blanket! In 1950 Doug raised the money to buy out the other members, and again entered the Clubman's TT, riding number 87, where he made the fastest practice lap and finished in 3rd place, in the process winning a free entry into that year's Manx Grand Prix.

When Doug and all the friends went over to the Isle of Man for the races, they stayed with Mr. and Mrs. Stanley at the Rookery Hotel, Palace View Terrace, Douglas, just off the Promenade next to the Falcon Cliff Lift. Doug was the Stanley's first competitor-resident, and when they saw the Norton, Mr. Stanley, in a typical example of Manx welcome and hospitality, moved his beloved Lanchester to the very end and next to the wall of the very large garage at his home, and handed the rest of the garage to Doug, the Norton, and the team to use as a workshop for the tuning and repairs and safe storage of the Norton.

Doug cleaned and polished the bike every day. When asked why he was so fussy he said it was the best way to make sure that all the nuts and bolts and attachments were okay. He felt happier that way and was proved right on the race-day when the bike finished in perfect condition.

Bill Hodge was the pit-stop man as he was the most unflappable man they knew! One of the pit-stops was rehearsed by using Stan Tyack's 10-feet long hand knitted scarf he always wore wrapped around his neck. Bill just pulled on it and applied it to the tank, lifted up the filler cap, timed the 15 seconds, closed the filler and Doug was on his way. That left a very satisfied Bill and a gasping Stan recovering from being half-strangled.

Stan is the last surviving member of the syndicate, and he remembers a story about the fuel in the filler. They had measured the amount of fuel required for one lap and intended to leave just that amount in the filler to put in for the last lap. After the race had started, Bill Hodge, who was in the pit, drained the excess fuel into a can and stowed it out of the way. Unfortunately, he was spotted by a pit official who made him put it back in the filler. "No fuel except in the proper place" was the rule, so without a means to measure the proper amount, he carried a lot more fuel round that last lap than he needed. He never found out if it did slow him down, but always believed that it had!

Doug finished 13th in the 1950 Manx Grand Prix and received a much-coveted replica. He also rode in the 1951 and 1952 Manx Grand Prix and received finishers' plaques. Out of interest, his expenses recorded for the 1950 Clubman's were: Norton £188, entry £6.35, tyres and tubes £8.00, front guard £1.25, oil £0.65, petrol £3.00, repairs £0.30, spares £1.00, hotel £11.25, insurance £3.75, goggles £1.00, carburettor parts £1.00, engine tune £16.00, oilskins and gloves £0.75, fares £1.75.

His love of the Isle of Man, the motorcycle racing, and the people never faded. He visited every year at Manx Grand Prix time, and for the TT and Southern 100 whenever he could afford to. His last visit was in 2004. Doug made many friends in and on the Island, and was always ready with his good friend the late Doug Rose of Castletown to help out with mechanical skills and advice in the true tradition and spirit of the Manx Grand Prix.

These are good, true stories that have brought back a lot of super memories. And as Stan Tyack has said, it has been a joy to recall such happy memories.

We (wife Grace and children Ray and Sue, and their families) will always love and be proud of him, and have lovely, happy memories of our Manx holidays."

My 1000cc Clubman's Rides
by Alex Phillip

I didn't have much time to prepare for the 1949 Clubman's. After the withdrawal of J.A.F. Blight as a result of a family bereavement, the Secretary of the Vincent HRD Owners Club Alan Jackson, wrote to me. I still have his letter, dated 26th May that year, in which he wrote "If you would like to take his place and would be able to leave for the I.O.M. not later than June 4th, please wire me at once".

I jumped at the chance at racing in the Isle of Man, and duly packed my tackle on the back of the bike and on the appointed date rode the 330 miles to Liverpool. I can well recall that day, it rained every mile of the way. I enjoyed excellent hospitality at Alan Jackson's home in Bramhall, Cheshire, and caught the Isle of Man Steam Packet ship next day. I was a wee bit mortified to see my pride and joy being bundled into a sling and lifted off by crane at Douglas Harbour.

Accommodation was already laid on at the Irwell Hotel on Douglas Promenade, it was a great location where large numbers of bikes and riders regularly gathered. Mine host at the Irwell, a Mr. Griffiths, was a professional masseur and many of my hero works riders used to come for regular treatment, it was great to meet them first hand. The Irwell staff, mostly family, were quite exceptional, accommodating our ungodly morning starts.

My only knowledge of the Island circuit was reading the excellent pre-war publication 'A Record Lap at 91 mph' by Harold Daniell. The first morning of the International Senior practice found me spectating at the 'Highlander'. Dawn had just broken when the first riders were heard in the distance, seconds later I was witnessing the greatest spectacle a motorbike enthusiast could ever wish to see. The AJS Porcupine's of Les Graham, Bill Doran and Ted Frend, followed by Harold Daniell, Artie Bell and Jack Brett on the Nortons, Fergus Anderson on the works Guzzi, and Dickie Dale on the Benelli. I was so taken aback with their speed and performance the hair was literally bristling on my neck. My first reaction was 'I think it would have been better if I had stayed at home'. However that experience convinced me it was

possible to do 'reasonably fast here', and with that in mind during all the practice sessions, I found myself improving at the 'Highlander' with every lap.

During my first official practice session there was quite a lot of mist on the Mountain, even as far down as the Waterworks. I was obviously trying to put in a reasonable lap to ensure qualifying, the strange thing about racing is when you are riding you never seem to be going fast enough, yet when spectating the speeds seem phenomenal!

I managed the first lap as I thought slowly and safely, and thought I'd better get a 'wee bit of a move on' during lap two. That certainly proved my downfall as the mist had cleared at the Waterworks, I approached far too fast and probably on the wrong line as the bend tightens up rapidly, bike cranked hard over, footrest scraping the road, with the straw bales and stone wall looming up. I was fortunate to escape with a broken finger but that was nothing compared with my absolute horror of damaging my HRD which was always in immaculate condition and had never been dropped before.

Here was I, almost in tears with bent forks and buckled front wheel, and my pride and joy looking decidedly second-hand. I managed to restart the bike and wobbled my way back to the pits, convinced my TT days were over. Much to my surprise I was surrounded by some Vincent personnel, one none other than Phil Irving who clapped me on the back saying "Well done Jock, you put in the fastest lap tonight on your first lap". I said sadly "I'm afraid it could be my last lap". Phil said not to worry, he'd lend me the forks and wheel out of the works sidecar outfit which he had on the Island, so after a late night fixing the bike I was all set for morning practice with a broken finger sticking through a hole in my glove.

The rest of '49 practice went pretty well but best of all was the tremendous camaraderie amongst the riders of every class making the whole event an especially enjoyable experience. Unfortunately during the race itself, when lying second to Chris Horn, I ran out of fuel due to the no refuelling rule. Despite my

Speed personified: Alex Phillip storms through Barregarrow.

extreme disappointment, the great experience 'refuelled' my determination to return to the Island. During the practice and race the bike 'ran like a train' with nothing more than tyres, chains and tuning. After the race it was a busy time restoring the bike back into road legal trim ready for the long ride home.

During the winter for the first time I stripped the engine which was found to be in excellent condition. Crankcases were mirror-polished inside and out, flywheels checked for balance. Certain modifications were allowed as my bike was one of the very early models, from memory engine number F10/AB313. I opened up and polished the inlet ports to accept Black Shadow carbs, the works recommended fitting modified timing gears and also a very beneficial higher ratio bottom gear to improve acceleration out of slow corners. I fabricated new full length straight-through individual exhaust pipes after experimenting

to arrive at the precise length for maximum power in conjunction with different slides in each carburettor, also needle settings and main jets, the engine was just assembled with meticulous care.

The original girder forks were replaced with Shadow Girdraulics together with a hydraulic damper on the rear suspension. Front mudguard was lowered to minimum clearance on the tyre, this allowed better cooling to the front cylinder. All brackets and ancillary parts were set up so they fitted with absolutely no strain, all bolts simply slid through, to prevent any fatigue fractures. Another modification was to fit cast iron brake drums in lieu of steel drums. Every Bowden control cable was checked, all nipples re-soldered ensuring cables were splayed properly at each end. Duplicate cables were routed alongside the originals as a precautionary measure. All essential nuts were drilled and secured with tying wire. I made a special seat similar to the AJS 7R accident I took the train to Stevenage to collect my restored Vincent, which I rode the best part of 500 miles home – it performed like a rocket ship.

Due to our very limited finances disappearing and only £1 5 shillings per week income, sadly I was forced to advertise my bike for sale. The response was very good and the keenest of all was a Lt.-Colonel Jack Churchill who turned out to be one of absolutely outstanding real life characters. I have some copies of articles describing his wartime exploits, and they include some outstanding deeds of bravery and skill, and having landed on 'D-Day' at Arromanches, I can really appreciate his great acts of bravery. It was a real pleasure to meet him then and also much later in his retirement.

For the record, I returned to spectate at the TT, and whilst on the IoM Steam Packet Co. ship I wandered around the deck looking at the various magnificent machines as we neared Douglas, and could hardly believe my eyes when I spotted an HRD registration number YJ 9840. I stayed with the bike until the owner – none other than Jack Churchill himself, returned. We were obviously delighted to meet and he arranged with me to have a run around the circuit on my winning machine which proved extraordinarily enjoyable. The bike was in beautiful condition, Jack had gold leaf transfers on top of the fuel tank to the effect '1950 1000cc Winner and Fastest Lap at 81.00'.

By 1952 both my injuries and my finances had improved so I borrowed my brother's old 500 Manx Norton with plunger rear springing. I removed the single-knocker engine and slotted in a fairly good double-knocker and entered for the Manx Grand Prix.

The Philip team after the winning ride. L to R: Alex, father and mechanic/friend, Jim Blair

During practice my primary chain broke at Glentramman. The chain cut through my boot, it locked up the transmission and I had the father and mother of all slides before stopping safely. I had to go to Ramsey Cottage Hospital to get nine stitches in my heel which made the remainder of my practice fairly limited. During an early morning practice I approached a rider near Ramsey, and even though he was on an AJS 7R and I only had a rear view it was the unmistakable 'J. Alexander'. I followed him round the remainder of the circuit, it was particularly misty on the Mountain so I eased off and allowed 'J.A' to disappear into the gloom. Later that day I spoke to him and said "You were setting a cracking pace in the mist". "Yes", he said a little ruefully, "I came round the three left-handers on the approach to Windy Corner, the mist was particularly bad and I said to myself 'Am I past the warning boards?' and decided that I wasn't and kept it wound on. The next I knew I was flying past the marshal's hut heading for the hills and heather. My word", he said, "I blessed those 7R brakes!"

During the race I was going quite well until I felt my left leg getting cold! I glanced down and to my horror the lower seam of my fuel tank had split and petrol was dripping down my leg. At this time I was at the Guthrie Memorial and once clear I gripped the bottom of the tank firmly with my left hand and rode single-handed, changing gear without the clutch until I reached Signpost. By this time the petrol had reached my stitched heel, it was simply, absolute murder! Thankfully I managed to negotiate Bedstead and the Nook single-handed in 2nd gear, being forced to use the clutch at Governors Bridge, and finally spluttered along Glencrutchery Road to finish 12th with my tank empty but well inside the time for those wonderful silver replicas.

By 1953 I was fortunate to be loaned a Featherbed rolling chassis from that great Scottish tuner Joe Potts, who sponsored Bob McIntyre. I installed the double-knocker engine, had a fair amount of success in local races, then entered for the '53 Manx. I was going really well, lying around 5th or 6th when I was overtaking a back-marker on the approach to Ramsey Hairpin, unfortunately he moved over and pushed me off. Being a slow speed corner I was uninjured but handlebars and control levers were bent, including the footbrake lever. I had managed to keep the engine running, got back on board, and on the way up to the Waterworks I was frantically trying to get some of the levers into a workable position. I was obviously annoyed and desperately wanted to make up time, and quite surprisingly put in my fastest time on the last lap and managed to finish 12th, once more well inside replica time.

In early '54 my finances had improved to the extent that I bought a new 350cc Featherbed Norton from Joe Potts, complete with two-leading-shoe front brake, a luxury I never had the benefit of on my 500cc Nortons. I took delivery of my new 350 just before the Scottish Speed Championship final at Beveridge Park, Kirkaldy, a tight road circuit I really enjoyed, and 'ran-in' my new bike illegally on quiet country roads. I entered both 350 and 500 races and after a great tussle with Alastair King I finished 2nd in the 350 Championship event. The experience of the bike and super front brake made me decide to use it in the 500cc event on this tight, twisty short circuit. After another great dice I managed to win the 500 Championship on my 350 – which gave me immense satisfaction to beat a rider of Alastair King's stature on his 500.

I finally returned to the Island for the 1954 Manx, for the first time entered in both 350 and 500 races. The weather never seemed to be too kind at the Manx, but my every-day riding in all weathers gave me an advantage in wet and misty conditions. I finished 6th in the Junior and 5th in the Senior on the Nortons, and was the first genuine private owner to finish in both races without any form of sponsorship. In fact, when the race officials asked "Where are your mechanics" I just smiled and proceeded to strip my own engine for measurement. How times have changed.

1950 Clubman's Senior (cont.)

25	R. Yates, Norton	35.15	**33.57**	35.30	34.49	2 19 31.0	64.94
26	V. G. Hyland, Norton	35.32	34.23	36.16	**33.27**	2 19 38.0	64.91
27	J. Bollington, Triumph	32.39	33.05	**30.37**	44.03	2 20 24.0	64.51
28	L. C. Newcombe, Triumph	36.05	35.38	34.37	**34.26**	2 20 46.0	64.36
29	W. Kay, BSA	34.31	**34.23**	36.35	36.12	2 21 41.0	63.94
30	H. Wall, Triumph	32.06	**31.04**	31.21	47.58	2 22 29.0	63.58
31	R. F. Keen, Triumph	35.46	36.16	35.58	**34.53**	2 22 53.0	63.40
32	F. F. Parry, Triumph	36.12	37.51	**34.01**	34.54	2 22 58.0	63.37
33	W. Hillary, Triumph	**34.20**	38.36	34.59	35.07	2 23 02.0	63.34
34	A. Newstead, AJS	35.41	36.44	36.02	**34.53**	2 23 20.0	63.19
35	H. J. Ollerenshaw, Vincent	34.27	**32.44**	41.08	35.38	2 23 57.0	62.92
36	H. E. Gilbert, Triumph	**31.24**	34.36	33.24	46.32	2 25 56.0	62.07
	I. B. Wicksteed, Triumph	28.55	29.04	**28.29**	R		
	F. C. J. Collings, Triumph	37.22	**35.49**	36.37	R		
	C. Scott, Norton	34.01	**32.06**	47.32	R		
	A. S. Herbert, Norton	29.57	**29.29**	R			
	A. S. Avis, Triumph	32.40	**30.59**	R			
	P. J. Orton, Vincent HRD	32.12	**31.51**	R			
	G. R. A. James, Triumph	33.57	**33.08**	R			
	D. C. Millar, AJS	36.47	**35.38**	R			
	M. Hird, Triumph	**34.01**	43.01	R			
	J. Curphey, Triumph	**31.40**	48.11	R			
	H. Beck, Vincent HRD	**32.07**	60.32	R			
	H. J. D. Boynton, Norton	29.19	R				
	M. S. Featherstone, Triumph	30.02	R				
	J. E. Brookes, BSA	30.22	R				
	R. F. Austin, Triumph	31.59	R				
	"W. Workman", Triumph	32.38	R				
	A. J. Pollitt, Norton	R					
	D. A. Gadd, Vincent HRD	R					
	J. Fisher, Triumph	R					
	R. V. Hunt, Triumph	R					
	R. E. Paxton, Triumph	R					
	W. F. DeZylva, Triumph	R					
	R. K. Pilling, Triumph	Exc					

RIDER AND MACHINE	FIRST LAP POSITION	LAP POSITIONS 1950 CLUBMAN'S SENIOR		RIDER AND FINAL POSITION	MACHINE
I B WICKSTEED TRIUMPH	1			1	P H CARTER NORTON
H J BOYNTON NORTON	2			2	A HILL TRIUMPH
A S HERBERT NORTON	3			3	K DIXON NORTON
A HILL TRIUMPH	4			4	I K ARBER NORTON
M FEATHERSTONE TRIUMPH	5			5	R W KERR NORTON
J E BROOKES B.S.A.	6			6	F PASSMORE NORTON

Phil Featherston takes his T100 Triumph round Governors Bridge. He later changed allegiance to Velocette which he rode in the MCC Lands End Trial.

1950 Clubman's 1000 c.c.

1	A. Phillip, Vincent HRD	29.37	28.21	29.23	**27.57**	1 55 18.0	78.58
2	" J. Alexander", Vincent HRD	29.17	**28.21**	34.06	29.08.2	2 00 52.2	74.94
3	F. J. Young, Vincent HRD	32.05	31.05	31.55	**30.34.2**	2 05 39.4	72.08
4	G. Lund, Vincent HRD	31.28	**31.07**	32.34	31.08	2 06 17.0	71.74
5	L. Carr, Vincent HRD	32.10	**30.15**	34.11	31.04.6	2 07 40.6	70.94
6	J. D. O. Davis, Vincent HRD	32.41	32.02	32.07	**31.53.2**	2 08 43.2	70.39
7	F. Taylor, Vincent HRD	33.18	34.07	32.55	**32.25.2**	2 12 45.2	68.24
	C. Howkins, Vincent HRD	29.57	**29.14**	R			
	J. B. Netherton, Vincent HRD	R					
	R. F. Organ, Vincent HRD	R					
	C. W. G. Taylor, Vincent HRD	R					

LAP POSITIONS
1950 CLUBMAN'S 1000 CC

RIDER AND MACHINE	FIRST LAP POSITION			RIDER AND FINAL POSITION	MACHINE
"J ALEXANDER" VINCENT HRD	1			1	A PHILLIP VINCENT HRD
A PHILLIP VINCENT HRD	2			2	"J ALEXANDER" VINCENT HRD
C HOWKINS VINCENT HRD	3		R	3	F J YOUNG VINCENT HRD
G LUND VINCENT HRD	4			4	G LUND VINCENT HRD
F J YOUNG VINCENT HRD	5			5	L CARR VINCENT HRD
L CARR VINCENT HRD	6			6	J D O DAVIS VINCENT HRD

The long kick start arm needed to bring the Stevenage v-twin to life swings in the breeze as F J Young sweeps down Bray Hill.

1951

FOUR - TAKE AWAY TWO,
AND SO NEAR FOR TRIUMPH

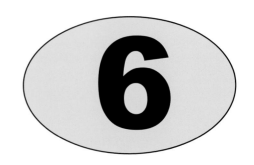

The classes and Regulations for the fifth Clubman's TT were essentially the same as for 1950, but the idea of a 'Clubman's Wednesday' had gone, with two of the four races moved to the Monday. This was to make room for the inclusion of the International 125cc race, a necessary addition to the programme to comply with FIM requirements. One minor change was the introduction of a lower capacity limit in each class, 240-250cc, 351-500cc and so on. However, two other seemingly minor changes combined to have a disproportionate effect on the races. First of these was the requirement for all machines to have been manufactured after 1st September 1945 (of the 17 entries in the 1950 Lightweight, something like half were on models which had not been produced since the war). The second was a change to the wording regarding the minimum number of entries required for a race for that class to be held. The change was from *"Unless twelve entries are received for any Race, that Race may not be held, or may be merged with another Race"*, to *"Unless twelve entries are received for any Race, that Race will not be held"*. By the closing date for entries, only eight had been received for the Lightweight, and as a consequence it was abandoned. Curiously though, the wording in the similar clause of the 1951 International Regulations remained as 'may not be held'. Similarly, at the close of entries the 1000cc race mustered eleven entries, so that too was scrubbed. It is hard to imagine that at the time of the framing of the new regulations, the likely implications hadn't occurred to anyone present.

So, for 1951, there would be just two Clubman's races, the Junior which was scheduled for the Monday afternoon following the International Junior, and the Senior for the Wednesday afternoon following the International Lightweight and Ultra-Lightweight.

Rider qualifications remained broadly similar to 1950, except that finishing in any three Manx Grand Prix's would bar a rider. Of greater significance was the introduction of minimum racing qualifications *"Any rider entered in the races for the first time must have had previous racing experience on a motorcycle with an engine capacity differing by not more than 150cc from that of the motorcycle entered in the Clubman's TT races, as follows:*

(a) He shall have competed and finished in two road races of not less than 10 miles each, promoted by the ACU, the Scottish ACU, or one of their affiliated Centres or clubs; or

(b) he shall have competed and finished in one road race and one race on an aerodrome circuit over a similar distance and similarly promoted, and shall be required to produce evidence of such experience".

'Pool' petrol was to be used, which was specified as having an octane rating between 70 and 75, and, as the Regulations stated *"likely to be nearer the lower rating than the higher"*. Entry fees had risen by 10 shillings to £6 17s, which included personal accident insurance premium, and payment for number plates and waistcoat.

Awards were as in previous years, £50.00 for the winner of each class down to £10.00 for 6th, and 25 free entries to the Manx Grand Prix (for the club) distributed between classes based on the number of starters in each race, and the Dunlop Trophy and replica for the rider improving on the lap record by the greatest amount, with replicas for those achieving similar in the other classes.

To qualify, every rider was to have completed three practice laps, one of which had to be in under 37 minutes for the Senior and 39 minutes for the Junior. Regulations regarding the machines were also almost unchanged, except that the battery carrier could be removed, and the rider could change the advance and retard control from automatic to manual and vice versa.

A welcome change was the re-introduction of the 15 minute warm-up prior to the start. Course alterations were few, and only a slight widening of the Quarter Bridge section changed the actual roads.

Entries and Practice

Numerically, total entries were similar to 1950, the Senior having grown from 66 to 82, the Junior shrinking from the maximum of 100 to 87. Machinery was dominated in the Senior class by Norton and Triumph, with 31 and 26 respectively, then BSA with 10, Matchless 7, AJS 4 and Vincent - HRD 3 (one entry was not taken up). In the Junior, BSA's successes led to their dominating the lists with 45, and Nortons were outnumbered by Douglas, 11 to 18, followed by AJS 5, Matchless 2, Royal Enfield 2, and Velocette 1 (three were not taken up).

A fair proportion of the Triumphs were Tiger 100's supplied with the new 'racing kit conversions', about whose performance rumours had been circulating

Manxman Billy Harding (Senior Norton) takes an unconventional line in an early morning practice session. Billy was son of Gilbert Harding, the Island's BSA dealer. For many of the Clubman races, BSA set up their spares and repair depot in the Harding workshop. Billy was also an accomplished trials and scrambles rider.

after factory testers had been 'spied' by enthusiasts putting the race-kitted models through their paces on roads across the Midlands. Certainly Triumph enthusiasts did not expect their marque to be beaten on speed that year. An innovation for 1951 was that the start line and the finish line were to be one and the same, not 70 yards separate as previous. Thus the circuit record time could be broken on a rider's first lap, and the new time would stand.

Names appearing in the Junior entry included Bernard Hargreaves, Derek Farrant, Derek Powell, Sam Seston, Frank Sheene (on one of the two Royal Enfields), John Clark, Eric Houseley, K.R.V. (Ken) James, and John Draper, the BSA works trials and scrambles star who had, a few weeks earlier, won the Scottish Six Days Trial, recording BSA's very first solo victory in that event. In the Senior list could be found Harry Plews, Sam Seston, Ivan Wicksteed, John Draper, the 1950 Lightweight winner Frank Fletcher, Alastair King, Jackie Wood, John Clark, Ivor Arber, Len Bolshaw, Willy Wilshere, and Frank Perris, later Suzuki teamster and manager of the John Player Norton team of the 1970's.

First practice for the clubmen was the early morning session on Saturday 26th May, and the weather conditions were calm and clear with dry roads, much improved from those which the 'International' competitors had endured the previous day. For the riders of some 1949 model Douglas machines, there was to be a scrutineering scare where the engines had been fitted with light alloy cylinder heads and fuel tanks. The ACU at first prevented them from practising as the parts were not catalogued within the required time period, and in fact they were only allowed to take part and race after the offending parts had been removed. *'The Motor Cycle'* dated 31st May contained the rather terse observation that *'Many felt, incidentally, that in such matters the ACU is not at all co-operative'*. An innovation for 1951 was that the first two practice laps times of any newcomer were not made public. The logic presumably was to reinforce the message for them not to go too fast until they had at least an idea of the course.

From the more experienced riders came some pretty quick laps, fastest of which was Wicksteed (Senior Triumph) with 28m 52s (78.44 mph), while

Ken James (Norton) was fastest Junior with 30m 14s (74.9 mph). Although the Triumph and the Norton headed the session in their respective classes, they were in fact the only examples of their marque in the top six, the rest of the Senior placings were taken by Nortons and Sam Seston's BSA, the Juniors comprised of three BSA's and two Douglas's. P. Shepley-Taylor (Senior Norton) approached Signpost far too fast, and by the time it became apparent that he couldn't make the corner he had passed the slip-road, and he hit the bank. He was able to pick up the fallen machine, re-start and continue. One rider to take a heavy fall was Henry Hall who suffered what was initially thought to be a fractured skull and other injuries when he came off his Junior BSA at Sulby Bridge. Later hospital reports on him were much better, the only breakage turning out to be a collar bone.

The storms returned for Sunday, but again cleared in time for Monday morning's second practice, leaving dry roads and calm conditions. A few miles of slightly reduced visibility over the Mountain was enough to lower the speeds slightly, and only F. O. Coleman (Senior BSA) got round in under the half-hour, with 29m 56s (75.65 mph), John Clark's Douglas putting in the fastest Junior lap at 31m 39s (71.54 mph). Spills were reported for R. Mawson (Senior Norton) at the Bungalow, A. Thomason (Junior BSA) at the Mountain Box, V. G. Hyland (Senior Norton) at Windy Corner, P. Beaney (Junior Norton) at the Cutting (Guthrie Memorial), and J. Bollington (Senior Triumph) at Brandish, none of which were serious in terms of rider injury, but their machinery was less fortunate, especially Bollington's Triumph which was extensively damaged. The *'TT Special'* reporter at Quarter Bridge was a little critical of John Draper on both laps, commenting on him as being *'jerky, as if still in a rough section of the Scottish!'* W. C. Hancock came off his Senior BSA at the Nook, but continued, as did J. B. Netherton (Senior Norton) who locked his back wheel approaching the same corner and ran into the bank.

The following day gave the clubmen an evening practice, held again in perfect conditions, and speeds were high, Wicksteed again fastest Senior with 27m 40s (81.84 mph) followed by Clark's Norton and

Coleman's BSA. Fastest Junior was Bernard Hargreaves (Douglas) putting in the only class lap in less than 30 minutes, with 29m 53s (75.77 mph). Throughout practice, his riding continued to draw favourable comment, particularly for his high cornering speed and flat-on-the-tank style. This being their only evening session, the 'Sulby Mile' timings and speeds were taken, and to the surprise of many it was not a Triumph which was the fastest, Wicksteed in fact second to Bob Ritchie's Norton, which 'clocked' 109.77 mph. Seventeen Seniors were timed at over the magic '100', four Triumphs, six Nortons, four BSA's, two Matchlesses and a Vincent. Two Juniors managed that feat, the BSA of G. R. Brown (104.07 mph) and the Norton of Ken James (100.00 mph). Compared to the 1950 results, when there had been a strong following wind, speeds in the Senior were down, but Brown's BSA was faster than any Junior the previous year. In fact, of the ten machines in that class over 95 mph, six were BSA's, two were Nortons, one an AJS and one a Douglas. Spills were reported for A.R. King (Senior Triumph), at Governors Bridge and who suffered concussion, R. Passmore (Senior Norton) who received leg abrasions when he contacted the wall at Cruickshank's leaving Ramsey, and A. E. Hilditch who was unhurt when he came off his Junior

A W Dobbs takes a rodeo ride past the Highlander on his Senior Matchless twin

Douglas at Kerrowmoar. Sadly, one fall was to have far more serious consequences. L. C. (Len) Bolshaw, who had finished 5th in the 1949 Lightweight Clubman's, ran off the road at the last left of the 32nd Milestone before Windy Corner and was killed instantly. A cattle dealer from Holmes Chapel in Cheshire, and entered by the Nantwich Club, he was a married man with three children.

More news of a distressing nature was to come through during the following (Wednesday) morning, with the death of John Simister following a roads-open accident on the Monday. Son of the well-known TT rider of the 1920's Tom Simister, the 26-year-old from Macclesfield had been a regular competitor in the Clubman's TT and in the Manx Grand Prix, and in 1951 was due to ride in the International TT. His brother Peter announced his withdrawal from the Junior race as a consequence, and the Macclesfield Club decided not to nominate a rider in his place. John had been travelling to lend assistance to his brother who had pulled over with machine trouble in the practice in the Ramsey area, when the accident, a collision with reserve Clubman rider Arthur Bint, happened.

Thursday morning's fourth session produced two outstanding performances in the Junior class, with reserve rider Brian Purslow (BSA) and Bernard Hargreaves both bettering the existing lap record, Purslow fastest with 29m 16s (77.61 mph). Wilf Harding's protégé, Manxman Jackie Wood (Norton) headed the Senior class with 28m 44s (78.80 mph). The only casualties of the morning were A. E. Clough (Senior BSA), who required medical assistance for a finger injury after a fall at the Nook, and J. F. Bean (Junior BSA) who also hurt a hand in a fall at Quarter Bridge, possibly as a result of a sticking throttle on his BSA. Certainly the engine did over-rev in the accident, whether as a result of impact with the road or beforehand, was not clear.

The 7th June issue of 'Motor Cycling' contained a paragraph comparing the abilities of different machines to take Ballaugh Bridge, entitled 'Frightening!'. *"Watchers at Ballaugh saw a wide variety of styles demonstrated and it is difficult to decide which got the bigger frights, some of the riders or some of the spectators. Here and there the professional touch could be seen, but, on the whole, it was a somewhat haphazard business. The BSA men seemed to adopt a peculiar style of their own, coming up to the bridge at an alarming angle and then suddenly jerking the machine upright. The resultant wobbles as the wheels touched down did not suggest that it was a very successful method. Unless handled with crass stupidity, the Nortons and Douglases took the section well, while the Matchless and AJS models, especially the twins, were really remarkable for their steadiness, straightening up effortlessly from the most painful-looking crash landings".*

Riders out for Friday morning's final practice continued to enjoy the ideal weather conditions, and Wicksteed again put in the fastest lap, although slightly down on Tuesday evening with 27m 56s (81.06 mph), while Purslow was again fastest Junior with 29m 53 (75.81 mph). Generally most treated this as a steady session, riders out to improve their course knowledge and bed in new chains and parts without risking too much. There was drama for race favourite Wicksteed when his Triumph's engine gave trouble, as did the similar machine of D. C. Birrell. N. Milburn (AJS) made painful contact with the bridge at Sulby, and A. J. Wellsted came off his Senior Triumph near Brandywell but was able to re-mount and complete the lap.

The Junior Race (Monday, 4th June)

Starters

	Rider	Club	Machine
1	G Arnold	Warrington & DMC	B.S.A.
2	D N Bradshaw	Burnley MC & LCC	Norton
3	B G Purslow	Worcester AC	B.S.A.
4	I G Matheson	Bradford Vagabonds MC	B.S.A.
5	D T Powell	Bournemouth MC	B.S.A.
6	G R Brown	Boston & DMC & LCC	B.S.A.
7	A Thomason	Warrington & DMC	B.S.A.
8	B J Hargreaves	Ribble Valley MC	Douglas
9	F T Gandy	Manor Motoring C	Douglas
10	G E Gibson	Loch Lomond MCC	B.S.A.
11	F Nowell	Preston & DMC	Norton
12	W S Corley	Mont' Christie MCC	B.S.A.
14	L J B R French	Norwood MC	Douglas
15	C H Fisher	Thornton Cleveleys MCC	B.S.A.
17	D Farrant	Tenterden & DMC & LCC	B.S.A.
19	J R Hill	Bristol MC & LCC	B.S.A.

21	K R E Prince	Loughborough & DMCC	B.S.A.
22	D K Morley	Ilkeston & DMC & LCC	B.S.A.
23	P Carr	Consett & DMC	Norton
24	P E Burns	Fleetwood MCC	B.S.A.
25	R D McCutcheon		
		Galloway & MC & CC	A.J.S.
26	S T Seston	Antelope MCC	B.S.A.
27	D E Bell	Hayes & DMCC	Matchless
28	J Blum	Blackpool MC & CC	Douglas
29	A McIvor	Manchester '17' MCC	Norton
30	C.M. Hopwood	Manchester '48th' MC	Velocette
31	A A Sanders	Coventry & Warks MC	B.S.A.
32	J Boulter	Gloucester & Cotswold MC	Douglas
33	A Hutchinson	East Lancs MC & LCC	B.S.A.
34	F Sheene	Sunbeam MCC	Royal Enfield
36	W C Reed	Stockport MCRC	Douglas
37	G Milner	Pickering & DMC	Douglas
38	K E Tully	East Grinstead & DMCC	A.J.S.
39	H Brown	Berwick & DMC	B.S.A.
40	B H King	Bedford Eagle MCC	B.S.A.
42	J F Bean	Stockton & DMC	B.S.A.
43	T W Brown	Newcastle & DMC	A.J.S.
45	A Newstead	Nottingham Tornado MC	A.J.S.
46	P R Sproat	Sunbury & DMC & LCC	Douglas
47	R H Holywell	Alnwick & DMC	Douglas
48	D G Chapman	South Reading MCC	Douglas
51	J R Clark	Waterlooville MCC	Douglas
52	P Beaney	Kenton & Kingsbury MCC	Norton
53	C E Robinson	Louth & DMCC	Douglas
54	E Houseley	Clay Cross & DMCC	B.S.A.
55	H A Nash	Solihull MCC	B.S.A.
56	E D Blackwell	Leamington Victory MCC	Douglas
57	J K Beckton	Middlesborough & DMC	B.S.A.
58	S Cooper	Banovallum MCC	Douglas
59	J H T Harris	Bridgnorth & DMC	B.S.A.
60	A W Akers	Dulwich & DMCC	B.S.A.
61	G J Draper	Cheltenham HG MC & LCC	Norton
62	B J Smith	Streatham & DMCC	B.S.A.
63	J Sutherland	St Helens & DAC	B.S.A.
64	S Graham	Lanarkshire MC & CC (Biggar)	
			B.S.A.
66	L H Stevenson	Haworth & DMC	B.S.A.
68	G E Collett	Southend & DMCC	B.S.A.
69	A C Turk	Hastings & DMCC	B.S.A.
70	B Duffy	Waterloo & DMC	Norton
71	P B Davis	Huddersfield MC	B.S.A.
72	K R V James	Ringwood MC & LCC	Norton

73	J Kirby	Farnham Royal MC & LCC	B.S.A.
74	C Bruce	Glasgow Lion MCC	Royal Enfield
76	D L Parris	Sanderstead & DM & MCC	Douglas
77	E H C Baker	Finedon Dolben MCC	B.S.A.
78	L Dunham	Thorne & DMC	A.J.S.
79	G E Read	Wolverhampton MC & CC	Norton
80	M R McGeagh	BMCRC	B.S.A.
81	J W Moore	Stocksbridge & DMC	B.S.A.
82	D Sheppard	Southall & DMCC	B.S.A.
83	L Carr	Seaton Delaval & DMC	B.S.A.
84	A E Hilditch	Crewe & S Cheshire MCC	Douglas
85	C E Staley	Salop MC	B.S.A.
86	G E Parry	Rhyl & DMC	B.S.A.
87	E J Goddard	High Peak MCC	B.S.A.

Of the original 87 entries, 76 made it to the weighing-in. Two were substitute riders for those originally named, with Brian Purslow replacing Lennox Broughton for the Worcester Auto Club, and Michael McGeagh replacing the injured Henry Hall for BMCRC. Non-starters announced were W. Fowler (BSA), G. Wright (BSA), S. Dawkins (BSA), B. C. Norwood (Douglas), P. Simister (BSA), H. Appleby (BSA), P. H. Waterman (Matchless), W. E. Golden (BSA), D. Spain (Norton), T. Baxter (BSA), T. C. J. Peacock (Douglas) and R. Brassington (Norton).

Start time was 2.30 pm, following the morning's Junior International, and weather conditions were almost perfect, the 'almost' meaning that so hot was the sun that there were warnings of patches of soft tar on parts of the course. In contrast to the chaotic scenes at the start of the previous year's races, almost all riders were able to kick-start and get away easily, thanks to the reinstated warm-up period. Despatched in groups of three at 15 second intervals, only G. Milner (Douglas), P. Beaney (Norton) and H. A. Nash experiencing delays, and even theirs were not too serious. First to reach Ballacraine was Brian Purslow, but there was an early concern for supporters of Ken James, whose 'clock' had not indicated him as having got that far. Amateur timing in Ramsey put Purslow and Hargreaves close on corrected time, but there had been a number of early retirements; Eric Houseley (BSA) at Union Mills with engine trouble, Brian Duffy (Norton) after a fall at Laurel Bank, rider ok, John Clark after suffering abrasions when his Douglas slid to earth entering Kirkmichael, J. Blum with a seized engine on his Douglas also in Kirkmichael, and S. Graham (BSA) who came off at Glen Helen and was treated in the hotel for minor injuries. Other first lap retirements for no specified reasons were A. A. Sanders (BSA), D. L. Parris (Douglas) and Frank Sheene (Royal Enfield). J. R. Hill took a spill from his BSA at Creg Willey's Hill, but was able to continue to the finish, even though his first lap took 57m 12s. First to complete the lap was Purslow, but Hargreaves had caught up on corrected time to lead him by 3 seconds, but both were pushed down the order by James. Not only had he not had trouble during the lap (the 'clock' had simply missed him), he had broken the lap record from a standing start by some 10 seconds.

First Lap Leaderboard

1	K.R.V. James (Norton)	29m 35s	(76.55 mph)
2	B. Hargreaves (Douglas)	29m 57s	(75.60 mph)
3	B. Purslow (BSA)	30m 00s	(75.60 mph)
4	A.C. Turk (BSA)	30m 05s	(75.28 mph)
5	D.T. Powell (BSA)	30m 12s	(74.98 mph)
6	(J.K. Beckton (BSA)	30m 22s	(74.57 mph)
6	(G. J. Draper (Norton)	30m 22s	(74.57 mph)

A number of riders pitted for fuel at the end of the first lap, including 4th place-man A. C. Turk, whose BSA tank was leaking. The first few miles of that second lap proved to be instrumental in setting the pattern of the race, as first the leader James was forced to stop by the 'Hawthorn' public house on the approach to Ballacraine to 'make adjustments', and then Hargreaves' superb ride on the Douglas came to an end, his 'clock' stopped at Kirkmichael. Other retirements included C. Bruce (Royal Enfield) at the pits, W. C. Reed (Douglas) after suffering cuts and abrasions in a fall at Hillberry, and C. E. Robinson (Douglas) at Governor's Bridge. Others to go out, but with un-specified problems, were F. T. Gandy (Douglas), F. Nowell (Norton), W. S. Corley (BSA), C. M. Hopwood (Velocette), G. Milner (Douglas), H. Brown (BSA), J. K. Beckton (BSA), L. Carr (BSA) and A. E. Hilditch (Douglas). At the end of the lap Purslow held a fairly comfortable lead as he went into the pits for fuel. With the delay to Turk and then the retirement of Derek Powell at the Guthrie Memorial with magneto trouble, John Draper moved up into 2nd place, and Derek Farrant into 3rd.

Second Lap Leaderboard

1	B. Purslow (BSA)	59m 40s	(75.89 mph)
2	G.J. Draper (Norton)	1h 0m 16s	(75.34 mph)
3	D. Farrant (BSA)	1h 0m 48s	(74.48 mph)
4	D.N. Bradshaw (Norton)	1h 0m 50s	(74.44 mph)
5	G.E. Read (Norton)	1h 0m 54s	(74.36 mph)
6	S.T. Seston (BSA)	1h 1m 8s	(74.07 mph)

Ken James was back in the race, but his second lap in 52m 15s had knocked him well down the order, and whatever the problem was, it returned on the fourth lap which took him over 46 minutes. He came into the pits to refuel but was obviously 'rattled' by his misfortune, and overshot his pit by quite a few yards, with the consequence of having then to manhandle the machine back the same distance. He eventually finished 41st and last, in a race for which he had been one of the clear favourites, and in which he had broken the lap record. Scant consolation, but no-one went faster during the race, and he retained the record lap. Purslow continued to lead on the roads and on corrected time, and a quick lap by Read lifted him above Draper into 2nd place, but Turk's race came to an end with a retirement at the Gooseneck. Others to drop out on that same lap were Ronnie McCutcheon (AJS), R. W. Holywell (Douglas), Don Chapman (Douglas) and Michael McGeagh (BSA).

Third Lap Leaderboard

1	B. Purslow (BSA)	1h 30m 3s	(75.43 mph)
2	G.E. Read (Norton)	1h 30m 44s	(74.86 mph)
3	G.J. Draper (Norton)	1h 31m 13s	(74.46 mph)
4	D.N. Bradshaw (Norton)	1h 31m 45s	(74.03 mph)
5	D. Farrant (BSA)	1h 31m 49s	(73.97 mph)
6	P.Carr (Norton)	1h 32m 41s	(73.28 mph)

Over forty seconds down on the leader starting the last lap, there was little possibility of Read challenging for the lead unless mechanical problems intervened. In fact, Read's final lap was over twenty seconds down on his third, and the 18-year-old Purslow ran out the winner with an increased margin.

In turn, any possibility of a challenge to his 2nd place from Draper effectively ended when the latter rider's Norton broke a footrest at that most inconvenient part of the circuit, flat out down Bray Hill. He was able to hold 3rd place to the end, but there were last lap retirements for G. R. Brown (BSA), A. Thomason (BSA), G. E. Gibson (BSA), J. Boulter (Douglas), P. R. Sproat (Douglas), A. W. Akers (BSA) and D. Sheppard (BSA), leaving 41 of the 76 starters to complete the course. Very sad news began to filter through after the race that D. L. Parris, of the Sanderstead club, who had received serious injuries in a first lap crash at the Bungalow, had succumbed to those injuries.

Finishing Order

1 B. Purslow (BSA)   2h 0m 10s   (75.36 mph)
2 G.E. Read (Norton)   2h 0m 56.6s   (74.87 mph)
3 G.J. Draper (Norton)   2h 1m 10.8s   (74.73 mph)
4 D.N. Bradshaw (Norton)   2h 1m 33.2s   (74.51 mph)
5 D. Farrant (BSA)   2h 1m 48.4s   (74.35 mph)
6 P.Carr (Norton)   2h 2m 42s   (73.81 mph)

Fastest Lap: K.R.V. James (1st lap) 29m 35s (76.55 mph) (Record)

The Senior Race (Wednesday, 6th June)

Starters

	Rider	Club	Machine
1	D J P Wilkins	Mendip Vale MC & LCC	Matchless
4	A J Hart	Chorley & DMC & LCC	Norton
5	R A Rowbottom		
		Scunthorpe MCC.	Matchless
6	J Ure	Glasgow Sporting MCC	B.S.A.
7	D R A James	Streatham & DMCC	Triumph
8	H Plews	Wakefield & DMSC	Norton
9	J C Duncan	Lincoln & DMC & LCC	Matchless
10	D A Gadd	Bristol MCC	Norton
11	B S Radford	Nottingham Tornado MC	Triumph
12	F G Perris	Chester MC	Triumph
14	P J Walsh	Solihull MCC	Triumph
15	C Scott	Sheffield MC & LCC	Norton
17	P J Price	Ashford Kent MC	Norton
18	J H Cooper	Bury & DMC	Norton
19	F C J Collings	West Bristol MC & LCC	Triumph
20	J L Kendall	Bayswater MCC	A.J.S.
21	S T Seston	Bourneville Works MC	B.S.A.
22	K D Waddington		
		Bradford & DMC	Triumph

The van reads 'F Purslow the Rider Agent'. So many riders had trade connections. Brian and brother Fron relax in the paddock after his winning ride with staff and members of the Worcester A.C.

23	I B Wicksteed	Royston & DMCC	Triumph	70	W Wilshere	Watford & DMC & LCC
24	J A Thomson	Croydon MC	A.J.S.	71	V G Hyland	North Hants MC

23 I B Wicksteed Royston & DMCC   Triumph
24 J A Thomson   Croydon MC   A.J.S.
25 J Havercroft   Hull MC Ltd   A.J.S.
26 P J Orton   Hinckley & DMC & LCC
                             Vincent H.R.D.
27 G N Camfield   X.H.G. Tiger MCC   Norton
28 J Wright   Wirral '100' MCC   B.S.A.
29 G J Draper   Cheltenham MC   Triumph
31 F Fletcher   West Leeds MC   Norton
32 K S Watling   South Leeds MC   Norton
33 J Cox   Manchester Eagle MC   Matchless
34 F Passmore   Hayes & DMCC   Norton
36 J J Wood   Peveril (IoM) MC & CC Norton
37 D C Birrell   Kircaldy & DMC   Triumph
38 R Yates   Mansfield & DMC & CC Norton
40 P Shepley-Taylor
                South Liverpool MC   Norton
42 J Bollington   Sheffield Ace MC   Triumph
43 T W Swarbrick Preston & DMC   B.S.A.
44 A C Whitehouse
                Castle Bromwich MC   Norton
45 W Howard   Warrington & DMC   Norton
47 'W Workman'   Rossendale & MC & LCC
                                   Triumph
48 R Kenworthy   Royton ATC MCC   Triumph
49 R L Jackson   Macclesfield MCC   Triumph
50 E G Oughton   West Leeds MC   Triumph
51 C Watson   North Lincs MC   Vincent
52 A S Avis   Border MC   Triumph
53 I K Arber   Wellingborough MCC   Norton
54 R F Keen   Sutton Coldfield & NBAC Norton
56 F O Coleman   Birmingham MCC   B.S.A.
57 W R Oldfield   Hyde MC   Triumph
58 J H Parker   Dunlop C & MCC   Norton
59 E J Bowman   Barham & DMC & LCC   Triumph
60 W C Hancock   Wallasey MC   B.S.A.
61 J B Netherton West Ham & DMC   Norton
62 E Pantlin   Hillingdon & Uxbridge MC Norton
63 A Bates   CSMA Ltd   B.S.A.
64 H J Ollerenshaw
                Hillsborough MCC   Vincent
65 R Mawson   Peveril (IoM) MC & CC Norton
66 A J Wellsted   Pathfinders & Derby MC Ltd
                                   Triumph
68 P J Pooley   Tollerton MCTC   Triumph
69 R F Austin   West Middlesex Amateur MCC
                                   Matchless

70 W Wilshere   Watford & DMC & LCC   Norton
71 V G Hyland   North Hants MC   Norton
72 W A Harding   Ramsey & DMC & LCC   Norton
73 L Newcombe   West Ealing MCC   Triumph
74 N Milburn   Darlington & DMC   A.J.S.
75 A W Dobbs   Bath & West of England MC
                                Matchless
76 J Hedley   Wood Green & DMC   Norton
77 A F J D Martin
                Leicester Query MC   Triumph
79 W J Keel   Folkestone MCC   Triumph
81 H Neal   Grasshopper (Romford) MCC
                                Norton
82 R Ritchie   Lanarkshire & DMC & CC Norton
83 G D Alcock   Northwich MC   Norton

The superb weather continued for the Senior, and again competitors were warned of the possibility of melting tar at Laurel Bank, the Ginger Hall area and at the Bedstead; the 'usual suspect' stretch of track for such warnings, between Birkin's Bend (Rhencullen) and Kirkmichael, was not mentioned. The public address announced thirteen non-starters, one of which was the last-minute withdrawal of the third-fastest man in practice, J. R. Clark (Norton). Others were A. C. R. Collins (Matchless), K. C. Brough (BSA), J. Ewer (BSA), R. J. Penney (Norton), A. R. King (Triumph), J. Mather (Norton), C. Howkins (BSA), 'T. Southward' (Triumph), A.R. Capner (Norton), T. Williams (Triumph), A. E. Clough (BSA) and of course the unfortunate L. C. Bolshaw. A change of rider representing the Bradford club brought in Bernard Hargreaves (Ariel twin) for K. D. Waddington (Triumph).

The combination of high ambient temperature and the reintroduction of the warm-up period made kickstarting less uncertain, and the only rider to experience a long delay in getting away was J. J. (Jackie) Wood (Norton). D. J. P Wilkins (Matchless) was the only one of the first group to make it to the start, and duly led on the road until joined by Bob Rowbottom (Matchless) and Harry Plews (Norton), the latter going well after losing a few seconds at the start. A. J. Wellsted had to change a plug at the foot of Bray Hill before getting the Triumph to pull as it should, while E. J. Bowman was forced out after a fall from his Triumph at Laurel Bank, possibly caught out by the melting tar, and was lucky to escape with just cuts and bruises. Rowbottom led Plews into Ramsey, followed by two higher-numbers, obviously going well, J. H. Cooper (Norton), and Ivan Wicksteed (Triumph). As the leaders approached the end of the first lap, Wicksteed was close behind Rowbottom on the road, but pulled into his pit to refuel, as did Cooper, whose stop was longer. Another late-number working his way through the field was Ivor Arber (Norton), and when the corrected times were posted he was seen to be in 2nd place, but some 50 seconds down on Wicksteed, even though the latter had lost some time slowing for the pit-stop. D. A. Gadd (Norton) approached

Governors Bridge far too fast but stayed aboard, narrowly missing the course marshal in the process, but then 'gave it a bit too much' in the Dip, and fell. He was unhurt, and was able to restart and re-join the race. F. Passmore was a retirement in Ramsey with what was described as 'chain trouble'.

First Lap Leaderboard

1	I. B. Wicksteed (Triumph)	27m 56s	(81.06 mph)
2	I. K. Arber (Norton)	28m 46s	(78.72 mph)
3	R. Ritchie (Norton)	28m 54s	(78.35 mph)
4	J. H. Cooper (Norton)	29m 9s	(77.68 mph)
5	G. J. Draper (Triumph)	29m 10s	(77.64 mph)
6	H. Plews (Norton)	29m 13s	(77.50 mph)

Just weeks after he won the Scottish Six Days trial on a BSA, John Draper took a brace of third places in the 1951 Clubman races. For the Junior, he rode an International Norton, in the Senior class he rode the Tiger 100, seen here at Cronk ny Mona.

131

Jack Wood at Quarter Bridge on his Senior Norton. His comments on the race were: "Dad bought the bike, I practiced, raced it, chap came round the evening after the race and bought the bike". The only true memory of the race was, being slightly short of stature, he had a problem kicking it into life. After the required three prods he wheeled it across to the pits, leant it against the pit wall where he was able to stand on the nearside footrest and give it a decent kick.

In later years, Jack rode for Geoff Duke, and was amongst the first riders to campaign the G50 Matchless. Later still Jack's expertise was put to good use as Clerk of the Course for the TT and the Manx Grand Prix for 17 years.

Wicksteed's first lap was dominant, and even though his speed was slower than Duke's of two years earlier, he was controlling the race. He maintained his advantage at nearly 50 seconds over 2nd place-man Arber round the second lap despite the fuel stop, but places were constantly changing in the following group who were all within seconds of each other, Cooper dropping down the order after his fuel stop. A. J. Hart and P. Shepley-Taylor (both Nortons) touched handlebars at Greeba and crashed, fortunately without serious injury, although both retired. Sam Seston (BSA) was initially reported as touring in to retire at Ramsey, but was able to effect a repair to whatever mechanical problem he had, eventually finishing 34th, his 'middle' two laps several minutes slower than his first and last. H. J. Ollerenshaw retired his Vincent Comet with engine trouble, while D. A. Gadd continued his eventful afternoon with another fall, this time when stopping

at the pits for fuel. Notwithstanding his adventures, he finished in a very creditable 20th place. A. Bates also hit trouble when stopping for fuel, as petrol from a split tank dropped onto a hot engine and his BSA Star Twin burst into flames. For a short while the pit area was in some state, as the fire brigade tackled the blaze while other riders pulled in to refuel, and marshals and officials tried to maintain some sort of order. Other second lap retirements were B. S. Radford (Triumph) near Brandywell, F. C. J. Collings (Triumph) at Governor's Bridge, 'W. Workman' (Triumph) at Hillberry, F. O. Coleman (BSA) unspecified, and W. Wilshere (Norton), the latter after a fall in Ramsey, resulting in a visit to the Cottage Hospital there with a cut nose.

Second Lap Leaderboard

1	I. B. Wicksteed (Triumph)	56m 8s	(80.67 mph)
2	I. K. Arber (Norton)	56m 55s	(79.56 mph)

3 H. Plews (Norton)	57m 28s	(78.80 mph)
4 R. Ritchie (Norton)	57m 34s	(78.66 mph)
5 G. J. Draper (Triumph)	57m 48s	(78.34 mph)
6 R. A. Rowbottom (Matchless)		
	58m 15s	(77.74 mph)

Wicksteed eased the pace slightly on the third lap, but actually increased his lead over Arber to a little over a minute as a result of the latter's fuel stop. D. C. Birrell (Triumph) overtook Rowbottom to take over the 6th leaderboard place, and Ritchie (an RAF serviceman stationed at nearby Jurby) moved up to 3rd, even though his lap was his slowest. The lap also brought a crop of retirements, although it has to be said that overall machine reliability in the Clubman's as a whole was good. In this particular race, 45 out of the 69 reached the finish, which was a better average than in the International races. None of which statistics of course helped those who did have to retire, including D. R. A. James (Triumph), B. J.

Hargreaves (Ariel), K. S. Watling (Norton), J Cocks (Matchless), W. Howard (Norton), E. G. Oughton (Triumph) D. J. P. Wilkins (Matchless) and A. J. Wellsted (Triumph).

Third Lap Leaderboard

1 I. B. Wicksteed (Triumph)	1h 24m 35s	(80.30 mph)
2 I. K. Arber (Norton)	1h 25m 38s	(79.32 mph)
3 R. Ritchie (Norton)	1h 26m 46s	(78.28 mph)
4 H. Plews (Norton)	1h 26m 58s	(78.10 mph)
5 G. J. Draper (Triumph)	1h 27m 3s	(78.02 mph)
6 D. C. Birrell (Triumph)	1h 28m 9s	(77.05 mph)

The fourth and final lap started with Ivan Wicksteed a minute ahead, an interval that seemed to be confirmed as he reached Ramsey, and, barring accident or mechanical trouble, it appeared to be a winning lead. The main interest centred on the continuing battle for the places, until unofficial timing over the Mountain showed that Arber was

Ivor Arber relaxes after his Senior Clubman win. Arber, a veteran of the R.A.F. took up bike racing after the war to recreate the buzz of flying Spitfires.

closing on the leader, and fast. For a rider to turn a one minute deficit into a 20-second advantage, and take a fall in the process, as Arber did at Governor's Bridge when only half-a-mile from the flag, was an almost impossible achievement. But achieve it he did, doubtless helped by Wicksteed slowing too much, and that in turn partly as a result of signals he was given at Ramsey. Arber's last lap, including the fall, was only 3.6 seconds slower than Wicksteed's first, and was actually one minute and 23 seconds faster than Wicksteed's final circuit. John Draper put in his fastest lap of the race on the last lap, 25 seconds faster than Ritchie or Plews, and leapfrogged both of them to claim 3rd place. There was the disappointment of last lap retirement for J. H. Cooper (Norton), who had been in 4th place on the opening lap, P. J. Orton (Vincent), J. B. Netherton (Norton), L. Newcombe (Triumph) and H. Neal (Norton).

Finishing Order

1 I. K. Arber (Norton)   1h 53m 37.6s (79.70 mph)
2 I. B. Wicksteed (Triumph) 1h 53m 57.6s (79.46 mph)
3 G. J. Draper (Triumph)   1h 55m 17s (78.56 mph)
4 R. Ritchie (Norton)   1h 55m 33.2s (78.37 mph)
5 H. Plews (Norton)   1h 55m 36.2s (78.34 mph)
6 J. J. Wood (Norton)   1h 56m 53s (77.53 mph)

Fastest Lap: I. B. Wicksteed (1st lap) 27m 56s (81.06 mph).

Dunlop Trophy: I. B. Wicksteed

Reflections

At the evening prize presentation, Ivan Wicksteed was sporting in the wake of his bitter disappointment, having thrown away a virtually certain victory, advising all *"I hope you will all see the moral of this, don't try to be so ruddy cunning"*. To sympathetic applause he added that his next biggest regret was that in finishing 2nd, he was barred from having another crack the following year. Ivor Arber blamed oil on the rear tyre for his spill, but said he had been very lucky to have kept the engine running when he fell. *'Motor Cycling'* had this to say on his victory *"Ivor Arber - who a few*

years ago won the Air Force Cross for successfully performing a task which many others would hesitate to undertake - has done the near-impossible for the second time in his life". Sadly the following year he was to lose his life in a crash at Hillberry in practice for the Manx Grand Prix, whilst riding one of Francis Beart's Nortons, when he apparently failed to react to the corner. Jeff Clew, in his biography of Francis Beart 'A Single Purpose', published by Haynes in 1978, said *"It was not until some time afterwards that he [Francis] learned that Arber had been involved in an aircraft accident whilst he was in the RAF and a doctor had forbidden him to drive a car, let alone a racing machine"*. Medical checks and safeguards, as well as the general perception of 'risk' in those days, were relatively simple and not very intrusive. Whatever the circumstances surrounding the accident it was a sad end to the life of a brave man and a rider of considerable ability.

1951 marked the half-way point in the eventual 'life' of the Clubman's, and after those five years differences in the manufacturer's approach to the event were becoming obvious. The commercial climate of the time was 'export-or-die', and there were shortages of certain motorcycles on the home market, particularly those models whose appeal was greatest to the American market, the very same sports machines that the Clubman's TT catered for. The publicity that a manufacturer could generate on the back of a TT win could not only help sales of the winning model, but all his range. It was not uncommon for an order for a new International Norton or Gold Star BSA not to be accepted unless it was the purchaser's intention to enter that year's Clubman's TT, or for those models to be delivered to dealers who were actively supporting the event, and who would 'arrange' that the purchaser was a suitable (and hopefully competitive) rider. Almost from the outset, the BSA management took an active interest in the event, and as well as personal attendances during practice and on race days for publicity, they also directed resources back in Small Heath toward achieving success. The sports 350 in the BSA catalogue of that time was the single-cylinder Gold Star, but the sports 500 was the A7 Star Twin, and the work of both the Development Shop and the Competition Shop reflected this policy. 'Fast but fragile' could be used to describe the twin's performances in Clubman's and open 500 class race set-up. Late in 1951, Roland Pike agreed to join BSA, beginning work in early 1952, and he states in the second (unpublished, but accessible on the internet) part of his autobiography dealing with the post-war years, that *"The primary aim of my Development Shop at BSA, apart from improving standard machines, was to win the Clubman's TT. For the Clubman's models we were always searching for a little more speed and of course reliability. This went hand-in-hand with American Class C AMA racing, since what was good for the Clubman's was also good for Class C"*. That then was the direction in which BSA were heading, even though the 500 Gold Star was to oust the A7 in the sporting role.

Slightly out of context perhaps, in that it partly refers to post-1951 races, the following extract from Roland's autobiography still makes for interesting reading. *"BSA did not dominate the early Clubman's TT races which were won mainly by Triumph and Norton. The 1949 race for 350cc was BSA's first victory. Many 350 BSA's were entered and few finished but that year the winner was a BSA. They had plunger rear suspension, leaked oil, and tended to blow oil out of the engine breather, to the extent of running low on oil, causing seizures etc. Nevertheless, the two or three best BSA's on that occasion did very well, competing against Velocette KSS models and 350 Norton Internationals.*

In 1952 BSA had hoped to provide a challenge in the 500cc Clubman's with an all alloy twin engine which would be promoted as the Gold Star Twin if successful. However the regulations prevented their use as it was not yet a production model. A few standard A7 500cc twins were built to Clubman's specifications, they pushed out 36-38 bhp which was about the same as the production Manx Norton, but in fact were unreliable and had a peaky performance, also did not handle as well as the single.

In 1953 it was the same story, the old CB 350 did quite well as did the 500cc singles of which there were two or three entered. The 500cc BSA twins were getting pretty unpopular by that time because when the crankshaft broke, they often destroyed the crankcases and fetched the rider off. If this happens at 100 mph it's pretty scary.

Triumphs were still going strong with their 500cc twins although they had their share of blown engines too. They won by the use of specially prepared hand-picked machines and some good riders".

Policy toward the Clubman's TT from the management of BSA's competitors is less easy to define. In the Junior class, Norton were unwilling (or financially unable) to develop the International, and the increasingly dated design was less and less competitive each year; AMC continued with the Model 16/G3, which achieved major successes in trials and scrambles at all levels including international, but was never catalogued as a Clubman's model, despite which individuals continued to score some excellent results; Velocette had been reduced from their 1948 success where they recorded 1st, 4th, 6th, 7th and 8th, to one machine entered and no finishers in 1951; Douglas brought enthusiasm with their 'Plus range, introduced in 1950, and based on the Mark III engine but with a tuned, high-compression motor. A lovely quote comes from Bob Currie in his book 'Great British Motorcycles of the Fifties', published by Hamlyn in 1980, *"In practice, it was said that all the 'Plus' engines were built to 90-Plus standard. If one reached 28 bhp on the brake (dynamometer) the bike was painted gold and called a 90-Plus; if it failed to reach this figure, the bike was painted maroon and termed an 80-Plus"*. There is no guaranteed correlation between enthusiasm and success in any sport, certainly not in the short term, and the 1951 results for Douglas show only 6th, 26th and 38th places, but encouragement should have been taken from the superb practice and early race performances of Clark and Hargreaves. Of the Triumph effort, there was none. The post-war twin cylinder Tiger 85, a high-performance 3T, never materialised, and the 3T itself refused to respond to any attempt at tuning. Bert Hopwood, in his definitive book 'Whatever Happened to the British Motorcycle Industry', published by Haynes/Foulis in 1981, says *"Small wonder that the machine, the 3T, never made the headlines, for it was quite impossible to coax a reasonable power figure from the engine in spite of all the wizardry that Freddie Clarke could muster. He finally gave up the struggle in despair"*. Of the other major manufacturer's, Ariel, Royal Enfield and Velocette, there was little or no factory involvement, and entries would appear to have been made by clubs and individuals who were enthusiastic for that particular 'marque'. From this it can be concluded that enthusiasm from the Board of Directors for the races was minimal, or they lacked confidence in their sports models to give a satisfactory account of themselves, or, most likely, that they could not afford to spend the money or divert the resources.

As would be expected, the attitudes of the manufacturer's toward the 500 class were pretty much the same, but the AMC story could have been so different. They seemed to have had the makings of an outstanding Clubman's racer in the G9, the machine from which the G45 was derived. Introduced at the 1948 London Earl's Court show, the twin-cylinder G9 engine differed in concept from the market-leading Triumph by having a centre bearing crankshaft, which enabled it, AMC claimed, *"..to operate to very high rpm while remaining rigid"*. *"Don't you believe it"* said Bob Currie in his companion publication 'Great British Motorcycles of the Sixties', also published by Hamlyn in 1980, *"Former Midland editor of 'Motor Cycling', Bernal Osborne, had one of the first Matchless twins - indeed the first one ever to be sold on the home market - as his staff machine, and the vibration was*

The ACU would have thrown the book at him for this! A bare-headed and retiring Charles Robinson freewheels his Douglas through Governors Bridge on his way to retiring his Douglas at the end of the first lap.

far worse than that of any Triumph, Ariel, BSA or Norton twin". The summer of 1951 saw the beefed-up G9 motor, a prototype G45, blow up spectacularly while being bench tested prior to that years Manx Grand Prix, and a steel crankshaft replaced the 'nodular' (spheroidal graphite) cast iron shaft for the rebuilt engine, with which Robin Sherry finished 4th in the race. (The following year it won the Senior MGP with Derek Farrant on board). It is easy to speculate on the possibilities of a G9 sports model using G45-developed parts and with some of the 7R/G45 cycle parts maybe available as options, as being able to offer a challenge to the venerable Nortons, possibly also the Triumphs. In fact Norton had their own twin by then, the Model 7 Dominator, introduced in late 1948/ early 1949. A glowing road test (as most were in those days) in 'The Motor Cycle' of 8th December 1949 included *"Acceleration through the gears when the entire engine performance was used was so zestful as to be almost breathtaking, and again gave the impression that this was an engine over 500cc"*. The 'give-away' came shortly after, with the mean maximum speed, the rider right down to it, quoted as being 92 mph, which compared unfavourably with Ritchie's Clubman's 'Inter' which was timed along the Sulby Straight at 109.77 mph. Ten years later, in the International Senior TT of 1961, the Dominator was to have its finest hour, when the 'Domiracer' derivative finished 3rd behind the Manxes of Hailwood and McIntyre, ridden by the great Tom Phillis.

Bert Hopwood was at Norton from 1947 to 1949, and in another quote from his book on those Norton days, he shows his pragmatic, finance-based view of racing: *"The production motorcycles on sale to the public bore no resemblance, of course, to the works racing machines, a handful of which were made each year. Yet such had been the company's racing successes, over a period of many years, that the rough, noisy and leaky production models were sold at the rate of just under 200 per week, to a long suffering, and slowly diminishing clientele.*

I was horrified to find that, for more years than most could remember, the company's design activity had been of the order of 90% racing and 10% product activity, so it is not surprising that the range of motorcycles on offer to the public had remained unchanged for many years while the company cavorted on the race track. I was hoping that this would soon be put into better perspective but I was to be disappointed,.... The Managing Director did not realise, until too late, that it was commercial suicide to have racing as a first priority".

1951 was the year that the Triumph Motor Cycle Co. was bought by BSA, although for a few years the new owners showed no intention of interfering with Meriden. BSA policy toward the Clubman's races has been described, but that of Triumph is less straightforward. They had won the Lightweight in 1947, and been well in the running in subsequent years. They didn't have a 350, but their 500 was fully competitive. Bert Hopwood again, from his time at Triumph after leaving Norton, *"As time went on and Triumph machines gained a greater reputation from successes in races and competitive events, [Edward] Turner would never listen to the many persuasive voices urging him to enter and support Grand Prix events such as the TT races. I feel now, as I did then, that this policy was absolutely right. Our strength and reputation lay with the many sporting Triumph owners who themselves entered and were successful in various competitive events throughout the world. This gave the product the publicity it needed and underlined its reliability, without having the problem of works supported race teams and their management. Furthermore, it left us free of the extreme demands which such projects would have made on the cream of our technical staff, to the possible detriment of the production programme".* Whilst the quote is primarily referring to Triumph involvement in the International TT and Grand Prix races, the sentence *"Our strength and reputation lay with the many sporting Triumph owners who themselves entered and were successful in various competitive events throughout the world"* is intriguing. It is difficult to imagine that in saying this he was somehow excluding Triumph performances in the Clubman's TT, but look elsewhere in his book for any reference to the Clubman's TT from his postwar spells not only at Triumph, but at Norton, AMC and BSA, and you will be disappointed. It apparently held little interest for him, and must have been viewed as having little use in terms of publicity, or

product development.

The confused picture of how the management at Triumph viewed development of its sports models is further illustrated by this quote, again from Bert Hopwood *"Freddie Clarke was a superb rider and he spent much time riding the enclosed version of the New Imperial in all weathers, making test after test with many modifications.....*

He had gone through many changes to steering angle and wheel trail and several other variations, which had transformed the handling ability of the motorcycle to such a degree that he felt that the Speed Twin and Tiger 100 machines, now being produced in substantial quantities, would benefit from a similar development programme.

It will be known to most Triumph enthusiasts of that era that our machines were far from outstanding in handling characteristics and indeed I had witnessed Freddie developing a lock to lock steering wobble a few weeks previously, while riding a very fast Tiger 100 machine. This was an unforgettable experience, with the handlebars of the motorcycle out of control, making loud clanging noises as they went from left to right lock in rapid succession.

I am sure this experience spurred on a programme of improved stability for the Triumph range of products but Turner would have none of it. Although he must have been aware of this shortcoming in an otherwise very satisfactory product range, he would never admit that the changes were necessary. The facts were that he was a fine rider himself and never got into any trouble but Clarke was also a very fine rider, and in addition, was capable of riding much faster than the boss.

Freddie so transformed the Triumph test machines with modifications to steering angle, engine position and trail that every tester and many others were agreed that the changes were a must and should be put into production with all urgency. But this was not to be, for Turner went near berserk when this was suggested. He had never found anything wrong and he ruled a no-change policy. It was a strange situation for a company to be producing motorcycles which were a little dangerous under certain conditions, with our own testers admitting the fault and the riding public knowing and accepting the fault purely because of the satisfaction they had with

P. J. Orton, Vincent	32.31	31.41	**31.07**	R
J. B. Netherton, Norton	**32.04**	32.06	40.10	R
L. Newcombe, Triumph	**32.25**	33.28	47.48	R
H. Neal, Norton	32.58	**31.50**	36.09	R
D. J. P. Wilkins, Matchless	30.32	**30.18**	R	
D. R. A. James, Triumph	32.42	**31.39**	R	
B. J. Hargreaves, Ariel	**31.03**	51.28	R	
K. S. Watling, Norton	**33.30**	47.39	R	
J. Cocks, Matchless	33.34	**30.04**	R	
W. Howard, Norton	**31.41**	31.52	R	
E. G. Oughton, Triumph	**31.02**	31.44	R	
A. Bates, BSA	31.40	**31.20**	R	
A. J. Wellsted, Triumph	**39.28**	42.31	R	
A. J. Hart, Norton	34.12	R		
B. S. Radford, Triumph	34.50	R		
F. C. J. Collings, Triumph	32.11	R		
P. Shepley-Taylor, Norton	31.38	R		
"W. Workman", Triumph	31.48	R		
F. O. Coleman, BSA	30.02	R		
H. J. Ollerenshaw, Vincent	31.04	R		
W. Wilshere, Norton	31.05	R		
F. Passmore, Norton	R			
E. J. Bowman, Triumph	R			

LAP POSITIONS

1951 CLUBMAN'S SENIOR

RIDER AND MACHINE	FIRST LAP POSITION		RIDER AND FINAL POSITION	MACHINE
I B WICKSTEED TRIUMPH	1		1	I K ARBER NORTON
I K ARBER NORTON	2		2	I B WICKSTEED TRIUMPH
R RITCHIE NORTON	3		3	G J DRAPER TRIUMPH
J H COOPER NORTON	4		4	R RITCHIE NORTON
G J DRAPER TRIUMPH	5		5	H PLEWS NORTON
H PLEWS NORTON	6		6	J J WOOD NORTON

1952

A WIN FOR TRIUMPH AT LAST, AND AN ISLAND DEBUT FOR 'BOB MAC'

There seems to have been little attempt to rally support for a return of either Lightweight or 1000cc races for 1952, and the format of race week mirrored 1951, with the Junior Clubman's on the Monday afternoon following the International Junior, and the Senior following the International Lightweight and Ultra-Lightweight on Wednesday afternoon. Pride of place of course went to the International Senior, which had Friday to itself.

Freddie Frith had been invited to make an inspection of the course over the close season, and a number of changes to the course had resulted, most notably on the Mountain section. At the Mountain Box, Stonebreakers Hut (Black Hut), Bungalow, Brandywell, 32nd and the section from Windy Corner through the 33rd and down to Keppel Gate, the wire fencing had been moved well back, and at the verge in places (the Bungalow, Brandywell, 32nd and 33rd) replaced by light wooden posts with a similar wooden 'rail' across the top. The rail and posts had been painted yellow to assist rider's navigation in mist or fog, and behind the posts run-off spaces had been cleared. The riders had found out that posts on their own did not sufficiently identify where the verge lay, when viewed against the skyline. Further down the Mountain, a red warning line had been painted across the road on the approach to Brandish Corner. Other improvements back at the Grandstand consisted of the creation of additional seating areas, and below the stand three wooden huts had been erected, a rider's washroom, an ambulance room, and a Scrutineer's headquarters. Hardly coming under the heading of 'course improvements', but resulting from resurfacing over the Mountain, was an abrupt change in road surface exiting the Dip at

Governor's Bridge. According to 'The Motor Cycle', the so-called non-skid surface all the way over the Mountain was maintained by the Manx Highway and Transport Board, while the Glencrutchery Road was the responsibility of Douglas Corporation. In a later issue, reporting practice week, and as if to illustrate the unpredictable grip the transition caused, it gave the examples of Clubman G. Arnold losing his BSA at that point when the road was wet, and of International competitor Tony McAlpine doing the same in the dry. Maybe the action of the throttle hand was the more likely link between the spills!

For those who were going to the Island, return ferry charges for a solo motorcycle were 26 shillings and 3 pence (26s 3d, about £1.31), 58s 3d for an outfit, both including crane charges, which in previous years had been charged separately. Petrol tanks of motorcycles had to be drained before embarking, for which the RAC charged 1s (although members were relieved of their petrol free-of-charge). Once on the Island, riders had to obtain

First Island appearance for a man who gained fame (infamy?) on three wheels. Owen Greenwood takes Quarter Bridge.

143

(Road Tax) Exemption Registration Certificates, and Temporary Driver's Licences issued by the Manx authorities either at a kiosk on the arrivals pier, or from the offices of the Highway and Transport Board. Fees were 2s 6d for a solo or outfit, 5s for a car, and then 1s for the driving licence. Passenger return fares on the ferry were 30s third class and 40s first class (there was no second class), while day excursions from Liverpool and Fleetwood were 15s third class and 19s first class. For the affluent, return air fares were £10 10s from London, £4 14s from Liverpool, £4 16s from Manchester and £3 7s from Belfast.

For those who were not able to go, the BBC Light Programme included live race coverage and results summaries not only for the International events, but also gave good coverage to the Clubman's races. To further assist visitors, the ACU published a new-style programme which for the first time covered all the races instead of a separate programme for each race day, and included a separate score card booklet and course map, features and photographs, and instructions to spectators on how to reach some of the more remote parts of the course. And all for the price of 2s 6d.

According to the published Regulations, competitors for the Clubman's would be supplied with 70-75 octane (Pool) petrol, whereas the International competitors would get 75-80, as in 1951. For some reason the *'TT Special'* misinterpreted an announcement on fuel and reported that all would receive the higher-octane fuel, and had to issue a retraction in the Monday issue under the heading 'Clanger'.

Entries and Practice

The Junior class was back to being over-subscribed, with 102 entries and 3 reserves. Two non-starters were announced before the start of practice, B. Norwood (Douglas) and A. G. Carr (AJS), and P. Pickerden and G. Bell (BSA) failed to provide evidence of previous race qualification and were excluded. Entry numbers were also up in the Senior class, 94 having been accepted, one of which fell foul of the same qualification requirements, T. F. Watson (Norton). These withdrawals immediately opened the way for Reserve 'A', which was P. Minion (Senior Norton) and Reserve 'B' D. W. G. Luke (Junior BSA), to take part in the races. Three consecutive successes in the Junior class, with Harold Clark, Brian Jackson and Brian Purslow, had enhanced the popularity of the 'Goldie' such that their contribution to the entry had risen from 45 in 1951, to 74. Norton slightly increased their number, from 11 to 14, and there were 4 AJS, 3 Matchless and 2 Royal Enfields. The real losers in the popularity stakes were Douglas, down from 18 to 5. The choice of machinery in the Senior class was broadly similar to 1951, with 39 from Norton, 30 from Triumph, 15 from BSA, 7 from Matchless and 2 from Vincent. Amongst the Junior riders were Bernard Hargreaves (one of the Douglas runners), Sam Seston, Derek Ennett, Eric Houseley, Derek Powell, K. V. R. (Ken) James, Harry Plews, Owen Greenwood (later a top-line sidecar driver and creator of the infamous Greenwood-Mini three-wheeler which was to cause such controversy in the 1960's), Bob Ritchie, Frank Sheene, Harry Voice and, given a late starting number (76), one Robert McGregor McIntyre. A similar

Frank Perris, another TT course debutee for 1952 later went on to become a Suzuki works rider, a Triumph Tiger 100 is a very different animal to the multi-speed Suzuki two-strokes

glance down the Senior line-up finds Willy Wilshere, Eric Houseley, Derek Farrant, John Clark, Jack Bottomley, Bernard Hargreaves, Frank Fox, Frank Perris, Derek Powell, Roy Ingram (later a TT and Continental Circus regular), Derek Ennett, Harry Plews, Eric Cheers, Bob Ritchie, Sam Seston, Louis Carr, Ken James, and Arthur Wellsted. Also listed, on a Senior Triumph, is David Tye, emulating what his BSA trials and scrambles team-mate John Draper had done the previous year.

An initial cause for concern for all competitors came from a quite unexpected source, the deposition of large amounts of rubber on the track in the middle of the high-speed left-hand sweep at Cronk-ny-Mona by sports cars practicing for the BRDC British Empire Trophy. The actual race, which was to run on the Thursday afternoon after the first International TT practice that morning, would put more rubber down in the same place. The course followed by the sports cars was similar to the first part of what was later to become the Clypse course, using the TT Grandstand area but turning right at Parkfield (St. Ninians crossroads), right at Willaston crossroads, and re-joining the TT course at Cronk-ny-Mona, where it turned right, thence via Signpost and Onchan back to the Glencrutchery Road. The Internationals had three practice sessions to cope with the hazard, the clubmen one, before the authorities responded by the commendably no-nonsense approach of re-surfacing the whole area on the Saturday after the car race. One of the competitors in the sports car race that year, driving an Aston-Martin, was a relative newcomer to racing on four wheels, Geoff Duke.

The first practice for the clubmen was on the morning of Saturday 31st May, and it was back to the traditional weather for Clubman's practice, foul! A total of 138 riders braved the elements, but no-one put in a lap anywhere near the half hour. Fastest was Harry Plews on his Senior Norton with 30m 51s (73.39 mph), Eric Houseley (BSA) fastest Junior with 32m 1s (70.72 mph). In reporting the practice sessions, *The Motor Cycle* of 5th June had a slightly different 'angle' on the weather *"Conditions could not have been better for the first Clubman's practice period last Saturday morning. Rain poured down steadily, and the wet roads made newcomers to*

the course duly cautious and forced them to take real note of its hazards. Two years ago the first three Clubman's practice periods were held over dry roads in good weather; then came a wet practice, and the ditches were littered with the machines of the over-confident". Whilst the comment contained some logic, it was not a view that many riders would have shared. *'Motor Cycling'* reported the rather strange fact that although the usual scene of misjudged approach speed for the clubmen was Signpost, this year there were precisely none in the opening session, but at the very next corner, Bedstead, just half-a-mile further on, *"no fewer than 14 were glad to find the gate open"*. Although the road has now been widened considerably at that point, and the wall and gate into the fields long gone, anyone repeating the performance of those 14 riders today would find themselves arriving at speed on the doorstep of one of the rather up-market suburban detached residences that now occupy the area. Two minor spills occurred a short distance further on, at Governors Bridge, G. Arnold requiring hospital treatment for ankle injuries when he hit the wall at the hairpin, and A.C. Peet who came off in the Dip, but re-mounted and continued. Both were riding Junior BSA's. R. Ellis had a fall at Kerrowmooar and escaped with minor injuries, although his Senior BSA was not so lucky and was extensively damaged.

As in previous years, the first two lap times put in by newcomers were not recorded. *'The 'TT Special'* reporter at Quarter Bridge commented *"R. McIntyre (BSA) went very close to the sandbags and turned toward Castletown, rejoining the course a few seconds later"*.

It just wouldn't have been the Clubman's without a scrutineering 'crisis', and this is how *'Motor Cycling'* reported the 1952 issue. *"So far the Clubman's scrutineering has passed off with comparative passivity; at any rate, no-one has actually shot Vic Anstice although some heat has been generated by his concern over short, clipped-to-the-fork-member-type handlebars. Since the Regulations say that controls may be modified to suit individual preferences and that handlebars may be of any shape or type, the subject provided much scope for a really hearty banging-on-the-bar-counter argument"*. Thus came into being another part of the

'Clubman's standard equipment', the clip-on handlebar, later to become 'coffee-bar standard equipment'.

The second practice was on the Monday morning, and the 162 riders were greeted by a cold wind, but the roads were mainly dry, just some patches of damp between Kirkmichael and Ramsey. Speeds were naturally up on the wet Saturday, and David Tye was fastest on his Senior Triumph with 28m 49s (78.56 mph), J.R. Clark fastest Junior with 29m 48s (75.98 mph). Spills were reported for E. Baxter (BSA) who was fortunate to avoid serious injury in a fall at Handley's Corner, B.W. Lack (Matchless) who was taken to hospital with suspected rib injuries and shock after coming off at the Nook, and F.C.J. Collings, who was taken to Ramsey Cottage Hospital with minor injuries after coming off his Norton between Waterworks Corner and the Gooseneck. R.F. Organ dropped his Junior BSA at Laurel Bank and sustained finger injuries, F.C. Pusey coming to grief at the same corner but without injury. Bob Ritchie made marshals, reporters and spectators on Bray Hill pay attention when his Norton ran into the gutter at the top and *"got into the mother of all wobbles, a real tank-slapper which lasted for about 200 yards; when he took the bottom bend he was still behaving like a bit of twisted elastic when released".* Seen in the timekeepers box later, he said he just couldn't do anything about it! The *'TT Special'* report of the second practice session tells of McIntyre's BSA being stranded *"near Brandish, where he had hit the bank with a footrest, but that rider was seen later in the Cadbury tent enjoying a cuppa".*

The third practice was the evening session on Tuesday, and the sunny but breezy conditions attracted 170 riders, who took part in a 'practice-start', setting off in groups of three, using the kick-starter. With the large number of riders out, the officials shortened the interval to 15 seconds halfway through the field. Writing in *'Motor Cycling'* Bob Holliday had the following comment on the 'dress-rehearsal', *"To me it demonstrated that an early number, and consequently a warm engine, is a distinct advantage, but I am still unconvinced that the grandstand spectacle of men hacking at reluctant motors is good publicity. I think the conventional run-and-bump start is a much smoother and prettier way of beginning a race. If kick-starters must be fitted to production machines – and surely they should – could not their efficacy be demonstrated to the scrutineers before the race starts; for example, on the commencement of the warming-up period".* Eric Houseley (BSA) set the fastest Junior lap at 29m 15s (77.41 mph), and the fastest Senior went to a new name to the top of the practice leaderboard, R.W.C. Kerr (Triumph), who lapped in 27m 43s (81.69 mph). The traditional timed-mile speed check on the evening session, run by the 'TT Special', had re-located from Sulby to the Mountain mile, because, according to the paper itself, *"today's lovely weather tempted us up the Mountain".* The timed section was a full bore run, slightly uphill, between the 27.5 mile and the 28.5 mile points, but directly into the stiff breeze which would have knocked off a few mph from everyone. Triumph's recorded the fastest three times, Kerr, Hargreaves and Houseley on board, Kerr's 113.23 almost 5 mph faster than the fastest BSA (John Wright in 4th place) and almost 8 mph quicker than the fastest Norton, J.H. Cooper in 7th. The Juniors struggled a little more against the gradient and headwind, only McIntyre's BSA beating the magic 'ton'. He was followed by a solid block of ten other BSA's before the fastest other-make, the Norton of P. Beaney with 94.60 mph. One reason for the decline in numbers of the Douglas was shown by the 'Mountain Mile' speed check, with the fastest 'Duggie' not living up to its Plus-90 tag, A.L. Burton registering 88.68 mph. Reports from around the course emphasized that the general standard of riding was very good indeed, but there were the almost inevitable spills around the course. R.A.D. Mawson (Senior Norton) hit the wall at Laurel Bank and was taken to Nobles Hospital with shock and bruising, D. Peacock (Junior BSA) came off at the Waterworks and was taken to the Cottage Hospital suffering a broken jaw and a lost tooth, while A. Jowett fell near the Guthrie Memorial and was treated for cuts and abrasions. Other minor falls were reported for H.D.S. Curzon and W.R. Smith (both Junior BSA's, and both at Braddan), H.R. Collier (Junior BSA) at Brandish, John Wright (Senior BSA) at Birkin's Bend (Rhencullen), and Derek Farrant dropped his Senior Norton at Governor's Bridge.

The next practice, on Thursday morning, was a wet and windy affair. Light rain as the competitors assembled turned into a downpour as the first riders were sent on their way. Added to the rain was poor visibility, over the Mountain it was at best 35 yards, and down to 10 yards in places. Eric Cheers was another new name to top a practice leaderboard, as Nortons headed both classes in the dreadful conditions, setting 31m 43s (71.31 mph) on his 500, while Harry Plews set the fastest Junior with 34m 02s (66.53 mph). A.N. Robinson (Junior BSA) misjudged the approach to Ballaugh and hit the wall beyond the bridge. He was taken to the Cottage hospital where his broken left collar bone was treated and re-set in double-quick time, and he was discharged before the close of practice! H. J. Cronan fell at Creg-ny-Baa but was unhurt, and was able to re-start his Triumph and complete the lap. 118 riders braved the conditions, and the 'TT Special' reporter (who set out to observe proceedings at Ballaugh, but was so wet by the time he got to Laurel Bank that he stayed there), 'awarded' every one of them a *"solid gold medal"* and called them *"ruddy heroes"*. His counterpart on the other side of the circuit at Governor's Bridge was moved to describe the rain *"It would not be true to say that it rained steadily all the time. It rained all the time, but it indulged in bursts of acceleration in second and third, so to speak, when it deluged".*

By contrast, the clubmen had perfect weather for their last practice, on Friday morning, and to enjoy the conditions 166 of them turned out to put in a total of 329 laps, a distance of 12,000 miles. K.V.R. (Ken) James was outstanding, putting in four laps, two on each of his Nortons. He was fastest in the Senior class, 5 seconds faster than Duke's record with 26m 58s (83.96 mph), and then on the 350 was one of four riders who beat his own record set the previous year, although McIntyre was 2 seconds faster with 28m 55s (78.30 mph). The other two were Ron Jones (BSA) and, getting a Matchless round at remarkable speed, Manxman Derek Ennett. In the Senior class the fastest Triumph was David Tye with 27m 12s (83.24 mph). Two accidents were reported, D. Webb came off his Senior Triumph at Keppel Gate and received rib injuries, and R.H. Smith crashed his Junior BSA at the Gooseneck, but escaped with a cut chin. Webb was taken to Nobles, Smith returned to the start in style, as passenger in the rescue car. G.D. Alcock almost succeeded in making the total three when he rode his Senior Norton up the bank at the very fast left hand Brandish Corner, and back down again onto the road, without even 'footing'. The dreaded last-practice-machine-trouble bit the BSA's of E. Baxter, P.H. Waterman, J. Kirby and D. Sheppard, and the Nortons of Sam Seston and Bob Ritchie.

The text refers to "The dreaded last-practice-machine-trouble" hitting D. Sheppard (BSA). It was more a case of D. Sheppard hitting the bank at Keppel Gate. The large picture shows him to be well off-line (inset) Sheppard inspects the sod bank. He was able to straighten the model and start the race.

Junior Race (Monday, 9th June)

Starters

No.	Rider	Club	Machine
1	R K Pilling	Bury & DMC	B.S.A.
2	B Millman	West of England MC	B.S.A.
3	K Smith	Barham & DMC & LCC	A.J.S.
4	B J Hargreaves	Accrington & DMC	Douglas
5	H Brown	Berwick & DMC	B.S.A.
6	S T Seston	Kings Norton MCC	B.S.A.
7	E Baxter	Triangle MCC (Ipswich)	B.S.A.
8	J D Poingdestre	Jersey MC & LCC	B.S.A.
9	P E Burns	Thornton Cleveleys MCC	B.S.A.
10	H A Appleby	Lewes Unity MCC	Norton
12	L Broughton	Southampton Vikings MC & LC	B.S.A.
14	D Ennett	Peveril (IoM) MC & LCC	Matchless
15	J E F Phillips	Swansea MC	B.S.A.
16	H A Nash	Solihull MCC	B.S.A.
18	F O Coleman	Birmingham MCC	Norton
20	C F Racle	Manchester Ace MCC	B.S.A.
21	A W Akers	Dulwich & DMCC	B.S.A.
22	E Houseley	Chesterfield & DMCC	B.S.A.
23	E Pantlin	Hillingdon & Uxbridge MC	A.J.S.
24	P H Waterman	Bristol MC & LCC	B.S.A.
25	A C Peet	Wirral '100' MC	B.S.A.
26	C F Jackson	Furness DMC	B.S.A.
27	H Nowell	Hutton & DMC	B.S.A.
28	D Sheppard	Southall & DMCC	B.S.A.
29	S Graham	Lanarkshire MC & CC (Biggar)	B.S.A.
30	D R Rose	Stewarts & Lloyds (Corby) MCC	B.S.A.
31	H Walmsley	Preston & DMC	Norton
32	J R Clark	Waterlooville MCC	Norton
33	D T Powell	Lymington & DMCC	B.S.A.
34	J Baybutt	Wigan Auto Club	B.S.A.
35	G E Parry	Rhyl & DMC	B.S.A.
36	H R Collier	Grasshopper MCC (Chingford)	B.S.A.
37	J Kirby	Windlesham & DMC & LCC	B.S.A.
38	K R V James	Ringwood MC & LCC	Norton
39	J Cunningham	South Liverpool MC	B.S.A.
40	H Plews	Wakefield & DMSC	Norton
41	D Wasley	Gloucester & Cotswold MC	Norton
42	R E G Phillips	Mansfield & DMC & LCC	Norton
43	E Cox	Cheadle Hulme MCC	A.J.S.
44	O E Greenwood		
		Leicester Query MC	B.S.A.
47	H Hunter	Portsmouth MC & LCC	B.S.A.
49	H D S Curzon	Wolverhampton MC & CC	B.S.A.
50	P M Elvin	Norwich Viking MCC	Douglas
51	R Capner	Whitehaven MC	B.S.A.
52	J W Moore	Stocksbridge & DMC	B.S.A.
53	C E Staley	Market Drayton & DMC & LCC	B.S.A.
54	H Evans	Darlington & DMC	B.S.A.
55	W A Roberts	Wrexham MC	B.S.A.
56	D G Chapman	South Reading MCC	Douglas
58	J T Hubbard	West Of England MC	B.S.A.
59	R Ritchie	O.W.L.S. MC	Norton
60	G Arnold	Warrington & DMC	B.S.A.
61	J Winterbottom	Sheffield North End MC & LCC	Royal Enfield
62	W R Anderson	Loughborough College MC	B.S.A.
63	P M Doncaster	Maun MCC Mansfield	B.S.A.
64	P Beaney	Kenton & Kingsbury MCC	Norton
65	G E Gibson	Loch Lomond MCC	B.S.A.
66	P K Cruse	Farnham Royal MC & LCC	B.S.A.
67	F Sheene	Stamford Bridge MCC	Royal Enfield
68	G Owen	Ramsey & DMCC	Matchless
69	H A Voice	Bishops Waltham MC	B.S.A.
70	H Williams	County Border Auto Club	B.S.A.
71	A L Burton	Southampton & DMCC	Douglas
72	G T Salt	Bridgnorth & DMC	B.S.A.
73	E D Blackwell	Leamington Victory MC & LCC	B.S.A.
74	C Ellerby	Scunthorpe MCC	B.S.A.
75	R Brassington	Potteries Clarion MC	Norton
76	R McIntyre	Mercury MCC (Glasgow)	B.S.A.
77	W R Smith	North Lincolnshire MC	B.S.A.
78	G R Brown	Boston & DMC & LCC	B.S.A.
79	R Jones	Salop MC	B.S.A.
80	A Johnstone	South Liverpool MC	B.S.A.
81	M E J Taft	Ilkeston MC & LCC	B.S.A.
82	A F J D Martin	Rugby MCC	B.S.A.
83	P B Davis	Huddersfield MCC	B.S.A.
84	W S Corley	Mont' Christie MCC	A.J.S.
85	A McIvor	Bolton MCC	Norton
86	D R Watson	Ravensbury MCC	B.S.A.
87	D A Gadd	Bristol MCC	Matchless
88	D W N Brereton	Waterloo & DMC	B.S.A.
89	A G Mollan	West Leeds MC	B.S.A.
90	B McGuinness	Moccasin MC & LCC	B.S.A.

91	H T Tyson	Wycombe & DMCC	B.S.A.
92	J Sutherland	Leigh & DMC	B.S.A.
93	J K Beckton	Middlesborough & DMC	B.S.A.
94	E B Jones	Manchester Eagle MCC	B.S.A.
95	B H King	Bedford Eagle MCC	B.S.A.
96	E B Carr	Ilkley & DMC	B.S.A.
97	E R Williams	Oswestry & DMC	B.S.A.
98	K R E Prince	Loughborough & DMCC	B.S.A.
99	D N Bradshaw	B.M.C.R.C.	Norton
100	G C A Murphy	Manor MC	B.S.A.
102	C H Fisher	Thornton Cleveleys MCC	B.S.A.
103	E Dawson	Huddersfield MC	B.S.A.
104	V J Holcroft	Leamington Victory MC & LCC	
			B.S.A.
105	F Nowell	Preston & DMC	Norton

The pit-road fuel containers were drained of their 80-octane contents from the morning's International Junior TT, and re-filled with the 'Pool' petrol for the clubmen. There were nine non-starters in all; in addition to the four already mentioned, R.F. Organ (BSA), R.H. Smith (BSA), A.N. Robinson (BSA), C.E. Robinson (Douglas) and E. Peacock (BSA) withdrew. This left 96 to face the start, which was delayed 15 minutes to 2.15 pm, the riders setting off in groups of three at 30 second intervals. Weather conditions were almost perfect for racing, dry and sunny with a moderate breeze. Most machines fired up without too much difficulty but C.F. Racle (BSA) lost nearly 4 minutes, including a plug change, before getting away, E.B. Carr and H.A. Nash lost the best part of a minute, while lesser delays affected H.D.S. Curzon, P.K. Cruse, G.C.A. Murphy and V.J. Holcroft (all BSA's). A. McIvor's Norton lost him 3 minutes. One of the first group away B. Millman (BSA) led into Ballacraine, into Ramsey, and by Cronk-ny-Mona had pulled out a 5 second lead over Pilling, with whom he had started, but the fancied runners were in the mid-numbers (Houseley 22, James 38, McIntyre 76). Father and son Nowell, riding a BSA and a Norton respectively got away well, although neither was destined to finish. A real family affair this, with two other sons manning their pits. The leaderboard at the end of the lap showed Houseley to have broken James's 1951 lap record by almost a minute, setting the new one at 28m 38s (79.09 mph), and in doing so had pulled out 12

seconds on 2nd placed McIntyre, who went in to refuel at the end of the lap. First lap retirements came for D. Sheppard (BSA) at Glen Vine, R. Capner (BSA) at Ballaspur, and J. Winterbottom (Royal Enfield) at Glen Helen, all with engine problems. At Sulby Bridge, B McGuinness (BSA) retired with a leaking oil tank, J. Kirby (BSA) at the pits, also with a leaking oil tank, after a long conversation with his pit attendant, C.F. Racle (BSA), P.M. Elvin (Douglas) and P.B. Davies (BSA) with unspecified troubles. Derek Wasley's Norton spluttered to a halt as it rounded Governor's Bridge, but he was able to restart it and complete the race, although that first lap was over 6 minutes slower than his subsequent best lap.

First Lap Leaderboard

1 E. Houseley (BSA)	28m 38s	(79.09 mph)
2 R. McIntyre (BSA)	28m 50s	(78.53 mph)
3 K.V.R. James (Norton)	28m 53s	(78.39 mph)
4 D.T. Powell (BSA)	29m 18s	(77.29 mph)
5 D. Ennett (Matchless)	29m 22s	(77.11 mph)
6 R. Ritchie (Norton)	29m 35s	(76.55 mph)

Houseley's second lap was slightly slower, and James's slightly quicker, the latter closing to within a second of Houseley by the end of the lap, before stopping for fuel. McIntyre dropped to 3rd, Powell's

Eric Houseley (BSA) had a flag-to-flag win in the Junior Clubman's

BSA and Ennett's Matchless remained in 4th and 5th places, Plews' Norton displacing Ritchie's similar machine in 6th. Laurel Bank saw the retirements of H. A. Appleby (Norton) and C. F. Jackson (BSA) with engine troubles. G. T. Salt (BSA) arrived at Governor's Bridge too fast, somehow made it round the hairpin, but was off line for the dip and slid down the camber into the wall. Uninjured, he re-started and rode to his pit, where he retired. A.C. Peet (BSA) retired at May Hill, Ramsey, with engine trouble, A. W. Akers (BSA) and D. G. Chapman (Douglas) at the pits with unspecified problems, J. D. Poingdestre (BSA) at the Stonebreakers Hut with a broken oil pipe, A. G. Mollan (BSA) at Hillberry, B. Millman (BSA) at Governors Bridge and H. Evans at the Gooseneck, again with unspecified problems, but all riders perfectly okay. Peter Cruse had been reported during the first lap as 'carrying out adjustments' in Kirkmichael village, and although he managed to get going to complete the lap in about an hour and a half, he called it a day and retired at the pits. The younger Nowell also retired on the second lap after his Norton suffered a puncture at Barregarroo, one of the fastest stretches of the course, but fortunately he was able to remain on board.

Second Lap Leaderboard

1	E. Houseley (BSA)	57m 32s	(78.71 mph)
2	K.V.R. James (Norton)	57m 33s	(78.69 mph)
3	R. McIntyre (BSA)	57m 45s	(78.41 mph)
4	D.T. Powell (BSA)	58m 14s	(77.76 mph)
5	D. Ennett (Matchless)	58m 31s	(77.39 mph)
6	H. Plews (Norton)	58m 41s	(77.16 mph)

Houseley's progress clock 'stuck' at Ballacraine, before moving directly to Ramsey, having apparently been missed at Kirkmichael, and he began the Mountain climb with only H. Brown (BSA) leading him on the road. Far from being in any trouble, he took more off the lap record on his third lap, completing the circuit in 28m 39s (79.51 mph), and extending his lead over James to 50 seconds, who, like McIntyre, had recorded his slowest lap of the race on the third lap. Houseley went through the Glencrutchery Road and into his final lap without pitting for fuel, and up into 5th place came the BSA

The stunning all-action style of Bob McIntyre as he flies through the Bray Hill dip.

of C.E. Staley. Elsewhere out on the course there were retirements for J. Cunningham (BSA), J. T. Hubbard (BSA) and P. Beaney (Norton).

Third Lap Leaderboard

1	E. Houseley (BSA)	1h 26m 1s	(78.96 mph)
2	K.V.R. James (Norton)	1h 26m 51s	(78.21 mph)
3	R. McIntyre (BSA)	1h 27m 1s	(78.05 mph)
4	D.T. Powell (BSA)	1h 27m 26s	(77.68 mph)
5	C.E. Staley (BSA)	1h 28m 8s	(77.68 mph)
6	D. Ennett (Matchless)	1h 28m 15s	(76.96 mph)

As McIntyre began his last lap, Houseley was entering Kirkmichael, and most of the amateur timekeepers around the course were watching for any closing of the gap between Houseley and James, and indeed it was closing, but not fast enough to seriously threaten. James's fourth lap was 11 seconds faster than Houseley, who finished a comfortable 40 seconds ahead. The real surprise of that final lap was the performance of the 3rd place-man McIntyre, who set another new lap record at 28m 16.4s (80.09 mph), the first over-80 mph lap by a 350, to lift himself into 2nd place, just 32 seconds behind the winner. There was disappointment for local man Ennett, who had his Matchless 'blow up' in Crosby village, and for 'Nowell-the-elder' who had experienced some trouble on his third lap, which he took 4 minutes longer to complete than his previous two, and who was eventually forced out on that last lap. Another AMC runner K. Smith (AJS) stopped during the lap, as did the BSA's of S. Graham, W.R. Anderson, E.D. Blackwell, H.T. Tyson, E.B. Carr and V.J. Holcroft.

The full merit of McIntyre's ride and his record last lap became known after the race, when it became clear that not only had his cylinder head gasket blown on the second lap, but that to get the motor to run cleanly he had had to partially close the air lever, losing 800 revs from the BSA, which made the *'Motor Cycling'* interviewer *"wonder what his last lap time would have been had his carburetion been spot-on"*.

Finishing Order

1	E. Houseley (BSA)	1h 54m 45.2s	(78.92 mph)
2	R. McIntyre (BSA)	1h 55m 17.4s	(78.57 mph)
3	K.V.R. James (Norton)	1h 55m 24.8s	(78.47 mph)
4	C.E. Staley (BSA)	1h 56m 53.6s	(77.52 mph)
5	D.T. Powell (BSA)	1h 57m 17.4s	(77.26 mph)
6	H. Plews (Norton)	1h 57m 45.2s	(76.92 mph)

Fastest Lap: R. McIntyre, (4th lap) 28m 16.4s (80.09 mph) (Record).

Senior Race (Wednesday, 11th June)

Starters

	Rider	Club	Machine
1	A Jowett	Bradford & DMC	Triumph
2	W H Wilshere	Watford & DMC & LCC	Norton
3	A M Cook	Lincoln & DMC & LCC	Triumph
4	E Houseley	Clay Cross & DMC	Triumph
5	D K Farrant	Tenterden & DMC & LCC	Norton
6	J R Clark	Waterlooville MCC	Norton
7	P K Cruse	Farnham Royal MC & LCC	B.S.A.
8	A S Avis	Border MC	Triumph
9	W S Corley	Mont' Christie MCC	Norton
10	J Bottomley	Stretford MC	Triumph
11	H J Ollerenshaw	Hillsborough MCC	Norton
12	W J Hill	Newbury & DMC	Triumph
14	J P Linskey	Southern MCC	Norton
15	B J Hargreaves	Bradford & DMC	Triumph
16	F M Fox	Wombwell & DMC & CC	Norton
17	C Watson	Vincent H.R.D. OC	Vincent
18	R Ellis	Sheffield Ace MC	B.S.A.
19	F G Perris	Westminster MCC	Triumph
20	B Freestone	Grimsby MC Ltd	Triumph
21	D Webb	St Helens & DAC	Triumph
22	A Newstead	Newark MC & LCC	B.S.A.
23	D T Powell	Lymington & DMC	B.S.A.
24	R A Ingram	Frome & D United MC & LCC	Matchless.
25	P J Walsh	Solihull MCC	Triumph
26	L D Boult	Antelope MCC (Coventry)	Triumph
27	L Broughton	Southampton Vikings MC & LCC	B.S.A.
28	E G Oughton	West Leeds MC	Triumph
29	R A D Mawson	Peveril (IoM) MC & CC	Norton
30	D Tye	Ilkeston & DMC & LCC	Triumph
31	W Zoellner	Runcorn & DMC	Norton
32	T Shelley	Wolverhampton MC & CC	B.S.A.
34	K R E Prince	Loughborough & DMCC	B.S.A.

36	D Ennett	Leyland AC	Matchless
37	R L Prosser	Southport MC & LCC	Triumph
39	H Brown	Berwick & DMC	Norton
40	J E Williams	C.S.M.A. Ltd	Triumph
41	D J P Wilkins	Mendip Vale MC & LCC	Norton
42	"W Workman"	Rossendale MC & LCC	Triumph
43	K A Taubman	Rawmarsh & DMC & LCC	Triumph
44	G R Brown	Boston & DMC & LCC	Matchless
45	J Lanyon	Guernsey MC & CC	Norton
46	J B Netherton	B.M.C.R.C.	Norton
47	H Neal	Grasshopper MCC (Romford)	Norton
48	D Andrews	Horsforth & DMC	Matchless
49	H Plews	Wakefield & DMSC	Norton
50	P J Orton	Hinckley & DMC & LC	Vincent
51	A E Clough	Winsford & DMC	Triumph
53	R H Modral	Darlington & DMC	Triumph
54	F C Pusey	Ormskirk & DAC	Vincent
55	F Passmore	Hayes & DMCC	Norton
56	W A Harding	Peveril (IoM) MC & CC	Norton
58	E Cheers	Chester MC	Norton
59	K D Waddington		
		Bradford & DMC	Triumph
60	R Ritchie	Lanarkshire & DMC & CC	Norton
61	R W C Kerr	Stranraer & DMCC	Triumph
63	D A Gadd	Bristol MCC	Norton
64	H F Hunter	Portsmouth MC & LCC	B.S.A.
65	A C Moore	Mont' Christie MCC	Norton
66	A F J D Martin	Rugby MCC	Triumph
67	K G Meadows	Wigan AC	Norton
69	C E Robinson	North Lincolnshire MC	Norton
70	H T Tyson	Wycombe & DMCC	B.S.A.
71	L Carr	Seaton Delaval & DMC	Norton
73	G D Alcock	Northwich MC	Norton
74	J Cox	Manchester Eagle MC	Matchless
76	J Wilkes	Solihull MCC	B.S.A.
77	J J E Porter	Norwood MC	B.S.A.
78	J Wright	Wirral '100' MC	B.S.A.
79	K V R James	Ringwood MC & LCC	Norton
80	D C Birrell	Kirkcaldy & DMC	Norton
81	J D Belcher	Gravesend Eagles MCC	Norton
82	I G Matheson	C.S.M.A.	B.S.A.
83	E J Goddard	High Peak MCC	Triumph
84	K Ratcliffe	Middlesborough & DMC	Norton
85	"T Southward"	Reading Ace MCC	Triumph
86	E Pantlin	Hillingdon & Uxbridge MC	Norton
87	K Clark	Hayes & DMC	Matchless
88	F O Coleman	Kings Norton MCC	Norton
89	F C J Collings	West Bristol MC & CC	Norton
90	J H Cooper	Bury & DMC	Norton
91	J S Hamilton	Ayr MCC	Triumph
92	A W Dobbs	Bath & West of England MC	Norton
93	P Minion	Pathfinders & Derby MC Ltd	Norton
94	K G Brough	Aldershot MCC	B.S.A.
95	G W Shekell	Worcester AC	Norton

The skies were cloudy but it was pleasantly warm as the 87 riders began the warm-up of their machines, and visibility was perfect. The forecast however, was not good, and rain had been predicted, possibly before the end of the race. As the field began to get away, the breeze seemed to strengthen, and the temperatures dropped a little. There were 7 non-starters, T.F. Watson has been mentioned, and he was joined by J. Hill (Norton), J. Hockin (Triumph), W. Spence (Triumph), B. W. Lack (Matchless), D.N. Bradshaw (Norton) and S.T. Seston (BSA). A. J. Wellsted was not listed as an official non-starter, but his name did not figure in the results. The International Lightweight TT run in the morning had been of shorter duration than the Junior International of the Monday, and there had therefore been no need to delay the start of the Senior Clubman's, which got away promptly at 2.00 pm. From the first group, Willy Wilshere (Norton) got away from the Triumphs of A.M. Cook and A. Jowett to head the field into Ballacraine (the latter one of three in the race using 5T's), but two other Nortons, those of W. S. Corley and H. J. Ollerenshaw, both needed some persuasion to fire up. H. T. Tyson unfortunately dropped his BSA in the efforts to get it started, but eventually got away. Two Norton riders, K. Ratcliffe and J. H. Cooper were left still kicking at their mounts when the last man, G. W. Shekell, got away on his. Cooper's delay was not too bad in the end, but Ratcliffe eventually got away to a big cheer from the sympathetic crowd in the Grandstand, 10 minutes after he should have gone. Cook led the field as it reached Ramsey, closely followed by Derek Farrant (Norton) and John Clark (Norton), who had started at numbers 5 and 6, but Monday's winner Eric Houseley was reported as touring there, his Triumph firing on only one cylinder. Possibly connected with Houseley's problems was the physical contact he had with Clark as they went round Handley's Corner on that first lap. Describing in the after-race interview what must have been a truly scary incident, Clark said that their machines had locked together on the approach, and had remained firmly interlocked for more than 40 yards, his own offside footrest being bent right back in the process. The very fast left and right sweep of Handley's, with its intimidating high wall on the inside of the course, is not a place to have any kind of problem, the idea of taking it at race speed whilst locked to another machine is not a pleasant one! In fact, Clark's eventual 3rd place was well earned, for as well as the Handley's incident, he had very nearly run out of road on the second lap at Quarry Bends, trying to gain momentum for the Sulby Straight, and had 'footed' his way out of trouble. Then on the last lap oil on his rear tyre had given him *"a very anxious moment"* at the Stone Bridge Bend (Bungalow Bridge or the Graham Memorial as it became).

The first actual retirement was another 'split-tank' victim, this time it was the oil tank of P. J. Walsh's Triumph, and he was soon joined by another Triumph, that of R. H. Modral in Kirkmichael with a

puncture. Clark and Farrant were the first to complete the lap, in close company, but the surprise was Bernard Hargreaves, who had struggled with an off-the-pace Douglas to finish 39th in the Junior race, but on his Senior Triumph had put in a first lap time of 27m 16s (83.05 mph), faster than 1951 speeds, but still not threatening Duke's 1949 time of 27m 3s. Hargreaves was 17 seconds ahead of Clark, who was in turn 2 seconds in front of Farrant. Ken James followed his strong performance in the Junior with a lap 4 seconds ahead of Clark to go into 2nd place. Houseley managed to nurse the Triumph back to the pits, where he retired, the stated reason being a broken oil pipe. D.A. Gadd retired his Norton at Ballaugh with clutch trouble, followed by D. Webb (Triumph) in the vicinity of Ramsey with plug trouble, and K. G. Brough came off his BSA in Glen Helen, retiring with minor abrasions. J. E. Williams (Triumph) and G. R. Brown (Matchless) were other first lap retirements, no reason specified, the latter reported to be sitting on the grass bank at Cronk-ny-Mona, watching the race and contentedly smoking a cigarette. Channel Islander J. Lanyon (Norton)

The Vincent Comet never achieved the Clubman success of its bigger brother. C Watson at Union Mills

retired after a spill at Signpost, seemingly without injury, but later reports had him 'comfortable' in hospital with back injuries.

First Lap Leaderboard

1	B.J. Hargreaves (Triumph)	27m 16s	(83.05 mph)
2	K.V.R. James (Norton)	27m 29s	(82.40 mph)
3	J.R. Clark (Norton)	27m 33s	(82.20 mph)
4	D.K. Farrant (Norton)	27m 35s	(82.10 mph)
5	D. Tye (Triumph)	27m 41s	(81.81 mph)
6	H. Plews (Norton)	27m 51s	(81.36 mph)

Two Triumphs and four Nortons in the first six, all lapping at over 80 mph, and only 34 seconds between them, the start of the second lap promised a good race, and the first two on the road, Clark and Farrant, were giving the crowd a close dice, very close at times. They went round the lap together, went into their pits to refuel at the same time, and came out still together. J. P. Linskey pitted his BSA

Brian Hargreaves seemed stunned by his victory in the Senior Clubmans.

at the end of the first lap with a split petrol tank, and was forced to retire there, and E. J. Goddard pushed his Triumph the last part of the lap to his pit, where, after a long discussion with his attendant, he too retired, apparently with float chamber problems. Clark and Farrant recorded exactly the same lap time, 27m 25s (82.60 mph), not only as each other, but with David Tye, who was just 6 seconds behind Farrant on corrected time, in 5th place. Even after two laps there was still only 38 seconds between the first six. First lap retiree J. E. Williams caused some amusement around the course when he sent a message to his wife via the Public Address commentator in Ramsey that he had only sprained a wrist, and was returning to Douglas on the 3.15 bus! Local hope Derek Ennett (Matchless) was reported as having stopped at Hillberry, and although he eventually made it to the pits, he got no further. R. Ellis (BSA) and H. J. Cronan (Triumph) were also second lap retirements.

Second Lap Leaderboard

1	B.J. Hargreaves (Triumph)	54m 45s	(82.71 mph)
2	K.V.R. James (Norton)	54m 49s	(82.61 mph)
3	J.R. Clark (Norton)	54m 58s	(82.39 mph)
4	D.K. Farrant (Norton)	55m 0s	(82.30 mph)
5	D. Tye (Triumph)	55m 6s	(82.18 mph)
6	H. Plews (Norton)	55m 23s	(81.76 mph)

The fast pace continued into the third lap, but positions remained more or less the same, the only change was a particularly quick lap by Jack Bottomley (Triumph) which saw him straight onto the leaderboard in 3rd place. Still only 12 seconds separated 3rd to 6th places. Hargreaves's lap time increased by 11 seconds over his previous, but there was no real threat from James, whose third lap was 30 seconds down on the leader, who appeared to be getting good signals, and who was controlling the race. As he hadn't stopped for fuel, spectators expected Hargreaves to pit at the end of the lap, but he gave his pit the 'thumbs-up' as he sped along the Glencrutchery Road and continued without stopping. Forced to drop out on the third lap were J.S. Hamilton, who left his Triumph between Quarter Bridge and Braddan, to walk 'home', P.K. Cruse, whose BSA stopped at the Highlander with magneto trouble, and R. F. Keen, who came off his Triumph at Windy Corner, without injury. W. J. Hill (Triumph), D. Andrews (Matchless), J. Wilkes (BSA) and H. T. Tyson (BSA) also retired with unspecified troubles.

Third lap Leaderboard

1 B.J. Hargreaves (Triumph)	1h 22m 23s	(82.45 mph)
2 K.V.R. James (Norton)	1h 22m 58s	(81.86 mph)
3 J. Bottomley (Triumph)	1h 23m 10s	(81.67 mph)
4 J.R. Clark (Norton)	1h 23m 14s	(81.60 mph)
5 D.K. Farrant (Norton)	1h 23m 18s	(81.54 mph)
6 D. Tye (Triumph)	1h 23m 22s	(81.47 mph)

There was no sign of the predicted rain as the Triumph supporters in the crowds anxiously followed Hargreaves's progress around the course, they had seen last lap reversals in the past, and those within earshot of a public address loudspeaker would have learnt that he had not taken on fuel. The spirited battle between Clark and Farrant who had started together and spent so much time in close company on the roads, began to resolve itself in Clark's favour, eventually taking 3rd place by a little under 20 seconds. The signal light indicating Hargreaves at Governors Bridge came on, and a short while later he crossed the line, taking the win with a margin of almost 40 seconds. The gap was less than he would have lost had he stopped to refuel, but his final lap was 3 seconds faster than James, which suggested that he was not over-concerned about running low on fuel, although a last lap excursion for James at Ballacraine when trying too hard to close the gap, didn't help his cause. The dreaded split tank disposed of David Tye, who was going so well in 6th place, bringing him to a halt at Handley's Corner. Other leaderboard men in trouble with (lack of) petrol were Harry Plews, who managed to coast and push his Norton home to finish 32nd, and Jack Bottomley, who was able to coast down the Mountain to conserve what little fuel he had left, and then drive the uphill bits, losing precious seconds in the process and dropping two places to 5th. R. W. C. Kerr benefited from Tye and Plews problems by getting his Triumph onto the leaderboard in 6th place. Willy Wilshere (Norton) was a last lap retirement, as were C. Watson (Vincent), H. F. Hunter (BSA) and A. F. J. D. Martin (Triumph). B. Freestone (Triumph)

completed the course but was excluded for receiving outside assistance.

After the race, Hargreaves reported a very enjoyable and trouble-free run on the Triumph, except for occasional difficulties engaging 3rd gear, and 'slightly-below-par' handling after the first lap, an observation that was soon explained by the fact that the drive-side rear wheel spindle nut was found to be missing! Further examination showed that the wheel had not in fact moved, and that chain tension was still good. Both the 2nd and 3rd Nortons had suffered from oil on the drive-side of the machines, caused not by oil leaks as such, but discharge past the drive-side crank bearing into the primary chain-case, thence outside and eventually onto the tyres.

Finishing Order

1 B.J. Hargreaves (Triumph)	1h 49m 50s	(82.45 mph)
2 K.V.R. James (Norton)	1h 50m 28.6s	(81.97 mph)
3 J.R. Clark (Norton)	1h 50m 32.6s	(81.92 mph)
4 D.K. Farrant (Norton)	1h 50m 52s	(81.68 mph)
5 J. Bottomley (Triumph)	1h 51m 8s	(81.49 mph)
6 R.W.C. Kerr (Triumph)	1h 51m 59s	(80.87 mph)

Fastest Lap: B. J. Hargreaves, (1st lap) 27m 16s (83.05 mph).

Reflections

Bob McIntyre's debut laps on the circuit with which his name would become forever associated, were eventful. In his book 'Bob McIntyre – The Flying Scot' (Breedon Books, 2006), Mick Walker tells of a spill that went unreported at the time, and how Bob himself described the incident. *"I did one lap and was full of the joys of spring. I roared down from Brandish to Hillberry with the intention of taking this fast right-hander flat out in top gear. I thought it could be done and it can be done. But I did not do it. I had forgotten to remove the centre-stand from the Gold Star! It grounded, lifted out the back end of the bike and I came off. I was doing 100 mph".*

Mick Walker then tells of a big scene between Bob and his sponsor/employer Sam Cooper, senior partner in the Cooper Brothers of Troon motorcycle business. Sam wanted to pull out there and then *"convinced that his young protégé would kill himself if he continued. Bob's determination won through, but he did agree to proceed with a little more caution thereafter".* There is a slight irony in the fact that Michelle Ann Duff, who had competed at the highest level in Grand Prix racing in the 1960's when known to the world as Mike Duff, had described her first meeting with hero McIntyre. His words of advice to the young Canadian on racing in the Isle of Man was *"Make haste slowly, laddie".* The title of her book is 'Make Haste Slowly' (mad8 publishing, 1999).

K.V.R. (Ken) James was employed and sponsored by Bob Foster. He finished the Clubman's with a 2nd and a 3rd place, and was widely tipped to win the Manx Grand Prix later that same year, and, on recommendation from Bob, took over Francis Beart's 350 following Arber's accident. Tragically for him, in what was to be a catastrophic year for Beart, he too lost his life in a practice accident only a few hundred yards further on from Arber's Hillberry crash. Reports of the time vary as to what exactly happened in the crash, which also involved T.W. Swarbrick. Jeff Clew, in his biography of Francis Beart says that James crashed and Swarbrick was unable to avoid the wreckage. Alan Brodrick also worked for Bob Foster at the time, and he understood (from Foster) that it was Swarbrick who was the first to fall, and that before a warning could be given, James came upon the fallen Norton in the middle of the track. Alan continues the story *"Years later, Bob Foster and myself were standing in the showroom talking of nothing much, when an elderly couple came in and started to chat to Bob. I stood apart but heard the lady say 'We were in touch with Ken again last night, he is very happy up there, and he, Jimmie Guthrie, Les Graham, Ted Mellors and quite a few others are coming down for the TT again this year'. Foster was looking at me warningly but I was not saying anything, and after the old couple had gone Foster said 'That was Ken James' parents.*

If anyone laughs at them or says anything to disillusion them, I'll kill them first and sack them later'. He went on to tell me that the tragic couple had got into the hands of an unscrupulous 'spiritualist' who had read up on TT history and memorised the names of a few long-dead TT riders to give colour to his story. 'The bastard ought to be locked up' said Foster, 'but what can you do? Ken was their only child and this spiritualistic rubbish is the only comfort they have". Bob Foster was a man who had competed in most forms of motorcycle sport with success. He was a successful dealer, who was then able to put back something into the sport, actively supporting and helping many Clubman's, Manx Grand Prix and TT riders. He acted as Travelling Marshal at the TT, sponsor, mentor, and above all a lifelong enthusiast for the sport of motorcycling. His Island career had begun in 1933, riding New Imperials in the Manx Grand Prix. The following year a New Imp took him to runner-up spot in the Lightweight, and he finished 6th in the Senior on a Sunbeam. He moved up to the TT, retiring the New Imp in 1935, but won the 1936 Lightweight for the Birmingham concern. In the years leading up to the Second World War, he rode works AJS's with less success, his best result being 13th in the 1939 Senior. The post-war years saw him ride Velocette, Triumph and Moto-Guzzi, winning the 1947 Junior for Velocette, which began a remarkable series of results on Velocettes in that class which resulted in 2nd the following year, then 6th, a retirement, and 6th in his final TT year of 1951. In 1950, despite his retirement in the TT, he won the rider's 350cc World Championship, and the manufacturer's for Velocette. Bob Foster passed away in 1985, around about the same time as 'Bob Foster Ltd., of Ashley Road, Parkstone, Dorset', closed its doors for good.

My 1952 Senior Clubman's Ride
by Frank Fox

My first race in the Island was the 1951 Junior Manx Grand Prix. I had joined the Crowe Edge Iron Works, near Holmfirth, and spotted a Manx Norton in the workshop. This was owned by Jack Bailey, a regular TT competitor. In those days I was riding trials and scrambles, and used to arrive at work on Monday with a well-used and abused bike. Jack said "Why don't you try some proper racing", my reply was "on what?" he pointed to the Manx and said "that". He had been watching my progress at weekends and thought I was a suitable pilot. A couple of shake-down rides and he packed me, the Manx, tools and suitcase off on the train bound for Liverpool. His parting words were "If you drop the bike - jump off the boat on the way home!".

I finished 27th, which attracted a piece in a local paper. Shortly afterwards I received a letter from Tom Garner of Barnsley, asking me to drop round. Tom was the largest area local agent for most of the British bikes and the reason for the call was to see if I would ride his International Norton in the Senior Clubman's. I knew that Clubman's entrants had to 'own' their bikes, proof was their name in the log book. "No problem" said Tom. He was on good terms with Alan Wilson of Norton, so I received a message in early May to go down to Bracebridge Street and collect my bike. It was handed over, with instructions not to go over 70 mph whilst running it in on the way home!

Back to base, lights, dynamo and number plates removed, a straight through pipe was fitted and away to the Island. I was entered by the Wombwell & D.M.C. & L.C.C.

Course knowledge from the previous years Manx was a great help; we had taken another Inter with us as a road hack. In those days you had to tax your bike on the Island. To cut down on costs, both the race bike and the hack had the same number plate. Most days a local constable would pop his head into the garage to check our progress, not once did he mention the duplicate bikes!

Tom had taken the works float, a Norton Big 4 with a box on the side to run about on. Most evenings we went along the prom to a restaurant near Summer Hill. One night, with about six bodies on board, I was persuaded to do two circuits of the policeman who directed the traffic at the bottom of Broadway, many years later he still remembered that stunt!

The bike ran faultlessly through practice, it was a 'dry' engine, some of the Inters were prone to weep oil from the camshaft, but this was as sweet as a nut.

Ferodo were based at Mylchreest Motors in those days, we took the front wheel along and they replaced the linings and skimmed them to size. In the latter stages of practice Tom had arranged for the bike to go to the Norton depot, based in a funeral parlour! They ran the rule over the bike, made sure everything was ok and we weighed in. Vic Anstice, Chief Scrutineer must have been in a foul mood that day, he got hold of a rear number plate and ripped it clean off! "Get it fixed", he said. We replaced it with the limited tools we had there, taped it up and it passed muster this time, someone must have rubbed him up the wrong way and he took it out on us!

It was a cold engine start for the Clubman's, in my days, so every time we got the bike out for practice, we made sure it would start well.

Come race day, it started first prod and I soon left my starting partners Watson and Ellis behind. Eric Houseley, who started No. 4 had a distinct green seat cover on his Triumph. He said "if you catch sight of the green cover, you're going bloody well. I was number 16, and passed him on the way into Ramsey on the first lap.

It was one of those few races where everything went so well, it is hard to remember anything outstanding. We had practiced pit stops during practice so we knew exactly the drill. The first and third laps were exactly the same time, lap two was slower due to the refuelling.

I finished 12th in the race, a very satisfactory ride, and when we got back to Barnsley, found that Tom could have sold that bike about twelve times over, such was the demand for the Inter. It was sold to a Roman Catholic priest, it replaced a Vincent!

The Clubman's ride was a good grounding for further Manx rides, later that year I finished 13th in the 1952 Senior Manx before winning the 1953 Junior Manx Grand Prix. I rode the TT from 1954 to 1960, and after a break of a few years I moved to the Island where I rode the Andreas Club and Southern 100 races on Yamaha and Weslake until finally hanging up my leathers in 1977. I had the occasional gallop in the Classic Parade, clocking a 92 mph lap in 1992 on a Norton Commando.

I can truthfully say I have enjoyed my racing years and still keep in touch with my many of my racing pals of yesteryear.

Frank looks to have the exit to Kate's Cottage well sorted in this practice shot

1952 Clubman's Junior

1.	E. Houseley, BSA	28.38	28.44	**28.29**	28.44.2	1 54 45.2	78.92
2.	R. McIntyre, BSA	28.50	28.55	29.16	**28.16.4**	1 55 17.4	78.57
3.	K. R. V. James, Norton	28.53	28.40	29.18	**28.33.6**	1 55 24.6	78.47
4.	C. E. Staley, BSA	30.05	29.03	29.00	**28.45.6**	1 56 53.6	77.52
5.	D. T. Powell, BSA	29.18	**28.56**	29.12	29.51.4	1 57 17.4	77.26
6.	H. Plews, Norton	29.41	**29.00**	30.16	28.48.2	1 57 45.2	76.92
7.	H. Brown, BSA	30.11	**29.08**	29.41	29.15.6	1 58 13.6	76.58
8.	R. Jones, BSA	30.24	29.21	**29.12**	29.22	1 58 19.0	76.54
9.	R. Ritchie, Norton	29.35	29.25	30.40	**29.10.4**	1 58 50.4	76.21
10.	E. B. Jones, BSA	30.10	30.23	29.18	**29.15**	1 59 06.0	76.04
11.	J. R. Clark, Norton	29.55	30.14	29.31	**29.29**	1 59 09.0	76.01
12.	L. Broughton, BSA	29.51	29.29	30.28	**29.24.6**	1 59 12.6	75.96
13.	H. A. Voice, BSA	30.05	29.26	30.18	**29.27.8**	1 59 16.8	75.93
14.	M. E. J. Taft, BSA	30.29	29.39	**29.25**	30.09.4	1 59 42.4	75.66
15.	S. T. Seston, BSA	30.23	30.08	29.53	**29.49**	2 00 13.0	75.33
16.	G. E. Parry, BSA	30.04	30.04	30.51	**29.25.4**	2 00 24.4	75.22
17.	G. Arnold, BSA	30.28	30.36	**29.49**	29.49	2 00 42.0	75.03
18.	W. A. Roberts, BSA	30.32	31.03	29.47	**29.33.6**	2 00 55.6	74.88
19.	G. R. Brown, BSA	30.19	29.51	31.15	**29.43**	2 01 08.0	74.76
20.	R. K. Pilling, BSA	30.19	30.05	30.53	**30.04.6**	2 01 21.6	74.62
21.	H. A. Nash, BSA	31.14	30.27	30.07	**29.46.8**	2 01 44.8	74.38
22.	K. R. E. Prince, BSA	30.23	**30.06**	30.57	30.20	2 01 46.0	74.37
23.	P. E. Burns, BSA	31.22	**30.07**	30.14	30.13.6	2 01 56.6	74.26
24.	J. K. Beckton, BSA	30.33	**30.10**	31.03	30.14	2 02 00.0	74.23
25.	P. H. Waterman, BSA	30.46	**29.29**	30.15	30.35.4	2 02 05.4	74.18
26.	F. O. Coleman, Norton	31.18	30.05	**29.55**	30.57	2 02 15.0	74.08
27.	A. Johnstone, BSA	30.40	**30.09**	31.30	30.12	2 02 31.0	73.92
28.	E. R. Williams, BSA	30.40	30.32	30.56	**30.30**	2 02 38.0	73.85
29.	A. F. J. D. Martin, BSA	31.31	30.32	**30.10**	30.52	2 03 05.0	73.58
30.	B. H. King, BSA	31.13	**30.31**	30.35	30.47	2 03 06.0	73.57
31.	C. Ellerby, BSA	30.35	30.07	**29.15**	33.17	2 03 14.0	73.49
32.	D. N. Bradshaw, Norton	31.34	**30.29**	31.07	30.35	2 03 45.0	73.18
33.	D. R. Rose, BSA	31.13	**30.14**	31.36	30.50.2	2 03 53.2	73.10
34.	H. Williams, BSA	31.04	30.56	**30.58**	30.58	2 03 56.0	73.07
35.	O. E. Greenwood, BSA	31.32	31.16	31.23	**29.41.6**	2 04 22.6	72.81
36.	A. R. Brassington, Norton	31.25	**30.25**	30.37	32.18	2 04 45.0	72.59
37.	H. Walmsley, Norton	31.32	30.57	**30.49**	31.47.4	2 05 05.4	72.40
38.	C. H. Fisher, BSA	31.18	30.44	32.50	**30.32**	2 05 24.0	72.22
39.	B. J. Hargreaves, Douglas	31.36	**30.42**	33.02	30.56.6	2 06 16.6	71.71
40.	J. Sutherland, BSA	31.46	**30.46**	31.15	32.38	2 06 25.0	71.64
41.	E. Baxter, BSA	31.12	**30.46**	33.07	31.21	2 06 26.0	71.63
42.	J. W. Moore, BSA	31.45	**30.42**	31.52	32.25	2 06 44.0	71.46
43.	H. Hunter, BSA	32.10	**31.15**	31.19	32.04	2 06 48.0	71.42
44.	R. E. G. Phillips, Norton	**31.31**	31.32	31.40	32.52	2 07 35.0	70.98
45.	W. R. Smith, BSA	32.31	32.11	31.36	**31.31**	2 07 49.0	70.85
46.	W. S. Corley, AJS	32.09	**31.24**	32.41	31.45	2 07 59.0	70.76
47.	J. Baybutt, BSA	32.29	31.49	**31.32**	32.14	2 08 04.0	70.71

48.	A. L. Burton, Douglas	32.14	**31.47**	32.14	31.50	2 08 05.0	70.70
49.	E. Dawson, BSA	32.57	31.53	32.24	**31.47**	2 09 01.0	70.19
50.	E. Pantlin, AJS	32.41	32.21	32.59	**32.09**	2 10 10.0	69.57
51.	V. E. F. Phillips, BSA	33.21	**31.51**	32.53	32.14	2 10 19.0	69.49
52.	G. Owen, Matchless	32.09	**31.57**	32.52	33.26	2 10 24.0	69.40
53.	E. Cox, AJS	33.11	32.50	33.28	**32.05**	2 11 34.0	68.83
54.	D. A. Gadd, Matchless	**32.26**	33.02	33.35	32.38	2 11 41.0	68.77
55.	G. E. Gibson, BSA	33.27	**32.43**	33.22	32.49	2 12 21.0	68.43
56.	G. C. A. Murphy, BSA	32.23	**31.27**	31.34	37.30	2 12 54.0	68.14
57.	H. R. Collier, BSA	33.42	33.23	34.25	**32.24**	2 13 54.0	67.64
58.	D. W. N. Brereton, BSA	34.02	33.27	33.54	**32.39**	2 14 02.0	67.57
59.	A. McIvor, Norton	36.20	33.46	34.08	**33.16**	2 17 30.0	65.86
60.	F. Sheene, Royal Enfield	35.45	34.19	35.11	**33.59**	2 19 14.0	65.04
61.	W. Wasley, Norton	39.46	33.32	34.42	**33.16**	2 21 16.0	64.11
62	P. M. Doncaster, BSA	**33.03**	33.50	35.07	40.27	2 22 27.0	63.57
63.	D. R. Watson, BSA	36.28	35.57	36.15	**34.21**	2 23 01.0	63.32
64.	H. D. S. Curzon, BSA	41.05	**39.48**	40.08	40.41	2 41 42.0	56.01
	K. Smith, AJS	31.02	**30.26**	33.50	R		
	D. Ennett, Matchless	29.22	**29.09**	29.44	R		
	H. Nowell, BSA	**33.03**	33.40	37.34	R		
	S. Graham, BSA	33.29	**32.49**	33.55	R		
	W. R. Anderson, BSA	**32.47**	32.58	33.13	R		
	E. D. Blackwell, BSA	30.49	29.54	**29.28**	R		
	H. T. Tyson, BSA	31.24	**30.30**	31.18	R		
	E. B. Carr, BSA	**33.39**	36.23	58.00	R		
	V. J. Holcroft, BSA	50.55	**35.49**	35.50	R		
	A. W. Akers, BSA	**30.25**	33.39	R			
	J. Cunningham, BSA	32.01	**31.30**	R			
	D. G. Chapman, Douglas	30.11	**29.23**	R			
	J. T. Hubbard, BSA	30.07	**29.55**	R			
	P. Beaney, Norton	**32.35**	32.39	R			
	J. D. Poingdestre, BSA	34.26	R				
	B. Millman, BSA	30.14	R				
	H. A. Appleby, Norton	32.58	R				
	A. C. Peet, BSA	31.19	R				
	C. F. Jackson, BSA	30.15	R				
	J. Kirby, BSA	35.30	R				
	H. Evans, BSA	32.40	R				
	P. K. Cruse, BSA	92.16	R				
	G. T. Salt, BSA	40.36	R				
	A. G. Mollan, BSA	33.17	R				
	F. Nowell, Norton	34.12	R				
	C. F. Racle, BSA	R					
	D. Sheppard, BSA	R					
	P. M. Elvin, Douglas	R					
	R. Capner, BSA	R					
	J. Winterbottom, Royal Enfield	R					
	P. B. Davies, BSA	R					
	B. McGuinness, BSA	R					

RIDER AND MACHINE	FIRST LAP POSITION	LAP POSITIONS 1952 CLUBMAN'S JUNIOR	RIDER AND FINAL POSITION	MACHINE
E HOUSELEY B.S.A.	1		1	E HOUSELEY B.S.A.
R MCINTYRE B.S.A.	2		2	R MCINTYRE B.S.A.
K V R JAMES NORTON	3		3	K V R JAMES NORTON
D T POWELL B.S.A.	4		4	C E STALEY B.S.A.
D ENNETT MATCHLESS	5		5	D T POWELL B.S.A.
R RITCHIE NORTON	6	R	6	H PLEWS NORTON

Frank Sheene (Royal Enfield, 67) leads his starting partners Goo Owen (Matchless,68) and Harry Voice (BSA, 69)

RIDER AND MACHINE	FIRST LAP POSITION	LAP POSITIONS 1952 CLUBMAN'S SENIOR	RIDER AND FINAL POSITION	MACHINE
B J HARGREAVES TRIUMPH	1		1	B J HARGREAVES TRIUMPH
K V R JAMES NORTON	2		2	K V R JAMES NORTON
J R CLARK NORTON	3		3	J R CLARK NORTON
D K FARRANT NORTON	4		4	D K FARRANT NORTON
D TYE TRIUMPH	5		5	J BOTTOMLEY TRIUMPH
H PLEWS NORTON	6	R	6	R W C KERR TRIUMPH

Local ace Derek Ennett on the fast but fragile Matchless twin leads E G Oughton (Triumph) out of Governors Bridge.

1953

CORONATION YEAR - AND A BSA
ON THE SENIOR LEADERBOARD

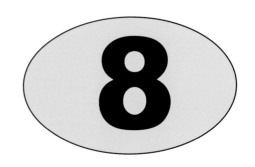

The 1953 Clubman's races followed the previous arrangement, with the Junior and re-introduced 1000cc events concurrently on the Monday afternoon following the Junior International, and the Senior on the Wednesday afternoon following the International 250 and 125cc races. It was thus made possible for riders to compete in both days racing, and therefore in more than one class. Although initially included, a Lightweight race never looked likely, as the minimum entries for a class to be run was twelve. In fact only one was received by the ACU, so that was that. 16 entered the 1000cc class, all on Vincents, 10 on Black Shadows and 6 on Rapide's. 56 of the 75 Junior entries were on BSA's, 12 on Nortons, with 3 on Douglas's, and 2 each on Matchless and AJS. In contrast the Senior was largely a Norton-Triumph affair, with 28 of the 62 entries on the former, and 18 on the Meriden twins. BSA made up another 8, Matchless and AJS a total of 6 equally split between the marques, and 2 Ariels.

The Norton Inter and the new BSA BB Gold Star were available with the new frames in 1953, the former benefiting from the Featherbed, and the latter the new all-welded duplex frame designated the BB32A, forerunner of the CB32 fitted to all the subsequent Clubman's Gold Stars until production ended.

The Regulation prohibiting a variation in exhaust port diameter was dropped, but still megaphones were barred, which apparent contradiction caused a little initial confusion, but in fact the end result was that the use of standard silencers was allowed, without making them compulsory. Fuel for 1953 would not be 70-75 octane 'Pool', for premium grades of Shell-Mex and BP, and Esso, were permissible, and these fuels would be provided to all competitors by the ACU for the races.

Entries and Practice

Entries included Harry Voice, Des Wright, Ivor Lloyd, Derek Powell, Owen Greenwood, Jimmy Drysdale, Ewen Haldane, Phil Palmer, Ellis Boyce, Frank Sheene, Sam Seston, Eddie Crooks, Jack Bottomley, Roy Ingram, Eric Cheers and Bob Keeler in the Junior, with Eddie Dow, Eddie Crooks, Terry Shepherd, Jack Bottomley, Sam Seston, Alf Hagon, Ron Jerrard, Bob Keeler, Alastair King, Derek Powell, Tom Ovens, Willy Wilshere and Eric Cheers contesting the Senior. Likely contenders for honours in the 1000 cc class were Richard Madsen-Mygdal, George Douglass and Hedley Cox. Two New Zealanders were entered,

One of the first overseas contingent to compete in the Clubman was Kiwi Neville Wooderson, seen here with his Junior G3L Matchless

one via the Auckland MCC was Neville Wooderson on a G3L Matchless in the Junior and a G9 in the Senior, and the other, Gavin Dunlop via the Tenterden MCC, again in the Junior and Senior classes, on 'Inter' Nortons.

Strong winds and heavy rain welcomed the riders at the start of the first practice, at first light on the morning of Saturday 30th May, and although the rain eased as the session progressed, the roads remained wet throughout. Many riders put in two laps, and while R. Ellis (Norton) was fastest in the Senior class with a time of 32m 10s (70.39 mph), Derek Powell was fastest overall, with 30m 44s (73.68 mph) on his Junior BSA. As the times for the first two laps of newcomers were not announced, only Richard

Madsen-Mygdal (on his third lap) and Frank Taylor were credited with times in the 1000 cc class, both taking it steady with lap times over 40 minutes. John Dulson was reported as having dropped his Junior Norton at Sulby, without injury, and J. I. Elliott stopped temporarily at his pit, having evidently taken a tumble somewhere, but continued.

There was some improvement in the weather for the second session on Monday morning, but not much. Showers of rain meant that the roads were wet in places, predominantly on the southern section of the course, and it remained cold and windy. Jack Bottomley initially struck problems with his Norton's gear linkage, but carried out repairs at Quarter Bridge, and then set fastest Senior lap with 28m 51s

Eddie Crooks rode his first TT in the 1953 Clubmans. His performances helped him to get into the Royal Signals and a place in the White Helmets Display Team. This in turn led to rides in the Army team in the International Six Days Trials, followed by rides for Reg Dearden in the TT, and finally a one-off works ride on the MZ in the 1960 TT. The Crooks Suzuki company he formed in Barrow in Furness achieved many Production TT and Manx Grand Prix successes.

(78.48 mph). Jimmy Drysdale led the Juniors with 29m 49s (75.94 mph), and Richard Madsen-Mygdal the 1000's with 29m 46s (76.06 mph). However, the big-guns class ended the day with two less competitors, when A. H. Frost crashed at Hillberry and suffered concussion and a broken collar bone, and later it was learned that F. E. Taylor had received news of a serious accident to his son, and had had to return home. G. C. A. Murphy had a lucky escape when he came off at the Verandah, demolishing part of the fence in the process, while his BSA was burnt out. Murphy was able to warn oncoming riders of the situation, then walked to 'civilisation' at the Bungalow. B. C. Norwood went through the fence between Keppel Gate and Kate's Cottage, and a couple of miles further round the course, Brandish claimed L. C. King and his Norton. Happily both riders escaped with minor injuries.

The weather for Wednesday evening's third practice was even worse, this time with mist accompanying the rain, and the rain getting heavier as the session went on. Familiar names topped the times, but in different classes, as Jack Bottomley was fastest Junior with 29m 57s (75.60 mph), again on a Norton, with Derek Powell next, and Derek Powell fastest Senior with 29m 15s (77.40 mph), this time on a Triumph, with Jack Bottomley close behind. George Douglass set fastest time for the 1000's, with 32m 18s (70.10 mph). The road and weather conditions probably contributed to some of the half-dozen reported accidents, thankfully none resulted in serious injuries. Two of the already depleted 1000 cc runners fell, A.W. Edgson at the Guthrie Memorial where he sustained ankle injuries, and G. Bradley received a broken wrist in a fall at Laurel Bank. V. Clifford dropped his Norton in a separate incident at the same corner, while in one of those strange coincidences that sometimes happen, K. R. Dunn and A. G. Mollan, both riding Junior BSA's, and who had consecutive numbers and so would have started the race together, both came off at Ginger Hall! J. Wooderson, who had posted fourth fastest Senior lap, was reported to have *"gone through a fence in the Mountain Box area, remounted and toured back to the pits"*.

The '*TT Special*' published speeds recorded during the third session over the Sulby mile, with light drizzle, wet roads and a fair headwind. Fastest was not in fact a '1000', but Angus Martin's Senior Triumph with 111.14 mph, followed by Eric Ellis's Vincent with 110.45 mph, and then with identical speeds of 109.9 mph, the Norton of Harry Plews and the BSA of Eddie Dow. Fifth fastest was the Junior BSA of Owen Greenwood with 107.81 mph.

At long last, on the Thursday morning, the clubmen were able to practice in decent weather conditions. Gone were the wind, rain and mist, in fact the roads were mainly dry with just a few damp patches to catch the unwary, but the high standard of riding exhibited by the riders continued, and no spills of any kind were reported. J. R. Mason almost spoiled the 'accident-free' session, when the rear tyre of his Ariel disintegrated right in the middle of the fast right-hander at Hillberry. Somehow he managed to stay on and keep it upright until he brought it to a stop at Cronk-ny-Mona. Fastest lap of the morning went to P. L. Peters, who took his 1000 Vincent round in 27m 46s (81.55 mph), still some 1m 18s outside Chris Horn's 1949 record lap. E. Ellis on another Vincent was second fastest, his 27m 55s (81.11 mph) being exactly the same as the fastest Senior, Eddie Dow's BSA. Derek Powell's Triumph was second fastest Senior, but he was again fastest Junior with 28m 44s (78.80 mph), 27.6 seconds outside Bob McIntyre's 1952 record.

Friday morning's final practice was dry but cold, with mist developing on the high ground, eventually restricting visibility from the Guthrie Memorial to the Bungalow. Even so, lap speeds were good, topped by J. Bottomley's Senior Norton with 28m 01s (80.82 mph), Dow second fastest and Alan Holmes third on a Norton. Douglass was fastest 1000 by almost a minute and a half, and a new name heading the Junior practice session board was P. E. Burns on his BSA, with a lap in 29m 14s (77.51 mph). The number of starters for the 1000 race was reduced further, when a high speed accident just before the Guthrie Memorial put Eric Ellis in Ramsey Cottage Hospital with serious spinal injuries. Thankfully, by the end of race-week he was reported as 'making good progress.' L. C. King suffered slight concussion and was taken to Noble's Hospital after he came off his Norton at Appledene, but he was found to have only minor injuries.

Another faller was A. M. Cook who dropped his Senior Norton somewhere on the Mountain, but was able to remount and ride back to the pits.

The fastest men by the end of practicing were therefore P. L. Peters (Vincent) in the 1000 cc class, Eddie Dow (BSA) in the Senior, and Derek Powell (BSA) in the Junior. The overall fastest lap was by the Vincent, nine seconds faster than the Senior BSA.

Hedley Cox, who, in 1951 built and raced an ingenious twin cylinder Velocette in the Manx Grand Prix, came off at the 33rd Milestone outside of official practice, and his chances of taking up his ride in the 1000 cc race were slim. The number of starters was thus reduced to eight.

Hedley Cox riding at Silverstone Saturday, qualifying for the 1953 Clubman's. A practice spill at the 33rd ruled him out his only TT ride.

The Junior Race (Monday, 8th June)

Starters

	Rider	Club	Machine
1	G T Salt	Bridgnorth & DMC	B.S.A.
2	E R Williams	Oswestry & DMC	B.S.A.
3	H Williams	Kings Norton MCC	B.S.A.
4	R A Russell	Kensal Rise & DMCC	B.S.A.
5	E Baxter	Triangle (Ipswich) MCC	B.S.A.
6	G A Northwood	Shropshire & Staffs. Bord MC & LCC	B.S.A.
7	A N Robinson	Antelope MCC (Coventry)	B.S.A.
8	E B Crooks	Ramsey & DMC & CC	Norton
9	G E Gibson	Loch Lomond MCC	B.S.A.
10	H A Voice	Bishops Waltham MC	B.S.A.
11	K R Dunn	North Leeds & DMC	B.S.A.
12	A G Mollan	West Leeds MC	B.S.A.
14	H Walmsley	Preston & DMC	Norton
16	K Smith	Barham & DMC & LCC	A.J.S.
17	J Sutherland	St Helens & DAC	B.S.A.
19	G R Dunlop	Tenterden & DMC & LCC	Norton
20	A F J D Martin	Rugby MC	B.S.A.
21	M E J Taft	Ilkeston & DMCC & LCC	B.S.A.
22	R Ellis	Sheffield Ace MC	B.S.A.
23	J N Wooderson	Auckland MCC (New Zealand)	Matchless
24	L Dunham	South Kirkby & DMC	B.S.A.
25	J Bottomley	Moccasin MC & LCC	Norton
26	E Cox	Cheadle Hulme & DMCC	A.J.S.
27	P E Burns	Thornton Cleveleys MCC	B.S.A.
28	G Owen	Ramsey & DMC & CC	Matchless
29	D A Wright	Runcorn & DMC	B.S.A.
30	B C Norwood	Kent & Sussex MCC	B.S.A.
31	J Benton	Wolverhampton MC & CC	B.S.A.
32	H Plews	Wakefield & DMSC	B.S.A.
34	I Lloyd	Holmsley & DMCC	B.S.A.
35	H Evans	Darlington & DMC	B.S.A.
37	D R Watson	Ravensbury MCC	B.S.A.
38	J V Hatcher	Weymouth & S,. Dorset MC & LCC	B.S.A.
39	D T Powell	Ringwood MC & LCC	B.S.A.
40	R Ingram	Frome & D. United MC & LCC	Norton
41	A S Bowie	Menstrie MCC	B.S.A.
42	E Cheers	Chester MC	Norton
43	E D Blackwell	Leamington Victory MC & LCC	B.S.A.
44	O E Greenwood	Leicester Query MC	B.S.A.
45	J Drysdale	Aberdeen & DMC	B.S.A.
46	D Webb	Saxon MCC	Norton
47	E McG. Haldane	Falkirk & DMC	B.S.A.
48	R Brassington	Potteries Clarion MC	Norton
49	W R Oldfield	Macclesfield MCC	B.S.A.
50	G Arnold	Warrington & DMC	B.S.A.
51	A L Burton	Southampton & DMCC	Norton
52	P Palmer	Huddersfield MC	B.S.A.

53	J R Dulson	South Liverpool MC	Norton
54	H A Nash	Kings Norton MCC	B.S.A.
56	R E Smith	Leatherhead & DMC	Norton
57	G R Brown	Boston & DMC & LCC	B.S.A.
58	S R Raynor	Notts & DMCC	B.S.A.
59	F McCormick	Dunfermline & DMCC	B.S.A.
60	J F Griffiths	Rhyl & DMC	B.S.A.
61	G C A Murphy	Manor MC	B.S.A.
62	J G Robertson	Alnwick & DMC	B.S.A.
63	H Smith (Jnr)	Golden Horse MCC	Douglas
64	R D Keeler	Ruislip & DMCC	Norton
65	J H T Harris	Louth & DMCC	B.S.A.
66	J Cunningham	South Liverpool MC	B.S.A.
67	A M Sutton	Castle (Colchester) MCC	B.S.A.
68	R Capner	Whitehaven MC	B.S.A.
69	E F H Boyce	Salop MC	B.S.A.
70	H R Collier	Mont' Christie MCC	B.S.A.
71	W R Smith	North Lincolnshire MC	B.S.A.
72	F Sheene	Stamford Bridge MCC	B.S.A.
73	A Scholefield	Accrington & DMCC	B.S.A.
74	S T Seston	Meteor MCC	B.S.A.
75	B Kershaw	Rochdale & DMC	B.S.A.
76	H McKenzie	Galloway MC & CC	B.S.A.

Non-starters announced were the BSA's of V. J. Holcroft and Doug Crennell, the Douglas's of Don Chapman and A. O. Duffy, and the Ariel of F. D. Jenkins. The superb weather from the morning's International Junior race continued, so much so that competitors assembling for the 2.00 pm start were warned of possible melting tar on the approach to Sulby Bridge. Starting arrangements were for groups of three at 30-second intervals, first away being George Salt, E. R. Williams and H. Williams, all on BSA's, and all got away without any difficulties. Most of the entry were able to avoid serious delays, but there were inevitably some whose luck was not in. Bernard Norwood lost 45 seconds before his BSA fired up, and two Norton riders who lost the best part of a minute at the start were John Dulson and one of the pre-race favourites Bob Keeler. Another of the likely contenders Jack Bottomley also lost precious seconds, but worst handicapped was W. R. Smith, whose BSA remained silent until a minute and a half had passed. At Kirkmichael, Ron Russell from the second starting group had made up the starting interval on the leading group, and led on the roads,

with P. E. Burns picking up places from his starting number of 27. Russell continued to lead on the roads into Ramsey, lost it to E. R. Williams over the mountain but then regained it by the end of the lap. Others who were noticeably fast and obviously making up ground on that first lap were Jack Bottomley, Eddie Crooks and Bob Foster's protégé Derek Powell. Once on the move, Bob Keeler had put in a near-record lap and re-gained some of the time lost at the start, even though he stopped for fuel at the end of the lap. As the first corrected times became known, Keeler was found to be in a joint 8th place with Russell, but the leader was Powell, with a 13-second advantage over Bottomley, and Burns 3rd. Burns was another to take on fuel early, but overshot and lost time pulling the BSA back to his pit. The first six places were separated only by 56 seconds.

First Lap Leaderboard.

1	D.T. Powell (BSA)	28m 20s	(79.93 mph)
2	J. Bottomley (Norton)	28m 33s	(79.32 mph)
3	P.E. Burns (BSA)	28m 36s	(79.18 mph)
4	O.E. Greenwood (BSA)	28m 44s	(78.81 mph)
5	I.I. Lloyd (BSA)	28m 51s	(78.49 mph)
6	P. Palmer (BSA)	28m 56s	(78.25 mph)

Machine reliability and staying power at sustained high speeds was again proving to be very good, with only two retirements from mechanical causes on that first lap, E. Cox at the pits with a split tank on his AJS, and the BSA of J. Sutherland reportedly stopped out on the course, without any details as to where or why. S.R. Raynor came off his BSA at Hillberry and retired as a consequence, Harry Voice stopped temporarily at the Bungalow to adjust his front brake. Leading positions remained as they were on the previous lap, with unofficial timekeeping indicating that Powell was pulling away from Bottomley. When the times were announced, Powell had increased his lead to 42 seconds and in the process broken Bob McIntyre's existing lap record with a time of 27m 58s (80.96 mph). Burns dropped from the leaderboard, elevating Owen Greenwood to 3rd place, and differing strategies over fuel stops brought the BSA's of H. McKenzie and Angus Martin onto the leaderboard at the end of the second lap, McKenzie having put in a very fast lap, lifting himself from 13th on the first lap to 4th. H. R. Collier retired his BSA at the pits with 'steering trouble', also dropping out on the lap were Goo Owen (Matchless) and Laurence Dunham (BSA). G. C. A. Murphy and J. V. Hatcher both overshot their pits, and lost time, but the latter must have had a more fundamental problem as he retired the BSA shortly after.

Second Lap Leaderboard.

1 D.T. Powell (BSA)	56m 18s	(80.43 mph)
2 J. Bottomley (Norton)	57m 00s	(79.44 mph)
3 O.E. Greenwood (BSA)	57m 43s	(78.46 mph)
4 H McKenzie (BSA)	57m 48s	(78.34 mph)
5 A.F.J. Martin (BSA)	58m 9s	(77.87 mph)
6 I.I. Lloyd (BSA)	58m 15s	(77.74 mph)

Keeler's spirited ride came to an end in the pits after the second lap, leaving Bottomley to uphold Norton fortunes against the tide of BSA's. Powell had steadily reduced the two minute starting interval between himself and 2nd man Bottomley, by Ramsey on the third lap he was right with the Norton, and by Cronk-ny-Mona had passed him. Bottomley regained the advantage as Powell lifted his goggles and pulled in to refuel. Despite the loss of use of his front brake during the third lap, a 28m 23s lap by Greenwood elevated him to 2nd place when the leaderboard was displayed, 11 seconds ahead of Bottomley. Russell retired on the Mountain with engine trouble, and E. D. Blackwell was reported as 'making adjustments' at Hillberry, without success apparently, as he retired at the pits shortly after. Another reported retirement was that of the surviving AJS of W. J. Keel at Laurel Bank, no cause was given, just that the rider was 'ok'. Happily he must have been able to cure the problem, as he eventually made it to the finish, and 33rd place. Bernard Norwood locked up his front wheel as he came in to refuel, and in coming off hit the pit wall quite hard. Despite his protests, he was prevented from rejoining the race by Scrutineer Vic Anstice because of damage sustained by the BSA. Other third lap retirees were J. N. Wooderson (Matchless), G. Arnold (BSA) and J. Cunningham (BSA). As the positions settled down following fuel stops, two new names appeared on the leaderboard, those of P. Palmer and A. M. Sutton, both on BSA's.

Third Lap Leaderboard.

1 D.T. Powell (BSA)	1h 24m 18s	(80.57 mph)
2 O.E. Greenwood (BSA)	1h 26m 6s	(78.89 mph)
3 J. Bottomley (Norton)	1h 26m 17s	(78.72 mph)
4 P. Palmer (BSA)	1h 26m 49s	(78.24 mph)
4 A.M. Sutton (BSA)	1h 26m 49s	(78.24 mph)
6 P.E. Burns (BSA)	1h 26m 51s	(78.21 mph)

Harry Voice retained his lead on the roads to the end, coming home in 8th place, followed by Bottomley and the winner Powell, who finished a minute and 20 seconds ahead of 2nd placeman Greenwood, who had survived a scare when he ran wide at Laurel Bank on the final lap. Greenwood held off Bottomley by the margin of only 3.6 seconds at the flag. The third lap tie for 4th place was resolved in favour of Palmer, 8 seconds ahead of Sutton, while Burns's eventful afternoon continued with a fall high on the Mountain road on the fast left-hander at the Stonebreakers Hut (or Black Hut) just before the Verandah, without serious injury. Another faller on the Mountain was Arthur Brassington, who dropped his Norton at the Mountain Box, while H. Walmsley pushed his Norton in from Hillberry to finish 48th and next to last. H. Evans' BSA ran out of fuel at Ramsey hairpin and he was forced to retire.

Bernard Norwood 'in discussion' with ACU officials after sliding off his Gold Star when coming in to refuel. They would not allow him to proceed.

Other retirements on that last lap were R. Ellis (BSA) with engine trouble at Glen Helen, and H. Smith parking the sole remaining Douglas near Handleys. A. L. Burton (Norton) and J. Drysdale (BSA) were additional retirements, and although no reasons were specified for their stops, the riders were reported as being 'ok'. As well as posting a new record lap, Powell's race average of 80.17 mph was in fact faster than Bob McIntyre's previous years lap record. Post-race machine examinations showed that Greenwood's BSA had at some point developed an oil leak from the pushrod tunnel, and the tank had been all but drained by the end of the race.

Finishing Order

1 D.T. Powell (BSA)	1h 52m 57.8s	(80.17 mph)
2 O.E. Greenwood (BSA)	1h 54m 18s	(79.23 mph)
3 J. Bottomley (Norton)	1h 54m 21.6s	(79.19 mph)
4 P. Palmer (BSA)	1h 54m 52s	(78.84 mph)
5 A.M. Sutton (BSA)	1h 55m 0s	(78.75 mph)
6 W.R. Oldfield (BSA)	1h 55m 37s	(78.33 mph)

Fastest Lap: D.T. Powell (2nd lap) 27m 58s (80.96 mph) (Record)

The Centre Team Prize was not awarded.

The 1000cc Race (Monday, 8th June)

Starters

Rider	Club	Machine
102 D L Buss	Vincent HRD OC	Vincent
103 L Floodgate	Vincent HRD OC	Vincent
104 L F Pittam	Vincent HRD OC	Vincent
105 P L Peters	Vincent HRD OC	Vincent
106 G P Clark	Hull AC & LCC	Vincent
107 J O Finch	Vincent HRD OC	Vincent
108 G P Douglass	Vincent HRD OC	Vincent
115 R Madsen-Mygdal	Vincent HRD OC	Vincent

Although scheduled in both 1951 and 1952, entries had fallen short of the number required to enable a separate class to be run for the 1000cc machines, so

Leaderboard men from the 1953 Junior Clubman. Left to right: Owen Greenwood (BSA), Jack Bottomley (Norton) and Derek Powell (BSA).

it was three years since the previous TT outing for the big machines. Supporters of the event must have been dismayed therefore by the eight non-starters, exactly half the field. The unfortunates were E. Ellis, A. W. Edgson, J.R. Thurston, A. H. Frost, H. J. Cox, F. E. Taylor, G. Bradley and J. Hawtin, all entered on Vincent - HRD's. The first of those who could make the start were sent off 5 minutes after the last of the Junior Clubmen had gone, J. O. Finch's machine proving reluctant to fire up, although he did eventually get away. The sparse field was quickly reduced still further when L. Floodgate came a cropper at Union Mills, and was fortunate to have suffered only a broken collar bone. The first runner to show was Richard Madsen-Mygdal (father of TT and Classic racer David), who had pulled out a 20 second advantage over 2nd place-man Geoffrey Clarke, and 36 seconds over George Douglass.

First Lap Leaderboard

1 R. Madsen-Mygdal (Vincent-HRD)
                        27m 41s   (81.81 mph)
2 G.P. Clark (Vincent-HRD) 28m 3s (80.72 mph)
3 G.P. Douglass (Vincent-HRD)
                        28m 17s   (80.07 mph)
4 P.L. Peters (Vincent-HRD) 30m 38s (73.95 mph)
5 D.L. Buss (Vincent-HRD)   31m 18s (72.32 mph)
6 L.F. Pittam(Vincent-HRD) 32m 32s (69.06 mph)

Clark was having slight twistgrip problems with his machine, and had slowed after a big 'moment' at Quarry bends. Perhaps also Douglass' 'Black Shadow' had a slight speed advantage over the 'Rapide', but there was no doubting that Douglass' 2nd lap was a quick one. Not only did his 27m 16s (82.46 mph) lap put him 46 seconds ahead of Clark, it put him in the lead when Madsen-Mygdal came off after tangling with a slower rider at Brandywell, fortunately receiving only minor injuries.

Second Lap Leaderboard

1 G.P. Douglass (Vincent-HRD)
                        55m 43s   (81.27 mph)
2 G.P. Clark (Vincent-HRD) 56m 29s (80.17 mph)
3 P.L. Peters (Vincent-HRD) 1h 0m 52s (74.40 mph)
4 D.L. Buss (Vincent-HRD)   1h 2m 40s (72.20 mph)
5 L.F. Pittam (Vincent-HRD) 1h 4m 23s (70.33 mph)

6 J.O. Finch (Vincent-HRD) 1h 8m 2s (66.55 mph)

Douglass extended his lead over Clark during the 3rd lap to over 2 minutes, and the already wide gap between Clark and 3rd place-man Peters also increased. There were no retirements or reported problems for the remaining six competitors on that lap.

Third Lap Leaderboard

1 G.P. Douglass (Vincent-HRD)
                        1h 23m 43s (81.13 mph)
2 G.P. Clark (Vincent-HRD) 1h 25m 51s (79.12 mph)
3 P.L. Peters (Vincent-HRD) 1h 31m 31s (74.22 mph)
4 D.L. Buss (Vincent-HRD)   1h 34m 54s (71.57 mph)
5 L.F. Pittam (Vincent-HRD) 1h 36m 23s (70.47 mph)
6 J.O. Finch (Vincent-HRD) 1h 41m 47s (66.73 mph)

The placings remained the same over the concluding lap, the gaps increasing slightly, except that was, for the battle which developed for 4th place between Buss and Pittam. This went right to the line, and after nearly two hours of racing the advantage went to Pittam by 1 second. Douglass's winning margin was exactly 3 minutes, and although his average speed was also a race record, his fastest lap (the fourth, 27m 21s (82.80 mph) was outside Chris Horn's 1949 record. Out of petrol, J. O. Finch pushed in his heavy machine, long after most of the crowd had gone, to finish in a distant 6th place.

Finishing Order

1 G.P. Douglass (Vincent-HRD)
                        1h 51m 4s   (81.54 mph)
2 G.P. Clark (Vincent-HRD) 1h 54m 4s (79.39 mph)
3 P.L. Peters (Vincent-HRD) 2h 1m 59s (74.24 mph)
4 L.F. Pittam (Vincent-HRD) 2h 6m 36s (71.53 mph)
5 D.L. Buss (Vincent-HRD)   2h 6m 37s (71.52 mph)
6 J.O. Finch (Vincent-HRD) 2h 34m 0s (58.81 mph)

Fastest Lap: G.P. Douglass (4th lap) 27m 21s (82.80 mph).

The 500cc Race (Thursday, 11th June)

	Rider	Starters Club	Machine
1	P Cooper	Middlesborough & DMC	Triumph

3	V Clifford	Wakefield & DMSC	Norton
4	W A Harding	Southern MCC	Norton
5	R Ellis	Sheffield North End MC & LCC	
			Norton
6	J Wright	Wirral '100' MC	B.S.A.
7	P J Pooley	South Liverpool MC	Triumph
8	H Plews	Wakefield & DMSC	Norton
9	K Smith	Barham & DMC & LCC	A.J.S.
10	L R King	Worcester AC	Triumph
11	E B Crooks	Peveril (IoM) MC & LCC	Norton
12	J N Wooderson	Auckland MCC (New Zealand)	
			Matchless
15	J R Mason	Accrington & DMCC	Ariel
16	W R Oldfield	Macclesfield MCC	Triumph
17	T S Shepherd	Wirral '100' MC	Norton
18	F O Coleman	Kings Norton MCC	Norton
19	E C Little	Liverpool Imperial MCC	Matchless
20	D Andrews	Horsforth & DMC	Matchless
21	R A D Mawson	Peveril (IoM) MC & LCC	Norton
22	W H Wilshere	Watford & DMC & LCC	Triumph

23	J Bottomley	Moccasin MC & LCC	Norton
24	G W Shekell	Cheltenham Home Guard MC & LCC	
			Norton
25	E Cheers	Chester MC	Triumph
26	A S Avis	Border MC	Triumph
27	J H T Harris	Louth & DMCC	Triumph
28	W Zoellner	Runcorn & DMC	Triumph
29	A E Hart	Manchester Pegasus MCC	Triumph
31	S T Seston	Birmingham MCC	Norton
32	P E Walsh	Solihull MCC	Norton
33	A J Hagon	Ilford Amateur MC	Norton
34	R Arthur	Golden Horse MCC	Norton
35	R E Jerrard	Southampton & DMCC	Norton
36	D T Powell	Ringwood MC & LCC	Triumph
37	K A Taubman	Rawmarsh & DMC & LCSC	Triumph
38	J I Elliott	Lewes Unity MCC	Ariel
39	I Lloyd	Holmsley & DMCC	Triumph
40	N George	Jersey MC & LCC	B.S.A.
41	A F J D Martin	Rugby MCC	Triumph
42	D Naylor	Castle (Colchester) MCC	B.S.A.
43	R D Keeler	Ruislip & DMCC	Norton
44	D S Cholerton	St Helens & DAC	Triumph
45	L C King	B.M.C.R.C.	Norton
46	A King	Mercury MCC (Glasgow)	Norton
47	J Walker	Peterborough MCC	Triumph
48	G R Dunlop	Tenterden & DMC & LCC	Norton
49	W E Dow	Castle (Colchester) MCC	B.S.A.
50	D Johnstone	Warrington & DMC	B.S.A.
51	P G K Baldwin	Sunbeam MCC	A.J.S.
52	T A Ovens	Cirencester MCC	Triumph
53	F D Jenkins	Peveril (IoM) MC & CC	Ariel
54	M W Gillingham		
		Sturminster Newton & DMC & LCC	
			Norton
55	A M Cook	Lincoln & DMC & LCC	Norton
56	A Newstead	Retford & DMC	B.S.A.
57	H B Winter	North Lancashire MC	Norton
58	T F Watson	Scunthorpe MCC	Norton
59	H F Hunter	Portsmouth MCRC	B.S.A.
61	R A Russell	Kensal Rise & DMC	A.J.S.
62	P Minion	Pathfinders & Derby MC	Norton
63	C Watson	North Lincolnshire MC	Norton

A delighted George Douglass reflects on his winning ride

Wednesday's International Lightweight race had gone ahead despite the mist and rain, after a one hour delay to the start, but by the time the race ended, a little after 1.00 pm, the visibility on the Mountain had fallen to 15-20 yards. By 3.00 pm, the 125cc International and Senior Clubman's races had been postponed to the following day. This caused difficulties, with the postponed races taking place on the same day as the weigh-in for the highlight of the week, the International Senior TT. The 125cc and Clubman's Senior prize distribution was also scheduled for that same evening, and as a consequence the Senior Clubman's was reduced to three laps.

Weather conditions were much improved on the Thursday, and the afternoon was sunny with clear skies, and a slight breeze to keep temperatures comfortable. Four non-starters were announced, M. D. King, C. McLean, G. Cooper and W. Scott, all on Nortons. Racing began at 12.30 pm, riders again in groups of three at 30-second intervals, P. Cooper (Triumph) and V. Clifford (Norton) getting things under way. Most got away well or without too much delay, but Ron Jerrard (Norton), J. I. Elliott (Ariel) and Alastair King (Norton) all lost precious seconds, and Manx butcher Bob Mawson had a major problem, losing about 5 minutes before his Norton fired up. Manxman Alan Holmes was the first to reach Kirkmichael, but New Zealander G.avin Dunlop got no further than Quarter Bridge where he

crashed his Norton, without injury. Junior winner Derek Powell started number 36, and set off as if he intended to repeat the performance. John Wright retired his BSA twin at Bishopscourt, and likely front-runner Jack Bottomley had a 'coming-together' with traffic policeman Len King's Triumph at Governors Bridge. King continued and finished in 15th place, but the Norton suffered damage in the ensuing fall, and Bottomley retired and walked the mile or so back to the pits. Another Manxman Eddie Crooks put in a very quick first lap, only 11 seconds outside Geoff Duke's 1949 record, and for a while it looked as though he might be in the lead, but when Bob Keeler's time came up he was 7 seconds faster. Appearing on the leaderboard in 3rd place only 8 seconds down on Crooks was Eddie Dow, a notable achievement as the Gold Star, despite its success as a 350, had not until that time been seen as a serious contender in the bigger class. That was about to change forever. A.E. Hart needed treatment after coming off his Triumph at Laurel Bank, and another faller was D. Johnstone who dropped his BSA in the Glentramman area, again escaping with minor injuries. Retirements during the lap were J. H. T. Harris (Triumph), F. D. Jenkins (Ariel) and H. B. Winter (Norton).

John Mason rounds Quarter Bridge on his Ariel Huntmaster twin.

1 R.D. Keeler (Norton)	27m 7s	(83.50 mph)
2 E.B. Crooks (Norton)	27m 17s	(83.15 mph)
3 W.E. Dow (BSA)	27m 25s	(82.60 mph)
4 D.T. Powell (Triumph)	27m 36s	(82.05 mph)
5 W.A. Holmes (Norton)	27m 39s	(81.89 mph)
6 W.R. Oldfield (Norton)	28m 3s	(80.72 mph)
6 H. Plews (Norton)	28m 3s	(80.72 mph)

Keeler's second lap was a terrific 26m 48s (84.49 mph), some 15 seconds inside Geoff Duke's 1949 record, and it put a little daylight between him and 2nd place, which by the end of the lap was Dow, who had a 21 second advantage over Crooks, who by that time was riding without a clutch. By the end of the lap Holmes had made up the 3 second deficit on Powell to tie. Tom Ovens retired after coming off his Triumph, but N. George re-joined the race after a fall at Quarter Bridge. Ron Russell was forced to stop at the pits and eventually pull out his AJS when it split a tank, H. B. Winters (Norton) retired at the Quarry Bends with engine trouble, and M. W. Gillingham retired his Norton at the pits. P. J. Pooley brought his Triumph into the pits, and stayed there. Also posted as 2nd lap retirements were Eric Cheers (Triumph), with engine trouble at the Mountain Box, P. Minion (Norton), with engine trouble at the Gooseneck, and A. M. Cook (Norton), who was reported as sitting on the bank at Brandish, near his silent Norton, making the best of his enforced retirement and enjoying watching the race. D. S. Cholerton (Triumph) was another retirement at the pits.

Second Lap Leaderboard

1 R.D. Keeler (Norton)	53m 55s	(83.98 mph)
2 W.E. Dow (BSA)	54m 16s	(83.45 mph)
3 E.B. Crooks (Norton)	54m 35s	(82.96 mph)
4 W.A. Holmes (Norton)	55m 6s	(82.18 mph)
4 D.T. Powell (Triumph)	55m 6s	(82.18 mph)
6 A. King (Norton)	55m 54s	(81.25 mph)

Unofficial timekeepers at Kirkmichael were ready with the stopwatches to measure Dow's progress, but they waited in vain, as he had, in his own words much later, *"overdone it"* in a big way at Laurel Bank. He was to be hospitalised for several months as a result. Holmes was first past the flag, followed by Crooks, but Keeler, with a last lap only fractionally outside his new record, had stretched his lead to a little over a minute at the end of the race. Holmes and Powell remained very close on corrected time, the verdict (and 3rd place on Dow's retirement) went to Holmes by just 3.6 seconds. Bob Mawson's Norton, which had lost him so much time at the start, had one more trick to play, and demanded to be pushed in from Governors Bridge. Unsurprisingly, he was last, but at least he was a finisher, which a few more unfortunates on that last lap were not. H.F. Hunter retired his BSA at the Gooseneck with engine trouble, and also out for unspecified reasons were W .J. Keel (AJS), W. Zoellner (Triumph) and I. Lloyd (Triumph).

Finishing Order

1 R.D. Keeler (Norton)	1h 20m 43.4s (84.14 mph)
2 E.B. Crooks (Norton)	1h 21m 49.3s (83.00 mph)
3 W.A. Holmes (Norton)	1h 22m 22.2s (82.46 mph)
4 D.T. Powell (Triumph)	1h 22m 25.8s (82.40 mph)
5 A. King (Norton)	1h 23m 4.2s (81.77 mph)
6 H. Plews (Norton)	1h 23m 24s (81.44 mph)

Fastest Lap: R.D. Keeler (2nd lap) 26m 48s (84.49 mph) (Record)

The Centre Team Award went to the Yorkshire Centre (R. Ellis, H. Plews and D. Andrews).

Reflections

Post-race machine examinations revealed that Keeler's Senior-winning Norton had been running perfectly, but only had about a pint of oil left in the tank. It was therefore just as well that the race distance had been shortened by a lap.

The winning average speed for the Junior was 80.17 mph, for the Senior 84.14 mph, and for the 1000 cc 81.54 mph. Fastest laps were respectively 80.96 mph, 82.80 mph, and 84.49 mph. The performance of the 1000's was somewhere between the Juniors and Seniors, although of course rider ability played a major part in determining lap times. They were a match for most 500's, spectacular, and popular with the spectators, but 1953 was to be the last throw of the dice for the 'big-uns'. Throughout the Clubman's series, the class had suffered from lack of numbers. The two who entered the first event in 1947 unfortunately didn't make the start but the following year showed what the Vincent's were capable of, with 1st, 2nd, 5th and 6th places in the Senior, and a record lap for George Brown 2½ mph faster than Eric Briggs' 1947 lap on his 500 Norton. 10 of the 31 finishers were on the Stevenage product, and the winner Jack Daniels nearly seven minutes ahead of the first 500, C.A. Stevens in 3rd place on his Norton. Thus encouraged, the ACU gave the 1000's their own race in 1949, and entry numbers were similar (11), and although race average speeds were down (Dennis Lashmar winning at 76.30 mph), Chris Horn's record lap of 26m 28s (85.57 mph) was faster than Geoff Duke's Senior (500) lap record of 27m 3s (83.70 mph). In fact, this incredible lap was never bettered by a 1000 cc machine, and wasn't bettered in the Clubman's until Alastair King's record Senior lap in 1954. Another separate 1000 race in 1950 attracted 13 entrants, Alex Phillip winning at 78.58 mph, with a fastest lap in 27m 57s (81.01 mph). This was faster than the winning 500 which was Phil Carter, who averaged 75.60 mph, while fastest lap was set by Ivan Wicksteed at 28m 29s (79.51 mph).

Not running with the 500's, but having their own class proved to be a mixed benefit. Fine if sufficient entries were received for the event to be staged, but if they weren't, the 1000's could not then drop into the Senior class, which had a capacity limit set at 500 cc. Which was exactly what happened in both 1951 and 1952, entries in each of those years falling below the threshold number of twelve. That sufficient entries were received by the ACU for the class to be reintroduced in 1953 was due, in the main, to considerable efforts by the Vincent Owners Club to rally support, but after that year the class was dropped.

The Vincent-HRD was the only competitive make of machine in the class, the odd Scott or Ariel were entered more out of an individual's enthusiasm for that marque than a desire to be able to compete for top honours.

David Wright, author of three books on Vincents, including 'Vincents, HRD's and the Isle of Man', published by Amulree in 1998, describes the Vincent

factory involvement in the Clubman's thus:

"Philip Vincent claimed his bikes were not designed for racing, but always sought maximum publicity from their successes.

He saw racing on the TT Course as a way of demonstrating the big Vincent's capability of maintaining high-speeds for a long period, hinting that he was not particularly interested in results.

There were two 1000cc Vincents entered in the 1947 Clubman's. One was a Series A Twin from the late 1930s and the other a new post-war Rapide sent to Whittakers of Blackpool. Vincents knew the Rapide was destined for the Clubman's and, like all its special performance models, it was taken to Gransden airfield for a test run. (Ordinary roadsters were just tested up the A1). Philip Vincent was present at the test run and had a bare-headed run on the bike. Unfortunately, the gearbox seized and although he rode it almost to a standstill, he was thrown off. The injuries he received affected his balance and put a stop to his riding.

The fellow who rode it for Whittaker's disgraced himself by not really trying in practice - press reports told of him riding one-handed in places - and did not qualify.

With regard to the 1948 event, Vincent employee at the time Cliff Brown (brother of George) and author of George's biography wrote: '.... Mr. Vincent decided that George and Phil Heath should ride them (1000 Twins) on the Island and after working hard on a couple of engines which had been rejected in road-tests as bad rattlers, I was happy . . .'

Phil Heath was in the 'Trade' and had long-standing connections with Vincents.

Vincent employee at the time, Ted Davis, rode in 1948 and tells how he and Phil Irving spent the week-end before the race working on his Twin and found another 10 mph.

1949 was the no refuelling fiasco.

1950 Vincents concentrated on their 'works' Grey Flash entries in the 'International' Senior TT.

I am not aware of any 500cc Vincent entries in the Clubman's receiving any special attention from the factory, but I'm sure if a private owner ordered a machine specifically for the Clubman's the factory gave it that little bit more attention. Of course, many of the Vincents raced in the Clubman's by true

Clubmen had done many road miles."

Unfortunately for all concerned, the Vincent factory was beginning to struggle financially in the early 1950's, and machine development was minimal. George Douglass's winning machine in 1953 was a 1949 'Black Shadow' with over 28,000 miles on the clock. A glance through the motorcycle press of late 1950 shows five British manufacturer's other than Vincent with over-500 cc machines catalogued. The Ariel Square Four was a full 1000 cc, the Panther Model 100 and Scott Flying Squirrel both 600 cc, but none of these could have been considered to have any race potential (Scott enthusiasts may wish to dispute that point). Triumph's Thunderbird and BSA's Golden Flash were not promoted primarily as sports machines let alone racers, but it would have been interesting to see how they performed against the Vincents. ACU minutes show that a proposal to include 1000's in the 1954 event was considered by the TT Sub-Committee at their meeting on 31st August 1953, and the Competitions Committee on 3rd September 1953. The motion was defeated by 5 votes to 3, and thus the chance was missed to swell the entry and to breathe new life into the 1000 cc class.

In contrast to the lack of development of the big vee-twins, the 350 class saw a concerted and sustained programme of improvement for the Gold Star. This period in BSA's history has been well documented over the years, as have the contributions made by the likes of Jack Amott, then Roland Pike, Cyril Halliburn, Reg Wilkes, Alan Sandilands et al. In 1953 the 350 Norton 'Inter' was still just about capable of putting up a fight against the Gold Star, but the machine of choice for the majority of the runners had become the BSA. Winning the Clubman's TT was a BSA management priority, and the development effort, which was centred around the 350 in the early years, began to bring reward.

'The Motor Cycle' of 18th June featured what was then a traditional post-race test of the TT-winning machines performed and written by the incomparable Vic Willoughby, and included Derek Powell's winning Gold Star.

"A few years ago there was a tremendously wide gulf between pure racing machines and those designed for road work and clubman racing. The gulf remains today, but the development of the 348 cc BSA Gold Star to its present pitch has narrowed it considerably.

D.T. Powell, an erstwhile Dorset farmer and now a motorcycle salesman at Bob Foster's Parkstone premises, provided proof of this when he brought his Gold Star home first in the Junior Clubman's at an average speed of 80.17 mph. Pulling a 5.05 to 1 top gear during the race, Powell was able to obtain 7,000 rpm on level stretches of road. This represents approximately 105 mph, a speed which I subsequently confirmed.

When I rode the BSA two days later, there was a notable absence of external oil and the machine had not been cleaned since the event. The only attention to the BSA before my test was the replacement of the petrol tank, which had split during the race. The sole modification from standard noted was the use of an Amal Grand Prix carburettor in place of a TT type.

I started the engine several times by means of the kick-starter, a feat which could be easily accomplished on near-full advance, provided only a small throttle opening was used and care taken not to over-flood the carburettor. Riding from Douglas to the Mountain I found the engine tractable and the exhaust reasonably quiet provided the rpm were kept below 4000. Around this engine speed, there was a fairly pronounced show of temperament but, as soon as the carburation had cleared, the power came in with a surge, racing fashion: 7,000 rpm is quoted as maximum permissible engine speed. Powell had his rev-meter so mounted that this figure was in the nine o'clock position. Consequently, when I was tucked well down, it was difficult to check this reading accurately. There was clearly audible indication from the valves whenever the engine speed exceeded 7,000 rpm so that only the most clueless would unwittingly over-rev the engine.

I was impressed by the potency of the pushrod engine. From rev-meter readings, it appeared to be as fast as the racing machine I had used in the Junior International event. Possibly its acceleration may not have been so good, though this is rather difficult to judge.

The handlebar position was high by pure racing machine standards, but the riding position was comfortable nevertheless. The 8-inch front brake was powerful, though it seemed to me to have a fractionally delayed action - possibly the result of a strenuous race.

The new pivoted-fork rear springing worked well.

A few bumps were apparent, but I have yet to meet the springing which absorbs all the Island's surface irregularities. Front fork action was soft and comfortable."

My 1953 Senior Clubman's Ride
by Alf Hagon

I entered the 1953 Senior Clubman's TT on a brand new International Norton, supplied by 'Maxie' Miller, who had a tool-making business in Romford. Maxie was a larger than life character who used to grass-track and road-race in the early 1950's. Sadly, he was killed in a light aeroplane accident only a few years later. The 'Inter' was a completely standard model complete with lights, and was run in by riding it up to Liverpool to catch the ferry. Once over there I shared a garage with Terry Shepherd who was riding another 'Inter' Norton, and who knew his way around the Island (he finished 6th in the Junior Manx Grand Prix later that same year). Terry helped me get settled in and showed me the way around the course on the back of a road bike. During the first practice the bike was found to be well under-geared, and in fact it over-revved on a couple of occasions and bent the valves. The front brake also tore itself to pieces. Norton's of course were in the Island and they fixed it up, but it was very slow compared to the Gold Stars. One lap I completely misjudged the approach to Signpost Corner in the mist and fog, but thankfully it was no problem as there was a slip road there, which is not often the case on the Mountain circuit. One lasting memory, from somewhere up on the Mountain, was being passed at lunatic speed by more experienced competitors in mist so thick you could hardly see the kerb. I was thinking to myself that they must have no brains, or else have radar!

In the race I got up to about 8th before a misfire set in, and I stopped to change a plug. Unfortunately, with not knowing the course too well, I stopped in a slightly uphill section of the course, which meant that the restart would have to be by kick, which I managed, but the misfire had been caused by the magneto points starting to close up, not the plug, so it was no improvement. The best I could do was press on and eventually finished 23rd. [Alf's first race lap was completed in 28m 41s, which, had he been able to continue at that speed, would have brought him home certainly in the first 10].

Alf is barely inches ahead of his starting partner Sam Seston as they peel into Union Mills.

Looking back on the Clubman's, it was a fantastic experience and one that I wouldn't have missed, but I had no desire to return the following year. That was in the early days of my racing career, doing speedway and grass-track as well as the occasional road-race (I did both the last grass-track meeting at Brands Hatch and its first road-race). In the two weeks that the Isle of Man took up, it was possible to ride in seven or eight grass and speedway meetings. The decision had to be made as to which direction my racing would go, and as grass-track and speedway had begun to take a larger part of me, I chose to go that route, followed a little later by sprinting of course.

The Isle of Man and the Clubman's TT
by Ewen Haldane

Picture this chap viewing a TT practice lap for the first time ever and wondering at his prospects on the following morning. Les Graham had just gone screaming past two other riders whilst negotiating St. Ninians crossroads, and left me with a decidedly drop-down stomach. I had completed thirty-odd laps of the circuit and had a good idea of the sequences of the bends. My two pals had plans to enter the 1953 Junior Clubman's event and I, never ever having dreamt of such an enterprise, decided to join them. Jimmy Drysdale and Sandy Bowie had been long time friends with this shared involvement with bikes. The months prior to the event had been devoted to learning as much as possible about the course. Geoff Duke's 'Castrol' pictures of some of the most demanding bends, their names all made mention of in various articles, and which were 'indelible' in our minds, proved to be of great worth during after-practice discussions. No less a person than our own Robert McGregor McIntyre spent four hours with us on the

May, 1953 - 'The Menstrie Lads', left to right, Jim Drysdale, Ewen Haldane and Sandy Bowie.

course and we really had no reason for not doing well. Ah well, there were faster men around and there was no glory. It may be of interest to the reader to learn of my introduction to Bob and the lead-on to his being of great help. My first ever race event took place at Crail aerodrome and, on returning to the pits from a practice session, I fell foul of another rider who had decided to do an about-turn to return to the circuit. My old Gold Star had no room to manoeuvre and hit the other machine amidships. I, appropriately as it was an aerodrome, went flying over the handlebars, and crash-landed on what seemed like all parts of my anatomy at the same time. I was ok physically, but was concerned for the state of my newly-acquired jodphur twills and flying jacket, and a great rage for the idiot causing this state. I think that, possibly, I ended up apologising more than my hero did. This then led to the four hours course lesson.

My old Goldie's frame was badly distorted as a result of the impact with the 7R. I don't know what its state was, but my next event was a sand race at St. Andrews and I finished last, the bike having left a double track in the sand. Anyway, that was my excuse, which meant nothing to the wee boy who approached me afterwards and told me that "You are some racer surr"! This led to me having a snail painted

Ewen cranks his 500 Gold Star into Union Mills, 1954 Senior Clubmans.

on my helmet and it remained there until I achieved a success.

Back to my first ever Isle of Man practice period. My less-than-happy state was made even more so as it was raining. Ye gods and little fishes! However, apart from one departure up the slip road at Ballacraine, all went well and there was excitement aplenty at the hotel breakfast table that morning. Breakfast talks always aroused interest in the rest of the guests, all of whom were race enthusiasts. The 'Rookery', Palace View Terrace, hosted by the most hospitable of couples, Mr. and Mrs. Stanley, was a popular stay place for Scottish supporters and there were a number of us Scottish riders in the hotel. Our table was at a window site and we would go to breakfast straight from practice (after two days they gave up on putting on fresh table cloths). On one such occasion a rider joined the one or two of us who had arrived earlier from practice and angrily told of an idiot who had passed four of them whilst negotiating the Quarry Bends. Those bends were vastly more difficult an encounter than those of today, and we, the other riders, made sympathetic noises wondering at the potential for unpleasant consequences. Later another rider arrived commenting on the poor standards of a number of riders he had encountered when passing through the Quarry Bends. The look of astonishment on his face is well remembered and this on account of the hilarity that his statement had provoked. Now, should I reveal the names? Well, why not. The first rider Jimmy Buchan, and the second chap Jimmy Drysdale.

BSA's Cyril Halliburn figured largely in our Gold Star days, and there was the memorable occasion when, at Oulton Park, my 350 blew up and he, in company with Jimmy Drysdale (then retired from racing on account of business commitments and home on holiday from Africa) worked all night at Cyril's home in order that I could compete at Snetterton that same weekend. I probably got more support from Cyril than deserved. On one occasion, for a Junior Manx, I was given a 350 engine with the assurance that it could safely be revved to eight thousand! Sadly it only lasted for three laps. Maybe a 14-stone 6-foot tall rider is not best suited to 350's. A bit more name-dropping! No less a person than

Roland Pike came to me at Oulton Park and complimented me on my riding. Heady stuff. He, as good as his word, sent on some special bits in order that I could use them at the next meeting. My recollection is that the parts were cam gear stuff and followers. The bike went well after this treatment.

I had a new 500 for the 1954 event. Interviewed after the event I was credited with having said that I had found the race to have been a dull affair. Utter nonsense. This was made by a reporter from 'The Motor Cycle', whereas the reporter from 'Motor Cycling' more correctly quoted me as saying that my ride had been a lonely one, there being three laps when I hadn't been near anyone. I was then overtaken by Ben Denton, and thereafter had some 'company'. I was advised by no less a person than Bob McIntyre to have care with reporters. I only took the Green'un ('Motor Cycling') as money was tight, and it was only recently that this came to light, and I was taken to task over describing an Isle of Man race as being dull. On my return from the Isle of Man, I had to sell my beautiful 500 as I was heavily in debt and could not afford the next payments.

During 1954 I received word that a prominent sports journalist would be pleased to have us come to Perth as he had a favour to ask of us. Jimmy, Sandy and I were duly introduced to the family, including a young Jimmy Buchan, with the request that we look after him during his introduction to the 1954 Junior event. Didn't need much looking after, did he! His dad, the journalist, had finished 3rd in a pre-war Manx Grand Prix. There must be something about this business of genes!

A verbal invite to visit the BSA factory one year found us journeying to Birmingham around New Year time, in Jimmy Drysdale's 1930's Lanchester. It was very special in that it had no side windows but so what, we were motorcyclists. On arrival at the factory we were conducted to some big-shot's office, and there, very brusquely told that there was no way that we could be shown around, and this despite explaining that we had travelled all that way. Nasty man. It was at this point that we were joined by Jimmy Davie, but it was a deflated group that made their way back to the main gate, there to be rescued by Cyril Halliburn. What followed was tea and buns and then a conducted tour by no less a person than Jeff Smith! Red carpet treatment, great stuff. The same could not be said about the return journey, as the weather had deteriorated from mild to severe – two days in bed recovering from hypothermia.

My 500 Gold Star came back into my life fifty years on from having ridden it. It had been found in some barn where it had been since 1963, and it had been bought and completely restored to as good as new and, thanks to my new sponsors Messrs. Webber and Walker, the former being the new owner and the pair founding a partnership in the restoration. I was reintroduced to my old bike at the Stafford show and did not imagine that I would have been so affected by that reunion. The fiftieth anniversary demonstration run is one that the memory of is everlasting, and my indebtedness to those two in unbounded. I reckon that I have been the luckiest of chaps to have had the privilege of competing on the world's greatest course.

Post-Script: Jimmy Davie

Following his 3rd place in the 1954 Junior Clubman's, Jimmy rode an AJS to 12th in the same years' Junior Manx Grand Prix. Sadly, his promising Island career was brought to an end on the second lap of the 1955 Junior MGP, when, in a fine 4th place, his AJS hit a fallen machine on Tower Bends, the fast sweeps leading up to the Gooseneck, and he died of injuries before reaching hospital. Any such incident is always tragic, it just seems particularly so when a rider is simply the victim of someone else's accident.

Jimmy Davie at Cronk ny Mona

My Clubman's TT Memories
by Derek Powell

The roads are closed, it is 6.00 am on a lovely summer's morning, and I am thundering through a sleepy village at 100 mph with an open exhaust bellowing beneath me. The Manx flies are building up on my goggles and screen, and there is the sweet smell of Castrol 'R' in the air from the bikes on the road ahead of me. These are the most wonderful moments of my life, Clubman's TT practice.

When I first started motorcycling I was a BSA fanatic. I loved the Gold Stars and travelled many miles to see them winning scrambles. I followed the Isle of Man races in various books and it became my ambition to go there and ride a Gold Star in the Clubman's TT.

In 1951 I got married and departed to the Island for my honeymoon complete with my ZB32 Gold Star. I knew the late Bob Foster very well, and he gave me a lot of help and support. Shortly after arrival in the Island Bob came to my garage and asked had I got the bike ready for practice in the morning. I pointed to the bike and he said "Good heavens, they won't let you out like that, your tyres are nearly bald". I answered that I couldn't afford new ones so he said "Get those wheels out and let me have them". He returned later with two new Dunlop racing tyres fitted, and said that Renold were coming to fit new chains for me, Mobil were bringing me some oil, KLG had some plugs for me and petrol is free at the start. What a wonderful world it used to be!

Derek Powell flies down Quarter Bridge Road.

The practice week went very well and I was soon on the leaderboard. Bob used to visit me in the middle of breakfast in our hotel and tell me I was going too quickly for a newcomer. He used to say "There are no gold medals for practice" - sound advice I think. The race started well for me, I was 5th at the end of the first lap, and moved up to 2nd on the second lap, but it wasn't to be. I retired at the Guthrie Memorial with a broken magneto shaft - thanks to 'help' from BSA. I had an alloy piston clamped in place of the dynamo which was okay, but BSA insisted on a 'works' block of wood being fitted instead. The heat from the engine shrunk the wood, and it all came loose!

In 1952 I went over with a BB32 Gold Star on which I had won the Clubman's race at Silverstone, and a special Star Twin in full Clubman's trim, with close-ratio box and TT carburettor. This went very well, and was timed at 112 mph on the Mountain Mile when the standard Star Twin would be good for 97 mph. I finished 8th on the twin and 5th on the 350, which was running very weak for some reason.

Moving on to 1953, this was my year! I had a swinging-arm BB32 Gold Star and a Triumph Tiger 100C for the two races. During practice week some BSA reps came to our garage and offered us a special engine for the 350cc race which, of course, we fitted. This motor promptly blew up in a big way, so we put back our original motor, which was running OK. The BSA was well on the leaderboard throughout practice, and I led the race from start to finish, and broke the lap record in the process. I finished with a bone dry petrol tank as it split on the second lap, and when I came in for an intended gallon of fuel, my mechanic Mitch insisted on filling the tank right to the brim, much to my annoyance. What I hadn't realised was that he was shielding a serious petrol leak by standing very close to the bike and holding his knee against the tank while doing the refuelling. Had the Stewards seen the petrol they would have excluded me. I had a slide at the 33rd and Keppel Gate was pretty scary. I took it easy at Brandish, thinking there was oil on the rear tyre, but it was of course, petrol. There is a measure of good luck attached to road racing success at times! Regarding the Senior Clubman's, most of the practices were wet and cold, and the Triumph was very good on wet roads and I was into fastest times, and I got the longest jump at the 'Highlander'. Race day however, was a problem for me. We had a heat wave, with warnings of wet tar all around the course, and the heat made the oil in the Triumph forks so thin that there was no damping, with that and the sprung hub (rubber spokes!) I had a very interesting ride, including a real tank-slapper through Union Mills which thrilled the spectators! However, I finished in 4th place. If only it had been cold or wet....

That year Bob Foster, my sponsor, was a Travelling Marshal and used a fantastic BSA Super Flash for his duties. This was a rare and exciting machine, which I purchased for my own use after the TT. The following year Bob used a special A7 Shooting Star with Daytona head and TT carb. This bike went like the clappers, so of course I purchased this one as well. I then discovered BSA had pinched the head back and put on a standard one, although it was still a good bike.

Looking back at the Gold Star and the T100C, my recollections are that there were very few twins that handled quite as well as the singles, but my experience of Triumphs ridden 'in anger' was that whatever they did, they were very safe, especially in the wet for some reason, just screw them on and they won't get out of control. The G45 Matchless twin was a good comparison with the G50 single, the twin went extremely well and should have been further developed. It was a pig to stop, and it was nicknamed the 'Galloping Camel'. The Tiger 100 C was a very fast bike, and set up nicely would give a B34 Gold Star a good run for its money, as I proved by winning the Clubman's event at Eppynt not long before the TT. I had several 1000 cc Vincents over the years and they could take control of their rider if ridden like a Goldie or a Tiger 100C!

That completed my Clubman's races, and I went on to the Manx Grand Prix. I have ridden in twenty-five races in the Island, and I love the place. I always had a road bike over there so I could enjoy the wonderful countryside such as at Sulby Glen, Druisdale and Injebreck, and take in the scenery. We made friends with some farmers at Ballaspit and they used to lend us their .22 rifle to go shooting on the mountain, having tremendous fun and 'burning boxes of ammo'. BSA presented me with a 'Sportsman 15' .22 rifle for winning the Clubman's on one of their bikes, the rifle has a silver plate let into the stock with the race success inscribed on it, which I still use to this day.

I have now got to the age of 77 and still enjoy bike riding, and have three bikes, unfortunately the standard of car driving has got so bad now that motorcycling is quite tricky, not like it used to be.

Life in the Island could be pretty exciting between races as most of the riders were well into practical jokes. There was a craze for water pistols for a year or two, I remember getting soaked several times when fights suddenly broke out, usually in the dining room. Then there were the 'whoopee cushions' which many riders carried already blown up ready for use in posh places, very embarrassing at times! The most foul joke was the little glass stink-bomb which would be carefully placed on the floor of a cinema or similar place, for someone to step on.

We used to have a lot of fun taking a passenger for a fast lap of the TT course, we knew our way around, they didn't. I took a policeman for a lap in my Austin-Healey 100 once and we broke every rule in the book to get the racing lines, he was absolutely gobsmacked! I took a friend of mine around in a Mini. He had a pipe in his mouth, and by the time we reached Ramsey he had bitten it off so many times he had to get a new one. The nasty trick was to let go of the steering wheel in the middle of the Verandah bends and pull out a note book or similar, which caused a real panic! I took a pillion rider for a lap one day on my Honda CBX six, and dropping down from Kate's Cottage to Creg-ny-Baa he really did think we were going right through the pub!

During the 2003 TT Lap of Honour, fifty years after the Junior win, I was able to ride again a 'closed-roads' lap of the Mountain Circuit on the very same Gold Star, restored by owner Peter Ayles and John Gardner. The memories came flooding back (and the old bike was still able to pull 7000 pm along the Sulby Straight, about 105 mph).

Derek with the rifle that BSA presented to him in 1953

My 1953 Clubman 1,000cc Ride
by Richard Madsen-Mygdal

My first Vincent was a new 1950 1000cc Rapide, which was replaced in 1951 with a new Black Shadow, bought from King's of Oxford. The Black Shadow was the 'Superbike' of its day, I remember showing off to a group of friends, gave it a big handful and dumping Stella straight off the back, she still remembers that incident!

I raced in the MCC Silverstone High Speed Trials, winning a first class award and Brand Hatch before deciding to enter the Clubman's. In those days it was a case of riding to the circuit, swapping silencer for straight-through pipe, taping the lights up and away we went. The only time this gave trouble was a very wet Thruxton meeting when the magneto flooded and refused to run on both cylinders, to get home we removed the back plug and chuffed back on a 'Comet'!

In 1952 I bought a new Black Shadow, (on hire-purchase) again from King's of Oxford. Having brought most of my bikes from them, I enquired whether they could assist me in any way. Howard King directed me to his salesman 'Hoppy'. His reply was they could not afford the bad publicity if anything went wrong. [A few years later 'Hoppy' - (Stan Hailwood) was supporting his son Mike to the hilt with the full backing from the firm!].

I raced the Black Shadow at the Silverstone Saturday meeting in April 1953, winning the Unlimited Clubman's event by quite a margin.

I was a member of the Oxford Section of the Vincent Owners Club, who were my entrants for the 1953 Clubman's race, after my good results, I was tipped by the Vincent Owners Club as a favourite to win the '53 Clubman's. Ted Hampshire, who worked in the experimental department at the Vincent factory in Stevenage, was a fellow section member, he gave the bike a good fettling before the race, he reckoned it was running well if he could balance an old three-penny bit on the oil tank cap whilst the engine was running. We fitted sidecar springs to the Girdraulics to get me better ground clearance.

Stella and I got married on a Wednesday, on the Friday after we were on the boat to the Island! A friend brought over the tools and spares on his sidecar outfit.

Our digs in Victoria Road cost us £3 a night, cash was tight so it was just as well that our expenses for the whole of the (wet!) practice period was a pair of Avon racing tyres and a pair of platinum pointed plugs. Practice was mostly wet, but I was making good times. When we weighed-in Stella pointed out a sign advertising insurance for racing bikes, cost £5. At that time, we were down to our last tenner, but she persuaded me to fork out for it (did she know something?).

Starting dead last on the road, I picked off a great deal of slower 1000s, plus many 350s that had started just before the 1000cc class. I was leading by 36 seconds at the end of the first lap. This had increased to 42 seconds by the Gooseneck, where friends were signalling for me. I was still catching and passing the 350 class at this time, and, approaching Brandywell and closing fast on a 350, he ignored racing's golden rule - stick to your line! Hearing the Shadow bearing down on him, the un-named rider took a wide line, just as I was trying to pass on the outside, I hit the gravel and down we went. Hindsight says I did not need to take such chances.

Stella went to collect the bike which was propped

against the wall, it did not look too bad from the offside, but the other side was different story - just as well she perusaded me to take out that insurance, the best fiver I ever spent!

I spent a few days in Noble's Hospital with a fractured skull and other injuries. My fellow hospital bed companions were George Brown, who had hit the blazing wreckage of Les Graham's MV at the bottom of Bray and Syd Lawton, who had tipped off at Creg ny Baa when horsing around with Norton team-mate Jack Brett.

Our money was all spent up, but the guest house owners let Stella stay without charge until I was fit enough to be discharged and then get back home by boat and train; we arrived back with three-ha'pence left in my pocket! The insurance paid to have the Black Shadow rebuilt at Vincent's

This was my only race on the TT course, I was fortunate to be sponsored by John Viccars on short-circuits for a few year on Norton and JV specials (the JV was a Triumph engine in a Norton frame, the Cooper 500cc car racing boys could not get engines, they had to buy a full Manx Norton and then throw the frame away!).

After a couple of years son David was born and we gave up racing, Stella took on a pub in Oxfordshire and I ran my haulage business.

Son David has proved his racing ability here by taking part in nearly 80 TT races, plus countless Manx Grand Prix and I still enjoy my bi-annual trips to the TT and Manx Grand Prix each year.

Richard Madsen-Mygdal presses on round Quarter Bridge

1953 Clubman's Junior

1.	D. T. Powell, BSA	28.20	**27.58**	28.00	28.39.8	1 52 57.8	80.17
2.	O. E. Greenwood, BSA	28.44	28.59	28.23	**28.12**	1 54 18.0	79.23
3.	J. Bottomley, Norton	28.33	28.27	29.17	**28.04.6**	1 54 21.6	79.09
4.	P. Palmer, BSA	28.56	29.32	28.21	**28.03**	1 54 52.0	78.84
5.	A. M. Sutton, BSA	29.01	29.35	28.13	**28.11**	1 55 00.0	78.75
6.	W. R. Oldfield, BSA	29.05	29.23	**28.31**	28.38	1 55 37.0	78.33
7.	I. Lloyd, BSA	28.51	29.24	**28.39**	28.46.4	1 55 40.4	78.29
8.	H. A. Voice, BSA	29.41	28.35	29.18	**28.09**	1 55 43.0	78.26
9.	H. McKenzie, BSA	29.10	28.38	29.37	**28.36**	1 56 01.0	78.06
10.	M. E. J. Taft, BSA	29.12	29.50	28.36	**28.28.8**	1 56 06.8	78.00
11.	A. F. J. D. Martin, BSA	29.12	28.57	29.28	**28.38**	1 56 15.0	77.92
12.	E. McG. Haldane, BSA	29.37	29.53	**28.25**	28.46.8	1 56 41.8	77.65
13.	R. Ingram, Norton	29.32	28.49	29.58	**28.34.2**	1 56 53.2	77.53
14.	J. H. T. Harris, BSA	29.29	29.27	**28.59**	29.04	1 56 59.0	77.47
15=	S. T. Seston, BSA	29.31	**28.59**	29.03	29.48	1 57 21.0	77.21
15=	G. R. Brown, BSA	29.49	30.00	**28.46**	**28.46**	1 57 21.0	77.21
17.	D. A. Wright, BSA	29.30	**29.04**	29.55	29.08.2	1 57 37.2	77.02
18.	G. T. Salt, BSA	29.55	29.42	29.27	**29.13.8**	1 58 17.8	76.55
19.	A. S. Bowie, BSA	29.20	30.47	**29.00**	29.18	1 58 25.0	76.48
20.	E. Baxter, BSA	29.36	**29.13**	30.13	29.42.8	1 58 44.8	76.27
21.	E. R. Williams, BSA	29.36	**29.33**	30.21	29.52	1 59 22.0	75.87
22.	G. C. A. Murphy, BSA	30.20	**29.30**	30.19	29.43	1 59 52.0	75.55
23.	E. Cheers, BSA	29.53	29.44	31.09	**29.11**	1 59 57.0	75.50
24.	H. Plews, BSA	30.02	30.12	**29.12**	30.40	2 00 06.0	75.40
25.	R. E. Smith, Norton	30.27	29.44	30.44	**29.33**	2 00 28.0	75.18
26.	H. A. Nash, BSA	30.11	**29.41**	29.46	30.51	2 00 29.0	75.17
27.	D. Webb, Norton	29.52	30.38	**29.28**	30.43	2 00 41.0	75.04
28.	G. A. Northwood, BSA	30.21	29.44	**29.39**	31.00	2 00 44.0	75.01
29.	A. Scholefield, BSA	30.44	**29.52**	29.54	30.32	2 01 02.0	74.82
30.	F. McCormick, BSA	30.53	31.13	30.05	**30.04**	2 02 15.0	74.08
31.	B. Kershaw, BSA	30.31	31.20	30.18	**30.10**	2 02 19.0	74.04
32.	H. Williams, BSA	30.29	30.37	**30.09**	31.11	2 02 26.0	73.97
33.	W. J. Keel. AJS	30.53	30.32	30.54	**30.15**	2 02 34.0	73.89
34.	E. F. H. Boyce, BSA	30.52	**29.51**	30.34	33.17	2 04 34.0	72.70
35.	E. B. Crooks, Norton	**29.02**	33.38	30.50	31.51	2 05 21.0	72.25
36.	K. R. Dunn, BSA	31.20	32.32	31.42	**30.47**	2 06 21.0	71.67
37.	G. E. Gibson, BSA	32.37	31.30	31.29	**31.11**	2 06 47.0	71.43
38.	A. N. Robinson, BSA	34.40	**30.51**	31.54	31.06	2 08 31.0	70.47
39.	A. G. Mollan, BSA	32.21	31.59	32.39	**31.37**	2 08 36.0	70.42
40.	F. Sheene, BSA	32.24	31.49	**31.34**	32.51	2 08 38.0	70.40
41.	W. R. Smith, BSA	32.05	33.25	33.06	**30.55**	2 09 31.0	69.92
42.	J. G. Robertson, BSA	32.42	**32.04**	32.44	33.25	2 10 55.0	69.17
43.	J. F. Griffiths, BSA	34.15	33.30	**32.31**	32.45	2 13 01.0	68.08
44.	J. Benton, BSA	**32.41**	32.46	35.04	34.09	2 14 40.0	67.25
45.	J. R. Dulson, Norton	35.07	33.50	**33.44**	34.28	2 17 09.0	66.03
46.	D. R. Watson, BSA	35.13	34.14	35.16	**33.39**	2 18 22.0	65.45
47.	G. R. Dunlop, Norton	**30.29**	31.01	34.51	42.25	2 18 46.0	65.26

48.	H. Walmsley, Norton	30.17	**29.50**	30.42	57.06	2 27 55.0	61.22
49.	R. Capner, BSA	30.57	**30.18**	33.25	55.19	2 29 59.0	60.38
	R. Ellis, BSA	**29.09**	29.54	29.38	R		
	P. E. Burns, BSA	28.36	29.47	**28.28**	R		
	B. C. Norwood. BSA	33.28	33.19	**33.18**	R		
	H. Evans, BSA	30.23	**29.46**	29.54	R		
	J. Drysdale, BSA	**29.10**	53.33	61.56	R		
	A. R. Brassington, Norton	30.36	**30.14**	31.05	R		
	A. L. Burton, Norton	30.22	**29.49**	30.55	R		
	R. A. Russell, BSA	**29.03**	34.41	R			
	J. N. Wooderson, Matchless	**31.20**	110.39	R			
	J. V. Hatcher, BSA	**31.28**	31.40	R			
	E. D. Blackwell, BSA	**30.40**	56.33	R			
	G. Arnold, BSA	**29.05**	29.21	R			
	H. Smith, Douglas	31.51	**31.23**	R			
	J. Cunningham, BSA	31.55	**30.51**	R			
	L. Dunham, BSA	30.09	R				
	E. Cox, AJS	38.16	R				
	G, Owen, Matchless	31.00	R				
	R. D. Keeler, Norton	29.03	R				
	H. R. Collier, AJS	44.05	R				
	J. Sutherland, BSA	R					
	S. R. Raynor, BSA	R					

LAP POSITIONS

1953 CLUBMAN'S JUNIOR

RIDER AND MACHINE	FIRST LAP POSITION		RIDER AND FINAL POSITION	MACHINE
D T POWELL B.S.A.	1		1	D T POWELL B.S.A.
J BOTTOMLEY NORTON	2		2	O E GREENWOOD B.S.A.
P E BURNS B.S.A.	3		3	J BOTTOMLEY NORTON
O E GREENWOOD B.S.A.	4		4	P PALMER B.S.A.
I I LLOYD B.S.A.	5		5	A M SUTTON B.S.A.
P PALMER B.S.A.	6		6	W R OLDFIELD B.S.A.

1953 Clubman's Senior

1.	R. D. Keeler, Norton	27.07	**26.48**	26.48.4	1 20 43.4	84.14
2.	E. B. Crooks, Norton	**27.14**	27.21	27.14.8	1 21 49.8	83.00
3.	W. A. Holmes, Norton	27.39	27.27	**27.16.2**	1 22 22.2	82.46
4.	D. T. Powell, Triumph	27.36	27.30	**27.19.8**	1 22 25.8	82.40
5.	A. King, Norton	28.07	27.37	**27.20.2**	1 23 04.2	81.77
6.	H. Plews, Norton	28.03	27.43	**27.38**	1 23 24.0	81.44
7.	W. R. Oldfield, Triumph	28.03	**27.45**	27.58.2	1 23 46.2	81.08
8.	R. Ellis, Norton	28.36	28.34	**28.27.8**	1 25 37.8	79.32
9.	G. W. Shekell, Norton	28.56	28.26	**28.18.4**	1 25 40.4	79.28
10.	S. T. Seston, Norton	28.48	28.37	**28.24**	1 25 49.0	79.15
11.	D. Andrews, Matchless	28.28	**28.17**	29.06.8	1 25 51.8	79.10
12.	R. E. Jerrard, Norton	29.07	**28.02**	29.10.4	1 26 19.4	78.68
13.	F. O. Coleman, Norton	28.56	28.45	**28.43.6**	1 26 24.6	78.60
14.	W. H. Wilshere, Triumph	29.07	29.09	**28.43.2**	1 26 59.2	78.08
15.	L. B. King, Triumph	**29.02**	29.06	29.17.2	1 27 25.2	77.70
16.	C. Watson, Norton	29.44	**29.08**	29.40.6	1 28 32.6	76.70
17.	D. Naylor, BSA	30.27	29.27	**29.15**	1 29 09.0	76.19
18.	P. G. K. Baldwin, AJS	30.02	**29.35**	29.37	1 29 14.0	76.12
19.	J. R. Mason, Ariel	30.16	**29.32**	29.36	1 29 24.0	75.98
20.	A. S. Avis, Triumph	**29.02**	30.09	30.34	1 29 45.0	75.68
21.	A. Newstead, BSA	30.34	29.55	**29.51**	1 30 20.0	75.19
22.	N. George, BSA	**29.03**	32.03	29.35	1 30 41.0	74.90
23.	T. S. Shepherd, Norton	31.56	30.37	**28.16**	1 30 49.0	74.79
24.	K. A. Taubman, Triumph	31.07	**30.23**	30.33	1 32 03.0	73.79
25.	R. Arthur, Norton	**29.54**	30.17	32.28	1 32 39.0	73.31
26.	E. C. Little, Matchless	30.27	**30.02**	32.29	1 32 58.0	73.06
27.	T. F. Watson, Norton	30.36	**30.20**	32.08	1 33 04.0	72.98
28.	J. N. Wooderson, Matchless	**29.09**	29.26	36.21	1 34 56.0	71.55
29.	A. J. Hagon, Norton	**28.41**	35.13	31.05	1 34 59.0	71.51
30.	J. I. Elliott, Ariel	**29.50**	30.51	34.58	1 35 39.0	71.01
31.	L. C. King, Norton	33.07	**32.40**	32.54	1 38 41.0	68.83
32.	V. Clifford, Norton	33.31	33.04	**32.44**	1 39 19.0	68.39
33.	P. E. Walsh, Norton	33.35	33.01	**32.45**	1 39 21.0	68.37
34.	A. F. J. D. Martin, Triumph	42.01	**28.58**	29.09	1 40 08.0	67.83
35.	J. Walker, Triumph	**32.06**	36.42	33.35	1 42 23.0	67.34
36.	P. Cooper, Triumph	**32.48**	35.20	35.00	1 43 08.0	65.86
37.	R. A. D. Mawson, Norton	35.58	**31.39**	39.37	1 47 14.0	63.34
	W. J. Keel, AJS	**28.51**	29.47	R		
	W. Zoellner, Triumph	**29.44**	79.47	R		
	I Lloyd, Triumph	28.41	**28.36**	R		
	D. S. Cholerton, Triumph	**31.03**	35.07	R		
	W. E. Dow, BSA	27.25	**26.51**	R		
	H. F. Hunter, BSA	30.27	**30.22**	R		
	P. J. Pooley, Triumph	42.33	R			
	E. Cheers, Triumph	28.52	R			
	T. A, Ovens, Triumph	33.54	R			
	M. W. Gillingham, Norton	38.37	R			

A.M. Cook, Norton	29.00	R
R. A. Russell, AJS	35.27	R
P. Minion, Norton	29.19	R
J. Wright, BSA	R	
J. Bottomley, Norton	R	
J. H. T. Harris, Triumph	R	
A. E. Hart, Triumph	R	
G. R. Dunlop, Norton	R	
D. Johnstone, BSA	R	
F. D. Jenkins, Ariel	R	
H. B. Winter, Norton	R	

LAP POSITIONS

1953 CLUBMAN'S SENIOR

RIDER AND MACHINE	FIRST LAP POSITION		FINAL POSITION	RIDER AND MACHINE
R D KEELER NORTON	1		1	R D KEELER NORTON
E B CROOKS NORTON	2	R	2	E B CROOKS NORTON
W E DOW B.S.A.	3		3	W A HOLMES NORTON
D T POWELL TRIUMPH	4		4	D T POWELL TRIUMPH
W A HOLMES TRIUMPH	5		5	A KING NORTON
W R OLDFIELD NORTON	6=		6	H PLEWS NORTON
H PLEWS	6=			

Bob Keeler leaves Governors Bridge, his was the last win by an International Norton in the Clubmans races.

1953 Clubman's 1000 c.c.

1.	G. P. Douglass, Vincent	28.17	27.26	28.00	**27.21**	1 51 04	81.54
2.	G. P. Clark, Vincent	**28.03**	28.26	29.22	28.13	1 54 04	79.39
3.	P. L. Peters, Vincent	30.38	**30.14**	30.39	30.28	2 01 59	74.24
4.	L. F. Pittam, Vincent	32.32	31.51	32.00	**30.13**	2 06. 36	71.53
5.	D. L. Buss, Vincent	**31.18**	31.22	32.14	31.43	2 06 37	71.52
6.	J. O. Finch, Vincent	34.56	**33.06**	33.45	52.13	2 34 00	58.81
	R. Madsen-Mygdal, Vincent	27.41	R				
	L. Floodgate, Vincent	R					

LAP POSITIONS

1953 CLUBMAN'S 1000CC

RIDER AND MACHINE	FIRST LAP POSITION		RIDER AND FINAL POSITION	MACHINE
R MADSEN-MYGDAL VINCENT-HRD	1		1	G P DOUGLASS VINCENT-HRD
G P CLARK VINCENT-HRD	2		2	G P CLARK VINCENT-HRD
G P DOUGLASS VINCENT-HRD	3		3	P L PETERS VINCENT-HRD
P L PETERS VINCENT-HRD	4		4	L F PITTAM VINCENT-HRD
D L BUSS VINCENT-HRD	5		5	D L BUSS VINCENT-HRD
L F PITTAM VINCENT-HRD	6		6	J O FINCH VINCENT-HRD

When Joe Finch pulled in to refuel his Vincent, he found the filler tank empty! Refuelling from what was left at an adjacent pit, Joe ran out at the Creg on the last lap and pushed the big v-twin into 6th (and last) place. The bike still exists and is ridden most weeks.

1954

CHANGING TIMES -
AND WHAT'S IN A NAME?

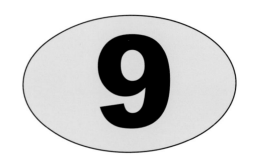

1954 saw the first signs of the tide starting to turn against the Clubman's TT. In the months following the 1953 event, the weekly magazines had reported that certain manufacturers had expressed a desire for the ending of the event (although they were never so indiscreet as to name any manufacturer). Reporting the annual meeting between the ACU Competitions Committee and representatives of the motorcycle industry held on 29th September 1953, Cyril Quantrill of *'Motor Cycling'* had this to say: *"The manufacturers – some at least – would, I believe, like to see the Clubman's TT abandoned or kept away from the International races, but members of the ACU pointed out at the meeting that they were primarily concerned with catering for the clubman who, they thought, wanted the Clubman's retained, and not with meeting the wishes of the manufacturers"*. An excellent and principled stand then by the ACU, but this was still serious for the future of the event. Not having direct support from major manufacturers was bad enough, but to have

One of the last of the Douglas riders; Don Chapman pictured at Cronk ny Mona.

them actively opposing the event did not augur well for the future.

Further pressure to 'marginalise' the Clubman's event came from an unexpected source. This was the need for major changes in the organisation and format of the International TT so as to accommodate the re-introduction of the 500cc Sidecar class, together with the introduction of the 10.79 mile Clypse course over which the sidecars were to race.

The arguments for and against the Clypse course being either necessary or desirable could fill another chapter, but an objective comment can be found in the Official Programme and Guide for the 1954 TT races, written by Graham Walker and titled *"A Cloud over the Mountain"*. In essence, he took the view that it's introduction had come about as a response to the changing face of European Grand Prix racing, moving away from the traditional International races each typically 220 – 260 miles long, toward shorter races, with a number of classes being able to be run on the same day in front of a paying gate, which in turn generated a source of prize money. This suited the manufacturers, who could better afford the time and reduced expense of the more 'packaged' events. Added to this was the undeniable spectator appeal of the sidecars, both on the Continent and in the UK, and there was pressure on the ACU to stage such an event, the last Sidecar TT having been run back in 1925. Graham Walker said *"I consider the ACU has acted wisely in selecting the new and shorter circuit for the 1954 experimental revival of the passenger event"*. He might have added 'pragmatically' or 'realistically' to 'wisely', because there was no doubt that the spectacle of watching the sidecars would have been diluted considerably if the sparse entry of 25 had been spread over the length of the Mountain Circuit.

If the need for the sidecars to have a new course

on which to make their return is accepted, then straightforward logistics begin to drive the programme, as it would be impossible to transfer road closures, marshals, and all the other paraphernalia of organisation between courses on the same day. The net result was that the Sidecar and Lightweight (125cc) TT's would have the Clypse course to themselves for one day, and because Manx Law did not then allow for the roads to be closed for more than three days in the week, one race-day would have to be moved out of race-week. No prizes then for guessing that it would be the 'Clubman's' which had to give way, shifted to the Thursday of practice week. Junior and Senior races were to be held on the same day, preventing any rider competing in both, which reduced the number of entries in each class, but at least they were still held over the Mountain Course.

These changes can be seen as part of the evolution of Grand Prix racing, and thus as being inevitable. Since 1949, the TT had been one of the FIM World Championship rounds, and the organising ACU had to respond to FIM policy and directives, but one example of the decline in status of the Clubman's TT which was not attributable to such external forces was the loss of the magic 'TT' designation for the Clubman's event. The pressure to make this change came from what would seem to be a most unlikely source, the Isle of Man Government's Manx Grand Prix Committee. The ACU minutes of a meeting between that Committee and the ACU TT Sub-Committee in the Exchange Station Hotel, Liverpool, on 31 October 1953, record that a member of the MGP Committee, the Rev. R.H. Reid had *"said that there was a body of opinion in the IoM which expressed the view that the close relation existing between the Clubman's Races and the Manx Grand Prix might eventually lead to a reduction in the grant made by the Manx Government to one or other of the events. He said that the 'TT' should be dropped from the title of the 'Clubman's TT Races' and that the Clubman's events should not be run concurrently with the International events."* Another of the MGP Committee Mr. R.P. Kennaugh then suggested combining the Clubman's Races with the Manx Grand Prix.

The Rev. R.H. Reid may or may not have personally held the views he was obliged to articulate, which would have been the views of the Manx Government, but the message he was carrying was clear. Firstly, that the Clubman's TT was to be 'distanced' from the International TT by staging it out of TT race-week, and by dropping the 'TT' status. Secondly, that the consequence of not complying with the request would be a likely reduction in the Government grant. This 'demotion' was based on an argument that would be heard again around the time of the final decision to abandon the series in 1957, that in effect, the very presence of the Clubman's within TT race-week detracted from the spectacle, even status, of the TT 'proper'. The argument continued that the time and place for learning the Mountain Course was during the Manx Grand Prix in September, whereas the TT was the showcase of road-racing for the world, and should consist of only the very best riders and machines. [The Rev. R.H. (Bertie) Reid was a well known supporter of motorcycle racing in the IoM. He was Chairman of the Manx Motorcycle Club, and held high-level posts in the TT and Manx Grand Prix organisations for many years. It is far more likely that he was acting as spokesman for the Government Committee than speaking his own thoughts on the Clubman's, a case of 'don't shoot (or blame) the messenger'].

Remarkably little opposition or comment was reported at the time, and what little criticism that did appear was directed toward the move of race day rather than the loss of status. For example, Frank Sheene was one of the few individuals brave enough to make his feelings public, with a letter published in the 14th January 1954 issue of *'Motor Cycling'*, and his criticism of the changes only related to the move of the Clubman's out of race-week. As he understandably asked, the number of entries for the Clubman's races would exceed the number for the sidecar race five times over, so shouldn't the sidecar races be held in practice week rather than the Clubman's?

Somewhat surprisingly, in the 26th November 1953 issue of *'Motor Cycling'*, the Editorial commenting on the ACU General Council decisions came out strongly in favour of the 'demotion' of the Clubman's, *"We applaud too, the decision to alter* the title of the clubman's [the lower case 'c' in clubman's is how the Editorial had it] *events to the Clubman's Trophy Races"*. No reasons or further comment were given. The Editor then was Graham Walker, his deputy Bob Holliday.

There was little to suggest a decline in popularity of the event amongst competitors, although it has to be admitted that the appeal to the general public would never be on the same scale as the all-out racing categories. There wasn't either any general feeling that sports machine events were at that time not being supported by the FIM or continental manufacturers. If anything the reverse was true, as the following comments (again from the Official 1954 TT Programme and Guide) from the then Editor of *'The Motor Cycle'* Harry Louis indicated: *"The latest step was the suggestion from the FIM Commission Technique last December that a start should be made in the progressive reduction of cylinder capacities. In 1956 the 500cc solo class should be abandoned; in 1957 the 350cc class, so that only the 125 and 250cc solo classes and the 500cc Sidecar class would remain.*

Parallel with the reduction in the number of racing classes should be the introduction of international races for sports machines: in 1956 a 'Sport International' class to which would be added, in 1957, classes for 350cc and 175cc machines.

These recommendations were shelved at the FIM Spring Congress last month, but the very fact that the Commission Technique put them forward is an indication of an important trend of thought".

"The proposals regarding international racing for sports machines deserve sympathetic consideration. On a national basis, events of this type have been keenly supported; for example, our own Clubman's Races and the Giro d'Italia in Italy (in the last Giro d'Italia,

held in April, there were 600 entries for a 2000 mile race over public roads). Sports-machine racing broadens the field; manufacturers who might never consider embarking on full-blooded racing policy will, as our own Clubman's events have shown, devote resources to providing suitable models, and the step to entering factory teams is a small one; enthusiastic private owners, debarred from taking an active part in current-type international racing on the score of cost might well be attracted by less expensive sports-machine events. Assuming the regulations were appropriately framed, sports machines would have closer resemblance to production machines than do pure racing models. This list gives some of the attractions and perhaps it is to the point to add that in the car racing sphere, sports-category events are successful and overshadow in prominence GP racing. For example, the world-famous Le Mans 24-hour race is for sports models".*

History would show that the years 1954 to 1957 were among the very best TT years ever, but in the latter part of 1953 the future of the TT was under very real threat from the FIM.

Enough politics for now, what of the racing?

Senior Clubman's race winner Alastair King draws a large audience of autograph hunters as he does a plug chop at the end of the Sulby Straight.

Entries and Practice

Prior to practice for the 1954 TT there were a number of significant alterations made to the Mountain circuit. Handley's Corner, the top of Baaregarroo, Ballaugh, Creg-ny-Baa, Signpost, Bedstead, and Governor's Bridge Dip had been modified by the Manx Highway Board, largely in the light of Geoff Duke's report recommendations following his December 1953 survey. 'Appledene', the white cottage which had given the name to the fast sweeps on the exit from Greeba Castle had been demolished the previous year, and the road set back, improving visibility considerably, and two 'leaps' flattened, at the Highlander, and nearer to Ballacraine at Ballagarraghyn. Warning boards had previously only been displayed on the approach to the best known corners, but their numbers were significantly increased before the 1954 event. The operators of the Glencrutchery Road scoreboards were given better shelter from the elements, and a new 'Dunlop' clock tower graced the scoreboard centre. However, the main course news for 1954 was the introduction of the 'Clypse' course for 125cc and Sidecar events.

The 1000cc class from 1953 was dropped, and the minimum number of entries required for each class was raised from 12 to 25. Published entry lists reached 63 for the Junior (350cc) event, 46 for the Senior (500cc), both down on previous years. From the *'TT Special'* Editorial of 5th June 1954 *"Arrangements for only two Clubman's events are laid on for 1954, in Junior and Senior categories. This is regretted by many, for there seems little doubt that a 'thousand' race would have been a different type of event from earlier races in this class - the 'Tiger 110' and 'Golden Flash' boys in particular were all set to dice heartily with the Vincenteers!"*

The Senior entry showed a healthy variety in machinery, with Nortons 17 numerically edging out the 14 from each of Triumph and BSA, plus a lone Ariel, but the Junior was dominated by BSA, all bar 8 riding the Small Heath machines. Of the 8, 6 were Norton and 2 were Douglas. Some names to note from the Junior list are Geoff Tanner, Jimmy Drysdale, Phil Palmer, Jimmy Davie, Roy Boughey, Jimmy Buchan, Frank Sheene, Des Wright and Fred Wallis. From the Senior come Dave Chadwick, Ewen Haldane, John Hurlstone, Eric Cheers, Ben Hazelwood, Gerry Turner, Howard German, Willy Wilshere, Syd Mizen, Sam Seston, Eddie Dow, Ben Denton and Alastair King.

It is usual now to recognise 1954 as a landmark year for BSA racing, with dominance at Daytona and the results which were to emerge from that year's Clubman's TT, but before the start of the June race fortnight, the larger Gold Star had never really been seen as a serious contender for Senior honours. The success of the 350 and Eddie Dow's

A J Gaunt (60) and James Coates weigh-in their Junior BSA Gold Stars.

temporary appearance on the 1953 Senior leaderboard had pointed the way, and indeed entries on the 500 Gold Star had increased, but the 1954 results would profoundly influence everyone involved with the races, whether rider, entrant, spectator or rival factory, until the demise of the event. Indeed, many would later blame the premature ending of the event on domination of the races by one make and model. Whatever way you look at it, the sustained work on both machines from Roland Pike's BSA development team really began to bear fruit with the emergence of the 1954 CB32 and CB34 machines.

Riders had to complete three laps in practice in order to qualify, one of which within the qualifying time for their class, 37 minutes for the Seniors, 39 minutes for the Juniors. Clubman's practice began on the morning of Friday 4th June, and the 113 riders found near perfect conditions, the only problem being low sun in places. First rider away just after 4.45 am was Alan Brodrick on his Junior Norton. As in earlier years, the first two laps of each newcomer were un-timed. 113 riders were out, 171 laps were completed and only one minor spill was recorded, that of policeman L. R. King, who came off his Senior Triumph at Cruickshanks on his first lap. Fastest Senior recorded was Alastair King with 27m 12s (83.25 mph), 24 seconds outside Bob Keeler's lap record from the previous year, and fastest Junior was Des Wright with 28m 41s (79.0 mph). Not listed in the entry, Reserve 'A' put in four respectable laps, with his two timed laps at 27m 58s and 27m 55s, and his riding attracting favourable comment all around the course. His name was P.H. (Percy) Tait.

Saturday's morning practice was held in dry but chilly and breezy conditions, and King recorded 26m 46s (84.60 mph) on his third lap, 2 seconds inside the Senior lap record. In the Junior, Phil Palmer's second lap was fastest at 27m 43s (81.71 mph), a full 15 seconds inside Derek Powell's record. Both were BSA mounted, as was Fred Wallis whose speed of 80.96 mph equalled the record. None the worse for his fall the previous day, L.R. King put in a couple of laps, each just over the half-hour. However, D.J. Hunt came off his Senior BSA at the Waterworks, and his injuries (a suspected broken pelvis) needed

the ambulance on the course which caused a delay for some riders in Ramsey.

Conditions had deteriorated by the time Monday morning practice came, with parts of the course damp, and although there was little actual rain, visibility over the Mountain road was poor. In the Junior class, Fred Wallis again set fastest lap at 30m 38s (73.92 mph) before a fall just before Laurel Bank. Far less fortunate in the same incident was Raymond Jeffrey Ashford, from Redlands, Bristol, who crashed his BSA on his third lap and sustained fatal injuries. Following close behind, Wallis was unable to avoid becoming involved in the accident, and suffered rib injuries. Other casualties of the session were A.R. Singer who was hospitalised with head injuries after a fall from his Junior BSA at Hillberry, K. Barfoot and R. Thompson who came off their Junior BSA's at Laurel Bank and the Black Hut (Stonebreakers Hut) respectively, fortunately neither suffering injury. In the Senior class, Ben Denton was fastest at 30m 20s, a speed of 74.66 mph, also BSA mounted. Another rider hospitalised, although as a result of a heart attack rather than an accident, was Bert Nowell. Earlier in the year, Bert was one of those who had written to 'Motor Cycling' expressing support for Frank Sheene in his stance against the moving of the Clubman's out of race-week.

Tuesday morning conditions were little better, with low cloud and showery rain, but thankfully the only reported incident was K.W. (Ken) James (this is a different Ken James to the 1952 Senior Clubman's runner-up, K.V.R.) who was fortunate to stay aboard his Junior BSA after contact with a stray sheep on the Mountain. Ben Denton was fastest Senior with 28m 08s (80.8 mph), with Jimmy Morton only fractionally slower on his BSA in the Junior, with 28m 09s (80.4 mph).

Denton also posted fastest Senior practice lap in Tuesday evening's final practice for the Clubmen, with 27m 14s (83.2 mph), followed by Ewen Haldane and Triumph-mounted Eric Cheers. Phil Palmer's fastest from Saturday morning still stood at the close of Junior practice, Sandy Bowie leading the session with a lap of 28m 11s (80.40 mph), 1 second faster than Jimmy Davie and 13 seconds faster than Morton, all Gold Star mounted.

The fact that no major scrutineering disputes were recorded was, in the opinion of *Motor Cycling*, down to two reasons. There was the undeniable high standard of preparation of the machines handed-in, but credit was also given to the 'fair scrutiny' and even-handed approach to the task by Chief Scrutineer, a Mr. Allan Mullee.

The Junior Race (Thursday, 10th June)

Starters

	Rider	Club	Machine
1	A F J D Martin	Rugby MCC	B.S.A.
2	J W Davie	Kirkcaldy & DMC	B.S.A.
3	G B Tanner	Ringwood MC & LCC	Norton
4	K Barfoot	South Liverpool MC	B.S.A.
7	H D Briggs	Meden Valley MCC	B.S.A.
9	J D Morton	Kilmarnock Tigers MCC	B.S.A.
11	J M Moore	Blackmore Vale MCC	B.S.A.
14	F Burgess	Hindley MC & LCC	B.S.A.
15	J Mockett	Mont' Christie MCC	Norton
16	A Scholefield	B.M.C.R.C.	B.S.A.
19	D Quayle	Peveril (IoM) MC & LCC	B.S.A.
20	A H B James	Burton MC & LCC	B.S.A.
21	W Gibson	Kilmarnock Tigers MCC	B.S.A.
23	H A Nash	Kings Norton MCC	B.S.A.
24	S Baskett	Wirral '100' MC	B.S.A.
25	J Clague	Peveril (IoM) MC & CC	B.S.A.
26	J R Dulson	South Liverpool MC	Norton
27	D J Smart	Bow District Garage MC	B.S.A.
28	J F Blake	Vagabonds MCC	B.S.A.
29	B S Radford	Ilkeston & DMC & LCC	B.S.A.
30	W Roberton	Falkirk & DMC	B.S.A.
31	R Whitehouse	Gravesend Eagles MCC	B.S.A.
32	W P Watson	Rochester, Chatham & DMC	B.S.A.
34	P Palmer	Wakefield & DMSC	B.S.A.
35	G Owen	Ramsey & DMC & CC	B.S.A.
36	R Boughey	St Helens & DAC	B.S.A.
37	J Powell	Waterloo & DMC	B.S.A.
38	J Muir	AA of Malaya	Norton
39	W Hillary	Rochdale & DMC	B.S.A.
40	K W James	Isle of Wight MCC	B.S.A.
41	J Buchan	Perth & DMC	B.S.A.
42	J Cunningham	South Liverpool MC	B.S.A.
43	G Arnold	Warrington & DMC	B.S.A.
45	F Sheene	Stamford Bridge MCC	B.S.A.
46	A W Brodrick	Darwen MC & CC	Norton
47	J H Morton	West Leeds MC	B.S.A.
48	J R Thurston	North Lincolnshire MC	B.S.A.
49	T R Graham	Dumfries & DMC & CC	B.S.A.
50	L Dunham	Thorne & DMC	A.J.S.
51	D A Wright	Chester MC	B.S.A.
52	A S Bowie	Montrose & DMC	Norton
53	D G Chapman	London Douglas MCC	Douglas
54	G A Northwood	Wrekin MC & CC	Norton
55	V J Holcroft	Berkswell & DMCC	B.S.A.
57	A W Edgson	Falcon (Croydon) MCC	B.S.A.
59	D Howe	North Bucks MC	B.S.A.
60	A J Gaunt	Whitehaven MC	B.S.A.
61	J E Coates	Rossendale MC & LCC	B.S.A.
62	G H Brooks	Runcorn & DMC	B.S.A.

Mechanical failures, accidents and failure-to-qualify reduced the 63 entrants in the Junior to 49 starters. Unusually, and a direct consequence of the move of the races out of the main raceweek, the Glencrutchery Road grandstand was manned by RAF servicemen from Jurby, the boy scouts having not been granted the extra day's holiday from school.

C. Willmore (Douglas), R. Ebbutt, J.J. Young, P. Whillier, K. Murphy and S. Wilcock failed to qualify, while Jimmy Drysdale, Fred Wallis, A.R. Singer, H. Nowell and R. Thompson (all BSA) were reported as remaining on the casualty list. B. Shaw (Norton), J. J. Young (BSA) and G. A Dormer (BSA) were declared non-starters, as of course was the unfortunate R.J. Ashford. Initially entered on a Norton, Des Wright switched to a BSA.

Riders began the warm-up of their machines just after 9.45 am, and were to be started in groups of three, at 30 second intervals, with the initial mandatory kick-start. After bad weather overnight, it was fine and dry at the appointed hour, although the start had been delayed by 15 minutes to enable the stiff westerly breeze to better dry the roads and clear the mist from the higher sections of the Mountain. The first trio to be flagged away at 10.15 am were all potential placemen or better, and Angus Martin's BSA fired up immediately, as did Geoff Tanner's Norton. Jimmy Davie's BSA was more reluctant, and the 45 seconds lost was to prove very significant come the end of the race. The BSAs of D. Quayle, W. Hillary and Goo Owen also gave trouble at the start, and in fact Quayle retired with clutch trouble at Laurel Bank, but Hillary's and Owen's machines recovered sufficiently to make it to the finish, Owen needing at least one stop en route. Tanner's Norton was first into Kirkmichael, and still led on the road at Ramsey, but from a rapidly closing Davie. The third of the first-away trio, Martin, was reportedly in trouble and 'touring' at Ramsey. He retired on the second lap. Another retirement in Ramsey was D.J. Smart, a London policeman, who dropped his BSA, suffering minor injuries. By the end of the lap, Tanner still led Davie, but by then the margin was down to 100 yards. Tanner's time from a standing start was only 11 seconds outside the record, Davie just three seconds slower. Later-starting Palmer's corrected time showed him to have knocked 7 seconds off the lap record, a time later equalled by No. 52 Sandy Bowie on another BSA. Wright's first lap was marginally outside the old record, but the surprise of that first lap was the 27m 43s (81.71 mph) set by the race leader George Arnold, 15 seconds inside the record on his BSA. Palmer and Wright refuelled at the end of the lap, whilst Martin and F. Burgess (BSA) retired, Martin with brake trouble, Burgess after a spill at the Bedstead. J. Clague (BSA) retired at Creg-ny-Baa with unspecified problems, and Jimmy Morton retired at the pits with engine trouble. Despite his setback at the start, Davie was on the leaderboard in 6th place.

First Lap Leaderboard.

1 G. Arnold (BSA)	27m 43s	(81.71 mph)
2=(P. Palmer (BSA)	27m 51s	(81.31 mph)
2=(A. S. Bowie (BSA)	27m 51s	(81.31 mph)
4 D.A. Wright (BSA)	27m 59s	(80.91 mph)
5 G. B. Tanner (Norton)	28m 9s	(80.44 mph)
6 J. W. Davie (BSA)	28m 12s	(80.30 mph)

Leading on the road at the end of the second lap was Davie, followed by Tanner and W. Gibson (BSA), who was 8th on corrected time, the latter two stopping to refuel. 5th through on the road and 5th on corrected time was Palmer. Arnold also refuelled at the end of the lap, still leading by 4 seconds from Bowie, who had yet to pit. In a similar position regarding the need for a fuel stop was Davie, whose second lap lowered the record to 27m 22s, a speed of 82.75 mph. Tanner's Norton held 4th spot, Jimmy Buchan's BSA 6th. Riding conditions were almost ideal from the second lap on, *'Motor Cycling's'* race report carried an interesting observation from the pit stops on the lack of the usual dead flies on number plates and goggles, putting the fact down to the brisk prevailing winds effectively 'grounding' the little menaces!

Main combatants in the 1954 Junior Clubman, pictured at Signpost Corner. Right, winner Phil Palmer, Left runner-up Des Wright.

1 G. Arnold (BSA)	55m 23s	(81.76 mph)
2 A. S. Bowie (BSA)	55m 27s	(81.67 mph)
3 J. W. Davie (BSA)	55m 34s	(81.49 mph)
4 G. B. Tanner (Norton)	55m 45s	(81.22 mph)
5 P. Palmer (BSA)	55m 52s	(81.05 mph)
6 J. Buchan (BSA)	55m 56s	(80.96 mph)

Arnold appeared to have developed a problem during the third lap, dropping five places, whereas Davie was flying, raising the lap record to 27m 19s (82.89 mph), and overhauling Bowie to take the lead. Reliability of these sports 350 machines had been shown to be very good, with less than half a dozen retirements by the end of the third lap. Davie stopped for fuel before the start of his last lap, but got away still in front of Tanner, followed by Gibson, Palmer, J.M. Moore (BSA), Arnold, Bowie and Wright. Palmer had lost time to the leaders on this lap, largely as a result of an off-road excursion at the Bungalow. J.H. Morton retired his BSA at Ballaugh with engine trouble.

Third Lap Leaderboard.

1 J. W. Davie (BSA)	1h 22m 53s	(81.95 mph)
2 A. S. Bowie (BSA)	1h 23m 00s	(81.83 mph)
3 P. Palmer (BSA)	1h 23m 19s	(81.52 mph)
4 D. A. Wright (BSA)	1h 23m 36s	(81.25 mph)
5 G. B. Tanner (Norton)	1h 23m 46s	(81.08 mph)
6 G. Arnold (BSA)	1h 23m 49s	(81.04 mph)

Not only were all the leader-board men close on corrected time entering the final lap, and no-one's place could be considered to be remotely secure, they were also sufficiently spread through the entry as to make amateur timekeeping difficult. Davie's last lap was slower because of the fuel stop, but he was first to cross the line, and for a while looked the likely winner, but Palmer's last lap of 27m 20s, just 1 second outside Davie's new record, gave him a fine 12s victory, but not from either of the third lap leaders, but from Wright, whose record last lap of 27m 15.8s (83.05 mph) elevated him to runner-up spot. Davie finished third, less than 3s behind Wright, and only 15s behind the winner, and was left to rue the time lost in starting his reluctant Goldie. Palmer's race average speed (81.83 mph) was faster than the previous year's fastest lap (80.96 mph). H.D. Briggs (BSA) was reported as a last lap retirement.

Finishing Order

1 P. Palmer (BSA)	1h 50m 39.4s	(81.83 mph)
2 D.A. Wright (BSA)	1h 50m 51.8s	(81.68 mph)
3 J.W. Davie (BSA)	1h 50m 54.4s	(81.66 mph)
4 A.S. Bowie (BSA)	1h 51m 01.6s	(81.56 mph)
5 G.B. Tanner (Norton)	1h 51m 04s	(81.54 mph)
6 G. Arnold (BSA)	1h 51m 30.8s	(81.21 mph)

Fastest Lap: D.A. Wright (4th lap) 27m 15.8s (83.05 mph) (Record)

The Centre Team Award went to the Scottish ACU team of J.W. Davie, J. Buchan and A.S. Bowie.

The Senior Race (Thursday, 10th June)

Starters

	Rider	Club	Machine
1	N F Sweetman	Wirral '100' MC	Ariel
2	P E Walsh	Solihull MCC	Norton
3	H McKenzie	Galloway MC & CC	Triumph
4	D V Chadwick	Cheadle Hulme MCC	Norton
5	E McG. Haldane		
		Menstrie MCC	B.S.A.
6	J E Guest	County Border AC	Norton
7	C Watson	North Lincolnshire MC	Norton
8	J B Denton	Bradford & DMC	B.S.A.
10	F O Coleman	Kings Norton MCC	B.S.A.
11	T F Watson	Scunthorpe MCC	Norton
12	J R Hurlstone	Vintage MCC	Triumph
14	E Cheers	Oswestry & DMC	Triumph
16	A Johnstone	South Liverpool MC	Triumph
18	W H Allen	Kings Norton MCC	Norton
19	T A Ovens	Cirencester MCC	Triumph
20	G J Turner	Edgware, Mill Hill & DMC	B.S.A.
21	G W Walker	Ely & DMCC	B.S.A.
22	L R King	Worcester AC	Triumph
23	H German	Mid Bucks MCC	Norton
24	A D Craib	Worksop & DMC	Norton
25	D S Cholerton	St Helens & DAC	Triumph
26	P Flaskett	Bristol MCC	B.S.A.
27	W H Wilshere	Watford & DMC & LCC	Triumph

28	F Bishop	Thornton Cleveley MCC	Norton
29	D Andrews	Horsforth & DMC	Norton
30	M R Baigent	Frome & D. United MCC	B.S.A.
31	J Hedley	B.M.C.R.C.	Norton
32	A H Frost	Thorne & DMC	Norton
33	W S Mizen	Southern MCC (IoM)	Triumph
34	W R Smith	North Lincolnshire MC	Triumph
36	A S Avis	Border MC	Triumph
37	W Barlow	Swinton & DMC	Norton
38	R Mawson	Peveril (IoM) MC & CC	Norton
39	S T Seston	Kings Norton MCC	B.S.A.
41	J F Hambling	Antelope MCC (Coventry)	B.S.A.
43	W E Dow	Leicester Query MCC	B.S.A.
45	G W Shekell	Worcester AC	Norton
46	A King	Mercury MCC (Glasgow)	B.S.A.
47	K Brough	Camborne-Redruth & DMC & LCC	
			Triumph

39 of the 46 entrants lined up for the 1.30pm start, and the fine weather conditions from the morning's race continued.

Non-starters were J. Newall (BSA), D. R. Andrews (BSA), P. Cooper (Triumph), B. E. Hazlewood (Triumph), D. J. Hunt (BSA), R. E. Jerrard and T.R. Cattell (both Nortons). Starting alongside Ewen Haldane in the second batch of three

riders, Chadwick lost a good 30 seconds before getting away. Although he regained the race lead by Ramsey, he lost it over the Mountain to Haldane, with Denton pushing him further back to 3rd. Flaskett's BSA and Hedley's Norton also lost several minutes at the start, but both eventually got away. Chadwick, Denton and Tait all pitted at the end of the first lap for fuel, but Haldane raced through setting a new lap record from a standing start of 26m 32s (85.34 mph). Remarkably, as he would have lost time slowing for his fuel stop, Denton was only 1 second down on Haldane. Starting number 46, King also took on fuel at the end of the first lap, and the timekeepers placed him 3rd, just 5 seconds behind the leader.

First Lap Leaderboard.
1 E. McG. Haldane (BSA)	26m 32s	(85.36 mph)
2 J. B. Denton (BSA)	26m 33s	(85.30 mph)
3 A. King (BSA)	26m 37s	(85.09 mph)
4 D. V. Chadwick (Norton)	26m 52s	(84.28 mph)
5=P. H. Tait (BSA)	26m 58s	(83.96 mph)
5=M. R. Baigent (BSA)	26m 58s	(83.96 mph)

1st and 2nd place-men remained the same during the second lap, but with a relatively slow 27m 48s lap, Chadwick dropped off the leaderboard, his 4th

Ewen Haldane restarts after the pit stop that potentially cost him the race.

Ben Denton hustles through Cronk ny Mona; he was on the leaderboard throughout the race

place taken by King. At the end of the lap Haldane went straight through, setting a new lap record of 26m 30s (85.38 mph), and leaving his fuel stop as late in the race as he could. Almost immediately, Baigent knocked 1 second off this to raise the lap record to 85.52 mph, and by his efforts claimed 3rd place from King. Syd Mizen (Triumph) became the second retirement, joining J.E. Guest whose Norton expired at the Quarry Bends on the first lap. A Johnstone's Triumph retired at the end of the second lap, having pushed in from Signpost.

Second Lap Leaderboard.
1 E. McG. Haldane (BSA)   53m 2s   (85.38 mph)
2 J. B. Denton (BSA)   53m 15s   (85.04 mph)
3 M. R. Baigent (BSA)   53m 27s   (84.72 mph)
4 A. King (BSA)   53m 28s   (84.70 mph)
5 T. A. Ovens (Triumph)   53m 41s   (84.35 mph)
6 P. H. Tait (BSA)   54m 8s   (83.65 mph)

Haldane's third lap was yet another record at 26m 25s, but almost immediately Denton went 2 seconds faster at 26m 23s (85.84 mph). Despite the lap time, it all went terribly wrong for Haldane at the end of the third lap. As he pulled in to refuel, he overshot his pit, taking over half a minute to get things sorted out, rejoining the race as Denton went flying through. G. J. Turner retired his BSA at the pits with engine trouble, and Sam Seston (BSA) was also reported stopped, and eventually as having retired.

First Triumph home was Tom Ovens in fourth place.

Third Lap Leaderboard.
1 E. McG. Haldane (BSA)   1h 19m 27s   (85.49 mph)
2 A. King (BSA)   1h 19m 35s   (85.35 mph)
3 J. B. Denton (BSA)   1h 19m 38s   (85.29 mph)
4 T. A. Ovens (Triumph)   1h 20m 12s   (84.69 mph)
5 M. R. Baigent (BSA)   1h 20m 30s   (84.38 mph)
6 P. H. Tait (BSA)   1h 20m 38s   (84.24 mph)

Beginning the last lap with more than his 30 second starting advantage and a clear road ahead of him, it looked as though the winner's trophy would be Denton's. Haldane caught Denton on the road and they battled it out all the way around the lap, eventually passing him, but Denton knew that all he had to do was to stay close to his rival and that he would have the advantage as a result of the starting interval. Advantage that was, over Haldane, but what of King? Dentons last lap again broke the record with 26m 3.6s (86.86 mph), and so set up a magnificent finish as King, still out on the course, was noted everywhere as being very smooth, and very, very fast. As he crossed the line, everyone knew it was a close-run result, and after an agonising wait over the timekeepers deliberations, the announcement came that with a new lap record on his final lap of 26m 1s (87.02 mph), King had taken victory from Denton by just over 5 seconds. Haldane was placed third, 31 seconds behind King, more or less the same time he had lost in the refuelling stop error. There were nine retirements from the thirty-nine starters, A. S. Avis (Triumph) retiring at the pits, and N. F. Sweetman (Ariel) at Hillberry on the third lap, G. W. Walker (BSA) at Guthries' on the last lap, while W. Barlow (Norton) was credited as having completed three laps.

Finishing Order
1 A. King (BSA)   1h 45m 36s   (85.76 mph)
2 J. B. Denton (BSA)   1h 45m 41.6s (85.68 mph)
3 E. McG. Haldane (BSA)   1h 46m 11.2s (85.26 mph)
4 T. A. Ovens (Triumph)   1h 46m 42.2s (84.87 mph)
5 M. R. Baigent (BSA)   1h 46m 51.8s (84.74 mph)
6 P. H. Tait (BSA)   1h 47m 5s   (84.58 mph)

Fastest Lap: A.King (4th lap) 26m 1.0s (87.02 mph) (Record).
The Centre Team Award went to the Scottish ACU (H.

McKenzie, E.McG. Haldane and A. King).

Reflections

As the earlier Junior race, the Senior Clubman's TT had been a tremendously close and exciting race, with the result in doubt right to the very end, few retirements, and nothing other than minor mishaps to report. To quote 'The Motor Cycle', "By and large this was the very finest race in Clubman's history, and it is not easy to recall a better-fought triangular battle even in the International sphere."

Four broadcasts on the BBC Radio's Light Programme gave mainland listeners over an hour's live commentary covering the start and finish of both races, and it is worth quoting from 'Motor Cycling's' editorial in the 17th June issue, to shed some light perhaps on their view on the impact of the broadcasts on the listening public, and of the status of the Clubman's TT as it was perceived at the time.

"A week ago today, millions of loudspeakers brought startling news into the homes of British motorcycle racing enthusiasts. Throughout the morning and afternoon of Thursday, June 10, the BBC's team of commentators kept the ether tense with accounts of a day's speed work on the Isle of Man Mountain Course which, for sheer drama, surpassed anything of the kind that has gone on the air for a very long time. And what caused the experts at the microphones to rise to such a pitch of excitement? Nothing more important than the Junior and Senior Clubman's Trophy Races.

The unwanted baby of motorcycle racing, enfant terrible for scrutineers, not good enough for TT week and not even sure of it's own name – the poor, despised, emaciated Clubman's it was that provided, in one day, two of the best races the Snaefell Circuit has ever known. High speed, well controlled, resulted in a plethora of records and an exceptionally low retirement rate with not a single serious mishap recorded in the 15,000-odd miles covered by some 100 competitors in the two events."

Two contemporary quotes illustrate, from different perspectives, the impact of the BSA domination of the races.

Firstly, the same issue of 'The Motor Cycle' which carried the race reports, included a perceptive and almost prophetic Editorial.

"A significant feature of the Clubman's races was the virtual monopoly of the leading places by one make of machine – BSA. All concerned with the design and production of these machines deserve the highest congratulations for having marketed such extremely efficient examples of pushrod-operated ohv engines, and thoroughly race-worthy complete motorcycles.

One inevitable question arises, as it has also arisen during the past few weeks concerning the world-famous Le Mans race for sports cars. Have the regulations governing the Clubman's Trophy Races led to the evolution of special machines which are too far removed from ordinary roadster machines? The conception when the Clubman's events were started in 1947 was to provide enthusiastic sporting motorcyclists with the opportunity of competing over the famous Manx circuit on machines of orthodox roadster type ('Manufacturers catalogued models, fully equipped'). The regulations impose certain restrictions to this end. Would it be desirable for the regulations to be more stringent? There are sound arguments both for and against, and the topic therefore merits close study by the Auto-Cycle Union."

Secondly, a caution to prospective owners within the official BSA sales brochures for the later (but little altered in specification) Gold Stars.

"The Clubman's model Gold Star has been developed for competition in road and short circuit events, and its specification is such that it is neither intended nor suitable for road use as a touring motorcycle". It is not clear when this caution first appeared in the sales literature, but it is probably safe to assume that it was after the last Clubman's TT had been run!

The underlying problems of scheduling the TT race-week in general, and the Clubman's races within that week, were summed up by Bob Currie, writing in the 'TT Special' two days after the Clubman's.

"Don't shoot the pianist. He's doing his best! So ran the motto of the rowdy saloons of the Wild West – yet no matter how many variations the ACU may wring from the original TT theme, there always seems to be a section of the audience with no ear for *music. This time it is the Clubmen who are letting fly with their six-shooters – and let it be said immediately that they have ample reason for feeling 'hard done by'. Shorn of the proud TT title that they have carried since their introduction in 1947, the Clubman's races have been unceremoniously bundled into the 'dark corner' of practice week. Without a chance to defend themselves, the Lightweight and 1000cc classes have been thrust out into the cold, cold snow, while the Junior and Senior classes were crammed into a single day, riders being barred from taking part in more than one race.*

Peeved? The Clubmen are furious! No wonder that entries for the two survivors of the Clubman's series were at the lowest level ever reached.

Under the present arrangement the average clubman wishing to make full use of the practising periods available to him, must forego the pleasure of watching the Senior TT, for not many can afford to take more than a fortnight's time off from normal work.

It may well be said that the Clubmen have been given a raw deal this year - but what can be done to rectify matters? This year the ACU has had to find room for an extra race – the Sidecar TT – and since it seems certain that this event will prove highly popular there will be little likelihood of dropping it from the programme and reverting to the 1953 schedule.

No, something else must go, and since there is little manufacturer support from Britain for the 125cc race, or the 250cc race either if it comes to that, there are many who feel that there is no point in retaining these races.

The only other alternative would seem to be to transfer the Clubman's races to September, when they could perhaps be run on the Wednesday of 'Manx Week'. This would certainly increase the interest of the September race period and may indeed prove to be the best possible solution to an awkward problem."

My 1954 Senior Clubman's Ride
by Howard German

My 1954 Clubman's TT ride began in 1953. No that is not double-dutch. It is true!

My 1953 Manx GP ride was so full of frustration and disappointment, that I was determined to get a good ride to justify all the time and money that had gone into the trip. The '53 Manx was my first visit to the Island and

after reading all the tales of the greats from 1907 onwards- I was determined to produce a good result for all the people who had helped me get this far. Alas it was not to be. The old 350cc Garden Gate Norton suffered from chronic vibration and broke it's frame every practice morning, and my Senior bike, a JV Special (a Triumph engined Manx) blew up in the last practice and was fixed by Triumphs and was told to take it easy. We had strengthened the Norton frame every day but in the race the vibration had to go

somewhere and on the third lap it broke the rear wheel spindle at the 33rd and that was that. I ran the newly rebuilt Triumph round and around the Island for two hours with my plimsolls stuffed up the meggas in all the villages, but it was still very tight. So the race was a high speed touring exercise just to get a finish in an IoM race. Result one Manx MCC finishing medal. 31st, not what I had come for.

Through the winter of 1953 I talked to everyone I could about a bike for 1954 but with no luck. At this time I only owned a 250 two-valve Rudge, which cost £40, and it was very good and held 250cc lap and race records at Brands, my spiritual home.

That winter the ACU revived a pre war event 'The Winter Ball' and it happened just before Christmas 1953. There I met a fellow 250cc Rudge exponent

Arnold Jones who had used his Rudge in the Isle of Man and we became friends. Arnold had just taken on the position of sales manager for Britax Accessories and his brief was to sell and publicise the Britax Ducati Cucciolo 49cc moped engine. Arnold set to and had a strengthened bicycle frame made and sold the bike and engine as a complete unit. The engine was very sophisticated and had pull rods and a two speed gearbox, which could be preselected, and was chain drive. Very advanced compared with the single speed moped engines that drove a bicycle through a friction drive on the tyre. Arnold suggested that we use two of these Cucciolos in the MCC Exeter Trial at New Year and this was one of the first publicity schemes that he dreamt up to put this product in the public eye. Space precludes I list the others.

Arnold had many contacts in the trade through his racing, and in the course of his visits to motorcycle shops to sell the Britax Cucciolos he learnt that Raymond Ways of Kilburn had an allocation of one Norton International Featherbed for 1954 but they could only have it if the machine was used in the Clubman's TT. Remember this was the age of export everything to pay our way in the world. Arnold reported this to me and a meeting was arranged with the manager and the deal was done. My cup runneth over as I was to collect the machine on the dock at Liverpool and I could take it to Nortons for any problems at Raymond Ways expense. What excitement particularly as Bob Keeler had won the 1953 500cc Clubman's on the same model and I was to have a potentially race winning bike.

At this time, through racing at Brands Hatch, I had met Frank Sheene who was a keen supporter of the IoM Clubman's races having raced a Douglas and an Enfield in previous years. Now he had purchased a new 350cc BSA Gold Star and we agreed to team up and travel and stay together for 1954.

I collected my bike at Liverpool all wrapped up in cardboard and factory packing and the first preparation jobs involved removing the stands, fitting a pad on the tank and making it fit me. First practices were all gently running in the long stroke (79mm x 100mm) and then getting down to some serious lapping. It soon became apparent the Norton would not live with the new 500cc BSA Gold Stars, and when Frank

and I both hit Sulby Straight together, his 350 Gold Star was 5mph quicker than my 500cc Inter. What disappointment after my high hopes.

Practice went as well as could be expected without too many snags. Most mornings would end with the Norton losing all its compression, and the Norton race mechanics accused me of running in the gutters and picking up gravel and stones into the inlet tract. I countered this argument by saying I was following Frank S. on his Goldie and his machine did not lose any compression. Oil tank frothing was another problem and a big thick pad of cloth over the oil tank filler 'cured' this. I had to replace one fuel pipe and used the Smiths armoured pipe that was covered in fine wire reinforcement to protect the soft hose inside. Tough stuff. Job done.

After practice reality dawned and a top ten place was the most likely finish that could be realised. Frank had had a smooth ride in the 350, finishing 25th in a BSA packed race, and had disappeared somewhere round the course to watch.

First lap was uneventful but I was making good progress and got on the pace until the end of the second lap, but as I crossed the finishing line, the engine coughed and slowed to a seemingly walking pace. Fuel starvation, I surmised, and frantically switched to reserve. No improvement. The bike coasted down Bray Hill and various scenarios rushed into my head. I tried to drive it, but by Braddan Bridge had decided that this was no way to go racing. I pulled in to the side road at Braddan, and Frank leapt out of the stands. The engine would run on small throttle openings, but no more, and Frank persuaded me that I could go to the finish like that and claim a finisher's award. And that was the way I finished the race, 27th and not last, so the first two laps must have been quite brisk.

The post mortem was very interesting. In fitting the Smiths armoured fuel pipe to the union a piece of the wire had been turned inside the pipe, and during the race broke off with vibration and found the main jet hole to rest in. Result no fuel.

Looking back, with hindsight, in my naivety and enthusiasm I had overlooked the short stroke revolution that had occurred, and my hopes were based on false premises. Nortons were in the same boat, as the old long stroke engine had won for years in the Manx and Internationals, and who could imagine a company like BSA building a racing bike.

The best part of this experience was that at 'The Winter Ball' I met a young lady who was to become my wife a few years later. That was the best result of 1954.

As I write this, my mind goes back to the ACU General Council meeting (1957?) that had to consider scrapping the IoM Clubman's series for good.

Frank Sheene and I had organised a strong campaign to keep these races going but unbeknown to us it had been predestined that they would go.

As a Committee member of the Vintage Club I was one of the VMCC representatives to the then all-powerful Council, but on the day of this meeting, I was wearing my 'Clubman's hat'. Frank and I had circulated our feelings, by letter, to all the Clubs who had supported the Clubman's and asked for their support in voting to keep the races going. Of course in those days such anarchy was severely frowned upon by the close, cliquey ACU Management Committee and all our lobbying was done without our names being publicised, and so no one knew the identity of the 'trouble makers' stirring up such revolutionary feelings.

The big day came and the matter was heatedly debated by the meeting. The strength of feeling was illustrated by the member for the Cheshire Centre who stood up and pronounced that in all the years of his attendance whilst representing his centre, he had never been told by his Centre

Committee which way to vote and they relied on his own sensible judgement. He then went on to announce that his centre had told him to vote for the continuation of the Clubman's races and he would do just that.

With that remark the ACU management Committee Chairman stood up and declared that this scurriless lobbying for the races had influenced too many people and if he could find the purveyors of this infamous propaganda he would have the culprits banned for life from the sport. So much for democracy. The vote when taken was very close, but lost, and so we lost another piece of our racing history. And I kept my head down and kept racing.

Howard checks if petrol tap has vibrated shut as his fuel-starved Inter splutters its way into the third lap.

My 1953 and 1954 Senior Clubman's Rides
by Sandy Bowie

I competed in '53 and '54, along with two good friends Jim Drysdale and Ewen Haldane; we worked in the same place and were members of the Menstrie MCC. I entered in '53 from the club, Jim got agreement from the Aberdeen & DMC and Ewen entered under the Falkirk & DMC. In '54 the Montrose MC allowed me to enter under their banner – but we were a'Menstrie lads at heart!!

Our first digs were in the 'Rookery' boarding house

at the foot of the Falcon Cliff pedestrian lift (the former demolished, the latter now derelict). We watched the International riders the evening before our first morning session – at the top of Bray Hill! Shouldn't have, they were fast, bl**dy fast!!

So, full of apprehension, excitement, nerves and whatever else, to my first early morning practice............don't remember much detail, except seeing a Vincent away up the hillside on the Mountain.

How did it get there? The après-practice breakfast gatherings were relaxed, with relief and much 'bullshooting' of course by some/all. The '53 race itself – what I do recall was that my pit-stop was an utter shambles!! No fault of my attendant, he was one of our club over to cheer us on. We topped up far too much petrol, then noticed the oil tank was smothered in oil (found out afterwards there was a crack in it) and the rear tyre was a wee bit lubricated – then topped up with the wrong oil giving a vegetable/mineral mix – or something. Hadn't a clue, just complete absence of preparation – but I finished!

The following year '54, no pit problems; just as well 'cos my 'attendant' was Jim Drysdale, on crutches, with an injury that prevented even him from starting. Now there's a first – and maybe only – time, of a pit attendant on crutches!

Both years kick-started first go, thankfully.

We drove the bikes from home to the ferry at Liverpool. On the way back in '53, early Sunday morning, a police car nabbed two of us, eventually, for speeding at Garstang.

I'll never forget that name! Fined of course.

The atmosphere both years was really something – the actual racing, needless to say, was exhilarating, exciting, frissons of fear and fright? Oh yes, best summed up by the modern phrase 'buzz'.

Jimmy Buchan and Jimmie Davie were part of the Scottish group, the latter an unforgettable character indeed!

What really made it for me was having my two companions, Jim and Ewen.

As happens in life, we went our separate ways after '54, but after many long years we met up again for a few days on the Island for this years' (2006) Manx – watching of course! Instant rapport. Aye, a 'Band of Brothers'.

My 1954 Senior Clubman's Ride
by Percy Tait

I only had the one ride in the Clubman's, that was the 1954 Senior. Being employed as a tester at Triumph, I was barred by the Regulations from riding that company's products, which is why I came to be entered on a BSA Gold Star, provided by Bob Foster. It was a long time ago, and a lot has happened since, so some of the details of what happened have been lost now. My entry was accepted as a reserve, and so it was not certain that I would get to ride in the race, but there weren't that many reserves and there would always be unfortunates who for some reason couldn't make it to the Island or who hit trouble during practice. This proved to be the case, the bike gave no trouble during practice, and I took the riding number 18. The race itself was quite straightforward, except that going down Bray Hill on the second lap both frame tubes broke near the upper engine mount, but in fact the handling was not too badly affected, and I was able to complete the race without too much difficulty, pleased to finish on the leaderboard in 6th place. I still have the plaque. I think the lug design was redesigned following a number of similar breakages. Later that same year I moved on to the Manx Grand Prix, and the International TT the following year.

1954 Clubman's Junior

1.	P. Palmer, BSA	27.51	28.01	27.27	**27.20.4**	1 50 39.4	81.83
2.	D. A. Wright, BSA	27.59	28.14	27.23	**27.15.8**	1 50 51.8	81.68
3.	J. W. Davie, BSA	28.12	27.22	27.19	**28.01.4**	1 50 54.4	81.66
4.	A. S. Bowie, BSA	27.51	27.36	**27.33**	28.01.6	1 51 01.6	81.56
5.	G. B. Tanner, Norton	28.09	27.36	28.01	**27.18**	1 51 04.0	81.54
6.	G. Arnold, BSA	27.43	**27.40**	28.26	27.41.8	1 51 30.8	81.21
7.	J. Buchan, BSA	28.21	**27.35**	28.28	27.44.6	1 52 08.6	80.75
8.	W. Gibson, BSA	28.24	28.12	28.36	**27.56**	1 53 08.0	80.05
9.	J. Muir, Norton	28.44	29.07	28.00	**27.47**	1 53 38.0	79.70
10.	W. Roberton, BSA	28.59	28.37	29.30	**28.27**	1 55 33.0	78.37
11.	G. H. Brooks, BSA	29.13	29.15	28.41	**28.24.6**	1 55 33.6	78.36
12.	J. E. Coates, BSA	29.14	**28.34**	29.28	28.35	1 55 51.0	78.17
13.	H. A. Nash, BSA	29.14	29.48	28.41	**28.38**	1 56 21.0	77.86
14.	K. W. James, BSA	29.38	29.01	29.46	**28.32.2**	1 56 57.2	77.48
15.	R. Boughey, BSA	29.52	30.17	29.04	**28.45.2**	1 57 58.2	76.76
16.	J. M. Moore, BSA	29.50	29.27	**29.15**	29.34	1 58 06.0	76.68
17.	T. R. Graham, BSA	30.34	29.28	29.56	**29.02**	1 59 00.0	76.10
17.	D. Howe, BSA	30.53	29.40	**29.09**	29.18	1 59 00.0	76.10
19.	B. S. Radford, BSA	30.56	29.46	29.27	**29.04.2**	1 59 13.2	75.95
20.	A. Scholefield, BSA	30.29	29.42	29.43	**29.33.6**	1 59 27.6	75.80
21.	G. A. Northwood, BSA	30.32	29.47	30.27	**29.11**	1 59 57.0	75.50
22.	J. R. Thurston, BSA	30.51	29.53	30.21	**29.13**	2 00 18.0	75.28
23.	D. G. Chapman, Douglas	30.16	**29.42**	30.17	30.32	2 00 47.0	74.98
24.	R. Whitehouse, BSA	30.26	29.55	31.26	**29.41.2**	2 01 28.2	74.55
25.	F. Sheene, BSA	31.33	**29.48**	31.10	29.57	2 02 28.0	73.95
26.	W. P. Watson, BSA	30.28	**30.09**	30.42	31.13	2 02 32.0	73.91
27.	G. Owen, BSA	37.47	29.35	28.38	**28.26**	2 04 26.0	72.78
28.	L. Dunham, AJS	31.22	**30.29**	31.51	30.53	2 04 35.0	72.69
29.	J. Cunningham, BSA	31.32	31.18	31.08	**30.45**	2 04 43.0	72.61
30.	A. W. Edgson, BSA	32.33	31.14	31.12	**30.07**	2 05 06.0	72.39
31.	A. H. B. James, BSA	32.19	31.23	32.08	**30.40**	2 06 30.0	71.59
32.	J. F. Blake, BSA	31.22	32.04	32.00	**31.16**	2 06 42.0	71.48
33.	J. Powell, BSA	32.09	31.33	31.48	**31.25**	2 06 55.0	71.35
34.	A. W. Brodrick, Norton	33.27	30.38	33.00	**30.25**	2 07 30.0	71.06
35.	A. J. Gaunt, BSA	32.30	**31.59**	32.11	32.19	2 08 59.0	70.21
36.	K. Barfoot, BSA	34.09	32.09	31.59	**31.50**	2 10 07.0	69.60
37.	J. Mockett, Norton	32.40	32.11	**32.01**	33.17	2 10 09.0	69.58
38.	S. Baskett, BSA	31.28	**31.25**	32.55	39.46	2 15 34.0	66.80
39.	J. R. Dulson, Norton	34.22	**33.09**	33.14	34.55	2 15 40.0	66.75
40.	W. Hillary, BSA	36.23	35.12	**33.48**	33.50	2 19 13.0	65.05
41.	V. J. Holcroft, BSA	**35.58**	36.12	36.45	36.44	2 25 39.0	62.18
	H. D. Briggs, BSA	31.48	**31.02**	34.18	R		
	A. F. J. D. Martin, BSA	37.32	R				
	J. H. Morton, BSA	30.02	R				
	J. D. Morton, BSA	R					
	F. Burgess, BSA	R					

D. Quayle, BSA	R
J. Clague, BSA	R
D. J. Smart, BSA	R

LAP POSITIONS

1954 CLUBMAN'S JUNIOR

RIDER AND MACHINE	FIRST LAP POSITION		RIDER AND FINAL POSITION	MACHINE
G ARNOLD B.S.A.	1		1	P PALMER B.S.A.
P PALMER B.S.A.	2=		2	D A WRIGHT B.S.A.
A S BOWIE B.S.A.	2=		3	J W DAVIE B.S.A.
D A WRIGHT B.S.A.	4		4	A S BOWIE B.S.A.
G B TANNER NORTON	5		5	G B TANNER NORTON
J W DAVIE B.S.A.	6		6	G ARNOLD B.S.A.

1954 Clubman's Senior

1.	A. King, BSA	26.37	26.51	26.07	**26.01**	1 45 36.0	85.76
2.	J. B. Denton, BSA	26.33	26.42	26.23	**26.03.6**	1 45 41.6	85.68
3.	E. McG. Haldane, BSA	26.32	26.30	**26.25**	26.45.2	1 46 12.2	85.26
4.	T. A. Ovens, Triumph	27.01	26.40	26.31	**26.30.2**	1 46 42.2	84.87
5.	M. R. Baigent, BSA	26.58	26.29	27.03	**26.21.8**	1 46 51.8	84.74
6.	P. H. Tait, BSA	26.58	27.10	26.30	**26.27**	1 47 05.0	84.58
7.	D. V. Chadwick, Norton	26.52	27.48	**26.50**	27.21.4	1 48 51.4	83.20
8.	E. Cheers, Triumph	27.59	28.10	27.16	**26.52.2**	1 50 17.2	82.10
9.	L. R. King, Triumph	27.43	27.35	27.57	**27.18**	1 50 33.0	81.92
10.	W. E. Dow, BSA	28.05	28.25	27.47	**27.28**	1 51 45.0	81.04
11.	H. McKenzie, Triumph	28.06	27.57	27.37	**28.06.8**	1 51 46.8	81.01
12.	G. W. Shekell, Norton	28.17	28.40	28.00	**27.54**	1 52 51.0	80.25
13.	D. Andrews, Norton	28.37	**28.03**	**28.03**	28.22	1 53 05.0	80.08
14.	F. O. Coleman, BSA	28.50	28.06	**28.02**	28.25.4	1 53 23.4	79.86
15.	W. H. Wilshere, Triumph	29.33	28.38	29.17	**28.17**	1 55 45.0	78.24
16.	J. R. Hurlstone, Triumph	29.43	29.55	29.05	**28.50.4**	1 57 33.4	77.06
17.	P. Flaskett, BSA	34.08	27.57	**27.46**	28.13	1 58 04.0	76.70
18.	J. F. Hambling, BSA	29.32	30.16	**29.10**	29.15	1 58 13.0	76.61
19.	T. F. Watson, Norton	29.53	30.02	**29.15**	29.18	1 58 28.0	76.44
20.	A. D. Craib, Norton	30.02	29.36	**29.03**	30.13	1 58 54.0	76.17
21.	C. Watson, Norton	29.36	**27.45**	28.50	33.00	1 59 11.0	75.98
22.	R. A. D. Mawson, Norton	31.08	30.23	29.57	**29.18**	2 00 46.0	74.99

23.	K. Brough, Triumph	31.41	30.46	30.35	**28.59**	2 02 01.0	74.22
24.	W. R. Smith, Triumph	30.46	30.47	**30.24**	30.45	2 02 42.0	73.81
25.	A. H. Frost, Norton	31.36	**31.06**	31.27	32.52	2 07 01.0	71.30
26.	F. O. Bishop, Norton	32.39	33.39	**31.50**	31.53	2 10 01.0	69.95
27.	H. D. German, Norton	**27.50**	28.51	38.48	36.44	2 12 13.0	68.49
28.	P. E. Walsh, Norton	34.33	**32.41**	34.11	33.24	2 14 49.0	67.17
29.	D. S. Cholerton, Triumph	31.39	31.47	**29.53**	42.49	2 16 08.0	66.52
30.	J. Hedley, Norton	39.03	33.59	**31.46**	31.55	2 16 43.0	66.24
	G. W. Walker, BSA	32.00	**30.25**	31.40	R		
	A. S. Avis, Triumph	**28.49**	29.08	38.28	R		
	W. Barlow, Norton	34.14	**32.44**	33.39	R		
	N. F. Sweetman, Ariel	**32.57**	36.33	R			
	G. J. Turner, BSA	**28.21**	28.39	R			
	S. T. Seston, BSA	29.25	**27.59**	R			
	A. Johnstone, Triumph	50.57	R				
	J. E. Guest, Norton	R					
	W. S. Mizen, Triumph	R					

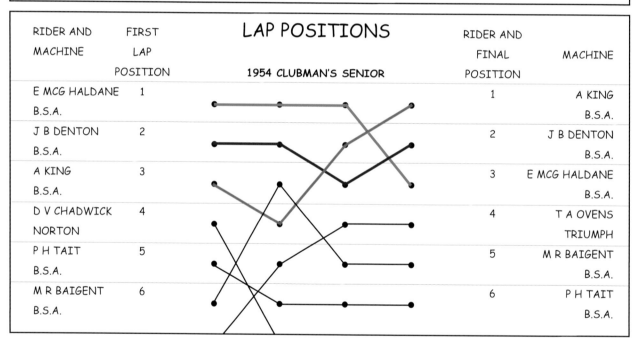

LAP POSITIONS

1954 CLUBMAN'S SENIOR

RIDER AND MACHINE	FIRST LAP POSITION		RIDER AND FINAL POSITION	MACHINE
E MCG HALDANE B.S.A.	1		1	A KING B.S.A.
J B DENTON B.S.A.	2		2	J B DENTON B.S.A.
A KING B.S.A.	3		3	E MCG HALDANE B.S.A.
D V CHADWICK NORTON	4		4	T A OVENS TRIUMPH
P H TAIT B.S.A.	5		5	M R BAIGENT B.S.A.
M R BAIGENT B.S.A.	6		6	P H TAIT B.S.A.

1955

THE CLYPSE YEAR

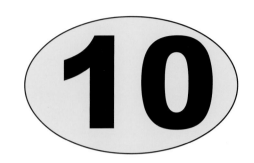

No longer called the Clubman's TT, not even the Clubman's Trophy, the 1955 Clubman's Race Meeting was even further devalued by the ACU in many people's view, by their decision to move the races to the Clypse course. The re-introduction to the International TT of the Sidecar class in 1954, and the decision to stage that event on the new Clypse course, had meant that the Ultra-Lightweight 125 TT also moved to the Clypse course. For 1955 the Clubman's TT was moved to the Clypse course, and also to the Saturday at the end of practice week. The move to this Saturday 'slot' meant that any postponement for weather became impossible, and the races would have to be abandoned. The flip-side of this was that the Clypse course only used the lower slopes of the Mountain, and was therefore less likely to suffer the low cloud and mist in the first place.

In his review of the 1955 Clubman's races for *'Motor Cycling'*, 9th June 1955, Geoff Duke had this to say. *"About 18 months ago I was asked to assist in choosing a circuit for the revival of the Sidecar TT. It was also decided at the time to run the smallest Grand Prix class, the 125, on the same circuit, to see if it also had any possibilities for solo class racing. This initial venture proved successful but the circuit required widening in places for safe overtaking.*

In spite of much work in this direction by the Manx authorities during the winter, I must admit to feeling rather shattered when I learned of the intention to use the Clypse Course for Clubman's events and, in particular, for the 500cc class. These machines, in many cases, have received engine developments far in excess of their stopping power. The addition of road equipment makes them heavier, harder to stop than ever and less easy to handle."

And from the same article, *"In addition the regulations now call for full road equipment, lights, dynamos, silencers etc. Even the compulsory use of centre-stands was in the original regulations! The last mentioned prompted me to write a letter to the secretary of the ACU a while ago, as I considered that the possibility of these stands digging in presented an un-necessary hazard."*

New for 1955 were restrictions on what equipment could be removed from the bike. The previous year allowed air cleaners, silencers, speedometers, luggage carriers, tool boxes, stands and battery carriers to be removed, but the 1955 Regulations only allowed for air cleaners and luggage carriers to go. Also in the new Regulations, the only equipment for which removal was mandatory were 'registration plates, rear lamps, horns, license holders and club badges other than transfers'. Rev-counters, rear springing and vents to clutch and chain-cases which in 1954 had come under the heading 'Permitted additions to equipment', were prohibited unless fitted as standard. Previous years had allowed alternative carburettors of the same make to be fitted, but for 1955 they had to be of the same make, type and fitting specified as original equipment. Other restrictions related to footrest details and positioning, and alloy rims could not be used unless fitted as original equipment.

Course improvements for 1955 included a widening of the road and pit access area on the Glencrutchery Road, and a new pedestrian bridge just beyond. The road widening referred to by Geoff Duke began just beyond Creg-ny-Baa, at Cronk-y-Garoo and at Morney 1, 3 and 4.

Races were to be over 9 laps of the 10.79 mile course, and because of the reduced race distance, re-fuelling was no longer required.

Entries and Practice

The entry fee remained at seven guineas, but entries were slow coming in. After a last-minute rush, 45 entries were eventually received for the Junior, all but 4 on BSA's, whereas in the Senior class just under half the 32 were similarly mounted, marque opposition coming from 12 Triumphs and 5 Nortons. A glance down the Junior entry list shows Jimmy Buchan, Ernie Washer, Fred Wallis, Alan Brodrick, Peter Ferbrache and Jimmie Morton, and in the Senior Eddie Dow, Jimmy Drysdale, and second rides for Fred Wallis and Peter Ferbrache, the only two riders taking advantage of this option. Entered by the Vintage MCC was *'Motor Cycling'* columnist John Griffith, who rode a Triumph T100 as part of an extended 'road test' of the model (the Road Test Report is included in the 21 July 1955 issue of that magazine).

Qualifying time was set at 14 minutes for both classes, with a minimum of five completed laps. First practice for the clubmen on the new course was on the evening of Saturday 28th May, and, breaking with what had seemed to be becoming a tradition, the two one-hour sessions were held in glorious sunshine, even a 'wet tar' sign shown to the riders warning of a possible hazard around the 5th Milestone and The Nook. The session began with a very uncharacteristic 'gaffe' by the driver of the 'Roads Closed' car, who evidently forgot that the Clypse course did not use the Dip at Governors Bridge. Having negotiated the hairpin and the left-hander in the Dip in style, he found his exit onto the Glencrutchery Road blocked by a barrier, much to his embarrassment. In the first one-hour practice, restricted to Juniors, the fastest lap was put up by South African Daniel Joubert on his BSA, with 9m 47s (66.30 mph).

In the second session, for Seniors, Menstrie club member Jimmy Drysdale was almost a casualty as he appeared to brush the wall on the apex of Parkfield with his shoulder, but it turned out to be just a close call, and he continued, to register fastest lap of the session with 9m 29s (68.46 mph).

Spills were reported concerning two riders, N. J. Davenport (Junior BSA) and D. C. L. Dalziel (Senior Triumph), both escaped with minor injuries. Neither accident happened on the new course, being at the Nook and Governors Bridge respectively. Davenport in fact walked the remaining mile to the pits, where a broken collar bone was diagnosed by the examining doctor.

Although minor in its nature, Dalziel's accident was to have repercussions in terms of the race regulations, as it was apparently caused by the centre-stand of his Triumph grounding. No doubt conscious of Geoff Duke's

D C L Dalziel at Signpost Corner (a left-hander on the Clypse course) during practice, his Triumph Tiger 100 still wearing the obligatory centre stand. Just a mile further on he had a spill at Governors Bridge which prompted the organisers to allow their removal.

earlier letter on the subject, the ACU acted with commendable speed, rescinding the rule in time for the evening practice on the following Monday afternoon. As was the norm, the times for the first two laps of newcomers were not reported.

Fine weather again greeted riders for Monday's second practice, and riders were warned of loose chippings on wet tar, this time at the entrance to Parkfield and at the Manx Arms in Onchan. Joubert was again fastest in the Junior session with 9m 35s (67.74 mph). Incidentally, *'The Motor Cycle's'* correspondent reporting practice, who had described Joubert's riding in the first session as *'inclined to be lurid'*, felt it necessary to re-categorise after the second session, up-grading it to *'inclined to be wild'*. In fairness, his cornering style was simply the more upright and occasional foot-down technique used by all on the loose surfaces common to racing back in his home country, something akin to American flat-tracking. In contrast, Jimmy Buchan's riding received particularly favourable comment from the *'TT Special'* reporters around the course. Jimmy Buchan and Peter Ferbrache were only slightly slower than Joubert on their BSA's. J. D. Morton dropped his BSA at Governors Bridge but remounted and continued. Jimmy Drysdale was again fastest Senior. Two spills were reported from the Ballacoar area in the Senior class, D.M. Snaith (BSA) escaped with concussion, but V.F. Kerbey was less fortunate, suffering what were thought to be serious head and spinal injuries. Later in the week came the good news that he was likely to be discharged from hospital within days. A number of riders found difficulty with the awkward downhill approach to the right-hand bend at Ballacoar, and several glanced off the bank on the exit. Hardest 'strike' was by J. J. Womack, who came to a stop after the impact, but he managed to tour back to the pits after regaining his composure, his machine seemingly okay except for a bent footrest. From all around the course came reports of silencers grounding, throwing up showers of sparks and looking spectacular, but not apparently causing too much concern for the riders.

Tuesday evening's third practice again enjoyed superb weather, and once again Joubert and Drysdale were fastest in their classes. Alan Brodrick came off his Junior BSA at Morney 3 and injured his shoulder,

B. A. Denniss crashed his Senior BSA at Cronk-y-Berry, near Cronk-ny-Mona. However, Saturday's Governors Bridge casualty D. C. L. Dalziel was back in action on his Triumph (now, like all the runners, without the offending centre-stand). Lap times were generally quicker than on the previous sessions, as riders became more accustomed to the circuit, and as the loose chippings on certain corners were dispersed, notably at Parkfield, The Manx Arms and Nursery Bends.

Thursday morning's final practice took place in cool but almost ideal conditions, only low sun causing any problems for riders as they left Creg-ny-Baa, heading east as they took the road cross-country toward Laxey. Joubert made it a clean sweep of the Junior class by again putting up fastest time, but Fred Wallis headed up the Senior class ahead of Dow and Drysdale. The only spill reported was that of R. Thompson, who came off his Junior BSA on the Ballacarrooin Hill section of the course, but he was unhurt and continued. H. E. Vine had a walking-pace 'off' when his BSA silencer grounded at Governors Bridge, lifting the rear wheel and spinning him around. He lost little time in recovering things and setting off again. Overall fastest in practice then were Joubert in the Junior with 9m 23s (69.2 mph), and Drysdale in the Senior with 9m 14s (70.25 mph).

The exuberant South African Daniel Joubert, pictured at Bedstead.

end of the 7th lap with the brake pedal having holed the primary chaincase. (A contemporary account placed the fall at Creg-ny-Baa, and suggested that a policeman on duty at the Nursery Bends had reported that the BSA was possibly not in a fit state to continue). David toured back in to retire, unaware that the black flag had been prepared for him at the Start/Finish.

Luckily the showers never developed into persistent rain, and the majority of the circuit remained dry to the end of the race. Both Buchan and Joubert were receiving signals, and were fully aware of the others progress. Although close on time, Buchan was able to control the race, easing a little to avoid mechanical problems or rider error in the closing stages. So it proved, and while Joubert was closing all the time it was not quickly enough. He crossed the line first, but lost out to Buchan on corrected time by some 16 seconds, Ferbrache coming home 3rd. In the final two laps James slowed a little, and finished back in 7th, while the scrap for 4th, 5th and 6th went to Thompson, only 1.5 seconds ahead of McLean, who was 7 seconds ahead of Hocking.

Originally hailing from Guernsey, Barry Cortvriend was one of many riders who enjoyed the racing patronage of former 350cc World Champion Bob Foster whilst working at his Poole motorcycle business.

Finishing Order

1 J. Buchan (BSA)	1h 25m 24s	(68.23 mph)
2 D. Joubert (BSA)	1h 25m 39.6s	(68.02mph)
3 P. Ferbrache (BSA)	1h 27m 54.8s	(66.28 mph)
4 R. Thompson (BSA)	1h 30m 13s	(64.59 mph)
5 C. McLean (BSA)	1h 30m 14.4s	(64.56 mph)
6 W. H. Hocking (BSA)	1h 30m 21.8s	(64.49 mph)

Fastest Lap: D. Joubert (7th lap) 9m 18s (69.78 mph) (Record).

The Centre Team Award was not awarded.

The Senior Race (Saturday, 4th June)

Starters

	Rider	Club	Machine
2	D C L Dalziel	B.M.C.R.C.	Triumph
3	H E Vine	Southend & DMCC	B.S.A.
7	W E Dow	Leicester Query MC	B.S.A.
8	G W Shekell	Worcester AC	Triumph
10	C Dearden	Rochdale & DMC	Triumph
12	L C St J Hawkins		
		Mendip Vale MCC & LCC	B.S.A.
14	A Ashley	Armthorpe Ace MCC	Triumph
15	R F Keen	Sutton Coldfield & NBAC	B.S.A.
16	J Drysdale	Menstrie MCC	B.S.A.
17	J P Griffith	Vintage MCC	Triumph
18	R Kelly	Southern MCC (IoM)	Triumph
19	I M Atkinson	Bradford & DMC	Triumph
20	D J Hunt	Braintree & DMCC	B.S.A.
21	D Merridan	Chalfont & Amersham AC	Triumph
22	D C Middleton	Salop MC	Triumph
23	P E Walsh	Solihull MCC	Norton
24	F Wallis	Nottingham Tornado MC	B.S.A.
27	J Hedley	Chase MCC	Norton
28	P Ferbrache	Wakefield & DMSC	B.S.A.
29	M W Gillingham		
		Sturminster Newton & DMC & LCC	Triumph
30	A H Mustard	Dunlop C & MCC	B.S.A.
31	R Preece	Stafford AC	Norton
32	D Andrews	Horsforth & DMC	B.S.A.

As the later finishers crossed the line at the end of the Junior race, the clouds began to break, and the sun made its first appearance of the day. The breeze helped dry the roads, and by the start at 6.30 pm conditions were generally very good for the 23 starters from the original 32 entries, 10 of whom were on BSA's, another 10 on Triumphs, and 3 on Nortons.

Non-starters were the BSA's of W. Mace, D. M. Snaith, B. A. Denniss, K. J. Bell and 'W. Cliff', the Triumphs of S. Snowden and V. F. Kerbey and the Nortons of B. Herbert and M. Redford.

The riders were again set off in groups of four, starting at 30 second intervals. First away were D. C. L. Dalziel (Triumph) and H. E. Vine (BSA), W. Mace and D. M. Snaith non-starting. Eddie Dow's BSA required a few kicks before starting, D. J. Hunt's BSA and P. E. Walsh's Norton took longer still, but one of the likely front-runners Peter Ferbrache lost about two minutes before getting away on his BSA. Fastest man in practice Jimmy Drysdale was also in trouble, getting away in good time but his BSA was misfiring badly away from the start. Dow led on the roads at the end of the first lap, 3rd on adjusted time behind Manxman Raymond Kelly, and leader Ian Atkinson, both on Triumphs, who started in the same group as each other, and with *'Motor Cycling'* correspondent John Griffith, who had fellow staffman Bernal Osborne pitting for him. Drysdale pulled into his pit at the end of the lap, but despite his difficulties managed to claim 7th place. Fred Wallis was 4th, and having a great dice for 5th and 6th places, as well as on the roads, were Andrew Mustard and Don Andrews, both on BSA's.

First Lap Leaderboard

1 I. M. Atkinson (Triumph)	9m 26s	(68.82 mph)
2 R. Kelly (Triumph)	9m 33s	(67.98mph)
3 W. E. Dow (BSA)	9m 37s	(67.505 mph)
4 F. Wallis (BSA)	9m 43s	(66.79 mph)
5 A. H. Mustard (BSA)	9m 48s	(66.18 mph)
6 D. Andrews (BSA)	9m 53s	(65.58 mph)

The pit stop for the unfortunate Drysdale lasted some four minutes, dropping him well down the order, and you can only begin to imagine his feelings when, as soon as the BSA fired up to rejoin the race, the misfire immediately returned. Dow increased his pace, passing Kelly and closing on Atkinson. Another to lose time in the pits was Alan Ashley,

who worked on his Triumph for over a minute before restarting, only reaching Creg-ny-Baa before retiring. To no-ones surprise, Drysdale pulled into his pit at the end of lap two, and lost a couple more minutes, but during that time he and his attendant had succeeded in identifying the problem as a loose contact breaker assembly. With the problem rectified, he set off, way behind, but at a tremendous pace. With the fastest lap of the race thus far on his third lap, Dow was the race leader by 4 seconds from Atkinson, while Ferbrache, after the time lost at the start lapping as fast as Dow, was not yet able to get into a leaderboard place. The leader was 4 seconds faster on his next lap, extending his lead over Atkinson to 10 seconds, but the absolute sensation of that fourth lap was the blistering 8m 56 secs lap record posted by Drysdale, the first sub-9 minute lap of the Clypse Course. By the end of the fifth lap Dow had increased his lead over Atkinson to 22 seconds, but again Drysdale was in near-record time at 8m 58 secs.

Fifth Lap Leaderboard

1 W. E. Dow (BSA)	46m 08s	(70.17 mph)
2 I. M. Atkinson (Triumph)	46m 30s	(69.62mph)

Surprise of the race was the pace of Manxman Raymond Kelly. Surprise, that is, to all except the local constabulary who were quite aware of his turn of speed! Had he not overshot the odd corner he would have probably finished higher than third.

3 R. Kelly (Triumph)	47m 08s	(68.68 mph)
4 F. Wallis (BSA)	47m 44s	(67.82 mph)
5 D. Andrews (BSA)	47m 46s	(67.77 mph)
6 A. H. Mustard (BSA)	47m 47s	(67.75 mph)

Pulling through the field in a similar fashion, albeit slower and with less of a deficit to catch up, was Ferbrache. He reached 5th place on the sixth lap, tying with Andrews, with Mustard and Wallis close behind. Unfortunately, Wallis's BSA then appeared to lose some of its top-end power, and he began to drop back, eventually taking 7th place. Drysdale was flying. He equalled his newly-set lap record on his sixth lap, and his seventh lap was only 2 seconds slower, consistently almost 10 seconds a lap quicker than the leader Dow. Meanwhile the Triumph of Crowther Dearden slowed with gearbox gremlins, but he was able to nurse it to the finish, as did David Merridan who lost time at the pits working on his Triumph (it would have to be Triumph with a name like that). As the race moved into the last lap, Ferbrache passed Wallis to take 4th place, then, shortly after Drysdale set off on his final lap, Eddie Dow crossed the finish line to win by over a minute from Atkinson and Kelly. Ferbrache finished 4th, and the race-long scrap between Mustard and Andrews,

which the crowd (and doubtless the riders) had thoroughly enjoyed, went to Andrews by 3 seconds. For the record, hero of the day and new lap record holder Drysdale came in 16th.

Finishing Order

1 W. E. Dow (BSA)	1h 22m 23s	(70.73 mph)
2 I. M. Atkinson (Triumph)	1h 23m 31s	(69.77mph)
3 R. Kelly (Triumph)	1h 24m 32s	(68.93 mph)
4 P. Ferbrache (BSA)	1h 25m 02s	(68.52 mph)
5 D. Andrews (BSA)	1h 25m 21s	(68.27 mph)
6 A. H. Mustard (BSA)	1h 25m 24s	(68.23 mph)

Fastest Lap: J. Drysdale (6th lap) 8m 56s (72.53 mph) (Record).

The Centre Team Award went to Midland Centre ACU (R.F.Keen, A.H. Mustard, R. Preece)

Reflections

Second-place man in the Junior Daniel Joubert must have cursed his luck, his machine or himself for the 50 seconds or so self-imposed handicap at the start of a race that he eventually lost by 16 seconds. Whether or not he could have won will never be known, as Buchan was receiving good signalling, and would have upped the pace had he been seriously threatened. There's no record of Daniel Joubert taking part in any other TT or Manx Grand Prix, although after the race he said he had greatly enjoyed the circuit and the race, even though he had never before raced on wet roads, and was troubled only by the misty conditions and the cold!

A less dramatic but similar 'if-only-it-had-started-first-kick' story came in the Senior race, where Peter Ferbrache would probably have claimed 3rd place had the BSA fired up when first asked.

However, by far the biggest 'what-if' story belongs to Jimmy Drysdale, whose times on those record laps once the loose contact-breaker assembly

Once the reluctant Gold Star started, Captain Eddie Dow took the lead on the third lap to record his only Island win. A true all-rounder, Eddie won a Gold Medal in the International Six Days Trial (also Gold Star mounted).

had been tightened, suggest that he would have been ahead of Eddie Dow at the finish. Dow's machine finished in near-perfect condition, and with little more than a check-over took part in the Thruxton Nine-hour endurance event, ridden again by Dow, partnered by Eddie Crooks, and won outright.

Post-race reaction to the Clypse course by the winners was, perhaps unsurprisingly, favourable. Eddie Dow, who had ridden in the Clubman's TT in 1953 and 1954 on the Mountain Course, and who had been critical of the decision to switch, went out of his way to retract some of that criticism. The fact was that in addition to the logistics associated with the running of the 125 and sidecar classes mentioned earlier, some of the motives behind the switch were sound. Demanding, but shorter and easier to learn for the newcomer, slower and arguably less unforgiving, its lower altitude meant that it could be used in some circumstances when the Mountain Circuit could not, the 1955 Junior being an obvious example. It was seen as an introduction to 'true' road-racing, in a more manageable form for riders and organisers alike, but did the reasoning and sober logic miss the entire point of the races, that of providing clubmen with the opportunity of tackling the ultimate motorcycling challenge? The editorial in 9th June issue of 'The Motor Cycle' pondered the question without any conclusion or expressed opinion. *"Since last November, when it first became known that the Auto-Cycle Union planned to run the Clubman's events on the Clypse course, critics have suggested that the races were doomed, largely because clubmen had been denied the prestige of riding over the world-famous Mountain Circuit. The fact that entries were fewer than in previous years implied that the critics*

A racing journalist; John Griffith of 'Motor Cycling' wrote a first-hand account of his Senior Clubman's ride.

were right. However, the shorter (10.79 mile) Clypse course can be learned by newcomers more easily than the 37.73 mile Mountain Circuit – this consideration alone is of real merit. Furthermore, competitors in both events undoubtedly enjoyed the racing. On the other hand, the opinion was expressed that since it will always be overshadowed by the glory of the Mountain Circuit, the Clypse substitute will not continue to draw representative entry lists. It is thought that many potential competitors might well weigh the time and cost involved, and decide instead to race on mainland circuits. The ACU should, perhaps, address an official questionnaire to all riders in this years Clubman's races as a policy guide for next year's events".

Contrast this with Geoff Duke's views in *'Motor Cycling'*, the very same day. *"Without a doubt the most universally unpopular change has been the move from the main TT circuit to the Clypse course! This is very largely responsible for the big decrease in entries for both races. The opportunity to try his hand on the famous TT circuit has been snatched away from the clubman for no accountable reason and he doesn't like it."*

The following week's Editorial in *'Motor Cycling'* set out a few simple questions. *"How to plan a simpler TT is one of the problems the 1955 event*

217

leaves behind. Others are:- Should the Clubmen use the Mountain or Clypse circuit? Should the Clubman's meeting be included in the TT at all? If not, could it be incorporated, as Geoff Duke has suggested, with the Manx Grand Prix? What do the Clubmen themselves want?"

My 1955 Senior Clubman's Ride
by Jimmy Drysdale

I had some advantages going into the 1955 Senior Clubman's TT. The Clypse circuit was new to everyone and I was a fast learner; on a very narrow and twisty road, mostly between banks, I saw my height, 6' 3", as something of an advantage, letting me see into the bends; it was also natural for me to use the back brake, letting me turn the bike relatively quickly which I saw as the way to go fast on this circuit.

Plus I had a very good bike. I rode it down from Scotland, learned the course, practised and finally raced it. I was totally at home with it. It was delivered to me with TT gearing and after the first practise I dropped this by half a tooth, because I wanted it to sing on the only real length of fast road, from the reverse entry into Hillberry into what was for us, the right-hander at the Creg. By happy coincidence, that gearing also suited me on the twisties. We made one other change late on the night before the race. The bike was a very, very bad kick-starter, the use of which was obligatory to get going in the race and so we took it to have a new magneto fitted. The bike became an instant one-kick starter and off we went to bed to sleep the sleep of the well prepared. Wrongly, as it turned out, because loose contact breaker points cost us a lengthy pit-stop in the race itself. That in itself had its plus point, because I restarted from the pits knowing that I could finish at best. While this was a big thing for me, as I had not done this in two previous attempts, the Junior in '53 and '54, it meant I restarted carefree, with only the problem of the road in front of me to think about. There is no better way to enjoy the Isle of Man. There were three places where I had been afraid of dirt out on the edges of the track but I had checked these out on my earlier laps. So I had a glorious time, all thanks to the Isle of Man. The only disappointment was the chequered flag. But that's the way it should be.

218

My Clubman's Rides
by Jimmy Buchan

The first shock came when I discovered that for 1954, all riders had to complete two 10-mile road races or three short-circuit events. The only road races within 250 miles of my home in Perth were at Esholt Park near Bradford.

It consisted of a blast up an old drive, a left turn through a farm yard, and then another blast, much slower this time because it was on a genuine tow path, with the canal on one side and a nine foot fence on the other!

A far cry from the Isle of Man, but it served its purpose.

My Gold Star was not ready until close to the time of our departure, and the only time I raced it was at my local track, Errol, the day before I sailed from Fleetwood. I managed to win the 350 Novice Race before I left.

The next week just flew past as we tried to learn the Mountain Course, checking the bike every day, and finally the four lap (150 miles) race.

Probably the thing that I remember best was the hot chocolate tent where many tales were swapped and no doubt embellished.

There was a strong Scottish contingent that year and we won both team prizes. Alastair King was 1st in the Senior, Ewen Haldane 3rd, and Alastair McKenzie 11th. In the Junior the placings were Jimmy Davie 3rd, Sandy Bowie 4th and myself 7th. We all sailed back to Ardrossan which saved two hundred miles on the journey, then rode the bikes home.

1955 followed much the same pattern, but it meant a move to the Clypse Course which had none of the character or tradition of the Mountain Course. We had to keep the lights, stands and a huge silencer on, instead of the snappy 6" straight-through exhaust of '54. We had to do 9 laps with no pit stops. I thought the best thing was to go really hard from the flag, and it paid off. I led all the way with a nice cushion of 15 to 25 seconds from the South African champion, Danny Joubert.

Overall, it was a fantastic experience. I just wish it had been over the 'big' course. Three months later I was back in the Island for the Manx Grand Prix and finished 4th in the Junior and 2nd in the Senior.

A year later I did the Junior and Senior Manx Grand Prix double.

The Gold Star was simply 'too good for its own good' and its domination was one of the reasons for the races being abandoned.

I would like to pay a small tribute to the landladies (and landlords) of the Island, who in practice week were up long before dawn, serving up the best tea and toast I have ever tasted! Our hotel was run by the Stanley family, and they charged £1.00 per day for dinner, bed and breakfast, including a cup of tea and toast when we got up for practice at 3.30 am. The usual rate was a guinea (a pound and a shilling) but they deducted one shilling a day as we were riders. We also had exclusive use of their magnificent double-garage on Dukes' Road - we could free-wheel back from the pits. During the day we were visited by the trade reps, Lew Ellis of Shell, Jimmy Hill of Castrol, Geoff Murdoch of Esso, with contracts to sign and petrol and oil to give away. No wonder we felt good!

What is it like to race on the Clypse Course?

When I first competed on the Island the year before, we were on the Mountain Course with its instantly recognisable features - Quarter Bridge, Ramsey Hairpin, Kate's Cottage; and of course the petrifying plunge down Bray Hill within seconds of the Start.

Instead, we now turned right at a filling station (still there) at St. Ninians crossroads, before the top of Bray and along a suburban street. Another right-hander at Willaston took us up to Cronk-ny-Mona onto the 'real' TT course, the only thing was, we went the wrong way, down to Hillberry then up to Brandish and Creg-ny-Baa. To try and keep the Gold Star buzzing on the long drag from Brandish I lowered the gearing, which also helped on the slow corners.

Another right-hander at the Creg took you into the unknown. In places the road had been widened to make life easier for the sidecars, and the road was mainly level or downhill all the way to Ballacoar, a tight right-hander with a deceptive approach over a blind summit. Then it was back among the high bankings, and the feeling of being hemmed in. Suddenly you popped out onto the Laxey-to-Douglas road and the full bore drive over Whitebridge and up into Onchan. The lower gearing caused the bike to over-rev to 8,000 rpm (112 mph) but I reckoned a short blast shouldn't harm it.

Hard on the brakes at the Manx Arms and up to the lovely sweeping Nursery Bends - that was more like

it. We rejoined the Mountain Course at Signpost, which became a left-hander with the approach now from Onchan, and the remainder of the 10.79 mile lap was on more familiar roads. Except that there was a final indignity still to be suffered, the world famous Dip at Governors Bridge was by-passed. Why? Don't ask me!

I was delighted to win, of course, but I have always felt it was devalued. The difference between the courses is perfectly demonstrated by a couple of statistics. On my first ride on the Mountain in 1954 I averaged 80.75 mph over four laps with one fuel stop. On the Clypse it was 68.33 over nine laps, with no fuel stop!

One image of the '55 Senior Clubman I will never forget was Jimmy Drysdale starting his reluctant 500 Gold Star. He simply launched into a non-stop series of kicks until it must have been doing 2,000 rpm plus and it just had to fire. It seemed to bend in the middle as Jimmy, six foot three inches and built to match, literally dared it not to go. We all cheered when it did, confident he would win once it had started, but new points fitted the night before worked loose and he had to pit twice before he was on full song.

He did have the consolation of winning the Dunlop Trophy for the fastest lap, but Captain Eddie Dow won the race comfortably.

Have you ever seen a Gold Star bend in the middle?

Well, I have.....

My Clubman's Rides
by David Hagen

To be in the Isle of Man during the TT was one of life's great joys and particularly so during the Golden Years of the 1950's, the age of the Manx Norton, the 7R, open megaphones, bump starts, early morning practice and the Cadbury Cocoa tent. The Clubman's races were a part of the Golden era as well. The Clubman's was for me, the focus of an odyssey which began on a gravel road in a small Oregon town and ended on the Glencrutchery Road.

My awareness of the Isle of Man and the TT began in picking up a copy of an American motor cycle magazine in the local drug store. Syd Lawton rounding Governors Bridge on a 7R AJS was pictured on the cover, the picture was amazingly powerful and looking back was surely the pivotal moment in my decision about racing.

The lead article featured the 1950 TT in the Isle of Man. The works featherbed Norton's made their winning debut led by Geoff Duke and Artie Bell. Printed on the final page was the subscription order blank for the two English motor cycle weeklies, 'Motor Cycling' and 'The Motor Cycle', I ordered both and for the next few years, these two publications were to play a key role in developing my anglicized view of motorcycle racing.

It is hard to believe that throughout the 1950's there was virtually no motor cycle road racing in all of the United States. By 1954 it seemed that any American who was seriously interested in racing would have to migrate to Britain. I wrote to Cyril Quantrill of 'Motor Cycling' describing how I thought it was possible to come to England and asked for his opinions and suggestions. He replied promptly, probably intrigued by my audacity and determination, he clearly had good contacts in racing circles and offered to find a club willing to act as a sponsor for the clubman's.

David Hagen at Union Mills in 1956, 50 years on, David returned to the Island for a nostalgic trip. The intervening years had dulled his memory somewhat, he could remember the major corners, but not the myriad of curves that made up the Clypse or Mountain circuits!

I arrived in London in early spring of 1955 and promptly made contact with The Mont' Christie motorcycle club who were willing to act as a sponsor for the Clubman's. An early stop was in Pall Mall at the ACU offices to acquire an ACU racing license. The manager of the British Moto Cross Des Nations team, Harold Taylor happened to be there and greeted me warmly, a good omen I thought. Mont' Chrisite Motor Cycle Club boasted half a dozen racers or ex racers among the membership including BWT (Benny) Rood, a master at building race winning 250cc Velocettes. Among his credits was winning the Governor's Handicap in the 1952 Ulster. I remember well the day we loaded Ben's old furniture van with his 250 Velocette, my Gold Star and a couple of 7Rs and drove to Snetterton for the day. This was my first experience on an English circuit and I droned around it, lap after lap enjoying the experience immensely. My first race took place at Thruxton where my performance was undistinguished. Also, making his track debut, in the same heat was Tony Godfrey who finished second on a famous bike, the ex Tommy Wood KTT Velocette. That day, 11 April, 1955 was a sad one however on the return home we learned Ray Amm had been killed at Imola in his debut on the MV.

Two weeks later Benny drove us all to Silverstone arriving on the Friday. My first task was to remove my wheels and take them to the Dunlop van to have new tyres fitted. The tyre fitter, sizing me up as an American, abruptly took a verbal swing at me, the message "it was because of Yanks just like you that I had to eat SPAM all during the war." The next day making a promising start in the 30-mile Clubman's race, things were looking good until I nearly rammed a slower rider on my line at Woodcote. Instead of pulling the bike over to the right I went wide to the left and onto the grass, and immediately hit a shallow ditch, propelling the bike into the air high enough, I was told, to make grandstand occupants leap to their feet. Miraculously staying on board. I continued on, chiding myself for going off course.

The drama at Silverstone that weekend which was played out in secret was all about the hush hush BSA four valve MC-1, Geoff Duke tested it at Oulton Park and entered it for Silverstone. While it had good speed, it had poor brakes and only four speeds, and

needed more engine development. The main competition was John Surtees on the new NSU Sport Max. Odds are Surtees would have won. Had Geoff won it would have been a major event in British motor cycling history.

A month later I stepped off the ferry in Douglas armed with a used BSA Gold Star and an entry in the Junior Clubman's. Arriving early, I found myself in the company of another early arrival Danny Joubert. Initially, we went out to learn the Clypse together. This pairing didn't work for long. Joubert was phenomenally fast and a trifle frightening! He was travelling at near racing speeds on open road. I left him to it!

On the day of the race, I sat in the front row pondering why I had been given number 2, Joubert was number 3. My Gold Star was an older model with the smaller carburetor and a quick starter. As the flag dropped, my Gold Star fired and I led the field for a few miles. I was running in the first dozen, but tiring. A spectator told me after the race he had watched the race from Nursery Bends and listened to a radio broadcast at the same time. When I arrived at Nursery Bends, the broadcaster shouted, *"and here comes the American and he is still on the wrong line!"* He seemed to know what he was talking about because I dropped it there on my next lap. The front wheel hit the kerb a glancing blow sending me end over end along the pavement without touching the stone wall. Running back I picked up the bike but the brake pedal has been smashed into the chain case and it was inoperable. A policeman ran up asking me if I was alright, and I said "yes" and rode off slowly to the grandstand to retire.

The damage to the bike was little more than cosmetic. Once repaired the bike was sold to a waiting buyer and I left town without it. Back in London, I wasted little time booking passage on a freighter which sailed from London Docks down the Thames, the ship was limited to 12 passengers, we ate with the Captain and had the run of the ship. It was tedious at times as we crawled across the Atlantic at less than 15 knots, reaching New York in a week and a half. I had plenty of time to work on a racing plan for 1956. I was amused at how little my relatives understood of my racing in England. They made comments like, "we're glad to see you, we're glad you are alright", "we are glad you got that racing business out of your system". Little did they know! I soon went to work in a local paper mill and continued to plan my second trip to England. For 1956 I ordered a brand new 500cc DBD Gold Star 'Clubman' direct from the factory to be delivered to a London area dealer, Sam Coles. After riding the Gold Star around London for a week and a day spent at Snetterton sorting things out, I tied all my belongings to the bike and headed for Liverpool.

In Clubman's trim the Gold Star was not the easiest bike to ride on the road. Especially when heavily laden. During the journey, it rained and the two lane roads were heavy with traffic, but how could I complain? I had a new motor cycle and I was on my way to the Isle of Man. And as Geoff Duke often said, I was "full of the joys of spring." As I arrived in Liverpool, and passed through the Mersey tunnel, I arrived at the docks where the ferry waited, four more hours and I would be in the Isle of Man!

During the weeks practice I was determined to be first away one morning. Arriving at the grandstand at 5:00 am I found two others already waiting in line. But as the gates swung open at 5:30 am, the other two stopped to tinker and I was first after all. I loved the feeling of being in front. Residents of the island are required to have their pets and farm animals confined during TT practice or races. Nevertheless, sometimes an animal is in the road when it shouldn't be. On this morning, rounding a very fast right hand bend I found a dog sitting at the side of the road in front of a farm gate, It was too late to take action. Fortunately the dog didn't step into the road. It does happen. In 1956 John Surtees smashed his MV in a collision with a cow in TT practice with fatal consequences to the cow.

This morning I went all the way around the course as far as the exit from the 'Creg' before I was passed by Bernard Codd. In a few moments Codd reached the start/finish, starting a second lap and I followed.

Bill Corley my mechanic had just arrived at the grandstands in time to see Codd flash through with me trailing. When Bill saw me in close proximity to Codd, he thought I was lapping at the same speed and was riding over my head. It took Bill a while to realize I had actually started well before Codd and wasn't riding over my head.

I had practiced kick-starting my bike days before the race, but when the time came to do it for real, could I do it? I couldn't! Needless to say, the two Triumphs in my row needed only one kick. I kicked and kicked for what seemed like minutes but was really 7 or 8 seconds before it started. On the first lap, I was crossing Greeba Bridge when Ron Jerrard blasted by me, got into a tank-slapping wobble and went on his way, at undiminished speed. When I got to Ballacraine he was out of sight.

On the second lap, I turned my head to one side just enough to have the wind catch my goggles, pulling one side of the lens out of its rubber frame leaving it flapping in the wind. I tried to force the lens back into its slot but couldn't. I debated whether to stop along the road and fix them or to stop in the pits and get a fresh pair. As I rode on, I realized I didn't have another pair and I rode on without stopping. There were not many corners in all of the TT course I felt I knew well. Worse case was all of Glen Helen, the best being Quarry Bends. As I approached the Quarry Bends on lap 2, I could feel a Triumph creep up along my right side. Apparently I had the peel off point well selected because I had pulled out 10 or 15 yards on the exit. The Triumph, ridden, I believe by Mike Brookes certainly had the steam but not the handling of the Gold Star. He passed me shortly but must have dropped out soon, maybe on Sulby.

On a day in June half a century ago motor cycle riders on standard machines set out to race three laps over the TT mountain circuit in the Isle of Man. As the last rider in the last race crossed the line, so ended a series of races known as the Clubman's TT. Reasons for the termination of these events are not clearly documented, however the races did serve the needs of several groups over the 10 years of its existence. For the club rider it was a chance to experience racing over the fabled mountain circuit and for another, the young rider with serious TT ambitions it was the first step. The history of the Clubman's deserves more recogition. It is entirely appropriate that we celebrate the 50th Anniversary of the last Clubman's races and to honor the clubmen who rode in them.

1955 Clubman's Junior

Pos	Rider, Make										Total	MPH
1.	J. Buchan, BSA	9.48	9.24	9.25	**9.22**	9.25	9.25	9.25	9.32	9.38	1 25 24	68.23
2.	D. Joubert, BSA	10.08	9.33	9.29	9.22	9.24	9.22	**9.18**	9.29	9.34.6	1 25 39.6	68.02
3.	P. Ferbrache, BSA	10.10	9.38	9.32	9.33	9.34	**9.31**	10.03	10.00	9.53.8	1 27 54.8	66.28
4.	R. Thompson, BSA	10.26	10.00	9.53	9.54	10.00	**9.45**	10.02	10.09	10.04	1 30 13	64.59
5.	C. McLean, BSA	10.25	9.58	9.56	9.58	9.57	**9.53**	9.59	10.07	10.01.4	1 30 14.4	64.56
6.	W. H. Hocking, BSA	10.07	9.57	**9.56**	**9.56**	9.57	9.58	10.24	10.00	10.06.8	1 30 21.8	64.49
7.	K. W. James, BSA	10.25	10.03	9.57	9.54	**9.49**	9.50	10.02	10.25	10.03	1 30 28	64.41
8.	D. Jervis, BSA	10.36	10.05	10.00	9.58	9.49	**9.48**	10.07	10.16	10.01.8	1 30 40.8	64.26
9.	T. E. Hutchinson, BSA	10.50	10.08	10.08	10.06	10.03	**10.02**	10.23	10.23	10.16.6	1 32 19.6	63.12
10.	R. M. Harding, BSA	10.47	10.01	10.02	11.53	**9.47**	9.54	10.16	10.04	9.53.2	1 32 37.2	62.91
11.	A. Culshaw, BSA	10.43	10.18	10.12	10.11	**10.10**	10.13	10.38	10.38	10.20	1 33 23	62.40
12.	G. Arnold, BSA	11.32	10.18	10.07	**10.01**	10.15	10.10	10.33	10.39	10.23.2	1 33 58.2	62.00
13.	T. Swinney, BSA	10.57	10.29	10.26	10.33	10.26	**10.24**	10.41	10.48	10.27	1 35 11	61.22
14.	R. B. Cortvriend, BSA	10.54	10.38	10.26	10.29	**10.24**	10.24	10.41	10.47	10.34	1 35 17	61.15
15.	J. D. Morton, BSA	10.54	10.41	10.42	10.30	**10.29**	10.31	10.38	10.34	10.32.4	1 35 31.4	60.99
16.	S. Baskett, BSA	10.52	10.32	10.36	10.34	**10.29**	10.43	10.54	10.51	10.36.6	1 36 07.6	60.61
17.	J. R. Thurston, BSA	10.59	10.44	10.46	10.41	10.37	10.45	10.53	**9.50**	11.27.2	1 36 42.2	60.25
18.	P. G. Kirkham, BSA	11.32	10.42	10.43	10.48	10.37	**10.35**	10.51	10.58	10.44	1 37 30	59.76
19.	W. D. Fellows, BSA	11.19	10.56	10.55	10.38	**10.34**	10.36	11.10	11.08	10.53	1 38 09	59.37
20.	J. J. Womack, BSA	11.11	10.48	10.52	10.51	**10.42**	10.53	11.05	10.59	10.53	1 38 14	59.31
21.	E. Peacock, BSA	11.15	**10.41**	10.50	10.45	10.45	11.09	11.00	11.05	10.55	1 38 25	59.20
22.	K. A. Lindsay, BSA	11.18	11.07	10.58	11.14	10.53	**10.52**	11.08	10.57	10.59	1 39 26	58.60
23.	P. B. James, BSA	11.13	10.52	10.53	10.49	**10.45**	11.16	11.19	11.23	11.03	1 39 33	58.53
24.	M. F. Sweetman, BSA	11.42	11.08	11.04	10.57	10.50	11.03	11.07	**9.58**	11.54	1 39 43	58.43
25.	D. J. Smart, BSA	18.22	10.18	10.15	10.15	10.12	10.14	10.16	**9.25**	11.17.2	1 40 34.2	57.93
26.	N. C. Fletcher, BSA	10.28	10.07	**10.04**	14.09	14.27	11.12	10.58	10.41	10.39	1 42 45	56.71
27.	G. A. Dormer, BSA	11.40	11.21	11.20	11.27	11.23	11.40	11.57	11.41	**11.19**	1 43 48	56.13
28.	F. Wakefield, Norton	12.04	11.33	11.33	11.32	11.35	11.27	11.28	**11.18**	11.30	1 44 00	56.03
29.	T. Brown, Douglas	16.18	12.55	10.21	**10.13**	10.16	13.10	10.33	10.20	10.15	1 44 21	55.84
30.	R. Maw, BSA	20.07	10.52	10.48	10.35	10.43	10.43	10.46	10.29	**10.24**	1 45 27	55.26
31.	N. H. Vivian, BSA	12.23	12.02	11.53	11.38	11.45	11.48	11.45	**11.35**	11.53	1 46 42	54.61
32.	J. Hutchison, Douglas	12.34	12.16	12.19	**12.09**	12.36	12.42	13.17	13.34	13.25	1 54 52	50.73
	D. Hagan, BSA	10.54	10.24	10.19	**10.16**	**10.16**	10.23	12.15	R			
	E. Unwin, BSA	10.47	10.02	9.56	9.44	9.39	**9.34**	R				
	A. J. Dean, Royal Enfield	10.48	10.37	10.27	**10.22**	10.36	R					
	E. J. Washer, BSA	9.53	9.43	9.30	**9.25**	9.27	R					
	N. Lay, BSA	10.26	10.02	**10.00**	15.03	R						
	N. Robertson, BSA	R										

LAP POSITIONS

1955 CLUBMAN'S JUNIOR

RIDER AND MACHINE	FIRST LAP POSITION		FINAL POSITION	RIDER AND MACHINE
J. BUCHAN B.S.A.	1		1	J. BUCHAN B.S.A.
E. WASHER B.S.A.	2		2	D. JOUBERT B.S.A.
W H HOCKING B.S.A.	3	R	3	P. FERBRACHE B.S.A.
D. JOUBERT B.S.A.	4		4	R THOMPSON B.S.A.
P. FERBRACHE B.S.A.	5		5	C MCLEAN B.S.A.
JAMES DAVIE B.S.A.	6=		6	W H HOCKING B.S.A.
K. JAMES B.S.A.	6=			

Marshals scurry to the aid of N C Fletcher, who clipped the kerb on the exit to Parkfield Corner.

1955 Clubman's Senior

1. W. E. Dow, BSA	9.37	9.11	9.07	9.08	9.05	**9.03**	9.04	9.04	9.04	1 22 23	70.73
2. I. M. Atkinson, Triumph	9.26	9.17	9.16	9.14	9.17	9.15	9.19	9.14	**9.13**	1 23 31	69.77
3. R. Kelly, Triumph	9.33	9.32	9.20	**9.16**	9.27	9.20	9.19	9.17	9.28	1 24 32	68.93
4. P. Ferbrache, BSA	11.21	**9.09**	**9.09**	**9.09**	9.10	9.17	9.15	9.16	9.16	1 25 02	68.52
5. D. Andrews, BSA	9.53	9.35	9.27	9.21	9.30	9.29	9.23	**9.19**	9.24	1 25 21	68.27
6. A. H. Mustard, BSA	9.48	9.36	9.31	9.22	9.30	9.29	9.22	9.27	**9.19**	1 25 24	68.23
7. F. Wallis, BSA	9.43	9.34	9.32	**9.25**	9.30	9.30	9.28	9.34	9.29.8	1 25 45.8	67.94
8. G. W. Shekell, Triumph	10.13	9.34	9.36	9.33	9.35	9.27	**9.22**	9.24	9.28	1 26 12	67.60
9. M. W. Gillingham, Triumph	10.18	9.42	**9.33**	9.34	9.41	9.41	9.39	9.36	9.34.8	1 27 18.8	66.73
10. D. J. Hunt, BSA	10.32	9.49	9.40	9.46	9.32	9.41	9.36	**9.29**	9.32.4	1 27 37.4	66.49
11. R. Preece, Norton	10.00	9.49	**9.42**	9.43	9.43	9.52	9.49	**9.42**	9.46	1 28 06	66.15
12. L. C. St. J. Hawkins, BSA	10.24	9.59	10.05	9.53	**9.51**	9.54	9.54	**9.51**	9.53	1 29.44	64.93
13. J. P. Griffith, Triumph	10.33	10.20	10.19	10.13	10.09	10.02	10.05	**9.56**	10.04	1 31 41	63.55
14. R. F. Keen, BSA	10.50	10.21	10.09	10.07	**10.02**	10.24	10.17	10.04	10.14.6	1 32 28.6	63.00
15. H. E. Vine, BSA	10.43	10.29	10.23	10.21	10.17	10.12	10.12	10.10	**10.09.6**	1 32 56.6	62.69
16. J. Drysdale, BSA	9.57	14.16	18.29	**8.56**	8.58	**8.56**	8.58	9.00	9.02	1 36 32	60.36
17. C. Dearden, Triumph	10.12	9.52	9.49	9.51	**9.46**	16.21	10.53	10.18	10.19	1 37 21	59.85
18. D. C. Middleton, Triumph	10.52	**10.43**	10.48	10.52	10.56	10.44	10.48	10.51	10.51	1 37 25	59.81
19. D. C. L. Dalziel, Triumph	11.15	11.11	11.03	10.50	10.53	10.42	10.46	10.44	**10.39**	1 38 03	59.43
20. D. Merridan, Triumph	10.35	10.06	9.51	9.55	10.03	18.28	**9.48**	9.57	9.49	1 38 32	59.13

Flagged off upon the completion of eight laps

P. E. Walsh, Norton	12.50	11.44	11.53	11.44	11.52	11.46	11.45	**11.33**
J. Hedley, Norton	**11.39**	**11.39**	11.44	11.51	**11.39**	11.41	11.48	12.02
A. Ashley, Triumph	11.10	**10.45**	R					

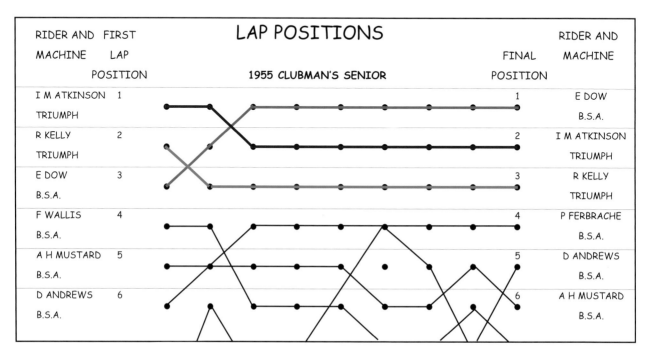

LAP POSITIONS
1955 CLUBMAN'S SENIOR

RIDER AND MACHINE	FIRST LAP POSITION		FINAL POSITION	RIDER AND MACHINE
I M ATKINSON TRIUMPH	1		1	E DOW B.S.A.
R KELLY TRIUMPH	2		2	I M ATKINSON TRIUMPH
E DOW B.S.A.	3		3	R KELLY TRIUMPH
F WALLIS B.S.A.	4		4	P FERBRACHE B.S.A.
A H MUSTARD B.S.A.	5		5	D ANDREWS B.S.A.
D ANDREWS B.S.A.	6		6	A H MUSTARD B.S.A.

1956

BACK ON THE MOUNTAIN

To the controllers of motorcycle sport in Britain, it was the 'ACU Clubman's Race', and the award for winning either class was the 'ACU Clubman's Cup'. To everyone else it was the 'Clubman's TT' and always would be.

Back on the Mountain Circuit (even though the Scorecard booklet in the 1956 Official Guide and Programme still had them on the Clypse Course), the Clubman's Trophy races were no longer any part of either TT practice or race week, but on the following

Thursday, just at the time that many spectators and trade representatives were leaving the Island, on the Saturday after the Senior International TT, Douglas began to fill with a different kind of enthusiast, those who wanted to see machines of the type which they owned, or dreamt of owning, competing over the same course and under the same conditions as the International TT. These spectators also were able to identify with the riders as being similar to themselves, possibly they knew and were friends

The solitary Velocette in a sea of BSA. John Righton waits in a crowded paddock alongside John Eckhart (Junior BSA). Standing behind the Viper is Arthur Taylor, Velocette dealer from Shipston on Stour, father-in-law of World Champion Cecil Sandford and partner in the Taylor-Dow Gold Star performance company with Eddie Dow.

with one or more of the riders, and might have been helping out in the pit. One thing is certain, many who came over specifically to watch the Clubman's races harboured thoughts (ranging from definite plans to unlikely dreams) of taking part themselves in following years.

Both races were to be held on the same day, but since they were reduced to three laps, riders could enter both if they so wished.

Some Clubman's competitors had arrived during the race-week, and taken the opportunity to observe the experts, then do some course learning on road bikes or in cars. Entry numbers were up on 1955 by some thirty-three, reflecting the unpopularity of the Clypse Course with competitors and entrants, partly because it lacked the challenge or prestige of the Mountain, but riding the shorter course did little for a rider in terms of preparation for the Manx Grand Prix or TT, which was surely in many riders' minds. The following comment on entries and spectator support is taken from *'The Motor Cycle'* of 21st June 1956. *"Though the increased size of the entry leaves no doubt as to the popularity among the riders of the return to the 37¾-mile Mountain Course, it remains a moot point whether it is wise to run races for relatively inexperienced riders on one of the world's most difficult courses. Last week, too, it was possible for the first time to assess the true spectator-appeal of the Clubman's races. In previous years they have* *basked in the reflected glory of the International events. This year, divorced from the TT races proper, they attracted only sparse crowds of spectators. Indeed, interest in the Clubman's events seemed to be confined almost solely to those who had direct connections with them".*

This seems a surprising and somewhat out-of-touch interpretation of the attendance figures, as it assumes that the average enthusiast did not have very limited holidays, nor did they have a job to go back to. Faced as they were then with TT practice week, TT race week <u>and</u> Clubman's week, there were very few who could afford and justify a whole week in the Island, let alone two or three. Not so surprising though, was the fact that those who wished to see the end of the Clubman's latched on to the poor attendance to further their argument.

Entries and Practice

Course improvements included a significant easing of what had hitherto been a sharp right-hand bend at Glen Vine, or Ballagarey as it now tends to be called (also called 'Ballascary' by some!). There was an entry of 68 for the Junior, and 42 for the Senior, with BSA Gold Stars dominant. In the Junior there were only 5 entries on other makes, 2 Velocettes, 2 Douglas and a solitary Norton. The Senior was slightly less of a BSA benefit with 11 'interlopers', 8 Triumphs and 3 Nortons. Names from the Junior entry included Bernard Codd, Dennis Pratt, Gerry Borland, Derrick Jervis, Alan Shepherd (whose entry via the Bradford Club is explained by the fact that Alan was then working as a motorcycle salesman at Allan Jefferies emporium in Shipley, Yorkshire), John Hurlstone,

Fred Wallis prepares to meet the setting sun as he leaves Quarter Bridge in a practice session. Fred later rode solo and sidecar TTs.

John Righton, Alan Brodrick, Fred Wallis, John Eckhart, Colin Moram, Ken James, Jimmy Morton and Dave Nourish. The Senior field contained second rides for Bernard Codd, Fred Wallis, Derrick Jervis and John Hurlstone, with Peter Cruse, David Hagen, Ron Jerrard, Maurice Candy, Mike Brookes and Ned Minihan. Riders who had failed to meet the ACU's racing experience qualification requirements, and who were therefore announced as non-starters, were B. Marshall, G. Lowe, R. McCrave, A. R. Singer and T. A. McCann in the Junior, and H. Synowiec, G. A. Turner and D. J. Ellis in the Senior.

Machine specifications had changed little from previous years, but 1956 was the first year that the machines would be tackling the Mountain Course complete with headlamps and dynamos. Stands could be removed. Notwithstanding the fact that the 'specs' had changed little, the appearance of some of the Gold Stars by this time, was distinctly 'purposeful'. The silencer body had taken the shape of a long, shallow taper, megaphone-style, with a domed end and smaller diameter tailpipe (the classic 'Goldie' silencer), a shape it was claimed that was developed to 'avoid contact with the kick-starter crank'. Most models had the new full-width 190 mm front brake, some had deep 'Lyta' light alloy fuel tanks with large cutaways for the rider's knees, and hump-back racing seats. The Senior Gold Stars sported the biggest racing carburettor available on the home market, a 1½ inch Amal GP. All were strictly above-board and legal, catalogued as options available to any purchaser.

That Saturday, the 9th of June, the weather in the Island was at its wonderful best, warm and sunny, with the cooling breeze dropping toward evening, and by the 6.30 pm start of the first practice, the conditions for spectators could not have been better. The Glencrutchery Road grandstand held a sizeable crowd for that first session, and good numbers were reported around the course. First rider away was John Eckhart on his Junior BSA, who set the tone with a copybook bump start and fast getaway for the first of four fast laps, including fastest Junior lap of the evening of 28m 51.6s (78.35 mph). He was followed closely by K. Nicholls also on a BSA, and the rest of the 'field', some riders using the kick-start they would have to employ on race day, some a

bump start, but the majority followed Eckhart's example. Fastest Senior was Ron Jerrard with a lap in 27m 41.8s (81.79 mph), amid rumours of a particularly fast lap by Bernard Codd. As the first two laps by Newcomers were not published, his 'official' time of 28m 50s put him 3rd fastest Senior of the session. Casualties from the evening were Drew Herdman, who suffered collar bone and wrist injuries when he came off his BSA in Glen Helen and was thrown over the wall, A. E. Culshaw (BSA) with a broken jaw after a fall at Brandish, and A. Smith (Velocette) with back injuries, a broken finger and abrasions in a spill at Cruikshanks, Ramsey. L. Chapman was the only Senior faller, after he clipped the kerb on the exit from Quarter Bridge. He escaped with facial abrasions, but his BSA was less fortunate, and needed front end repairs.

Monday dawned dry and sunny, perfect for the 89 riders who turned out for the first morning session. American David Hagen was first to get away on his Senior BSA, followed a little later by similarly-mounted Bernard Codd, whose riding had already put him right up amongst the favourites to win later in the week. His pace around the course was described as 'seemingly effortless', and his second lap of 26m 40.2s (84.42 mph) set fastest of the morning, with E. Unwin (BSA) fastest in the Junior class, somewhat slower at 29m 16s (77.37 mph). It was rumoured at the time that Bernard's Saturday

T. Brown waits to start a practice lap on his 90 Plus Douglas. Unspecified problems made him a non-starter.

night high-speed demonstration had earned him a reprimand from his mentor Austin Munks, maybe for 'showing his hand' too early. Saturday faller L. Chapman was happily out again, riding with a little more respect for the course than shown in the first session. Three further falls were reported during the morning, two in the Senior class at the Waterworks, with K. Latham (Norton) and H. Russell (Triumph) receiving minor cuts and abrasions, and T. Mash came off his Junior BSA at Keppel Gate without injury. The *'TT Special'* offered the opinion that the fine weather and the prospect of a particularly enjoyable morning's ride had tempted some riders to attempt an extra unplanned lap, which had resulted in a small 'rash' of retirements on the Mountain in the closing stages, out of fuel.

The evening session that same day was again blessed with perfect weather conditions, in contrast to the thunderstorms hitting the south-east of England, as *'The Motor Cycle'* correspondent took some pleasure in reporting! As a rehearsal for the race start, riders were formed up and flagged off in groups of four, and were to use the kick-start. Out this time on his Junior BSA, Codd set the fastest lap in the class at 27m 56.4s (81.06 mph). Derrick Jervis was fastest Senior with a lap of 27m 20.0s (82.85 mph). Sadly, the evening was marred by an accident late in the session at Ballaugh Bridge, when David Merridan, a dairyman from High Wycombe in Buckinghamshire, failed to slow his Senior BSA sufficiently for the bridge on his 3rd lap. His machine leapt high in the air and, unable to control the landing, he hit a wall and was killed outright. Less serious casualties of the evening were C. Huxley who damaged a finger in a fall at Brandish, and R. A. Holland who fell at Sarah's Cottage, both riding Junior BSA's.

The fine weather came to an end that evening, and conditions that faced the 67 riders the next morning were very different. Although the roads were generally dry, it was cool and breezy, with cloud on Snaefell restricting visibility in some places to 20 yards. Speeds were remarkably good in the circumstances, Codd again the fastest Junior at 29m 17.2s (77.33 mph), and this time fastest Senior was Ron Jerrard (BSA) with 27m 56.6s (81.04 mph). Second fastest in the Junior was Alan Shepherd, on

the solitary Norton.

Wednesday began cool and bright in Douglas, but Snaefell was shrouded in mist as competitors set off for the final practice session. Peter Cruse (BSA) clocked fastest Senior time with 27m 51s (81.30 mph), and in doing so lifted himself to 4th fastest Senior over all sessions. J. E. Coates (BSA) was a new name on the practice leaderboard, second fastest to Bernard Codd, who almost as expected, was fastest Junior of the morning at 28m 46s (78.70 mph). Speeds improved as the mist gradually cleared from the Mountain, but for many riders the most important thing was to avoid mechanical problems, as there would have been very little time to put things right before the weigh-in at 10.00 am the same morning. Almost inevitably, there were unfortunates who did hit trouble, including K. Nicholls, N. J. Davenport, G. Coombes and C. Huxley, all on Junior BSA's except G. Coombes who was on a 500). Misfortunes of a more self-inflicted nature befell A. Jackson who struck the wall at Sulby Bridge, without injury, but needing replacement forks for his Junior BSA.

The Junior Race (Thursday, 14th June)

Starters

	Rider	Club	Machine
1	P G Kirkham	Oswestry & DMC	B.S.A.
2	W D Fellows	Stockton & DMC	B.S.A.
5	B R Cortvriend	Ringwood MC & LCC	B.S.A.
6	P B James	Birmingham MCC	B.S.A.
7	N J Davenport	Warrington & DMC	B.S.A.
8	B D Codd	Louth & DMCC	B.S.A.
9	N Lay	Southampton & DMCC	B.S.A.
10	D Pratt	West Leeds MC	B.S.A.
11	D D Shand	Hawick & Border C & MCC	B.S.A.
12	G A Borland	Stevenston & DMCC	B.S.A.
14	C Huxley	Hebdon Royd & DMCC	B.S.A.
15	D Jervis	Chesterfield & DMCC	B.S.A.
16	H Riley	Bolton MCC	B.S.A.
17	K Nicholls	Preston & DMCC	B.S.A.
18	J D Hamilton	Southampton & DMCC	B.S.A.
19	R G Sutcliffe	Bankstown-Wiley Park MCC	B.S.A.
20	N H Vivian	South Reading MCC	B.S.A.
21	J E Coates	Barnoldswick & DMC	B.S.A.
22	K A Lindsay	Rye & DMCC	B.S.A.

23	E Unwin	Worksop & DMC	B.S.A.
24	C McLean	Glasgow Speedway MCC	B.S.A.
25	A Shepherd	Bradford & DMC	Norton
26	A W G Walczak		
		Stratford-on-Avon MC & CC	B.S.A.
27	R J Brinnand	Salop MC	B.S.A.
28	G E Briggs	North Lancs MC	B.S.A.
30	H D Briggs	Meden Valley MCC	B.S.A.
31	G Bell	Whitehaven MC	B.S.A.
32	W A Cooper	Bankstown-Wiley Park MCC	B.S.A.
33	N Robertson	Lion MCC	B.S.A.
34	J F Righton	Stratford-on-Avon MC & LCC	
			Velocette
35	S L F Orson	Rochester Chatham & DMC	B.S.A.
36	R A Holland	Shirley MCC	B.S.A.
39	G Arnold	Warrington & DMC	B.S.A.
40	S Baskett	Wirral '100' MC	B.S.A.
41	P R Hodgson	Reigate, Redhill, North Downs MC	
			B.S.A.
42	A W Brodrick	X.H.G. Tiger MCC	B.S.A.
43	P E Walsh	Solihull MCC	B.S.A.
44	G A Dormer	Reading Ace MCC	B.S.A.
45	L Bull	Surrey Hills MC	B.S.A.
48	R Thompson	Ledbury Cobras MC & LCC	B.S.A.
50	M R Oram	Maidenhead MC & LCC	B.S.A.
51	F Wallis	Nottingham Tornado MC	B.S.A.
52	J Eckhart	Leicester Query MC	B.S.A.
53	C G Moram	Farnham Royal MC & LCC	B.S.A.
54	L S Rutherford		
		Bermondsey MCC	B.S.A.
55	D F Thomson	Dalmarnock MCC	B.S.A.
58	E P Davies	Southampton & DMCC	B.S.A.
59	K W James	Isle of Wight MC	B.S.A.
60	T Folwell	Ruislip & DMCC	B.S.A.
62	N F Sweetman		
		Wirral '100' MC	B.S.A.
63	N C Fletcher	Bury & DMC	B.S.A.
64	J Hill	Craven & DMC	B.S.A.
66	J D Morton	Kilmarnock Tigers MCC	B.S.A.
67	D H Nourish	Nottingham Tornado MC	B.S.A.
69	A Jackson	Sutton Coldfield & NBAC	B.S.A.

Almost ideal weather conditions greeted riders, warm, dry and sunny, but with a stiff north-westerly breeze. Of the 68 entries, some 55 had made it through to race-day. Non-starters announced were J. Hutchinson, J. R. Hurlstone (who only fielded his Senior machine), A. Smith, M. D. Smith, A. Herdman and A. E. Culshaw (who were injured in practice), and for reasons not known, T. Brown and T. Mash elected not to ride, although it might be assumed that the latter's decision was not unconnected with his fall earlier in practice. The additional effect of these withdrawals was a reduction in the (already low) machine opposition to the Gold Star, both Douglas's and a Velocette out before the race started, leaving solitary examples of 'Inter' Norton (Alan Shepherd) and Velocette Viper (John Righton) to battle the BSA's. However, the two interlopers had fared well in practice, and were expected to be leaderboard contenders during the race. With dry roads, and two years machine development since the last Clubman's on the Mountain Circuit, records were expected to be threatened in both classes. For some unaccountable reason, the race Regulations had stipulated that refuelling must be by means of two-gallon cans with suitable pourers. Sanity prevailed, but only after demands from the petrol companies that on safety grounds the quick-fill canisters already provided, should be used! In actual fact, for a three-lap race, few required refuelling.

Promptly at 11.00 am, the first group, which in fact consisted of two riders, P. G. Kirkham and W. D. Fellows, was flagged away by the starter Mr. Lumby. The former got away cleanly, but Fellows lost time trying to start his BSA, eventually getting away at more or less the same time as the second group, 30 seconds later, from which race favourite Codd made a textbook start. Slow starts also affected G. E. Briggs and H. D. Briggs (not believed to be related), who both had to move away from their starting 'blocks' to make way for the next group. D. Nourish, R. J. Brinnand and S. C. F. Orton all lost time at the start, as did veteran and likely leaderboard man Fred Wallis only much more so, losing three minutes. In effect, his competitive race was over before it even started, although it was fortunate indeed for the eventual winners of the East Midland Centre Team that Wallis did get away, as their other riders were destined to finish 1st and 2nd in the race.

Before Kirkmichael, Codd led on the roads, and came through the Grandstand area to complete the standing start lap in a record 27m 30.4s (82.33 mph), before anyone else was even signalled at Signpost. Shepherd's Norton, which was reported around the course as being noticeably quieter, and slower, than the front-running BSAs, appeared to be in 2nd place, until the later-starting John Eckhart came through 24 seconds faster. Shepherd had quickly made up the 30 second starting advantage held by E. Unwin, but he was unable to get away, and the pair then enjoyed an on-the-road dice which lasted until the end of the race, passing and re-passing many times during the three laps.

First lap retirements were J. Hill, who came off at Glentramman, 'rider ok' as the expression was (and still is), and K. Nicholls whose clutch gave out at Governors Bridge. A far sadder retirement was that of Peter George Kirkham, a 24-year old motor mechanic from Llanymynech, Montgomeryshire (now Powys), who crashed at the fast left-hander following the Waterworks, and was killed instantly. The Oswestry club member had finished 18th in the previous years Junior Clubman's. John Righton, pulled in at the Gooseneck to report the unfortunate incident, sacrificing a leaderboard place in the process.

First Lap Leaderboard

1. B. D. Codd (BSA)	27m 30.4s	(82.33 mph)
2. J. Eckhart (BSA)	28m 04.4s	(80.65 mph)
3. A. Shepherd (Norton)	28m 39.8s	(79.05 mph)
4. D. Jervis (BSA)	28m 56.8s	(78.22 mph)
5. E. Unwin (BSA)	29m 13.2s	(77.49 mph)
6. J. D. Morton (BSA)	29m 15.0s	(77.42 mph)

Looking every inch a winner, Codd continued his fast, controlled pace on the second lap, just 3 seconds slower than the opener, leaving the rest of the field to fight for the places, although there was no change in the leaderboard places during the lap. Jervis was running 2nd on the road, 4th on corrected time, while Righton, only 1 second off the leaderboard despite his first lap stop, was forced to stop at the pits to remove engine oil from the back end of his Velocette. N. J. Davenport retired in the vicinity of Union Mills with 'engine noises', and A. Jackson was unhurt in a spill at the Waterworks.

Second Lap Leaderboard

1 B. D. Codd (BSA)	55m 3.8s	(82.23 mph)
2 J. Eckhart (BSA)	55m 51.0s	(81.08 mph)
3 A. Shepherd (Norton)	57m 5.4s	(79.22 mph)

The scrap of the Junior race. E. Unwin (BSA) leads Alan Shepherd (Norton) on the road, but was behind on time.

4 D. Jervis (BSA)	57m 34.8s	(78.64 mph)
5 E. Unwin (BSA)	57m 41.8s	(78.48 mph)
6 J. D. Morton (BSA)	57m 54.4s	(78.20 mph)

Eckhart began the third and final lap in as seemingly secure a 2nd place as Codd was secure in the lead. The battle behind them was closely fought, and although places remained unchanged to the flag, only some 50 seconds covered the next four places. Alan Shepherd's three-year-old Norton broke the BSA monopoly by holding on to a fine 3rd place, despite losing his goggles at the Gooseneck on the last lap, giving the first hint as to the great future that lay ahead for the Grange-over-Sands rider. As reward for his efforts in hanging on to Shepherd on the road, Unwin pipped Jervis for 4th place by the margin of just 0.8 seconds. Surprisingly, none of the first three finishers had any previous Isle of Man racing experience. Overall, 50 of the 55 starters completed the race.

Finishing Order

| 1 B. D. Codd (BSA) | 1h 22m 40.4s (82.02 mph) |
| 2 J. Eckhart (BSA) | 1h 23m 30.0s (81.34 mph) |

3 A. Shepherd (Norton)	1h 25m 43.2s (79.24 mph)
4 E. Unwin (BSA)	1h 26m 8.0s (78.86 mph)
5 D. Jervis (BSA)	1h 26m 8.8s (78.84 mph)
6 J. D. Morton (BSA)	1h 26m 21.2s (78.66 mph)

Fastest Lap: B.D. Codd (1st lap) 27m 30.4s (82.33 mph).

The Centre Team Award went to East Midland Centre, ACU (B. D. Codd, J. Eckhart, F. Wallis).

The Senior Race (Thursday, 14th June)

Starters

	Rider	Club	Machine
1	D Andrews	Horsforth & DMC	B.S.A.
2	B Payton	Worcester AC	B.S.A.
4	P G Hyde	Horsham & DMC & LCC	Triumph
6	V Naintre	Westminster Racing MCC	B.S.A.
7	P K Cruse	Slough & DMC & LCC	B.S.A.
8	B D Codd	Louth & DMCC	B.S.A.
9	F Wallis	Nottingham Tornado MCC	B.S.A.
10	A H Jenkins	Bristol MCC	B.S.A.
11	R F Keen	Sutton Coldfield & NBAC	B.S.A.
12	G Coombes	Bankstown-Wiley Park MCC	B.S.A.

Not being nicked! Bernard Codd is escorted into the winners enclosure after the Junior race.

14	C Dearden	Rochdale & DMC	Triumph
15	G Arnold	Warrington & DMC	B.S.A.
16	A H Mustard	Dunlop Car & MCC	B.S.A.
17	D Jervis	Chesterfield & DMCC	B.S.A.
18	D J Smart	Leicester Query MC	B.S.A.
19	B W Newman	Southampton Vikings MC & LCC	
			B.S.A.
21	W J Hill	Newbury & DMC	B.S.A.
22	A Ashley	Armthorpe Ace MC	Triumph
25	D Hagen	Mont' Christie MCC	B.S.A.
26	R Smith	Blyth & DMC	Triumph
28	J R Hurlstone	B.M.C.R.C.	Triumph
29	R E Jerrard	Southampton & DMCC	B.S.A.
30	R Preece	Stafford AC	B.S.A.
31	M J Candy	Maidstone Aces MCC	B.S.A.
34	B F Herbert	Bulldog MC & MCC	Norton
36	M W Munday	Portsmouth MCRC	B.S.A.
37	M W Gillingham		
		Sturminster Newton & DMCC & LCC	
			Triumph
38	P A Alexander	Bayswater MCC	B.S.A.
39	M T Brookes	Shirley MCC	Triumph
40	L C St J Hawkins		
		Mendip Vale MC & LCC	B.S.A.
41	E Minihan	Winsford & DMC	B.S.A.
42	D Howe	North Bucks MC	B.S.A.

The weather never even looked like it might break during race-day, and the beautiful conditions continued into the afternoon for the 2.00 pm start. 32 of the 42 entries were listed as starters, joining the three non-starters already mentioned were G. Lowe, L. Chapman, A. R. F. Morris, K. Latham, M. Redford and H. Russell, plus of course, the unfortunate David Merridan.

First away without trouble was P. C. Hyde on his Triumph, with the BSA's of D. Andrews and B. Payton taking a little longer, and in fact passed by Peter Cruse and Bernard Codd of the second group before they reached St. Ninians crossroads, although the engine of Cruse's bike was hesitant and misfiring as he pulled away. Quite a number of the other machines showed a reluctance to fire up, Ned Minihan losing half a minute and Bob Keen losing over four minutes before they all eventually got away. By Ballacraine, Codd was leading on the roads and riding superbly, fully justifying those who had

been predicting a 'Double' for the protege of Austin Munks. Twenty-six minutes and fifteen-point-two seconds after he was flagged away, Codd crossed the line to start his second lap, Ron Jerrard 27 seconds down in 2nd place, Derrick Jervis a further 35 seconds adrift in 3rd. Peter Cruse (BSA), who had been a leaderboard man in practice, was forced to retire at the pits with a split oil tank, and another first lap retiree was V. Naintre (BSA), at the Quarry Bends with engine trouble. Delayed starter Bob Keen got only as far as Quarter Bridge before stopping again for a few minutes, but then he restarted, and in fact made it to the finish on his still misfiring Goldie. Fred Wallis and Tony Jenkins started together in the third group, and completed the lap still together, Wallis marginally in front. G. Arnold came off his BSA at Governors Bridge, but was able to re-start, remount and continue.

First Lap Leaderboard

1	B. D. Codd (BSA)	26m 15.2s	(86.26 mph)
2	R. E. Jerrard (BSA)	26m 42.2s	(84.81 mph)
3	D. Jervis (BSA)	27m 16.4s	(83.03 mph)
4	F. Wallis (BSA)	27m 28.6s	(82.42 mph)
5	A. H. Jenkins (BSA)	27m 29.0s	(82.40 mph)
6	M. T. Brookes (Triumph)	27m 53.2s	(81.20 mph)

In the earlier Junior race, Codd had been able to ease the pace slightly on his second lap, but the challenge of experienced Mountain Course competitor Jerrard was real, and Codd increased the pace, not knowing then that the second-placed BSA was suffering 'self-change' gearbox problems for a large part of the race. Positions behind the first two leaders moved up one during the second lap, as a consequence of the unfortunate retirement of Derrick Jervis, who stopped at Sulby with engine trouble. Codd's lap of 26m 10.4s was close to the existing record, and his lead extended over Jerrard to some 47 seconds. The Triumph challenge looked unlikely to amount to a serious threat to the BSA's, with only Mike Brookes on the leaderboard, next came John Hurlstone in 10th. As *'Motor Cycling's'* race reporter observed, *"several BSA's again have the slight misfire which has bothered them all week, but they are all still very fast"*. The hotly-disputed battle for 3rd between Wallis and Jenkins continued, for which the crowd were showing their appreciation all round the 37 ¾ miles lap, and they entered their final lap still with just yards in it.

Second Lap Leaderboard

1 B. D. Codd (BSA)	52m 25.6s	(86.37 mph)
2 R. E. Jerrard (BSA)	53m 13.0s	(85.09 mph)
3 F. Wallis (BSA)	54m 22.2s	(83.29 mph)
4 A. H. Jenkins (BSA)	54m 22.4s	(83.28 mph)
5 M. T. Brookes (Triumph)	55m 22.4s	(81.78 mph)
6 D. J. Smart (BSA)	55m 44.0s	(81.25 mph)

The leader maintained his consistent lapping over the final lap, finishing over a minute ahead of Jerrard, who was in turn 1½ minutes ahead of the Wallis - Jenkins scrap, which went all the way to the flag, Jenkins taking 3rd by the margin of just under 2 seconds, probably the biggest it had been throughout the race. The solitary leaderboard opposition to the BSA's, Brookes' Triumph, was reported stopped at the Bungalow with clutch trouble. Then, amid cheers not only on the Mountain road, but from spectators around the course listening to the commentary over the loudspeaker system, he got the Triumph moving again. Utterly determined to finish, he managed to push and coast the last few miles to claim a gallant 26th place. His misfortune brought G. Coombes into 6th, and Hurlstone was the first non-BSA finisher, coming home 7th. B. Payton (BSA) was a last lap retirement, stopping at the Gooseneck with engine trouble, only the fourth retirement from the 32 starters.

Finishing Order

1 B. D. Codd (BSA)	1h 18m 40.6s (86.33 mph)
2 R. E. Jerrard (BSA)	1h 18m 46.8s (85.13 mph)
3 A. H. Jenkins (BSA)	1h 21m 22.4 (83.47 mph)
4 F. Wallis (BSA)	1h 21m 24.2s (83.44 mph)
5 D. J. Smart (BSA)	1h 23m 15.0s (81.59 mph)
6 G. Coombes (BSA)	1h 24m 4.8s (80.78 mph)

Fastest Lap: B. D. Codd (2nd lap) 26m 10.4s (86.52 mph).

The Centre Team Award went to Southern Centre ACU (W .J. Hull, R. E. Jerrard, B.W. Newman).

Mike Brookes' Triumph was the sole contender amongst a tide of BSA Gold Stars, until lack of fuel meant a very long push to the finish (and a standing ovation for his effort)

Reflections

Bernard Codd's performance was nothing short of remarkable, for in addition to being a newcomer to the Isle of Man, he had started racing only the previous August. It was the manner of his winning rides which marked him out as something special, talent that Sam Coupland and Austin Munks had spotted from the beginning. His laps were consistently fast, and if his fastest was marginally down on Alastair King in 1954, it has to be remembered that Regulations for the earlier races had allowed for the removal of silencers and electrical equipment, whereas for 1956 road-legal silencers and full electrical equipment were required (well, almost, rear lamps and horns could be removed). He was already an accomplished trials rider, riding James and Norton machines under the Austin Munks banner. Austin ordered two new Gold Stars from the factory early in 1956, and Bernard took five weeks off the family farm, to prepare for the races. Many, many laps of the Mountain Course were covered, by car with Austin, Bill Lomas and Geoff Duke, or on a Matchless road bike. After the

Bernard Codd heads for the finish of his second winning ride of the day, a feat he shares with Mike Hailwood, Charlie Williams and Graeme McGregor.

Clubman's, Bernard rode Manx Nortons for Austin, with successes against recognised stars of the day. Later the same year he finished third in the Junior Manx Grand Prix, but retired in the Senior. His last Island appearance was in the 1957 Golden Jubilee Senior TT, finishing 11th. A month later, his racing career came to an end when he was hit by a following rider at the Crystal Palace track in London. At the time of the accident, negotiations were taking place for him to sign to ride a factory Gilera. What might have been, never had the chance to start.

Looking back over the 1956 Clubman's TT, it had to be said that the racing for the positions (with some exceptions) wasn't breathtakingly close, but as *'Motor Cycling'* put it, *"Determination to finish always gets applause - and what a big hand they gave Brookes as he comes in, alternately running and walking with the Triumph which he had pushed a very long way. That, perhaps, represents the spirit of the 'Clubman's' as the event was originally conceived: the spirit of contest between enthusiasts to win, or to justify belief in their own skill or endurance and their faith in standard machines of varying character. This year came the culmination of a persistent drift toward a quite different state of affairs in which that all-essential rivalry is lacking and which, as we in Douglas have witnessed today, public interest has correspondingly flagged. But there is nothing wrong with the fundamental spirit of the race and if, in these less fruitful seasons, events like today's Senior can produce men of the calibre of Bernard Codd, then probably there is nothing very much amiss with the Clubman's Races or with the security of their future".*

In those days, overt criticism by the motorcycling press of a manufacturer's policies or products simply did not happen, but it doesn't take much reading between the lines of the comments in *'Motor Cycling'* to imagine it to be a plea for other manufacturer's to rise to the BSA challenge and offer competitive machines capable of providing a race for the all-conquering Gold Stars. The inference was also clear, that if no such competition were to be forthcoming, public interest in the event would continue to wane, and there would be little future for the races.

Why the Clubman's?
by John Hurlstone

It was the only affordable entry to racing in the Isle of Man. My racing debut was delayed like so many by National Service, coming home with savings of £15 was not a lot of help, but I was able to purchase a vintage bike. A poster of Harold Daniell 'That lap at 91' was on the shed wall, and I read and re-read everything that had been written about the TT course. A friend loaned me money toward the deposit on something more modern to help me keep up with them. A 1950 Thunderbird was bought, a brilliant machine, and with silencers removed and clip-ons fitted, otherwise standard, two races were entered at the end of 1953. But I wanted to go the Island so for 1954 a new T100 was ordered from Rex Judd's, the Thunderbird in as a first deposit with Judd's salesman Stan Pike, then save the rest of the deposit through the winter. A few problems still, you had to have a club enter you, and I was only in the Vintage Club, who at that time were not into post-1930 bikes, but 'Titch' Allen talked them round. The next problem was that you needed to do two qualifying races, and I had no bike. There were many calls to Triumph's, and I asked Percy Tait at a Crystal Palace race meeting to chase it up, and finally they sent it by train to Euston. Gerry Turner and I went to collect it at night. Lovely – twin carbs, close gears, rev-counter, straight-through pipes – and a tiny drop of petrol left in it, so we just had to start it under the Euston Arch!

We did the qualifying races at Brands Hatch with Isle of Man gearing, Gerry won one on his Gold Star,

then both off to the Island by train, pushing the bikes from Liverpool Lime Street station to the docks for the ferry. We arrived at the hotel in Ballanard Road (you take the right turn at St. Ninian's crossroads at the top of Bray Hill), to find the Surtees family installed. In the Island we met the Triumph men Frank Baker (who had worked with Noel Pope at Brooklands), and Stan Truslove – great people. Practice went well, no road bike to learn the circuit on, just a few laps on the racer. I only knew the famous corners, and was rubbish everywhere else, but I got a mention in the 'TT Special' that I had 'cornered in real International style'. Jack Surtees said "That means nothing". I said "Well it does to me, Jack. It's nice to read when one's a novice, better than reading that you are rubbish".

Near the end of practice a few of us told Frank that our bikes were not as fast. Wise Frank said "You've got used to the speed. What revs are you getting on Sulby? The same? There you are then, 120 mph. Not bad." Handling was good in '54 with no lights etc.

1955 was the year of the Clypse course – no thanks. That won't help with learning the Mountain Course, so into the 'Manx'. Had a rod through the cases in the middle of Bray in practice, Frank said put the engine on a plane to Coventry, and he brought it back in the boot of his car. My mechanic left a lump of gasket in the jet well so it ran on one cylinder for most of the race (are you out there Vincent?).

In 1956 I again met Frank while at Silverstone with my scruffy Triumph, he said "You had better let us have that". For the 1956 Clubman's we needed silencers, dynamo and lights, and it came back like new, the head was a different colour, made of a different alloy. Rode the bike to the Island, it was still doing 120 on the Sulby straight with silencers and very small bore pipes, but the handling was terrible. The late Mike Brookes went faster but took risks I wouldn't. When I rode a slow Manx Norton in the Manx it only did 112 mph, but I lapped a lot faster. When I told Frank that I should have raced a Gold Star, the conversation was short and to the point. He said "How much did your racing cost?" "Nothing" I replied. "Well shut up then!"

I then went on to buy two new Nortons for the Manx in 1957 from the great Harold Daniell, a lovely man despite what you read in today's books, ask John Holder. Esso's Geoff Murdoch had his runners go round the course with Jack Brett, who said that the race was won on the slow corners, then went out in his race and fell off at Sulby Bridge. But he was right, nobody cornered like they did at short circuits.

Being at the Clubman's enabled a 'peasant' to watch Werner Haas, Ray Amm etc. and meet McIntyre, King and many fine fellows, all on hp [hire puchase]!

Great days, and great memories.

Classic style from John Hurlstone at Union Mills

My Clubman's Rides
by Alan Brodrick

The Clubman's was often a more interesting race than the TT proper, which had become a procession of Manx Nortons, 7R AJS's and a few Velocettes. You could see the ordinary 'over-the-counter' motorcycles, mostly popular British machines, being ridden extremely quickly. Nearly every bike you could buy found some enthusiast to ride it in the 'Clubman's', and there were some very unlikely entrants.

It had been prophesied that the TT Course 'would run red with the blood of all these novice riders', but this did not happen, even though the lap speeds were not a lot less than they were in the true TT races.

I had ridden my race-kitted Tiger 100 in the Manx Grand Prix the previous year, and retired with a split oil tank. For 1954 I bought a 350 'International' from Bob Foster, which had been ridden by Ken James into third place behind Eric Houseley and Bob McIntyre in the 1952 Junior Clubman's. It was unburstable and handled well, although it had the old 'Garden-Gate' frame and not the 'Featherbed'. Unfortunately the new BSA 'Clubman's' Gold Stars appeared that year, they were a thinly-disguised racing machine with a close-ratio gearbox and were about ten mph faster than anything else. Even Geoff Tanner, who later won the Senior and Junior Manx Grand Prix, and was seventh in the 1954 Junior TT, could only finish fourth, behind three less skilful chaps on Gold Stars. I finished about half way down the list.

I had a new 350 Gold Star for 1955; I was by then working for Bob Foster in Poole, and Bob let my colleague Barry Cortvriend and myself have our new BSA's at cost price, gave us the TT fortnight off (this, at the busiest time of the year), lent us their big van to carry the bikes, paid our boat fares and hotel expenses, and sent his best mechanic, Larry Mitchell, to look after us. All this was done for two undistinguished chaps who were going to be lucky to finish the race without falling off. He was also supporting two 'proper' riders then, Derek Powell and Percy Tait, on a couple of Nortons each. Derek had won the Junior Clubman's on a BSA in 1953 and was second in the 1954 Senior Manx. Percy was a first-class racer too...

My Gold Star never gave the slightest trouble, but Barry's machine seized up within minutes of being started for the first time. The outrigger plate that supported the timing gear was distorted. It was replaced under guarantee of course, but he had many annoying troubles with this machine.

The Clubman's TT was run over the Clypse course that year, like the Sidecar and the Lightweight TT's. Many riders were disappointed with this, as 'The Island' meant only the traditional 37¾ mile Mountain Circuit, and only just enough entries were received to justify running the 'Clubman's' at all. We felt that any race in 'The Island' should be supported and entered. I liked the 'Clypse'. Although it was only a little under eleven miles long, it ran over unspoilt narrow roads, bordered with stone walls, very like what the TT Course had once been.

On the first evening of the practice period, Barry and I were two of the few who did ten laps, and I was on the practice leaderboard. On the next Practice I hit the wall at a corner called 'Morney 3', wrecked the BSA and dislocated my left shoulder. Bob Foster was riding as a Travelling Marshal that year and was sent out, on his BSA Shooting Star, to investigate. He laughed heartily when he saw me. "Silly bugger! Coming all this way and then falling off. Get on the back!", and we went off to Nobles Hospital where they reset my shoulder. The BSA team on the Island quickly rebuilt the Gold Star with a new frame, forks and many other parts, but I had to watch the races instead of riding, and I set off for Poole at the end of TT week.

The hospital had bandaged me like a mummy, but I took these wrappings off and used only a sling, I could not have ridden otherwise. I should have put the bike on the train at Liverpool, but foolishly elected to ride the 250 miles to Poole. I found it too painful to keep my hand on the left-hand handlebar, so put that arm in a sling after getting under way and through the gears, then rode one-handed; not easy with the Gold Star's cramped riding position, but at least I was able to change gear without using the clutch, thanks to the close-ratio box. There were no motorways then, but I got through the towns and the traffic well enough. Not my most enjoyable ride.

Bob Foster made a 'ladder' with rungs about an inch apart and put it on the wall in the shop. Dickie Dale had broken his arm in a car crash on his way to the TT, lived nearby, and called frequently at the shop. Foster told us "Get those slings off, and walk your fingers up my ladder!" Good therapy.

There had been a 1,000cc Clubman's event, discontinued because it became a procession of big Vincents although someone once entered an Ariel Square Four. Those heroes who rode Shadows and Rapides in this race were very brave men, they seemed to be working hard all the time.

I had a new Gold Star for 1956. There was nothing wrong with the earlier model but the 1956 machines had a full-width front brake, we all wanted the very latest thing, but the new brake was not as good as the earlier one, and gave a lot of trouble before it could be made to work properly. I rode it in the

Clubman's that year, which was the last of the series, and by then it had become a procession of Gold Stars in both 350 and 500cc classes.

This was my last race too (finishing safely, not very far up) as in 1957 I married my long-suffering fiancé, who had stood, uncomplaining, spectating at race meetings and listening to boring motorcycle talk (Golden Wedding this year!).

Gold Stars were always in short supply, but Bob Foster had pulled a few strings and was able to advertise 'immediate delivery'. A young man in Warrington wrote to say that he could not get delivery in under three months anywhere. He wanted a new 500 and had a one-year-old Velocette Viper to exchange. I was a Bolton lad, my parents still lived there, and I was going home for Christmas in a fortnight, so I suggested that I made the trip on Christmas Eve on a new Gold Star, dropping it off in Warrington as I passed through on my way back on Boxing Day. He readily agreed, as he would be spared a 300-mile journey to Poole. We were unusually busy on Christmas Eve and I did not get away until 3 pm. By Ringwood, a few miles out, I noticed that the dynamo had stopped charging and that the lights were failing. Ignition was no trouble as Gold Stars had a very good magneto, but you do need lights on a dark night. I carried on with only the pilot light, but soon even this 'glow-worm' went out, so I pressed on regardless, without lights, through Salisbury and Amesbury and over Birdlip to Cheltenham, no Motorways then. Fortunately traffic was light and near Marlborough a Morgan 4/4 overtook me and I tucked in behind and followed him for an hour or so. He turned off eventually, but I was now in a better lit area and could see and be seen, fortunately not by the police. I went through Warrington and Leigh to Bolton, arriving about 9 pm, to find two friends waiting patiently. "What kept you?" they asked. I started to tell them of this epic ride but they cut me short. "You want locking up for that. Get changed, we are going out aren't we?" I was more ready for bed than for booze, but enjoyed a Christmas pint or two, getting home at 2 am.

I cleaned the Gold Star the next day and set off early on Boxing Day to meet the customer. His Velocette was in perfect order and worth a lot more than we had quoted, but he was not happy about accepting a new machine with a duff dynamo and a flat battery. I was polite but firm. "I rode this thing 300 miles without lights the other night so that you would not be disappointed. All you need to do tomorrow is to go to your Lucas Depot, show them the BSA Guarantee, and they will change the dynamo whilst you wait". They did too! We shook hands, I had a mug of tea with plenty of rum in it, and set off on the Velocette. The roads were empty and the towns deserted because of the Boxing Day holiday, and I had a marvellous ride to Poole, the Velo feeling as if steering itself. The weather was mild and dry and as I passed our shop I looked at the big BSA clock outside. Half past five, not bad going I thought, still rather light for five thirty. I looked again to see that it was only half past four, and that I'd made the best time I ever was to do on that run. I once got within half an hour of it on a Trophy Triumph., and the slowest time ever was on a Vincent Rapide.

A Clubman's Gold Star is now an antique, too valuable to ride. A pity, as once clear of traffic, with the close-ratio box, they were a delight on the open road.

Alan Brodrick at White Gates, Ramsey. Alan is a regular contributor to motorcycle magazines with tales of his motorcycling past, both as a competitor and also tales from working in 'the trade'.

1956 Clubman's Junior

1.	B. D. Codd, BSA	**27.30.4**	27.33.4	27.44.6	1 22 48.4	82.02
2.	J. Eckart, BSA	28.04.4	27.46.6	**27.39**	1 23 30.0	81.34
3.	A. Shepherd, Norton	28.39.8	**28.29.6**	28.33.8	1 25 43.2	79.24
4.	E. Unwin, BSA	29.13.2	28.28.6	**28.26.2**	1 26 08.0	78.86
5.	D. Jervis, BSA	28.56.8	28.38	**28.34**	1 26 08.8	78.84
6.	J. D. Morton, BSA	29.15.0	28.39.4	**28.26.8**	1 24 21.2	78.66
7.	J. E. Coates, BSA	29.18.2	28.47.2	**28.39**	1 26 44.4	78.31
8.	N. Robertson, BSA	29.22.6	29.07.4	**29.00.6**	1 27 30.6	77.62
9.	K. W. James, BSA	29.17.8	29.17.8	**29.04**	1 27 39.6	77.48
10.	D. Pratt, BSA	29.21.8	**29.13**	29.18	1 27 52.8	77.29
11.	R. Thompson, BSA	29.29	29.23.8	**29.11.8**	1 28 04.6	77.11
12.	G. Bell, BSA	29.40	29.20	**29.04.8**	1 28 04.8	77.11
13.	S. L. F. Orson, BSA	29.29.4	**29.28.8**	29.30.6	1 28 28.8	76.76
14.	C. McLean, BSA	29.31	**29.28**	29.36.6	1 28 35.6	76.67
15.	E. P. Davies, BSA	29.50.8	**29.23.4**	29.24.2	1 28 38.4	76.63
16.	C. J. Moram, BSA	29.59	29.26	**29.22**	1 28 47.0	76.50
17.	G. A. Borland, BSA	29.48	**29.43.2**	29.51.8	1 29 23.0	75.99
18.	R G. Sutcliffe, BSA	30.00	29.50.4	**29.39.4**	1 29 29.8	75.89
19.	D. F. Thomson, BSA	29.52	29.54.2	**29.49.6**	1 29 35.8	75.81
20.	D. H. Nourish, BSA	30.25	29.43.8	**29.28.8**	1 29 37.6	75.78
21.	B. R. Cortvriend, BSA	29.55.8	**29.50**	29.57.6	1 29 43.4	75.70
22.	W. A. Cooper, BSA	30.05.6	**29.47.6**	29.54.2	1 29 47.4	75.65
23.	J. F. Righton, Velocette	29.16	**28.57**	31.35.2	1 29 48.2	75.64
24.	F. Wallis, BSA	32.33.6	28.48.2	**28.39.4**	1 30 01.2	75.45
25.	W. D. Fellows, BSA	30.33.8	29.56.2	**29.35.8**	1 30 05.8	75.38
26.	G. Arnold, BSA	30.32.2	**29.52.2**	29.52.8	1 30 17.2	75.23
27.	D. D. Shand, BSA	30.37.0	30.13.8	**29.43.2**	1 30 34.0	75.00
28.	R. J. Brinnand, BSA	31.06.2	29.59.2	**29.55.4**	1 31 00.8	74.62
29.	S. Baskett, BSA	30.35	**30.06.0**	30.21.4	1 31 02.4	74.61
30.	P. R. Hodgson, BSA	31.19.8	30.25.2	**29.33.0**	1 31 18.0	74.39
31.	C. Huxley, BSA	30.51	**30.21.2**	30.27	1 31 39.2	74.11
32.	A. W. Brodrick, BSA	30.56.6	30.23.4	**30.19.8**	1 31 39.8	74.10
33.	H. Riley, BSA	30.42.2	**30.21.2**	30.56.8	1 32 00.2	73.83
34.	P. B. James, BSA	31.28.4	30.25.8	**30.15.4**	1 32 09.6	73.70
35.	N. Lay, BSA	30.55.6	**30.46**	30.46.4	1 32 28.0	73.46
36.	N. F. Sweetman, BSA	31.22.8	30.42.4	**30.31.4**	1 32 36.6	73.34
37.	A. W. G. Walczak, BSA	31.25.2	30.50	**30.32.8**	1 32 48.0	73.19
38.	N. C. Fletcher, BSA	31.58.6	31.11.2	**30.20.6**	1 33 30.4	72.64
39.	J. D. Hamilton, BSA	31.45.6	31.30.4	**31.18**	1 34 34.0	71.82
40.	G. E. Briggs, BSA	33.42.8	30.50.6	**30.04.2**	1 34 37.6	71.78
41.	T. Folwell, BSA	**31.45**	31.55	32.00.6	1 35 40.6	70.99
42.	H. D. Briggs, BSA	34.25.8	**30.57.4**	31.11.6	1 36 34.8	70.32
43.	R. A. Holland, BSA	**32.32**	32.20.8	32.34.2	1 37 27.0	69.70
44.	L. Bull, BSA	**32.22**	33.00	33.08.2	1 38 30.2	68.96
45.	G. A. Dormer, BSA	33.27	32.59.4	**32.41**	1 39 07.4	68.52

46. L. S. Rutherford, BSA	40.14	**30.01.2**	30.14.8	1 40 30.0	67.58
47. P. E. Walsh, BSA	33.41.8	33.29.4	**33.24**	1 40 35.2	67.53
48. K. A. Lindsay, BSA	33.47.6	33.31.4	**33.28**	1 40 47.0	67.39
49. M. R. Oram, BSA	34.09.2	34.39.8	34.40.4	1 43 29.4	65.63
50. N. H. Vivian, BSA	34.50	34.50.2	**33.52.6**	1 43 32.8	65.59
N. J. Davenport, BSA	29.59.8	R			
A. Jackson, BSA	31.54.6	R			
P. G. Kirkham, BSA	R				
K. Nicholls, BSA	R				
J. Hill, BSA	R				

LAP POSITIONS

RIDER AND MACHINE	FIRST LAP POSITION	1956 CLUBMAN'S JUNIOR	FINAL POSITION		RIDER AND MACHINE
B D CODD B.S.A.	1			1	B D CODD B.S.A.
J ECKHART B.S.A.	2			2	J ECKHART B.S.A.
A SHEPHERD NORTON	3			3	A SHEPHERD NORTON
D JERVIS B.S.A.	4			4	E UNWIN B.S.A.
E UNWIN B.S.A.	5			5	D JERVIS B.S.A.
J D MORTON B.S.A.	6			6	J D MORTON B.S.A.

1956 Clubman's Senior

1. B. D. Codd, BSA	26 15.2	**26 10.4**	26 15.0	1 18 40.6	86.33
2. R. E. Jerrard, BSA	26 42.2	**26 30.8**	26 33.8	1 19 46.8	85.13
3. A. H. Jenkins, BSA	27 29.0	**26 53.4**	27.00	1 21 22.4	83.47
4. F. Wallis, BSA	27.28.6	**26.53.6**	27.02	1 21 24.2	83.44
5. D. J. Smart, BSA	28.12.8	27.31.2	**27.31**	1 23 15.0	81.59
6. G. Coombes, BSA	28.29.2	27.59.4	**27.36.2**	1 24 04.8	80.78
7. J. R. Hurlstone, Triumph	28.32	27.56	**27.45.4**	1 24 13.4	80.65
8. W. J. Hill, BSA	28.45	28.09.4	**27.42**	1 24 36.4	80.28
9. B. W. Newman, BSA	28.40.2	28.07.6	**27.57.4**	1 24 45.2	80.14
10. D. Andrews, BSA	28.48.2	**28.02.2**	28.06	1 24 56.4	79.96
11. R. Preece, BSA	28.45.8	28.21.8	**28.00.6**	1 25 08.2	79.28
12. D. Hagan, BSA	28.57.4	28.28	28.09	1 25 34.4	79.37
13. A. H. Mustard, BSA	29.07.8	28.24	**28.11.2**	1 25 43.0	79.24
14. P. A. Alexander, BSA	28.54.8	28.38.0	**28.24.8**	1 25 57.6	79.01

15. E. Minihan, BSA	29.34	**28.20.4**	28.21	1 26 15.4	78.74
16. M. J. Candy, BSA	29.06	28.46.6	**28.34.8**	1 26 27.4	78.56
17. D. Howe, BSA	29.17.2	28.47.8	**28.37.0**	1 26 42.0	78.34
18. L. C. St. J. Hawkins, BSA	29.30.8	28.55.8	**28.23.8**	1 26 50.4	78.22
19. P. G. Hyde, Triumph	29.34.6	29.12.4	**29.09.6**	1 27 56.6	77.23
20. M. W. Gillingham, Triumph	30.01.0	29.26.2	**29.11.2**	1 28 38.4	76.63
21. G. Arnold, BSA	28.57.8	31.20.6	**28.52.4**	1 29 10.8	76.16
22. A. Ashley, Triumph	30.44.6	29.47.8	**29.09.6**	1 29 42.0	75.72
23. C. Dearden, Triumph	30.41.2	30.01.8	**29.59.4**	1 30 42.4	74.88
24. M. W. Munday, BSA	31.20.2	30.28.6	**30.12.8**	1 32.01.6	73.80
25. R. Smith, Triumph	34.42	**29.56.4**	31.13.2	1 35 51.6	70.85
26. M. T. Brookes, Triumph	27.53.2	**27.29.2**	41.34.8	1 36 57.2	70.06
27. R. F. Keen, BSA	36.39.4	**32.07.0**	32.26.2	1 41 12.6	67.11
28. B. F. Herbert, Norton	**33.35.6**	33.56.8	34.39.6	1 42 12.0	66.46
B. Payton, BSA	29.57.4	**29.19**	R		
P. K. Cruse, BSA	29 37.2	R			
D. Jervis, BSA	27.16.4	R			

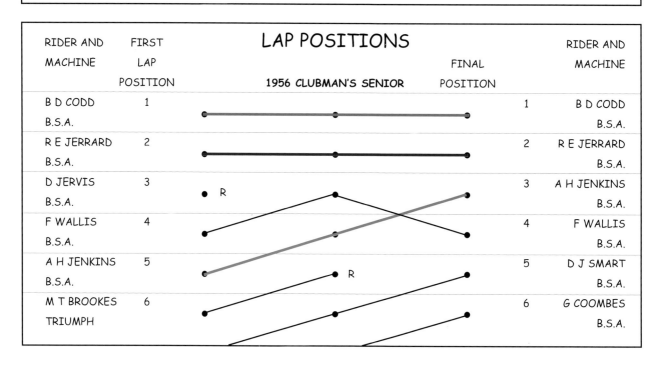

LAP POSITIONS

1956 CLUBMAN'S SENIOR

RIDER AND MACHINE	FIRST LAP POSITION		FINAL POSITION	RIDER AND MACHINE
B D CODD B.S.A.	1		1	B D CODD B.S.A.
R E JERRARD B.S.A.	2		2	R E JERRARD B.S.A.
D JERVIS B.S.A.	3		3	A H JENKINS B.S.A.
F WALLIS B.S.A.	4		4	F WALLIS B.S.A.
A H JENKINS B.S.A.	5		5	D J SMART B.S.A.
M T BROOKES TRIUMPH	6		6	G COOMBES B.S.A.

CHAPTER 12

THE PROBLEMS INCREASE - HOW AND WHY IT ALL ENDED

Before describing the circumstances and events that led to the ending of the Clubman's TT (or Clubman's Trophy, or Clubman's Cup), it is worth recalling the way the event was viewed at the time. The following, quoted in full from the Thursday 14th June 1956 *'TT Special'* (the day of what turned out to be the very last Clubman's races), presents the arguments, difficulties and discussion points from the time, and was written by Bob Currie.

THE CLUBMAN'S – AND THE FUTURE

There is a well known saying to the effect that the Lord Mayor's Show is followed by a vehicle from the Borough Sanitary Department. Last week we had the TT Races, in all their pomp and ceremony; today the procession comes to an end with the Clubman's 350cc and Clubman's 500cc the official designation of the events, though to us they remain the Junior and Senior Clubman's TT. But make no mistake, the famous cleansing vehicle is not yet in sight.

The Clubman's races, of which today's are but the tenth of a series which began away back in 1947, have always been something of a Cinderella by any standard: but Cinderella in the favourite children's story did eventually reach the Ball and meet her handsome prince. For the Clubmen, alas, the fairy godmother has apparently made a delayed start. Pantomime, yes - very much so - but fairy tale - no, more's the pity.

Nine years ago the TT Races came back to the Isle of Man after the long war years; enthusiasm was high, but the war had taken its toll, and many of those who were star riders in 1939 had aged a little in the meantime. It was obvious that some sort of nursery would have to be started - a school for the TT riders of the future: so the Clubman's TT was devised, in which the average rider, using the average road-going machine, could try his luck over the Mountain Course.

The start of it all

The first Clubman's TT of 1947, slipped shyly into the programme without benefit of a fanfare of trumpets, was in effect, just a single race with three separate classes - Senior, Junior and Lightweight, running concurrently. The Senior class, by the way, was for 'Up to 1,000cc' machines, though in fact there were only two 'thousands' entered and neither of them actually started. Both Junior and Senior competitors were set to cover four laps of the Mountain Course, while the Lightweight runners had to do three.

There were 64 entries, all told – quite a promising start – of which the eight Lightweights were sent off at intervals, followed after a few minutes break by the Juniors, and in due course by the Seniors.

So far, so good, but the event got away on the wrong foot, for this arrangement meant that a 500 c.c. rider had to plough through the 350 c.c. field, and perhaps through the 'two-fifties' too. It might have been better to do things the other way round, by sending the bigger machines away first, but that is a minor quibble; the main thing was that the series caught the imagination of the Clubman, and it seemed that the ACU had a 'hit' on their hands.

Through the years which followed, however, chopping and changing altered the positioning, the scope and the whole general character of the events. Through it all the Clubmen played the game despite all the apparent discouragements, and support was at a high level

Out in the cold

The ACU, however, were doubtless pre-occupied with weightier matters, and the re-introduction of the Sidecar TT in 1954 dealt a very heavy blow to the Clubman's TT. The resurrected three-wheeler dice had to be accommodated somehow, so poor Cinderella went out into the cold, cold snow - to the

Thursday of 'Practice Week'.

This in itself was an insult, but to make matters worse the title of 'Clubman's TT' was taken away, to be replaced by the unfamiliar 'Clubman's Trophy' styling. In these circumstances it was not surprising that entries were well down; only two races - Junior and Senior - were now to be permitted, and riders were given the option of competing in one or the other of them, but not in both.

And yet, when it came to the point, the two races were as closely contested and as exciting as any that had gone before. The glamour had been removed - by order - but at least there was some little consolation in that the course was still The Course.

More salt was yet to be rubbed into the wound – lorry loads of it, in fact, for by last year the series which had started so bravely way back in 1947 had degenerated into a pathetic little short-circuit meeting – a Saturday evening affair, run off over the new Clypse Circuit. The only comfort that the Clubmen could retain was that they were still, at least, in the Isle of Man.

"Scrap the Clypse"

MOTOR CYCLING   August 23, 1956

NO "CLUBMAN'S" for NEXT YEAR'S T.T.?

THERE will probably be no 'Clubman's' races in the Isle of Man in 1957, Golden Jubilee of the T.T.; the A.-C.U. will not countenance pools betting on motorcycle meetings; the Union is not to disaffiliate from the F.I.M. but national clubs such as those of Australia and New Zealand may be asked to consider direct affiliation to the Federation in order to ensure adequate representation of British Empire interests on the international body. These were three of the most important decisions passed by the General Council of the Auto-Cycle Union at its meeting last Friday in the Royal Automobile Club, London.

Whereas the Council's previous meeting must have been one of the rowdiest on record, this, by contrast, was surely one of the quietest, the delegates respecting the written advice of their chairman, Prof. A. M. Low, to conduct themselves in such a manner that their motives could not be misconstrued and, so far as possible, to speak only once to any motion, however much provoked by other speakers. The absence of Prof Low because of illness was deeply regretted and, as senior vice-president, Mr. J. D. Woodhouse took the chair at the outset, handing over to senior vice-chairman Mr. N. E. Dixon before the Competitions Committee minutes were presented.

"Friend at Court"

For his spirited defence of the cause of motorcycling sport during the House of Lords debate on the new Road Traffic Bill, the Council offered its unanimous thanks and appreciation to the Union's president, Lord Brabazon of Tara, P.C., M.C., and applauded the manner in which he had been briefed by secretary S. T. Huggett. Speaking of the effects of the new Act which became operative on August 2 last, the secretary said that he had been advised by the Ministry of Transport that the provisions requiring organizers to obtain permission from local highway authorities before using footpaths and bridleways for motorcycle events might not be fully effective for at least two months, since local councils had yet to institute the machinery for dealing with applications. The Ordnance Survey department had been approached with the object of ensuring clear demarcation of such tracks on future editions of their one-inch maps and he understood that similar requests had been made by certain local authorities.

There was some criticism of the fact that earlier in the day the Competitions Committee had made various recommendations concerning the 1957 T.T., before the subject had been considered by the T.T. sub-committee. However, Mr. Dixon pointed out that the Competitions Committee had been asked for its advice and that the various points raised would be considered by the sub-committee.

The Competitions Committee was anxious to retain the Clubman's, but felt that these races had departed far from the spirit in which they were originally intended. Therefore, in order to break the continuity of what was felt to be an undesirable development and to give the sub-committee a reasonable opportunity to reshape the races purely and simply as events for clubmen on ordinary touring machines—as initially conceived—it recommended that they should not be held next year. Speaking of the Clubman's, Cheshire Centre delegate J. Smith said that the races had been interfered with far too much during recent years, largely because of the introduction of the sidecar T.T., and strongly opposed any suggestion that the series should be abandoned. He saw a significant connection between the introduction of sidecar races and the decline of public interest in the T.T. In reply, Mr. Dixon said that there was not the slightest intention of abandoning the Clubman's and that the day might come when they would be the mainstay of the T.T. programme.

A man can stand so much and no more. If the Clubman's races were to survive at all, it was obvious that they must revert to the Mountain Course: yet how could it be done? The Clubman's answer -"scrap the 125c.c. and Sidecar events, and to heck with the FIM!" – was unacceptable, so a compromise was evolved, which placed the Clubman's races (not even the Clubman's Trophy Races now) right out of the TT period altogether. And there we have it – like it or lump it.

Have the races served their original purpose? Yes, by gosh, they have! Geoff Duke, Bob McIntyre, Derek Ennett, Derek Powell, John Clark, Cecil Sandford, Phil Carter – all these, and many more of proven capability now racing in International events had their schooling in the Clubman's classes. In todays list of entries there may be the stars of the future: they may not even finish in a particularly high position - Carter was 28th in the 1948 Senior Clubman's: Sandford was fifth in the 1949 Junior – but watch their progress in the years to come !

Certainly it's an impressive list, and on that showing alone the events have proved their worth – yet the Dismal Jimmies sadly shake their heads and murmur that "the Clubman's has had it. Take it away and bury it in a dark corner-preferably in Manx Grand Prix week." Why on earth should we? The plain truth is that the series has never received full publicity; this, we feel, is the main reason for any falling-off in support.

Why, for instance, was the title of 'Clubman's TT' taken away? Because the events are no longer contained within TT week? Phooey to that one! 'TT' in case the ACU has forgotten stands for 'Tourist Trophy' – and the machines which the Clubmen ride are more nearly touring models than any of those which yearly contest the Senior International race. Stick that in your megaphone and silence it !

Now what?

All right, let's be objective about it, it is plain that the races must continue over the Mountain Course – the feeble entry list for 1955 underlined that particular theory – and yet room has to be found somewhere. If the 125cc and Sidecar International events are to be retained, then it is equally plain that a date outside TT week proper must be found for the Clubman's series. The Thursday of Practice Week *has been tried – the Saturday before Race Week has been tried – and today yet a third solution is offered.*

That it is not the complete answer has been amply evident during the past few days of practicing. Whereas large groups of spectators could be seen all round the course during the early morning International practices, few - very few - have risen early to watch the Clubmen: those stalwarts who have taken the trouble are more often that not interested in one particular rider only - a clubmate of theirs, for whom they are perhaps carrying out timing operations or a plug check.

Now it is race day - and just look at the empty grandstands; the enthusiasts who crowded into the Island in their thousands last week have sailed away on the Saturday boats, most of the traders and other big-wigs have mainly made off in the direction of other venues, and the whole set-up has fallen flat on its face. It is too slight an affair to follow the Senior TT, too much of an anti-climax.

Island headaches

Consider again the 1955 races; at first sight the Saturday before TT week seems a most attractive proposition - enthusiasm is abroad in the air, crowds are pouring into the Island - yet there is one very large horsefly crawling around in the ointment. The use of the Island's roads as a racing circuit, attractive as it may seem to us, tends to tie the entire transport system into reef knots – and Saturday is the day when incoming steamers bring over crowds of holidaymakers, and take back those who must regretfully say "au revoir" to the Island and get back to work.

Consequently those who may be bound to or from Peel, Kirk Michael or other distant parts, are apt to be mightily annoyed at our interference with their liberty. The Clypse Circuit, admittedly, reduced this particular nuisance – but we have already indicated our opinion in that respect.

Over to you!

It's a thorny problem, isn't it! Can you - our readers - suggest a workable solution? Think it over - have a full scale clubroom discussion if you like – and send us your views on the subject. We, for our part, will do our best to publish them in the forthcoming Manx Grand Prix issues; - and who knows?- the ultimate solution may emerge.

HOW IT ENDED

The General Council of the ACU assembled for its annual meeting in the Royal Automobile Club (RAC) Headquarters in London on Friday 17th August 1956, and an item high on the agenda was the future of the Clubman's. From the start there seems to have been an uneasy feeling that the outcome of some of the agenda items had been 'pre-ordained' by the Committee. 'Motor Cycling' reported immediate criticism raised by some of the delegates that the Competitions Committee had made recommendations regarding the 1957 TT before the subject had been considered by the TT Sub-Committee. Senior Vice Chairman Norman Dixon countered this by saying that the Competitions Committee had been asked for its advice, and that the points raised would be considered by the TT sub-committee at their meeting a week later, (a committee of which he would also be Chairman).

From the ACU minutes of this meeting

"Mr. J. Smith (in response to the Chairman's invitation), said that the abandoning of the Clubman's Races was, in his opinion, a retrograde step. For these races, in the past few years, the regulations had been continually changing, the courses had been switched over and now it would appear that the Competitions Committee had dictated the decision to the TT Sub-Committee.

The Chairman explained that the question of 'dictation' did not arise. The TT Sub-Committee had felt that before the 1957 programme was framed they should have the views of the Competitions Committee. That Committee had felt that the best interests of the Clubman's would be served by having a complete severance so that in the interval an opportunity could be given to review the regulations........ so as to get nearer to the original concept of the Races in 1947.

Mr. Smith said that if he had the Chairman's assurance that the Clubman's would be brought back again in 1958, he would be happy, but he had the feeling that if the Clubman's was not run in 1957 it would be finally abandoned.

The Chairman replied that the abolition of the Clubman's was not in their minds, and indeed, they thought that the Clubman's might be their main anchor at some future date, but it had got into such a state that a re-start from the bottom would make it safe for the future."

Reporting the General Council meeting, *'Motor Cycling'* dated 23rd August 1956 had this to say:

"The Competitions Committee was anxious to retain the Clubman's, but felt that these races had departed far from the spirit in which they were originally intended. Therefore, in order to break the continuity of what was felt to be an undesirable development and to give the sub-committee a reasonable opportunity to reshape the races purely and simply as events for clubmen on ordinary touring machines - as initially conceived - it recommended that they should not be held next year. Speaking of the Clubman's, Cheshire Centre delegate J. Smith said that the races had been interfered with far too much during recent years, largely because of the introduction of the Sidecar TT, and strongly opposed any suggestion that the series should be abandoned. He saw a significant connection between the introduction of sidecar races and the decline of public interest in the TT. In reply, Mr. Dixon said that there was not the slightest intention of abandoning the Clubman's and that the day might come when they would be the mainstay of the TT programme".

There is no ambiguity in those words, no scope for misinterpretation. The ACU, through the Competitions Committee, wanted the races discontinued in their current format and re-modelled. There was no mention there of any overcrowded schedule for the Golden Jubilee TT, no mention of an overstretched organisation, or any other aspect of the administration of the races. In the eyes of the ACU, the races in their then current format were unacceptable. The thoughts expressed at the meeting by Mr. Smith were similar to those by Bob Currie, but at least the delegates had gone away holding on to the assurance from Norman Dixon that the Clubman's would not be abandoned, that after a break and a re-think, the races would return.

The ACU made their position clear to the Manx authorities at a meeting of the Tynwald Races Committee, held in the Tynwald Committee Rooms on Wednesday 5th September 1956, *"As to the Clubman's Race, Mr. Dixon said the ACU had decided not to hold this in 1957. There was no question of abandoning it, but the ACU felt that this Race had got off the rails somewhat and they intended having a complete review of the whole position. The suspension of the Race in 1957 would give the ACU the necessary breathing space to go into the whole set-up and to consider the position fully".*

The 1957 Golden Jubilee TT Races were an all-round success, with good crowds and Bob McIntyre's historic 100 mph lap on the Gilera, and after it was over, thoughts turned to the following year. However, instead of the Tynwald Races Committee negotiating the running of the 1958 TT with the ACU, there was a new body, the IoM Race Committee of the Tourist Board, and whether or not connected to that change, there was a marked hardening of attitudes from the IoM authorities, especially toward the Clubman's. From the minutes of the ACU Sub-Committee meeting of 1st October 1957 comes a caution *"The Chairman [Norman Dixon] expressed the personal view ………….that the vast amount of mutual goodwill and confidence which had been built up over the years by personal contacts between that Committee [the Tynwald Races Committee] and representatives of the Union now appeared to have been lost. Other members expressed similar views…"* On the specific subject of the Clubman's, the ACU minutes say *"The views of the Tourist Board concerning the tentative proposal to organize the Clubman's Races on the Mountain Circuit in 1958 were discussed at length. The Chairman reviewed the history of the Clubman's Races and the present position of road racing in general and he mentioned the possible compulsory introduction of a 'Sports Machine' class in International events. The declared withdrawal of leading Foreign Manufacturers from International racing may indicate that future Classic events would have to rely solely on 'sports machines' for entries.*

After considerable discussion, it was unanimously agreed to adhere to the previous decision to hold the Clubman's Races for two classes to be run concurrently on the Saturday evening prior to TT week."

There was obvious concern at the ACU over whether the Tourist Board would approve the programme of races for 1958 (the inclusion of the

Clubman's being the biggest stumbling-block), and a later item in the same minutes was a proposed visit by the ACU Chairman and Secretary to the Isle of Man in early November in order to *"amplify the views of this Committee"*.

Before that came about, a significant day of meetings of the TT Sub-Committee took place at the Exchange Station Hotel, Liverpool, on Friday 1st November 1957. The Chairman was again Norman Dixon, with Vic Anstice, Les Archer (Snr), Jack Smith and C.H. King representing the ACU, J.M. Cain (Member of the House of Keys, the Manx Parliament), H.K. Corlett, H.C. Kerruish, W.E. Quayle, H.M. Rowell and L. Bond representing the Tourist Board. The first issues for the meeting, relating to the use of the Clypse Course and the various protocols involved in ACU contact with the IoM Highway and Transport Board, and Douglas Corporation, were soon dealt with satisfactorily, but then discussion turned to the Clubman's. Reproduced below is a selection of the minutes covering those exchanges. Space precludes quoting the minutes in full, but the selection does not bias the argument, the statements are clear and unequivocal.

"Mr. Corlett said the Board was most anxious that the previous happy relationship between the Isle of Man and the ACU should continue. There was a strong feeling that the Clubman's Races should not be held. He had understood that before the re-introduction of these Races, the matter would be discussed with the Board, but the first intimation it had was the copy of a letter to the Highway Board setting out the tentative programme of races for 1958.

Mr. Kerruish said that his Committee had been told by Tynwald that it must not under any conditions countenance the re-introduction of the Clubman's Races, and Mr. Cain expressed the view that the 1957 programme of races had proved most successful and the Clubman's Races had no other object than to give a number of relatively inexperienced drivers a ride around the TT Course.

The Chairman pointed out that the Clubman's Races had only been suspended for 1957. The General Council had sought an assurance that these Races were not being abandoned, but merely suspended so that the regulations could be overhauled and brought more into line with the original concept. This assurance had been given to the General Council, the governing body of the Union and representing over 800 clubs.

Mr. Kerruish said that the enthusiasm of the Clubmen had not been reflected in the attendance at these races which had received poor support and he asked whether the TT Sub-Committee was in a position to give an assurance to the General Council in view of the fact that the Isle of Man authorities were involved financially in any decision.

In reply to Mr. Rowell, the Chairman re-iterated that it was the declared intention of the Sub-Committee to re-draft the regulations of the Clubman's Races so as to revert to the original purpose of these races.

Mr. Cain enquired as to the cost of promoting the Clubman's Races but Mr. Kerruish said that more important than the cost of the races was the adverse publicity which these races created and the fact that the major races were in danger of losing their appeal through the introduction of other minor races.

The Chairman said he found it difficult to believe that people had been kept away from the TT because of the Clubman's Races, and Mr. Smith said that only when the tourist figures to the Island were going down was the Clubman's Races blamed, but these races must in any case attract a certain amount of support.

Mr. Corlett also expressed the opinion that there was a danger of the Clubman's Races undermining the International event and so ultimately bring about the collapse of the TT Races.

Mr. Quayle enquired whether the Newcomers Race included in the 1957 Manx Grand Prix would cover the purpose of the Clubman's Races and Mr. Bond asked whether the difficulty could be resolved if an opportunity was given for the Clubman's Races to be held in September.

Mr. Smith, commenting on these suggestions, said that in June not only did a driver in the Clubman's Races have an opportunity of riding over the Mountain Course, but he was able to obtain a certain amount of assistance from accessory firms and, also, see the International Races.

Mr. Cain asked for information on the decisions of the FIM with regard to 'Sports Machine' races and, in reply, the Secretary stated that whilst at the moment the inclusion of this type of racing in Classic events was not compulsory there was an increasing tendency to make it so.

Mr. Cain then referred to the Government Grant in relation to the Clubman's Races and said undoubtedly, this aspect would be raised by Tynwald and the Tourist Board would be criticized if it recommended any increase in the amount of the grant to cover the cost of the Clubman's Races.

The Chairman stated that it was difficult to estimate the additional cost of these races, but there would be some saving if the races are held within the TT period.

Mr. Kerruish said that Tynwald would not accept the Clubman's Races at any price and enquired what the position would be if in April next, the Tynwald reduced the amount of its financial grant. It would be understood that the Tourist Board could not force a decision through Tynwald and the Board would be foolish to ignore their views. There was a growing opposition to the Clubman's Races and these races were not required.

Mr. Corlett said he supported the views expressed by Mr. Kerruish and he felt it was the duty of the representatives to state, in the clearest possible terms, the position of the Tourist Board. He would like to be able to say that the Clubman's Races will definitely not be held in 1958, but that it was not possible to state that these races would not be run again. In the Isle of Man, the opposition to these races was general and was gathering momentum. This attitude was also largely held by members of Tynwald.

The Chairman said that the Board must convince Tynwald that International racing was likely to suffer from the recent withdrawal of foreign manufacturers and it may well be that in a future year the 500cc class will be discontinued in favour of a 'Sports Machine' class and that this may be followed by the dropping of the 350cc class. In that event it would be most advantageous for the Union to have already had experience in organizing sports machine type races suitable to fill the gaps created.

Mr. Smith reviewed the reasons for the introduction of the Clubman's Races originally and said that it may be through a trade recession and the consequent reduction of entries for International races we would then be only too pleased to have the Clubman's Races.

The Chairman enquired whether the Board would have the same objections if the Clubman's Races were to be held on the Monday of TT week, and Mr. Cain said the Board was against the continuance of these Races. Mr. Anstice regretted the views expressed by the Board, and Mr. King said he had no doubt that any attempt to convince the General Council not to promote the Clubman's Races would fail.

Mr. Kerruish said that over the years, there had been a feeling of growing resentment against the Clubman's Races and he felt that Tynwald would not agree to the holding of these Races. The Tourist Board and the Highway Board would not be able to act contrary to the wishes of Tynwald."

The meeting terminated at 4.05 pm, the Tourist Board representatives having to return to the Island, except for Mr. Cain, who stayed for the evening continuation of the meeting, and which began at 9.00 pm. After the 'full and frank exchange of views' as it might be called now, it was left to Mr. Cain to re-state the opposition of the Board to *"the holding of these races in any form in association with the International Races"*. The only real outcome of the evening meeting was a resolution *"to suggest to the Tourist Board that, in addition to the International Races, there shall be a National or International Race (exactly which remains to be decided) conforming as closely as possible to the FIM 'Sports Machine' Regulations, to be run on either Saturday 31st May, or the afternoon of Monday 2nd June."*

Such was the climate of the relationship between the ACU and the Tourist Board, that even this attempt to break the deadlock caused problems. At first, the Tourist Board appeared to accept the resolution, but in a follow-up letter made it conditional on the Regulations and arrangements for that race being submitted to the Board for approval prior to any announcement being made. Never before had the ACU had to submit supplementary Regulations for approval, and the Chairman *"felt that the ACU could not accede to the Board's request"*.

Amid further bickering between the two

Committees over statements being issued to the press without prior consultation of the other party, the TT Sub-Committee were left to lick their wounds, and wonder how to deal with the decisions of the Tourist Board in the light of assurances they had given to the ACU General Council *"that the Clubman's Races had not been abandoned but left in abeyance for 1957 only"*. The only outcome was a letter to the Tourist Board formally expressing the regret of the Committee that the Board had rejected the proposals for the Clubman's Race during the 1958 TT period.

On 7th November 1957, *'The Motor Cycle'* reported that the 1958 TT races had been the subject of discussions between the TT Sub-Committee of the ACU and the Isle of Man Tourist Board, and that the Clubman's was an on-going subject of negotiation. This was followed in the same magazine two weeks later by the following *"It is apparent from statements made by the Isle of Man Tourist Board and the Auto Cycle Union that a serious difference of opinion has arisen over the staging of the Clubman's Races in 1958. The IoM authorities would prefer to consider a sports machine event based on the regulations drawn up by the Federation Internationale Motocycliste. But the ACU is duty bound to meet the wishes expressed by centre delegates and to honour an undertaking that the Clubman's events would be held over for 1957 only. Both points of view are understandable but difficult to reconcile.*

Doubtless the IoM reaction is governed to some extent by the fact that past Clubman's Races have never drawn big crowds. On the other hand, the ACU has always had in mind the laudable object that racing clubmen regard their IoM events as stepping stones to more important contests such as the Manx Grand Prix and the TT. But might not the same purpose be achieved by the ACU sponsoring special races for clubmen riding suitably equipped machines on mainland circuits? With the co-operation of established organising clubs there is no reason why the number of races should not be such that they would provide clubmen with even better opportunities of gaining experience than the IoM events have done."

The same day issue of *'Motor Cycling'* carried the following. *"Readers will have been waiting anxiously for news concerning the future of the* Clubman's Races in the Isle of Man but, as is pointed out in our Editorial page in this issue, there seems to be some disagreement on the subject between the Auto Cycle Union and the IoM Tourist Board. The matter was capitalised when, last week, these two bodies issued respective statements, each of which is produced herewith:-

Statement by ACU issued November 14th;
'The Isle of Man Tourist Board has refused to agree to the holding of the Clubman's Race in the Isle of Man in 1958. The Isle of Man Tourist Board has agreed, however, to the alternative of holding another short race, of a form to be decided, on Monday afternoon, June 2, 1958.'

Statement by IoM Tourist Board issued November 15th;
'The Auto-Cycle Union has issued a statement relating to the 1958 TT Races, upon which the Isle of Man Races Committee feel that they should make some comment.

On February 11, 1957, the Auto-Cycle Union gave a written assurance to the Isle of Man Races Committee that they would be fully consulted before any decision to revive the Clubman's race was taken.

On August 16, 1957, the Auto-Cycle Union inquired from the Isle of Man Highway and Transport Board whether road closing orders could be arranged for a Clubman's Race on the Mountain Circuit on the evening of Saturday, May 31, 1958. A copy of the letter was sent to the Races Committee by the Auto-Cycle Union for information.

On September 10, 1957, the Races Committee wrote to the Auto-Cycle Union saying that, with the information then at the disposal of the Committee, they felt that they would have difficulty in agreeing with any proposals to revive this race.

On October 16, 1957, following the Auto-Cycle Union meeting on October 1 which was attended by a representative of the Races Committee, the Committee listed its reasons for objecting to a revival of the Clubman's Race and informed the Auto-Cycle Union that they felt that the event should not be revived and expressed the hope that the Auto-Cycle Union would concur with them in this decision.

At the same time the Committee indicated that they were aware that developments in the field of motorcycle racing made it likely that, in the near future, racing on sports machines might become part of an International meeting and the Committee was prepared to discuss this as a separate matter.

The Auto-Cycle Union insisted on running a Clubman's Race in 1958 and, in order to give them every opportunity of presenting their case, five members of the Races Committee made a special journey to Liverpool on November 1st, 1957, to meet the Auto-Cycle Union TT Sub-Committee.

On November 4, 1957, the Auto-Cycle Union proposed in a letter 'that in addition to the International Races, there shall be a National or International Race (exactly which remains to be decided) conforming as closely as possible to the FIM Sports Machine regulations, to be run on either Saturday, May 31, or the afternoon of Monday, June 2.

On November 12, 1957, the Isle of Man Races Committee informed the Auto-Cycle Union that they wished to do their utmost to meet their requirements and accordingly were agreeable to make the afternoon of Monday, June 2, available for a race on the line suggested, subject to the regulations and arrangements being submitted to the Race Committee for approval prior to any announcement being made.

There the matter now stands, with the Isle of Man authorities awaiting the proposals of the Auto-Cycle Union.

The Isle of Man Race Committee can only repeat the assurance they have already given that they wish to do their utmost to meet the views of the Auto-Cycle Union".

Those were the formally stated positions of the two sides, Bob Holliday summed up the situation in his Editorial in that same 21nd November issue of 'Motor Cycling'.

"A suspicion that there had been a major clash of opinion between the Isle of Man authorities and the Auto-Cycle Union, over the 1958 TT races, arose when, following a recent Liverpool meeting of representatives of both sides, a universal 'my lips are sealed' attitude was presented to all attempts by the Press to discover what plans had been made for the 1958 Clubman's Races.

That suspicion was confirmed last week when first the ACU, and then the IoM Races Committee, issued statements [as above]. *Little or no reading between the lines is needed to see what has happened. The Union, mindful of its duty to its 800-odd constituent clubs, wanted to continue the Clubman's series. Indeed, it had virtually promised to do so and a date for the event was tentatively announced.*

But the Islanders do not like the Clubman's. They have maintained that it has failed in one of its original purposes, which was to enlist the interests of the manufacturer's; that the amount of spectator (visitor) support it commands is so small that the time and effort required to run the race are not worth while; that there is always a danger that accidents to novice riders will bring bad publicity.

Being the holder of the purse strings, the Race Committee pays the piper – no Clubman's, or no grant. And the tune it calls is a 'Sports Machine' race based on the recent complicated FIM proposals, which were held in abeyance at the Paris Autumn Congress in favour of 'production' racing. Having, it would seem, no choice in the matter, the Union, becoming increasingly accustomed to rebuffs, has agreed to run an event of this sort on Monday, June 2, 1958. Even the ACU suggestion of Saturday, May 31, was vetoed. Until it is known exactly what constitutes a Sports Machine race it is difficult to assess the value of this event, but certain aspects can be considered. For one thing it is hard to understand how the accident danger is to be reduced, or spectator appeal increased, if the machines are to remain, in practically all respects, perfectly standard, 'over the counter' road going products. And what class of rider is envisaged for this Monday afternoon affair? Clearly it can hardly be intended for 'professionals only' because a large proportion of the eligible 'professionals' will already have ridden in the Junior TT, and FIM regulations would prohibit them from taking part in a second race on the same day. Must it not seem, therefore, that although the Races Committee refuses to have a Clubman's Race as such, it is proposing a race for Clubman-type machines ridden by clubmen? But are such riders likely to expend the money and time required to compete in a single race?

Then there is the problem of machine examination. If the proposed Sports Machine race is a mixed class event of, say, 350 and 500cc models, there will be at least six and, including possible additional fastest-lappers, perhaps eight, mounts at the end of the day requiring the complete strip-down and exact examination that is implicit in a production-machine type of race.

But above all is the question, is it wise to tack onto an important race, such as the Junior TT, something that, from the spectators point of view, must inevitably be in the nature of an anti-climax? Who, save the projectionists, would ever see the advertising trailers if they were screened after the big picture?"

It was downhill all the way from then on. The ACU Sub-Committee met again on 2nd December, discussed the matter of the 'additional race', and unanimously recommended that *"Having reconsidered the proposed 1958 Programme of Races in the Isle of Man and taking into consideration the IoM Tourist Board's objections to the Clubman's Races, and the manufacturer's apparent lack of interest in the proposed 'Sports Machine' race, we advised the Competitions Committee not to proceed with the extra race in 1958.*

The possibility of staging a Clubman's Race on the mainland in 1958 might, however, be considered".

The Competitions Committee met on 12th December and adopted the recommendation

WHY IT ENDED

The background to the IoM Tourist Board / Races Committee position was that, despite the improved attendances for the celebratory Golden Jubilee races, the figures for TT attendance were becoming cause for real concern. During the 1956 pre-TT weekend the steamers brought across 11,000 visitors – 3,000 fewer than in 1955 (when a rail strike had affected numbers), and 7,000 fewer than in 1954 or 1953. Thursday night 'Senior' sailings and flights brought a combined total of 10,000, 25% fewer than when the strike was on and less than half the 1954 total. The shifting of the Clubman's in 1956 to the week after the International had separated out and inadvertently highlighted the number of spectators drawn specifically by that event – the special steamers laid on from Liverpool and Fleetwood for the Thursday

Clubman's races had brought over respectively 80 and 75 visitors. (This latter 'revelation' was given some publicity at the time, and would have lent considerable weight to the anti-Clubman's lobby, but is of course, misleading. Apart from the fact that many people whose main interest was in the Clubman's would have already been over for the International, one can speculate on the effects of taking any individual race out of TT race week and staging it in isolation a week later; it is highly probable that the number of day-excursionists for any such race would be disproportionately low).

However, the Island grant to the organisers (the ACU) for staging the TT was £10,000 in 1956, and naturally the IoM authorities required a return on that investment. In those pre-offshore-finance days the IoM economy depended heavily on tourism, and the extensions of the traditional tourist season, brought about at the beginning by the TT, and at the end by the Manx Grand Prix, were financially significant.

Also by the mid 1950's, it was apparent that the attitude of 'the Trade' toward the Clubman's had changed from enthusiastic and supportive, to one the *'Motor Cycling'* Yearbook for 1956 described thus *"...the Trade element, which would cheerfully eliminate the Clubman's events on the score that they interfere with and undermine the prestige value of the TT races."* It is left for us now to wonder who was meant by 'Trade element', but it would have been unlikely to have been major accessory manufacturers, or tyre or fuel/oil companies. The only alternative would be the manufacturers, the erstwhile competition for BSA, but of those only AMC and Norton were in a position to benefit from the 'prestige value of the TT races', as by then they were the only British manufacturers competing seriously for top honours in the International events.

It is not difficult to imagine the rival manufacturers, having seen their own highly-vaunted sports models publicly humiliated by the Gold Stars year after year adding to the debate, and lobbying the ACU to find a reason to call a halt. There is probably some truth in this as well, and certainly AMC were of the opinion that the Regulations allowed for, even encouraged, racers disguised as roadsters to compete. Norton had no budget left after Joe Craig had taken the race-shop share, and Triumph's ambivalent approach to racing continued. The mental image of Edward Turner in hushed and earnest conversation with members of the ACU Competitions Committee at trade dinners and industry functions, persuading them over a gin and tonic that they should stop this annual humbling of his beloved twins by the 'cheat singles' is fanciful – but entertaining nonetheless.

What was clear was that the ACU had a problem on their hands. They were committed to the long-term success of the International TT, that was clear, and to ensure that success they needed the presence of the crowd-pulling continental works teams. The TT was a considerable investment both in terms of money and time for these teams, and to maintain the incentive for them to compete, the TT had to retain its status as a round counting toward the World Championship, and in doing that it had to comply with FIM rules and include the 125cc and Sidecar classes. On the other hand, to provide a training ground for TT riders of the future, there was a need for non-international status events over the Mountain circuit to provide that 'training ground'. Of course it could be argued that the Manx Grand Prix fitted that bill, and to a great extent it did, but the Clubman's had a role to play in providing the vital first step for many a talented but impecunious 'hopeful'. The original aim of the Clubman's had been to allow that first step to be taken using ride-to-work, or at least weekend 'sports' motorcycles. The Clubman's TT had evolved, and like all 'formula' race series before and since, the competing machines had developed, within the Rules, to be as competitive as their entrants and riders could make them. In short, they became more and more specialised. BSA and their Gold Star had gone further down the road of development toward the ultimate Clubman's racer than any of the other factories, to the extent that by 1956 it had become almost totally dominant in both remaining classes. The net result of this was that any rider hoping to be able to be competitive in the Clubman's simply had to buy a Gold Star, and the argument then went that he might be better served spending the same money on a purpose-designed racer, even if second-hand, and entering the Manx Grand Prix.

If it is accepted that the underlying reason for the demise of the Clubman's races was the lack of spectators drawn specifically by that event, it is necessary to look at why the appeal had gone. A reason often quoted has been that same domination of the races by the BSA Gold Star. There is an obvious truth in this, but it is over-simplistic to put this down as the main cause. Such domination is undesirable and detracts from spectator appeal, but, providing the racing is close and of good quality, one-model races do at least have the advantage that they provide a 'level playing field' on which to compare riders abilities. The Manx Grand Prix's of the 1960's (where there were effectively only two models competing in the Junior and Senior classes) or the 1970's (where there was only the TZ Yamaha which was competitive in Lightweight, Junior and even Senior classes some years) didn't put the races into terminal decline.

There are other contributory factors, and the ACU are far from being blameless. As Bob Currie had pointed out, the lack of any decent publicity (or 'promotion' as it would be termed today), the constant changes to the timetable, running the Clubman's in practice week, on the same day in race-week, on different days in race-week, and finally in the week following race-week, did not convey any message of permanence, and inferred a fundamental lack of support. Bob Holliday, in his book 'Racing Round the Island', published by David and Charles in 1976 wrote *"The much harrassed Clubman... had been chivvied from Thursday before the race week to the Thursday after and had been switched from Mountain to Clypse and back to the Mountain. At one time a four class event, it had now shrunk to two. There had been ... inumerable changes in race distance and methods of despatch from one at a time to four in a group. Endless arguments arose over catalogue specifications and in the end one indisputable fact emerged - that BSA Gold Stars were virtually unbeatable"*.

The ACU had given *"a written assurance to the Isle of Man Race Committee that they would be fully consulted before any decision to revive the Clubman's race was taken"*. It would appear that this was ignored, forgotten, or possibly the ACU did not believe there would be a problem in re-instating the races for 1958. The Manx authorities, through their representatives on the Races Committee, had made it clear that they wanted the Clubman's to be re-modelled along FIM 'Sports Machine' lines, and not only were the ACU obliged to listen (he who pays the piper... as Bob Holliday had said), they had pledged to consult before re-instating them in any form. Whether the 'Sports Machine' race format had merit or not, even whether it was viable or not, is debatable, but for the ACU to do nothing and then submit an application for road closures for an unchanged Clubman's Race was an affront to the Races Committee, and the IoM authorities, and they reacted accordingly. In view of the fairly minor differences (this is an assumption, as the detailed format of the 'Sports Machine' races never became clear) between the 'Sports Machine' and Clubman's requirements, it is difficult to understand why the ACU didn't simply agree to work with the IoM Races Committee (and the FIM) to try to make a go of it. That way they would be assured of complete support from both those organisations, the *undesirable development* of the races would be arrested, and they were being actually presented with the ideal opportunity to *re-shape the races'*. The ACU had little to fear in terms of adverse manufacturer reaction to rule change, as only one of them (BSA) would be likely to be upset by a change to the formula, and if it were to change surely that could only encourage the others to rejoin the event.

The inescapable truth behind all the words was that if the other manufacturer's could not or would not take up the challenge and compete with BSA, and thereby increase spectator appeal (and numbers), then the races had indeed run their allotted course, and their ending was inevitable.

Races over the IoM Mountain Course for production sports machines (using a formula, at least for machine eligibility, which was probably not too far removed from the FIM 'Sports Machine' format) returned with the advent of the Production TT in 1967. Then, with International riders, and National riders with proven Isle of Man pedigree, spectator and factory interest was re-kindled, and the event was a success for many years. The Production TT immediately embraced the bigger capacity machines, the 650's, 750's and later bigger still, and it is hard to avoid the feeling that the ACU 'missed a trick' by not opening up the Senior Clubman's class to the emerging 600's and 650's of the day.

Could the Clubman's have been saved by a move to September, to become part of the Manx Grand Prix? It was reported at the time that the grass roots feeling was against such a move, but it should be remembered that the inferred alternative was 'or leave them where they are?' Few folk then would have known, or even suspected, that the actual alternative was 'or lose them altogether'. What actually happened in 1957 was that, with the absence of the Clubman's in June, the Manx Grand Prix later that year was simply deluged with entries, so much so that the organisers (the Manx MCC) added two 'Newcomers' races to the programme, with successful riders being invited to remain and run in the MGP proper. In so doing, almost painlessly, the aims of the Tourist Board Races Committee and the ACU Competitions Committee (i.e. removal of the Clubman's from TT calendar, and a re-packaging of the event) had been accomplished. Essentially the Newcomers MGP events took over from the Clubman's, and the following year were continued as the 'Snaefell' races.

The need of the riders for Mountain Circuit experience was thus satisfied, but what of the manufacturers and the machines? In 1955 the Southampton & DMC had initiated the 9-hours (later to become the 500-Miles) endurance race for what were essentially Clubman's specification bikes, which, over the longer distances involved, were not so one-make-one-model dominated. The Gold Star did take class and overall wins, but so did others, and both public and trade interest was high and remained so for many years (although it must be said that on-the-day attendance figures were never large).

All in all, it would seem to have been a rather satisfactory conclusion for all parties, and the only 'casualty' in the end was, sadly, the axeing of the Isle of Man Clubman's.

After all the talk, the arguments, statements and counter-statements, what exactly did take the place of the Clubman's on the vacant Monday afternoon of the 1958 race-week? Precisely - nothing, there was no *"National or International Race conforming as closely as possible to the FIM 'Sports Machine'*

Regulations". The International Junior TT took on the same scheduling as Friday's Senior, over 7 laps, but beginning at a later time of 11.00am, and was the only race that day. From *'The Motor Cycle'* dated 19th December 1957: *"At a meeting of the Auto-Cycle Union Competitions Committee last Thursday, the following recommendation from the TT Sub-Committee was approved:*

Having re-considered the proposed 1958 programme of races in the Isle of Man, the Isle of Man Tourist Board's objection to the Clubman's Races and the manufacturer's apparent lack of interest in the proposed sports-machine race, we [the TT Sub-Committee] advise the Competitions Committee not to proceed with the extra race in 1958. The possibility of staging a Clubman's Race on the mainland in 1958 might, however, be considered."

It is not insignificant that, in so dropping the idea of the 'extra race in 1958', the ACU quoted one of the main reasons *"the manufacturer's apparent lack of interest"*.

The Clubman's name was later 'auctioned off' by the ACU, to be taken up by the Cheshire Centre of the Union, who had been at the forefront of the support for the race to remain in the Isle of Man, and who beat off rival 'bids' from BMCRC (offering Silverstone) and Scarborough & DMC (offering Olivers Mount). The ACU Clubman's re-emerged in a totally different form, a one-day meeting at Oulton Park, with an all-action days racing leading to the National Clubman's championship. Heats and finals were held for all solo classes, including production classes (and sidecars later), and the glory-day one-chance-is-all-you-get format provided great racing for up to three hundred riders. In 1959 the Clubman's went to Silverstone, then back on a long term footing to a Whit Monday slot at Oulton Park. Writing his programme notes for the 1961 event, Denys Ainsworth of the Daily Express said *"For it is no accident that stars of the future come from the Clubman's. The races were conceived by the Auto-Cycle Union in 1947 to give the amateurs a chance to prove themselves in conditions similar to those under which the big boys gain their glory. Geoff Duke, Bob McIntyre, Jimmy Buchan, Alastair King, Phil Carter – and now Phil Read* [who won both Junior and Senior events in 1960] *all started their roads to glory in the Clubman's"*. From the entry for 1961 he then picked out two names that he would be watching with particular interest *"for they carry the names of two famous riders who have each been honoured by the sport to which they gave their lives"*. These two, then at the very beginning of their racing careers, were Stuart Graham and Jimmy Guthrie (Jnr).

The Clubman's continued in the same form until the late 1970's before giving way to the more modern ACU Clubman's Championships spread over a number of weekends and at circuits all over the country.

As a single event in the sporting calendar, the Clubman's is now long gone, but for all those whose enthusiasm for motor cycles, for the Isle of Man races, and motorcycle racing in general brought them into contact with the series, the Clubman's TT will never be forgotten.

'The Clubman's is dead, long live the Clubman's'.

INDEX OF STARTERS

Adcock, K G
1949 J 42   Royal Enfield
Akers, A W
1951 J R   B.S.A.
1952 J R   B.S.A.
Alcock, Geoff
1951 S 15   Norton
1952 S 36   Norton
'Alexander, J'
1950 1000 2   Vincent HRD
Alexander, Peter
1956 S 14   B.S.A.
Anderson, W R
1952 J R   B.S.A.
Andrew, Edwin
1948 S 10   Norton
1949 S 6   Norton
Andrews, Don
1952 S R   Matchless
1953 S 11   Matchless
1954 S 13   Norton
1955 S 5   B.S.A.
1956 S 10   B.S.A.
Appleby, H A
1952 J R   Norton
Arber, Ivor
1949 S 27   Norton
1950 S 4   Norton
1951 S 1   Norton
Archer, Les R
1947 L 3   Velocette
Arnold, C
1950 J R   Velocette
Arnold, George
1951 J 36   B.S.A.
1952 J 17   B.S.A.
1953 J R   B.S.A.
1954 J 6   B.S.A.
1955 J 12   B.S.A.
1956 J 26   B.S.A.
1956 S 21   B.S.A.
Arthur, R
1953 S 25   Norton
Ashley, Alan
1955 S R   Triumph
1956 S 22   Triumph
Atkinson, Ian
1955 S 2   Triumph
Auld, W A G
1949 J R   Matchless
Austin, Roland
1949 S R   Triumph
1950 S R   Triumph
1951 S 27   Matchless
Avis, Stanley
1950 S R   Triumph
1951 S 22   Triumph
1952 S 52   Triumph
1953 S 20   Triumph
1954 S R   Triumph

Bacon, Bert
1947 S 9   Norton
Bagshaw, Peter
1950 J 40   A.J.S.
Baigent, M R
1954 S 5   B.S.A.
Baker, Eric
1949 J 48   B.S.A.
1950 J 33   B.S.A.
1951 J 27   B.S.A.
Baldwin, Peter
1953 S 18   A J S.
Barfoot, Ken
1954 J 36   B.S.A.
Barker, George
1950 L R   Velocette
Barker, Walter
1949 J 29   B.S.A.
1950 J 19   B.S.A.
Barlow, W
1954 S R   Norton
Barton, Arthur
1949 L 6   Triumph
Basinger, J F
1949 J 37   Velocette
1950 J R   B.S.A.
Baskett, Stanley
1954 J 38   B.S.A.
1955 J 16   B.S.A.
1956 J 29   B.S.A.
Bassett, A D
1948 J R   B.S.A.
1950 J R   B.S.A.
Bateman, A R
1947 S R   Ariel
Bates, Arthur
1950 J 27   Douglas
1951 S R   B.S.A.
Baxter, E
1952 J 41   B.S.A.
1953 J 20   B.S.A.
Baybutt, Jim
1952 J 47   B.S.A.
Bean, John
1950 J R   B.S.A.
1951 J 18   B.S.A.
Beaney, Peter
1950 J 43   Norton
1951 J 16   Norton
1952 J R   Norton
Beck, Harry
1950 S R   Vincent HRD
Beckett, W F
1948 S 19   Vincent HRD
Beckton, James
1947 J 12   Triumph
1948 J 12   Triumph
1949 S R   Ariel
1951 J R   B.S.A.
1952 J 24   B.S.A.

1953 J 24   B.S.A.
Belcher, J D
1952 S 28   Norton
Bell, D E
1951 J 19   Matchless
Bell, Gordon
1956 J 12   B.S.A.
Benton, J
1953 J 44   B.S.A.
Bertorelli, Leo
1949 J 28   Royal Enfield
Birrell, David
1951 S 9   Triumph
1952 S 15   Norton
Bishop, F O
1954 S 26   Norton
Blackwell, E D
1951 J 26   Douglas
1952 J R   B.S.A.
1953 J R   B.S.A.
Blake, J F
1954 J 32   B.S.A.
Blum, Jack
1951 J R   Douglas
Bogie, David
1950 S 13   BSA
Bollington, James
1950 S 27   Triumph
1951 S 39   Triumph
Bolshaw, Len
1949 L 5   Triumph
1950 L R   Triumph
Borland, Gerry
1956 J 17   B.S.A.
Bottomley, Jack
1949 S R   B.S.A.
1952 S 5   Triumph
1953 J 3   Norton
1953 S R   Norton
Boughey, Roy
1954 J 15   B.S.A.
Boult, Dean
1949 J 31   B.S.A.
1950 L 4   Triumph
1952 S 47   Triumph
Boulter, Jon
1950 J 45   Douglas
1951 J R   Douglas
Bowie, Sandy
1953 J 19   B.S.A.
1954 J 4   B.S.A.
Bowman, Eric
1948 J R   A.J.S.
1949 J 57   A.J.S.
1951 S R   Triumph
Boyce, Ellis
1953 J 34   B.S.A.
Boynton, John
1948 S R   B.S.A.
1950 S R   Norton

Bradley, G
1953 1000 R   Vincent
Bradshaw, D N
1951 J 4   Norton
1952 J 32   Norton
Brassington, Arthur
1949 J 9   Norton
Brassington, Raymond
1950 J 25   Norton
1952 J 36   Norton
1953 J R   Norton
Brereton, D W N
1948 L R   Velocette
1949 S 18   Triumph
1952 J 58   B.S.A.
Briggs, Eric
1947 S 1   Norton
Briggs, Gordon
1956 J 40   B.S.A.
Briggs, Harry
1954 J R   B.S.A.
1956 J 42   B.S.A.
Brinnand, Richard
1956 J 28   B.S.A.
Briscoe, R D
1949 J 10   Norton
Broadey, A
1948 J 20   Norton
Brodrick, Alan
1954 J 34   Norton
1956 J 32   B.S.A.
Brookes, John
1949 S R   B.S.A.
1950 S R   B.S.A.
Brookes, Mike
1956 S 26   Triumph
Brooks, G H
1954 J 11   B.S.A.
Brough, Ken
1952 S R   B.S.A.
1954 S 23   Triumph
Broughton, Lennox
1950 J 52   Douglas
1952 J 12   B.S.A.
1952 S 51   B.S.A.
Brown, Doug
1949 J 20   Norton
1950 J 3   Norton
Brown, G R
1950 J 36   B.S.A.
1951 J R   B.S.A.
1952 J 19   B.S.A.
1952 S R   Matchless
1953 J 15=   B.S.A.
Brown, George
1948 S 6   Vincent HRD
1949 1000 5   Vincent HRD
Brown, Harry
1950 J 7   B.S.A.
1951 J R   B.S.A.

1952　J 7　　　B.S.A.
1952　S 21　　Norton
Brown, Tommy
1950　L R　　Excelsior
1951　J 25　　A.J.S.
1955　J 29　　Douglas
Bruce, Charlie
1949　J R　　A.J.S.
1950　J R　　Royal Enfield
1951　J R　　Royal Enfield
Buchan, Jimmy
1954　J 7　　B.S.A.
1955　J 1　　B.S.A.
Buck, John
1950　S 18　　Norton
Bull, L
1956　J 44　　B.S.A.
Burgess, F
1954　J R　　B.S.A.
Burns, Frederick
1949　J 26　　B.S.A.
Burns, P E
1951　J 22　　B.S.A.
1952　J 23　　B.S.A.
1953　J R　　B.S.A.
Burrows, John
1949　S R　　Triumph
Burton, Adrian
1948　S R　　B.S.A.
1949　J R　　B.S.A.
1950　J 35　　Douglas
1952　J 48　　Douglas
1953　J R　　Norton
Buss, D L
1953　1000 5　Vincent

Camfield, G N
1949　J R　　Douglas
1950　J R　　Douglas
1951　S 16　　Norton
Camier, Bill
1949　J R　　Norton
Candy, Maurice
1956　S 16　　B.S.A.
Cannell, Jack
1947　S 11　　Triumph
Cantrill, Jack
1950　J 23　　B.S.A.
Capner, Roy
1952　J R　　B.S.A.
1953　J 49　　B.S.A.
Carr, D
1951　J 6　　Norton
Carr, E B
1952　J R　　B.S.A.
Carr, Jack
1948　S 11　　Vincent HRD
1949　S 7　　Vincent HRD
1950　S 20　　B.S.A.
Carr, Louis
1950　1000 5　Vincent HRD
1951　J R　　B.S.A.
1952　S 41　　Norton

Carter, Leo
1950　J 53　　Douglas
Carter, Phil
1948　S 27　　Norton
1949　S 4　　Norton
1950　S 1　　Norton
Carvill, Ron
1948　L 3　　Triumph
Chadwick, Dave
1954　S 7　　Norton
Chapman, Don
1951　J R　　Douglas
1952　J R　　Douglas
1954　J 23　　Douglas
Cheney, Eric
1947　J 9　　Triumph
Cheers, Eric
1952　S 49　　Norton
1953　J 23　　Norton
1953　S R　　Triumph
1954　S 8　　Triumph
Chefneux, Maurice
1949　S 23　　Triumph
1950　J R　　Douglas
Cholerton, D S
1953　S R　　Triumph
1954　S 29　　Triumph
Choules, Ronald
1950　J 42　　B.S.A.
Clague, J
1954　J R　　B.S.A.
Clark, G P
1953　1000 2　Vincent
Clark, Harold
1948　S 7　　Norton
1949　J 1　　B.S.A.
Clark, John
1950　J 4　　Douglas
1951　J R　　Douglas
1952　J 11　　Norton
1952　S 3　　Norton
Clark, K
1952　S 33　　Matchless
Clegg, Tom
1950　J R　　B.S.A.
Clifford, V
1953　S 32　　Norton
Clough, Arthur
1952　S 59　　Triumph
Coates, James
1954　J 12　　B.S.A.
1956　J 7　　B.S.A.
Cocks, J
1951　S R　　Matchless
Codd, Bernard
1956　J 1　　B.S.A.
1956　S 1　　B.S.A.
Coleman, Frank
1949　J 18　　Velocette
1950　S 15　　B.S.A.
1951　S R　　B.S.A.
1952　J 26　　Norton
1952　S 37　　Norton

1953　S 13　　Norton
1954　S 14　　B.S.A.
Collett, G E
1951　J 37　　B.S.A.
Collier, Henry
1952　J 57　　B.S.A.
1953　J R　　B.S.A.
Collings, E F
1949　J 7　　Velocette
Collings, Fred
1950　S R　　Triumph
1951　S R　　Triumph
1952　S 45　　Norton
Collins, A C R
1950　J R　　B.S.A.
Colver, Jack
1948　S 20　　Matchless
Cook, Tony
1952　S 9　　Triumph
1953　S R　　Norton
Cook, J F
1949　J R　　Matchless
Cookson, Tommy
1949　J 12　　Norton
1950　J 18　　Norton
Coombes, Geoffrey
1956　S 6　　B.S.A.
Cooper, J H
1950　J R　　Velocette
1951　S R　　Norton
1952　S 13　　Norton
Cooper, P
1953　S 36　　Triumph
Cooper, Stan
1950　J 30=　Douglas
1951　J 7　　Douglas
Cooper, W A
1956　J 22　　B.S.A.
Cope, Frank
1948　L 6　　Velocette
1949　L 7　　Excelsior
Corlett, Ted
1951　J 37　　B.S.A.
Corley, W S
1949　J 36　　A.J.S.
1950　J 15　　Norton
1951　J R　　B.S.A.
1952　J 46　　A.J.S.
1952　S 27　　Norton
Cortvriend, Barry
1955　J 14　　B.S.A.
1956　J 21　　B.S.A.
Cousins, P
1948　S R　　Vincent HRD
Cowling, John
1950　J R　　Douglas
Cox, E
1952　J 53　　A.J.S.
1953　J R　　A J S.
Cox, H J
1953　1000 R　Vincent
Cox, John
1950　J 12　　B.S.A.

1952　S 25　　Matchless
Craib, A D
1954　S 20　　Norton
Crebbin, Peter
1949　S 5　　Triumph
Crighton, A G
1948　L 4　　Velocette
Crocker, Alan
1947　S R.　　Triumph
1948　S 26　　Vincent HRD
Cronan, H J
1952　S R　　Triumph
Crooks, Eddie
1953　J 35　　Norton
1953　S 2　　Norton
Crossley, Don
1947　L 4　　Velocette
1948　S 16　　Triumph
Cruse, Peter
1952　J R　　B.S.A.
1952　S R　　B.S.A.
1956　S R　　B.S.A.
Culshaw, Alan
1955　J 11　　B.S.A.
Cunningham, J
1952　J R　　B.S.A.
1953　J R　　B.S.A.
1954　J 29　　B.S.A.
Curphey, John
1950　S R　　Triumph
Curzon, H D S
1952　J 64　　B.S.A.

Dalziel, D C L
1955　S 19　　Triumph
Daniels, Jack
1948　S 1　　Vincent HRD
Davenport, Norman
1956　J R　　B.S.A.
Davie, Jimmy
1950　J 32　　B.S.A.
1954　J 3　　B.S.A.
Davies, Eugene
1956　J 15　　B.S.A.
Davies, P B
1950　J 44　　B.S.A.
1951　J 11　　B.S.A.
1952　J R　　B.S.A.
Davis, C W
1949　J 39　　B.S.A.
1950　J 56　　B.S.A.
Davis, Dion
1950　1000 6　Vincent HRD
David, Ted
1948　S 5　　Vincent HRD
Dawson, E
1952　J 49　　B.S.A.
Dean, A J
1955　J R　　Royal Enfield
Dear, Rowland
1950　J R　　B.S.A.
Dearden, Crowther
1955　S 17　　Triumph

1956   S 23   Triumph

Dehany, Bill
1948   L 2   Excelsior

Denton, Ben
1954   S 2   B.S.A.

Desborough, Frank
1950   L R   Velocette

DeZylva, W F
1950   S R   Triumph

Difazio, Jack
1948   J R   B.S.A.
1949   J 17   B.S.A.
1950   J 11   Norton

Dixon, Ken
1950   S 3   Norton

Dobbs, A W
1951   S 14   Matchless
1952   S 10   Norton

Dobson, Wilf
1950   S 19   Norton

Doncaster, Peter
1952   J 62   B.S.A.

Dormer, Gerald
1955   J 27   B.S.A.
1956   J 45   B.S.A.

Douglass, George
1953   1000 1   Vincent

Dow, Eddie
1953   S R   B.S.A.
1954   S 10   B.S.A.
1955   S 1   B.S.A.

Downing, H P
1947   L 7   Velocette

Draper, John
1951   J 3   Norton
1951   S 3   Triumph

Drysdale, Ian
1948   J 5   A.J.S.

Drysdale, Jimmy
1953   J R   B.S.A.
1955   S 16   B.S.A.

Duffy, Brian
1951   J R   Norton

Duke, Geoff
1949   S 1   Norton

Dulson, John
1949   L 10   Velocette
1950   L 3   Velocette
1953   J 45   Norton
1954   J 39   Norton

Duncan, John
1950   S 17   B.S.A.
1951   S 21   Matchless

Dunham, Laurence
1950   J R   A.J.S.
1951   J 20   A.J.S.
1953   J R   B.S.A.
1954   J 28   A J S.

Dunlop, Gavin
1953   J 47   Norton
1953   S R   Norton

Dunn, K R
1953   J 36   B.S.A.

Eckhart, John
1956   J 2   B.S.A.

Edgar, E
1949   J 41   A.J.S.

Edgson, Eddie
1954   J 30   B.S.A.

Ellerby, Cliff
1950   J R   Velocette
1952   J 31   B.S.A.

Elliot, John
1953   S 30   Ariel

Ellis, R
1952   S R   B.S.A.
1953   J R   B.S.A.
1953   S 8   Norton

Ellison, George
1950   J 26   Norton

Elvin, P M
1952   J R   Douglas

Ennett, Derek
1952   J R   Matchless
1952   S R   Matchless

Evans, H
1952   J R   B.S.A.
1953   J R   B.S.A.

Evans, Wilmot
1947   J R   Matchless
1948   J R   Matchless

Fairbairn, Freddie
1947   S 6   Norton
1948   S 9   Vincent HRD

Farrant, Derek
1951   J 5   B.S.A.
1952   S 4   Norton

Featherstone, Mick
1949   S R   Triumph
1950   S R   Triumph

Fellows, W D
1955   J 19   B.S.A.
1956   J 25   B.S.A.

Ferbrache, Peter
1955   J 3   B.S.A.
1955   S 4   B.S.A.

Fetherston, Phil
1950   S 8   Triumph

Finch, Joe
1953   1000 6   Vincent

Fish, R W
1947   L 5   Velocette

Fisher, C H
1951   J 13   B.S.A.
1952   J 38   B.S.A.

Fisher, J
1949   S 17   Triumph
1950   S R   Triumph

Fisher, John
1948   J 15   Ariel
1949   J 11   B.S.A.

Flaskett, P H
1954   S 17   B.S.A.

Fletcher, Frank
1948   L R   Excelsior
1950   L 1   Excelsior
1951   S 17   Norton

Fletcher, N C
1955   J 26   B.S.A.
1956   J 38   B.S.A.

Floodgate, Les
1953   1000 R   Vincent

Folwell, Terry
1956   J 41   B.S.A.

Fox, Frank
1952   S 11   Norton

'Franklen, Sid'
1949   J 24   A.J.S.

French, L J B R
1948   S 30   Norton
1949   S 29   Triumph
1950   J R   Douglas
1951   J 38   Douglas

Frost, Arthur
1953   1000 R   Vincent
1954   S 25   Norton

Gadd, D A
1950   S R   Vincent HRD
1951   S 20   Norton
1952   J 54   Matchless
1952   S R   Norton

Gandy, F T
1951   J R   Douglas

Gaunt, A J
1954   J 35   B.S.A.

George, N
1953   S 22   B.S.A.

German, Howard
1954   S 27   Norton

Gibson, G E
1951   J R   B.S.A.
1952   J 55   B.S.A.
1953   J 37   B.S.A.

Gibson, Willie
1954   J 8   B.S.A.

Gilbert, Ted
1950   S 36   Triumph

Gillingham, M W
1953   S R   Norton
1955   S 9   Triumph
1956   S 20   Triumph

Goddard, E J
1951   J 28   B.S.A.
1952   S R   Triumph

Gowling, J A
1950   J R   Douglas

Graham, S
1951   J R   B.S.A.
1952   J R   B.S.A.

Graham, Tom
1954   J 17=   B.S.A.

Grant, Harry
1949   J R   A.J.S.

Gray, D H R
1949   J 23   A.J.S.

Green, John

1949   J 55   Triumph

Greenwood, Owen
1952   J 35   B.S.A.
1953   J 2   B.S.A.

Griffith, John
1955   S 13   Triumph

Griffiths, Cyril
1950   J 16   Douglas

Griffiths, J F
1953   J 43   B.S.A.

Guest, J E
1954   S R   Norton

Hagen, David
1955   J R   B.S.A.
1956   S 12   B.S.A.

Hagon, Alf
1953   S 29   Norton

Haines, Frank
1949   J 53   B.S.A.

Haines, J D
1949   J R   B.S.A.

Haldane, Ewen
1953   J 12   B.S.A.
1954   S 3   B.S.A.

Hallett, Ray
1949   J 4   B.S.A.

Hambling, J F
1954   S 18   B.S.A.

Hamilton, J D
1956   J 39   B.S.A.

Hamilton, J S
1952   S R   Triumph

Hancock, Walter
1951   S 36   B.S.A.

Harding, Jack
1949   1000 R   Vincent HRD

Harding, Richard
1955   J 10   B.S.A.

Harding, Billy
1951   S 12   Norton
1952   S 20   Norton

Hargreaves, Bernard
1949   L 3   Velocette
1950   L R   Velocette
1951   J R   Douglas
1951   S R   Ariel
1952   J 39   Douglas
1952   S 1   Triumph

Harris, J H T
1951   J 15   B.S.A.
1953   J 14   B.S.A.
1953   S R   Triumph

Harrison, Jack
1948   S 18   Ariel

Hart, A E
1953   S R   Triumph

Hart, A J
1950   J R   Velocette
1951   S R   Norton

Hartley, William
1949   S 15   Triumph

Hartree, O P

1947 J 6 — Velocette

Harvey, Eric
1949 J R — B.S.A.

Hatcher, J V
1953 J R — B.S.A.

Havercroft, Jack
1950 J 46 — A.J.S.
1951 S 29 — A.J.S.

Hawkins, L C St. J
1955 S 12 — B.S.A.
1956 S 18 — B.S.A.

Hawton, J
1953 1000 R — Vincent

Hazlehurst, Ronnie
1948 J 1 — Velocette

Heath, A E
1950 J 48 — Norton

Heath, Phil
1947 S 15 — Norton
1948 S 2 — Vincent HRD

Hedley, James
1950 J R — Douglas
1951 S 42 — Norton
1954 S 30 — Norton
1955 S R — Norton

Henthorn, Arnold
1948 L 8 — Velocette
1949 L 13 — Velocette

Herbert, Angus
1948 J 13 — Matchless
1949 J R — Matchless
1950 S R — Norton

Herbert, Brian
1956 S 28 — Norton

Hilditch, A E
1951 J R — Douglas

Hilditch, Fred
1950 J 49 — Douglas

Hill, Allen
1950 S 2 — Triumph

Hill, Jack
1956 J R — B.S.A.

Hill, J R
1951 J 40 — B.S.A.

Hill, W J
1949 J 35 — Douglas
1952 S R — Triumph
1956 S 8 — B.S.A.

Hillary, W
1950 S 33 — Triumph
1954 J 40 — B.S.A.

Hird, Maurice
1950 S R — Triumph

Hockin, J
1950 J R — Douglas

Hocking, W H
1955 J 6 — B.S.A.

Hodgson, P R
1956 J 30 — B.S.A.

Hodgson, Tom
1948 S 22 — Triumph
1949 S 13 — Triumph

Holcroft, V J

1949 L R — Velocette
1952 J R — B.S.A.
1954 J 41 — B.S.A.

Holding, H R
1947 J R — B.S.A.

Holland, R A
1956 J 43 — B.S.A.

Holmes, Alan
1953 S 3 — Norton

Holywell, R W
1949 S 25 — Triumph
1951 J R — Douglas

Hopwood, Cyril
1949 J 54 — Royal Enfield
1951 J R — Velocette

Horn, Chris
1948 S 8 — Vincent HRD
1949 1000 R — Vincent HRD

Houseley, Eric
1951 J 17 — B.S.A.
1951 J R — B.S.A.
1952 J 1 — B.S.A.
1952 S R — Triumph

Howard, Bill
1950 S 24 — B.S.A.
1951 S R — Norton

Howe, David
1954 J 17= — B.S.A.
1956 S 17 — B.S.A.

Howkins, Charles
1948 S R — Ariel
1949 1000 4 — Ariel
1950 1000 R — Vincent HRD

Hubbard, J T
1952 J R — B.S.A.

Hunt, D J
1955 S 10 — B.S.A.

Hunt, R V
1950 S R — Triumph

Hunter, H
1952 J 43 — B.S.A.

Hunter, H F
1947 S 12 — A.J.S.
1948 S 25 — Triumph
1949 S R — B.S.A.
1952 S R — B.S.A.
1953 S R — B.S.A.

Hurlstone, John
1954 S 16 — Triumph
1956 S 7 — Triumph

Hutchinson. Arthur
1950 L 5 — Velocette
1951 J 30 — B.S.A.

Hutchinson, John
1955 J 32 — Douglas

Hutchinson, T E
1955 J 9 — B.S.A.

Hutt, Wilfred
1950 J 34 — Douglas

Huxley, Cyril
1956 J 31 — B.S.A.

Hyde, P G
1956 S 19 — Triumph

Hyland, Victor
1950 S 26 — Norton
1951 S 28 — Norton

Ingram, Roy
1952 S 38 — Matchless
1953 J 13 — Norton

Iremonger-Watts, Hilary
1947 S 7 — Triumph
1949 L R — Triumph

Jackson, Albert
1956 J R — B.S.A.

Jackson, Brian
1949 J 25 — A.J.S.
1950 J 1 — B.S.A.

Jackson, C F
1952 J R — B.S.A.

Jackson, J F
1948 J 4 — Velocette

Jackson, R L
1951 S 25 — B.S.A.

James, A H B
1954 J 31 — B.S.A.

James, Derek
1951 S R — Triumph

James, G R A
1950 S R — Triumph

James, Ken (K V R)
1949 S 31 — A.J.S.
1950 J R — B.S.A.
1951 J 41 — Norton
1952 J 3 — Norton
1952 S 2 — Norton

James, Ken (K W)
1954 J 14 — B.S.A.
1955 J 7 — B.S.A.
1956 J 9 — B.S.A.

James, Peter
1955 J 23 — B.S.A.
1956 J 34 — B.S.A.

Jefferies, Allan
1947 S 2 — Triumph
1948 S R — Triumph
1949 S 2 — Triumph

Jenkins, Freddie
1953 S R — Ariel

Jenkins, Tony
1956 S 3 — B.S.A.

Jenness, Bill
1947 L 6 — Excelsior
1948 L R — Triumph
1949 L R — Triumph

Jerrard, Ron
1953 S 12 — Norton
1956 S 2 — B.S.A.

Jervis, Derrick
1955 J 8 — B.S.A.
1956 J 5 — B.S.A.
1956 S R — B.S.A.

Johnstone, Andrew
1947 J 13 — Excelsior
1949 S 9 — Triumph

1950 S 7 — Triumph
1952 J 27 — B.S.A.
1954 S R — Triumph

Johnstone, D
1953 S R — B.S.A.

Jones, Eric
1952 J 10 — B.S.A.

Jones, R
1950 J R — B.S.A.
1952 J 8 — B.S.A.

Joubert, Daniel
1955 J 2 — B.S.A.

Jowett, A
1952 S 42 — Triumph

Julian, Cyril
1948 J 8 — Velocette
1949 J 33 — B.S.A.

Kay, William
1950 S 29 — B.S.A.

Keel, W J
1951 S 23 — Triumph
1953 J 33 — A.J.S.
1953 S R — A J S.

Keeler, Bob
1953 J R — Norton
1953 S 1 — Norton

Keen, Robert
1950 S 31 — Triumph
1951 S 40 — Norton
1952 S R — Triumph
1955 S 14 — B.S.A.
1956 S 27 — B.S.A.

Kelly, Roger
1955 S 3 — Triumph

Kempson, Ted
1950 S 14 — Norton

Kendall, John
1950 J 41 — B.S.A.
1951 S 24 — A.J.S.

Kenworthy, Robert
1949 S 26 — Triumph
1951 S 43 — Triumph

Kerr, Robert
1949 S 28 — Norton
1950 S 5 — Norton
1952 S 6 — Triumph

Kershaw, B
1953 J 32 — B.S.A.

Keys, Basil
1947 L 2 — A.J.S.

King, Alan
1948 S 29 — Triumph

King, Alastair
1953 S 5 — Norton
1954 S 1 — B.S.A.

King, B H
1951 J 31 — B.S.A.
1952 J 30 — B.S.A.

King, Len
1953 S 15 — Triumph
1954 S 9 — Triumph

King, L C

1953   S 31   Norton

King, Robert
1948   J R   B.S.A.
1949   J 51   Matchless
1950   J 14   B.S.A.

Kirby, Ernest
1949   S 19   Triumph

Kirby, J
1951   J 32   B.S.A.
1952   J R   B.S.A.

Kirby, Norman
1947   S R   B.S.A.

Kirkham, P G
1955   J 18   B.S.A.
1956   J R   B.S.A.

Klinge, Arthur
1948   J 21   B.S.A.
1949   J 52   B.S.A.
1950   J R   Norton

Lamb, W M
1948   S R   Norton

Lanyon, J
1952   S R   Norton

Lashmar, Dennis
1949   1000 1   Vincent HRD

Lavington, Arthur
1949   J R   Velocette

Lawton, Syd
1947   S 8   Rudge

Lay, Norman
1955   J R   B.S.A.
1956   J 35   B.S.A.

Leech, W V S
1950   J R   B.S.A.

Leigh, George
1947   S 5   Norton
1948   S R   Norton

Liddiard, Anthony
1950   L R   Velocette

Lindsay, Ken
1955   J 22   B.S.A.
1956   J 48   B.S.A.

Lingard, Philip
1947   S 14   Norton

Linskey, Jimmy
1952   S R   B.S.A.

Little, E C
1953   S 26   Matchless

Lockwood, Monty
1948   L 1   Excelsior

Lomas, Bill
1949   J R   Royal Enfield

Lloyd, Ivor
1953   J 7   B.S.A.
1953   S R   Triumph

Lund, Gerald
1951   1000 4   Vincent HRD

McCormick, F
1953   J 30   B.S.A.

McCutcheon, Ronnie
1951   J R   A.J.S.

McDonald, Reg
1949   S 21   Norton

McGeagh, Michael
1950   J R   B.S.A.
1951   J R   B.S.A.

McGuffie, Ian
1950   J 2   B.S.A.

McGuinness, B
1952   J R   B.S.A.

McIntyre, Bob
1952   J 2   B.S.A.

McIvor, A
1950   J R   Norton
1951   J 34   Norton
1952   J 59   Norton

McKenzie, H
1953   J 9   B.S.A.
1954   S 11   Triumph

McLean, Charles
1955   J 5   B.S.A.
1956   J 14   B.S.A.

McLeod, W M
1948   J 14   A.J.S.

McMeeken, James
1949   J 49   A.J.S.

McVeigh, Jack
1948   L R   Triumph
1949   L 8   Triumph

McVeigh, Bill
1947   L 1   Triumph
1948   S 4   Triumph

Macartney, Carleton
1950   J 10   B.S.A.

Madsen-Mygdal, Richard
1953   1000 R   Vincent

Manning, Geoff
1949   1000 R   Vincent HRD

Marshall, Douglas
1949   S R   Triumph

Marshall, J. Howard
1947   S R   Scott

Martin, Angus
1951   S 35   Triumph
1952   J 29   B.S.A.
1952   S R   Triumph
1953   J 11   B.S.A.
1953   S 34   Triumph
1954   J R   B.S.A.

Mason, John
1953   S 19   Ariel

Matheson, I G
1951   J 29   B.S.A.
1952   S 23   B.S.A.

Maw, R
1955   J 30   B.S.A.

Mawson, Bob
1951   S 38   Norton
1952   S 56   Norton
1953   S 37   Norton
1954   S 22   Norton

Meadows, K G
1952   S 16   Norton

Merridan, David

1955   S 20   Triumph

Middleton, D C
1955   S 18   Triumph

Milburn, N
1951   S 44   A.J.S.

Millar, D C
1950   S R   A.J.S.

Millman, B
1952   J R   B.S.A.

Mills, Herbie
1950   S 11   Triumph

Milne, Sid
1948   J 17   EMC
1950   J 51   EMC

Milner, George
1949   J 13   B.S.A.
1950   J R   Douglas
1951   J R   Douglas

Minihan, Ned
1956   S 15   B.S.A.

Minion, Peter
1952   S 50   Norton
1953   S R   Norton

Mizen, Sid
1954   S R   Triumph

Mockett, J
1954   J 37   Norton

Modral, R H
1952   S R   Triumph

Mollan, Tony
1950   J 54   B.S.A.
1952   J R   B.S.A.
1953   J 39   B.S.A.

Moncrieff, David
1948   J R   B.S.A.
1949   J R   B.S.A.

Moore, A C
1952   S 55   Norton

Moore, J M
1954   J 16   B.S.A.

Moore, Joe
1947   J R   B.S.A.
1950   J R   B.S.A.
1951   J 8   B.S.A.
1952   J 42   B.S.A.

Moram, Colin
1956   J 16   B.S.A.

Morgan, Dennis
1948   J 9   A.J.S.
1949   J 32   A.J.S.

Morley, D K
1951   J 10   B.S.A.

Morris, Bert
1949   J 19   B.S.A.

Morrow, A E.
1950   J R   Douglas

Morton, Jimmy (J D)
1954   J R   B.S.A.
1955   J 15   B.S.A.
1956   J 6   B.S.A.

Morton, J H
1954   J R   B.S.A.

Moss, P

1947   J 7   B.S.A.

Mouat, R W
1949   J 46   A.J.S.

Muir, J
1954   J 9   Norton

Munday, Michael
1956   S 24   B.S.A.

Mundy, Bill
1948   J R   A.J.S.
1949   J R   A.J.S.

Murphy, George
1952   J 56   B.S.A.
1953   J 22   B.S.A.

Mustard, Andrew
1955   S 6   B.S.A.
1956   S 13   B.S.A.

Mustard, Donald
1950   L R   Velocette

Myers, Bill
1947   S 10   Rudge

Naintre, Victor
1956   S R   B.S.A.

Nash, Harry
1951   J 14   B.S.A.
1952   J 21   B.S.A.
1953   J 26   B.S.A.
1954   J 13   B.S.A.

Naylor, D
1953   S 17   B.S.A.

Neal, H
1951   S R   Norton
1952   S 40   Norton

Netherton, Jack
1949   1000 R   Vincent HRD
1950   1000 R   Vincent HRD
1951   S R   Norton
1952   S 31   Norton

Netherwood, W J
1948   S 17   Norton

Newcombe, Len
1949   S 22   Triumph
1950   S 28   Triumph
1951   S R   Triumph

Newman, Brian
1956   S 9   B.S.A.

Newstead, Arthur
1950   S 34   A.J.S.
1951   J 33   A J S.
1952   S 30   B.S.A.
1953   S 21   B.S.A.

Nicholls, Keith
1956   J R   B.S.A.

Northwood, George
1949   L 9   Velocette
1953   J 28   B.S.A.
1954   J 21   B.S.A.

Norwood, Bernard
1950   J R   Douglas
1953   J R   B.S.A.

Nourish, Dave
1956   J 20   B.S.A.

Nowell, Bert

1950 J 47 Norton
1952 J R B.S.A.

Nowell, F
1951 J R Norton
1952 J R Norton

Oldfield, Russell
1951 S 8 Triumph
1953 J 6 B.S.A.
1953 S 7 Triumph

Ollerenshaw, Henry
1950 S 35 Vincent HRD
1951 S R Vincent
1952 S 46 Norton

Oram, Malcolm
1956 J 49 B.S.A.

Organ, Roy
1950 1000 R Vincent HRD

Orson, S L F
1956 J 13 B.S.A.

Orton, Jack
1950 S R Vincent HRD
1951 S R Vincent
1952 S 26 Vincent

Osborne, N
1948 S 23 Triumph

Oughton, E G
1951 S R Triumph
1952 S 17 Triumph

Ovens, Tom
1953 S R Triumph
1954 S 4 Triumph

Owen, Goo
1952 J 52 Matchless
1953 J R Matchless
1954 J 27 B.S.A.

Pache, Jacques
1949 S R Triumph

Pados, Ferenc
1949 J 16 Douglas

Palmer, Phil
1953 J 4 B.S.A.
1954 J 1 B.S.A.

Pantlin, Eric
1951 S 30 Norton
1952 J 50 A.J.S.
1952 S 22 Norton

Parker, J H
1951 S 45 Norton

Parkinson, Denis
1947 J 1 Norton

Parris, Doug
1951 J R Douglas

Parry, Frank
1950 S 32 Triumph

Parry, G E
1951 J 23 B.S.A.
1952 J 16 B.S.A.

Parsons, George
1947 S 3 Ariel

Parsons, S
1948 S 31 Triumph

Passmore, Fred
1949 S R Norton
1950 S 6 Norton
1951 S R Norton
1952 S 29 Norton

Payton, Barry
1956 S R B.S.A.

Paxton, Roger
1949 S 16 Triumph
1950 S R Triumph

Peacock, E
1955 J 21 B.S.A.

Peatman, A
1948 J 18 A.J.S.

Peet, A C
1952 J R B.S.A.

Pennycook, Bob
1947 J 6 Norton
1948 J R Norton

Perris, Frank
1951 S 32 Triumph
1952 S 18 Triumph

Peterkin, E N
1948 J 11 A.J.S.

Peters, P L
1953 1000 3 Vincent

Peverett, L
1947 J 10 A.J.S.

Phillip, Alex
1949 1000 R Vincent HRD
1950 1000 1 Vincent HRD

Phillips, R E G
1952 J 44 Norton

Phillips, V E F
1952 J 51 B.S.A.

Pilling, Harvey
1947 J R Norton

Pilling, Reg
1950 S Exc. Triumph
1952 J 20 B.S.A.
1953 J 20 B.S.A.

Pink, Ted
1947 J R Norton
1949 J 6 Norton

Pittam, L F
1953 1000 4 Vincent

Plews, Harry
1950 S 9 Norton
1951 S 5 Norton
1952 J 6 Norton
1952 S 32 Norton
1953 J 24 B.S.A.
1953 S 6 Norton

Poingdestre, J D
1952 J R B.S.A.

Pollitt, Arthur
1950 S R Norton

Pooley, Peter
1951 S 26 Triumph
1953 S R Triumph

Porter, James
1950 S 23 A.J.S.
1952 S 34 B.S.A.

Porter, Ross
1949 J 56 B.S.A.
1950 L R Triumph

Powell, Derek
1951 J R B.S.A.
1952 J 5 B.S.A.
1952 S 8 B.S.A.
1953 J 1 B.S.A.
1953 S 4 Triumph

Powell, J
1954 J 33 B.S.A.

Pratt, Bob
1947 J 2 Norton
1948 J R Norton

Pratt, Dennis
1956 J 10 B.S.A.

Preece, Roy
1955 S 11 Norton
1956 S 11 B.S.A.

Price, Leo
1949 J 47 B.S.A.
1950 J 21= B.S.A.

Price, P J
1950 J 24 Norton
1951 S 18

Prince, Ken
1951 J 24 B.S.A.
1952 S 14 B.S.A.
1952 J 22 B.S.A.

Proctor, Ernie
1949 J 43 Matchless

Prosser, R L
1952 S 44 Triumph

Purslow, Brian
1951 J 1 B.S.A.

Purslow, Fron
1947 J 5 B.S.A.
1949 L R B.S.A.

Pusey, Fred
1952 S 54 Vincent

Quayle, D
1954 J R B.S.A.

Quine, Edgar
1947 J R Triumph

Racle, C F
1952 J R B.S.A.

Radford, B S
1951 S R Triumph
1954 J 19 B.S.A.

Ratcliffe, Ken
1952 S 57 Norton

Raynor, Alan
1949 J 34 Norton
1950 J 21= Norton

Raynor, S R
1953 J R B.S.A.

Read, Geoffrey
1951 J 2 Norton

Reed, Walter
1948 S R Norton
1949 J 8 Norton

1950 J R Douglas
1951 J R Douglas

Rees, Elwyn
1950 J 20 A.J.S.

Reeve, William
1947 S R Excelsior
1949 J 15 B.S.A.

Righton, John
1956 J 23 Velocette

Riley, Harold
1956 J 33 B.S.A.

Ritchie, Bob
1951 S 4 Norton
1952 J 9 Norton
1952 S 7 Norton

Ritchie, Dennis
1949 L 2 Velocette

Roberton, Bill
1954 J 10 B.S.A.

Roberts, H
1948 J 16 A.J.S.

Roberts, W A
1952 J 18 B.S.A.

Robertson, J G
1953 J 42 B.S.A.

Robertson, Norman
1955 J R B.S.A.
1956 J 8 B.S.A.

Robinson, A N
1953 J 38 B.S.A.

Robinson, Charles
1950 J 5 Douglas
1951 J R Douglas
1952 S 53 Norton

Robinson, G W
1948 J 2 A.J.S.
1949 J 30 Norton

Rose, Doug
1952 J 33 B.S.A.

Rowbottom, Bob
1948 J R A.J.S.
1950 S 12 Triumph
1951 S 7 Matchless

Russell, R A
1953 J R B.S.A.
1953 S R A.J.S.

Rutherford, Len
1956 J 46 B.S.A.

Salt, George
1952 J R B.S.A.
1953 J 18 B.S.A.

Sanders, Alan
1948 S 12 Triumph
1949 S 14 Triumph
1951 J R B.S.A.

Sandford, Cecil
1948 J R Velocette
1949 J 5 Velocette

Scholefield, A
1953 J 29 B.S.A.
1954 J 20 B.S.A.

Scott, Cyril

1950	S R	Norton
1951	S 33	Norton

Seston, Sam
1949	J 44	Royal Enfield
1950	J 13	Norton
1951	J 12	B.S.A.
1951	S 34	B.S.A.
1952	J 15	B.S.A.
1953	J 15=	B.S.A.
1953	S 10	Norton
1954	S R	B.S.A.

Shand, David
1956	J 27	B.S.A.

Sheene, Frank
1950	J 55	Douglas
1951	J R	Royal Enfield
1952	J 60	Royal Enfield
1953	J 40	B.S.A.
1954	J 25	B.S.A.

Shekell, G W
1952	S 19	Norton
1953	S 9	Norton
1954	S 12	Norton
1955	S 8	Triumph

Shelley, J
1952	S 39	B.S.A.

Shepherd, Alan
1956	J 3	Norton

Shepherd, Terry
1953	S 23	Norton

Shepley-Taylor, P
1951	S R	Norton

Sheppard, D
1951	J R	B.S.A.
1952	J R	B.S.A.

Sherry, Robin
1949	S 8	Triumph

Sifleet, Richard
1948	S R	Triumph

Silk, Tom
1950	J R	B.S.A.

Silva, Collin
1950	J R	B.S.A.

Simister, John
1947	J 4	Norton
1949	J 2	Norton

Simister, Philip
1950	J 6	Norton

Slater, George
1949	S 30	Triumph

Sleightholme, Wilf
1947	J 3	A.J.S.
1948	J R	A.J.S.

Slinn, Reg
1948	J R	B.S.A.

Smart, Dennis
1954	J R	B.S.A.
1955	J 25	B.S.A.
1956	S 5	B.S.A.

Smith, A M S
1948	S 15	Norton

Smith, B J
1950	J 37	Norton
1951	J 17	B.S.A.

Smith, Jack
1948	L 5	Velocette
1949	L 11	Excelsior

Smith, John
1949	S 12	Norton

Smith, H
1953	J R	Douglas

Smith, K
1952	J R	A.J.S.

Smith, Ron
1956	S 25	Triumph

Smith, Roy
1953	J 25	Norton

Smith, W R
1952	J 45	B.S.A.
1953	J 41	B.S.A.
1954	S 24	Triumph

'Southward, T'
1950	S 21	Triumph
1952	S 48	Triumph

Spavin, R W
1947	J R	Velocette

Sproat, P R
1951	J R	Douglas

Staley, C E
1951	J 9	B.S.A.
1952	J 4	B.S.A.

Starr, Leo
1949	S 3	Triumph

Stephen, Harry
1950	J R	B.S.A.

Stevens, Cyril
1948	S 3	Norton

Stevens, James
1947	S R	B.S.A.

Stevenson, Leslie
1950	J R	B.S.A.
1951	J 21	B.S.A.

Sunderland, Milton
1947	J 8	Norton
1948	J 3	Norton
1949	J 14	Norton

Sutcliffe, Ron
1956	J 18	B.S.A.

Sutherland, J
1951	J 39	B.S.A.
1952	J 40	B.S.A.
1953	J R	B.S.A.

Sutton, A M
1953	J 5	B.S.A.

Swarbrick, T W
1949	L 12	Excelsior
1951	S 11	B.S.A.

Sweetman, Norman
1954	S R	Ariel
1955	J 24	B.S.A.
1956	J 36	B.S.A.

Swinney, T
1955	J 13	B.S.A.

Symonds, Arthur
1947	J 11	Excelsior

Tait, Percy
1954	S 6	B.S.A.

Taft, Cyril
1949	L 1	Excelsior

Taft, M E J
1952	J 14	B.S.A.
1953	J 10	B.S.A.

Talbot, K
1949	J 21	Velocette

Tanner, Geoff
1954	J 5	Norton

Taubman, Ken
1952	S 58	Triumph
1953	S 24	Triumph

Taylor, Alan
1949	J 3	Norton

Taylor, C W G
1950	1000 R	Vincent HRD

Taylor, Frank
1950	1000 7	Vincent HRD
1953	1000 R	Vincent

Telfer, Ian
1948	L R	Velocette

Terry, Jack
1947	J R	Ariel
1948	J 19	Ariel

Thomason, A
1951	J R	B.S.A.

Thompson, R
1955	J 4	B.S.A.
1956	J 11	B.S.A.

Thomson, Daniel
1956	J 19	B.S.A.

Thomson, James
1949	J 45	A.J.S.
1950	J 38	A.J.S.
1951	S 37	A.J.S.

Thomson, Ronald
1950	J 39	B.S.A.

Thurston, Jack
1953	1000 R	Vincent
1954	J 22	B.S.A.
1955	J 17	B.S.A.

Tolley, Dick
1947	S R	Ariel

Tully, K E
1951	J 35	A.J.S.

Turk, Allen
1950	J 28	A.J.S.
1951	J R	B.S.A.

Turner, G J
1954	S R	B.S.A.

Tye, David
1952	S R	Triumph

Tyson, H T
1952	J R	B.S.A.
1952	S R	B.S.A.

Unwin, Eric
1955	J R	B.S.A.
1956	J 4	B.S.A.

Ure, John
1950	J 30=	B.S.A.

Uttley, Len
1948	S R	Norton
1949	S 20	Norton

'Vernon, R J'
1948	S 13	Vincent HRD

Vine, H E
1955	S 15	B.S.A.

Vinall, Harry
1950	J R	B.S.A.

Vivian, Neil
1955	J 31	B.S.A.
1956	J 50	B.S.A.

Voice, Harry
1952	J 13	B.S.A.
1953	J 8	B.S.A.

Waddington, Ken
1952	S 43	Triumph

Wade, John
1950	J R	B.S.A.

Wakefield, George
1948	L R	Triumph
1949	L 4	Triumph
1950	L R	Panther

Wakefield, F
1955	J 28	Norton

Walczak, Adalbert ('Addy')
1956	J 37	B.S.A.

Walker, G W
1954	S R	B.S.A.

Walker, J
1953	S 35	Triumph

Walker, Roy
1948	S 14	Norton

Wall, Harold
1950	S 30	Triumph

Wallis, Fred
1955	S 7	B.S.A.
1956	J 24	B.S.A.
1956	S 4	B.S.A.

Walmsley, Harry
1949	J 38	Velocette
1952	J 37	Norton
1953	J 48	Norton

Walsh, Peter
1953	S 33	Norton
1954	S 28	Norton
1955	S R	Norton
1956	J 47	B.S.A.

Walsh, Pat
1951	S 41	Triumph
1952	S R	Triumph

Warburton, Harold
1948	L R	Excelsior

Warr, Jack
1949	J R	Velocette

Warren, J D
1949	J R	B.S.A.

Washer, Ernie
1955	J R	B.S.A.

Wasley, W
1952	J 61	Norton

Waterman, P H				1948	S 24		Norton	1952	J 34		B.S.A.	1953	S 28		Matchless
1947	S 4		A.J.S.	1949	J 27		Norton	1953	J 32		B.S.A.	**Woods, Stanley**			
1952	J 25		B.S.A.	1950	J 9		Norton	**Williams, H L**				1949	S R		Triumph
Watling, Ken				**Westfield, Tom**				1950	S 10		Norton	**'Workman, W'**			
1949	S 24		Norton	1948	J Exc.		Triumph	**Williams, J E**				1950	S R		Triumph
1950	J 29		B.S.A.	**Wheeler, Arthur**				1952	S R		Triumph	1951	S R		Triumph
1951	S R		Norton	1947	L R		Excelsior	**Williams, Trevor**				1952	S 35		Triumph
Watson, C				1948	J 7		Velocette	1950	J R		B.S.A.	**Wright, Des**			
1951	S 31		Vincent	**Whelan, Don**				**Willis, Ken**				1953	J 17		B.S.A.
1952	S R		Vincent	1948	S 29		Rudge	1950	J 8		B.S.A.	1954	J 2		B.S.A.
1953	S 16		Triumph	**White, J W**				**Wilshere, Willy**				**Wright, James**			
1954	S 21		Norton	1947	S 13		Triumph	1947	J 10		Ariel	1949	1000 2		Vincent HRD
Watson, D R				**Whitehouse, A C**				1949	J 22		Triumph	**Wright, John**			
1952	J 63		B.S.A.	1951	S 19		Norton	1950	J R		Triumph	1949	S 11		B.S.A.
1953	J 46		B.S.A.	**Whitehouse, Ralph**				1951	S R		Norton	1950	S 16		B.S.A.
Watson, T F				1954	J 24		B.S.A.	1952	S R		Norton	1951	S 10		B.S.A.
1953	S 27		Norton	**Wicksteed, Ivan**				1953	S 14		Triumph	1952	S 24		B.S.A.
1954	S 19		Norton	1950	S R		Triumph	1954	S 15		Triumph	1953	S R		B.S.A.
Watson, W P				1951	S 2		Triumph	**Wilson, Pat**				**Wycherley, T G**			
1954	J 26		B.S.A.	**Wilcocks, Douglas**				1949	1000 3		Vincent HRD	1948	S 21		Ariel
Wayne, Donald				1949	J R		Velocette	**Winter, H B**				**Yates, Roy**			
1949	S R		Norton	**Wilkes, Jack**				1953	S R		Norton	1950	S 25		Norton
Webb, D				1952	S R		B.S.A.	**Winterbottom, J**				1951	S 13		Norton
1952	S R		Triumph	**Wilkins, David**				1952	J R		Royal Enfield	**Young, Fred**			
1953	J 27		Norton	1949	S 10		Triumph	**Womack, J J**				1950	1000 3		Vincent HRD
Weller, Frank				1950	S 22		Triumph	1955	J 20		B.S.A.	**Zoellner, Werner**			
1949	J 40		Norton	1951	S R		Matchless	**Wood, Jack**				1950	J 50		B.S.A.
Wellsted, Arthur				1952	S 12		Norton	1951	S 6		Norton	1952	S 60		Norton
1950	L 2		Triumph	**Williams, E R**				**Wood, W F**				1953	S R		Triumph
1951	S R		Triumph	1952	J 28		B.S.A.	1949	J 50		Douglas				
Wenman, John				1953	J 21		B.S.A.	**Wooderson, Neville**							
1947	S R		Sunbeam	**Williams, H**				1953	J R		Matchless				

As Jack Cannell, first Clubman rider to take to the track for practice, was the first Clubman rider to feature in this book, so Brian Herbert (Norton), who finished 28th and last in the 1956 Senior Clubman's, brings the book to a close.